The Legal Environment and Risks for Foreign Investment in China

Shoushuang Li

The Legal Environment and Risks for Foreign Investment in China

Springer

Shoushuang Li
12/F Oriental Kenzo Office Building
48 Dongzhimenwai Avenue
Beijing 100027
China
lishoushuang@gmail.com

ISBN 978-3-642-08011-7 e-ISBN 978-3-540-48377-9

Springer is part of Springer Science+Business Media

springer.com

Cover-design: Erich Kirchner, Heidelberg

Foreword

It is my great pleasure to introduce *The Legal Environment and Risks for Foreign Investment in China* by Shoushuang Li, a star young lawyer in Beijing. Mr. Li has a wealth of experience in foreign investment law and joint ventures, which he brings to bear in his analysis of this dynamic and critical field.

China's investment climate continues to evolve. Less than thirty years after the introduction of market reforms, China has become one of the world's most attractive investment locations. The legal system has developed a good deal, although there are still plenty of pitfalls that await investors who are not sufficiently careful. Foreign observers of the legal system remain divided as to whether the proverbial glass is half full, or rather half empty—some believe that China's efforts to develop the rule of law have already born fruit while others are more skeptical.

Li's strength is to combine the specific details of the various regimes governing investment in China with a broader perspective on risk management. He begins with an introduction to general issues related to foreign investment, tax law, land use right and labor law. These are likely to be of concern to investors in a wide array of fields. He then goes on to provide a wealth of detail on particular sectors of education, water, and insurance. While these sectors each have their own particular regulatory dynamics, they are also representative of many others that face similar problems. In particular, education and water involve special issues related to the provision of public goods that were traditionally monopolized by the state. Insurance on the other hand is generally viewed as best provided by market forces. The risks in all three sectors, however, demonstrate the distinctive features of the Chinese transition currently under way. Managers need to be aware not only of the general problems of doing business in China, but also the specific characteristics of the sector in which they plan to operate.

Li's concluding section ably demonstrates how managers and lawyers can reduce the risks associated with investment in China. Any investor will want to know about the options in case the deal goes bad, and China provides an array of dispute resolution choices that need to be considered before the investment occurs. These options are themselves evolving over time. With a guide as able as Mr. Li, investors can maximize the probability of a productive investment experience in the World's most dynamic marketplace.

Tom Ginsburg
Professor
Director, Program in Asian Law, Politics and Society
University of Illinois, College of Law

Preface

Investment in China: The Opportunities Co-exist with Risks

"The single most important thing to happen in our lifetime will be the emergence of China."

—— John Thornton[1]

The high costs of business regulation, a poor institutional framework, weak property rights *and an unstable macroeconomic environment are major obstacles to doing business in transition countries.*

—— The European Bank for Reconstruction and Development[2]

John Thornton, a former President of Goldman Sachs, once observed, "The single most important thing to happen in our lifetime will be the emergence of China." China is the new growth frontier of the global economy, and the investment opportunities that it presents are perhaps the greatest of the 21st Century. In a country of 1.3 billion people, with annual GDP growth twice that of the US (consistently 7-9%), it is clear that there is no stopping China's emergence as a major player. Successful investors will need to learn the nature of the opportunities that abound today so as to profit from growth tomorrow. Those who ignore the China opportunity will simply be left behind as the economy continues to excel and their competition soar to new heights.

There are of course two sides to the coin, and numerous pitfalls on the path to prosperity in China. The miraculous numbers cannot disguise the problems associated with the country's developmental transition period. In the "transition report 2005: Business in Transition" issued by the European Bank for Reconstruction and Development (EBRD), it is observed that the world's transition countries have made significant progress, but still lag behind mature market economies in most aspects of their business environments. The high costs of business regulation, a poor institutional framework, weak property rights and an unstable macroeco-

---

1 Former President of Goldman Sachs (Now a Professor at Tsinghua University).

2 The European Bank for Reconstruction and Development. *Transition report 2005: Business in transition*, download from http://www.ebrd.com/pubs/econo/6520.htm (last visit in Nov. 2005).

nomic environment all emerge from the survey as major obstacles to doing business in these transition economies.

In addition, there is concern about problems particular to China which obstructs the progress of the economy. For example, the multiple and legally-undefined roles of state-owned enterprises often perplex foreign investors. Meanwhile, traditional Chinese mono-culture has been replaced by a diversified system of values embracing foreign elements. Thus, more and more conflicts arise between the east and west, the host country and her rich foreign guests, leading to a variety of investment risks. In general, China cannot leapfrog this special phase featuring a transition from partial to complete rule-of-law. In particular, there are a large number of potential legal risks associated with the process of incorporating and operating a Chinese-Foreign joint venture or other businesses of a similar form.[3]

When it comes to risk management, most foreign entrepreneurs have a wealth of experience, plentiful resources and academic studies to hand. They would like to pay more attention to risk management and control in business of running joint ventures in China, whereas the legal risk otherwise is to some extent overlooked. Though this latter issue has been explored to an extent, there is still a lack of adequate depth. Foreign investors often play games with supervisory institutions and local authorities, walking the line between legitimacy and illegality. From the outset, these investors often set out ambitious plans that involve using contacts within local and central governments, or relying on their Chinese partners. These kinds of business relationships take the form of an extension to an individual's private circle, and are more grounded on the discretion of officials or the good faith of Chinese partners than business norms and legal institutions. By its nature these arrangements are vulnerable to unpredictable political and legal risks. Even if these risks are taken it into account in the course of making investment decisions, the serious scarcity of knowledge concerning this issue can not effectively make them to dodge the legal risks. There are still contradictions between various levels of laws and regulations as well as gaps. This causes some outside investors to hesitate, leading to the loss of dozens of opportunities. Other investors have paid a high price for poorly-advised investments due to misunderstanding or ignoring Chinese legal risks.

Aside from statutes, and the rules of central and local government, foreign investors inevitably come across judicial interpretations, administrative policies and counsel opinions. Equally, special Chinese environmental features such as complicated land ownership, socialist public ownership and state-owned enterprises

[3] See also Research results of Geringer, Kogut, Killing. Geringer, J. M. & C. A. Frayne (1990), Human resource management and international joint venture control: A parent company perspective, *Management International Review,* 30:103–120; Kogut, B. (1989), Why joint ventures die so quickly? *Chief Executive*, May/June issue: 70–73; Killing, P. (1988), Understanding alliances: The role of task and organizational complexity, In: *Cooperative Strategies in International Business*. F. Contractor & P. Lorange (Eds), Lexington: Lexington Books.

may confuse foreign guests. Often "under-table rules" virtually govern China's economic and social development. Defaulting on these rules will result in disqualification, forfeit, and even eviction.

According to Jack Welch "One should not be afraid of the legal risk itself, but the ignorance of it". The Chinese legal environment itself should not be blamed for foreign investors' losses. Rather, the legal risks hidden in the environment need to be far better understood. Whether dormant risks will become active depends on the knowledge and reflexes of foreign investors. The aim of this book is to advise on the many kinds of legal risk behind China's prosperity and to explore legal risk mitigating and management measures to be applied within China's unique legal environment.

Shoushuang Li October 2006

Acknowledgements

The book is intended to discover specific legal risks hidden in all phases through a selective introduction of China's legal environment for foreign investment. Also, my goal for this book tries to guide the foreign investors in discerning and making appropriate steps against the aforesaid risks, to avoid following the same mistakes by others and better achieve their ends.

The inspiration of this project started in mid 2005 was initially born in a conversation with Mr. Wu Hangbin, an editor in China Economic Press. Previouly, I wrote this book in Chinese. However, that I finally translated it into English is far attributed to Mrs. Brigitte Reschke in Springer for her kindly publishing offer.

During the years of 2005 and 2006, I was at all times pondering on an unprecedented situation—law-booming in China. Many important commercial laws and regulations including Company Law, Securities Law, Bankrupcy Law were promulgated with totally new revisions. Accordingly, I made onerous efforts in researching, analysing, rewriting to make this book updated.

I gratefully acknowledge the significant efforts of Mr. Wang Chunyang and Mrs. Gu Huaning helping me translate parts of the book.

Earlier draft of this book was proofread in painstaking detail respectively by Daniel Russel, Tamsin Westley, Grace Wang, Diana Shu, Owen Lee. Special supports were received from Adam Guli, Li Jing, Li Yunchi and Luoling to help me find them. I will always be thankful to them, whereas any remaining errors are solely my responsibility.

Special thanks are due to Prof. Tom Ginsburg in University of Illinois College of Law for his encouraging comments. I also owe thanks to the continuous help and encouragement from Mr. Yukio Nagasawa and Mrs. Maho Nakamura.

Li Longliang, Shi Minglei, Zhang Shucheng, Zhang Shiwei, Qian Weiqing, Lv Liangbiao, Song Yunfeng and many other persons have once supported this project. I would like to express my appreciation and gratitude to all of them.

Finally, my special thanks to my parents and Zhangya whose constant understanding, endurance, encouragement and selfless supports have always been an unfailing source of strength and persistence made me survive this project. They have my love and deep gratitude.

Shoushuang Li October 2006

Acknowledgements

The book is intended to discover specific legal risks hidden in all places through a selective introduction of China's legal environment for foreign investment. Also my goal for this book tries to guide the foreign investors in discerning and making appropriate steps against the aforesaid risks, to avoid following the same mistakes by others, and better achieve their ends.

The inspiration of this project started in mid-2005 was actually born in a conversation with Mr. Wu Hang, an editor in China Economic Press. Previously, I wrote this book in Chinese. However, that I finally translated it into English is attributed to Mrs. Brigitte Reschke in Springer for her kindly publishing offer.

During the years of 2005 and 2006, I was at all times pondering on an unprecedented situation – law-booming in China. Many important commercial laws and regulations including Company Law, Securities Law, Bankruptcy Law, were promulgated with totally new revisions. Accordingly, I made onerous efforts in researching and rewriting to make this book updated.

I gratefully acknowledge the significant efforts of Mr. Wang Chunying and Ms. Lin Huanan helping me translate parts of the book.

Earlier draft of this book was proofread in patient and detail respectively by Daniel Russel, Tamara Wheeler, Greg Wheeler, Diane Shin Owyang. The special supports were received from Angela Chan, Li Ting, Lu Yimoh and Linlin to help me find them. I will always be thankful to them, whereas any remaining errors are solely my responsibility.

Special thanks are due to Prof. Tom Ginsburg in University of Illinois College of Law for his encouraging comments. I also owe thanks to the continuous help and encouragement from Mr. Yukio Nagasawa and Mrs. Hatto Nakamura.

Li Longliang, Shi Minglei, Zhang Shuoheng, Zhang Shiwei, Qian Weiqing, Lv Hanbing, Song Yuntong and many other persons have once supported this project. I would like to express my appreciation and gratitude to all of them.

Finally, my special thanks to my parents and Zhangye whose constant understanding, endurance, encouragement and selfless supports have always been an unfailing source of strength and persistence made me survive this project. They have my love and deep gratitude.

Shenghuang Li October 2006

Table of Contents

Part Two:

Legal Risks in Operation of Foreign-Invested Enterprises

Abbreviations

AIC	Administration of Industry and Commerce
CBRC	China Banking Regulatory Commission
CIRC	China Insurance Regulatory Commission
CJV	Sino-foreign Cooperative Joint Venture
CPC	Community Party of China
CSRC	China Securities Regulatory Commission
FESCO	Foreign Enterprises Services Company
FISC	Foreign-Invested Joint Stock Limited Company
EJV	Sino-foreign Equity Joint Venture
FIE	Foreign-Invested Enterprise
GAC	General Administration of Customs
HC	Holding Company
JV	Joint Venture
LLC	Limited Liability Company
M&A	Mergers and Acquisitions
MOFCOM	Ministry of Commerce
MOLR	Ministry of Land and Resources
NDRC	National Development and Reform Commission
NEPC	National Economic Planning Commission
PBC	People's Bank of China
PRC	People's Republic of China
QFII	Qualified Foreign Institutional Investor
Rep Office	Representative Office
RMB	Renminbi, the official currency of China
SAEP	State Administration of Environmental Protection
SAFE	State Administration of Foreign Exchange
SAIC	State Administration of Industry and Commerce
SASAC	State-Owned Assets Supervision and Administration Commission
SAT	State Administration of Taxation

SETC	State Economic and Trade Commission
SOE	State-Owned Enterprises
VAT	Value Added Tax
WFOE	Wholly Foreign-Owned Enterprises
WTO	World Trade Organization

1 Introduction: The Legal Risks of Foreign Investment in China

"Nothing is a risk in itself; there is no risk in reality. But on the other hand, anything can be a risk; it all depends on how one analyses the danger, consider the event."

—— François Ewald[1]

"Human Beings are not born for solving universal problems, but may find out where the problems come, so limit them in an understandable range."

—— Goethe's talk to Eckermann[2]

1.1 Definition of Legal Risk of Foreign Investment

1.1.1 Risk and Legal Risk

Risk

The word "risk", in Ewald's study, originated from the Italian word "rischio", which was used in early transactions in the maritime and insurance industries. This original usage of the word referred to natural disasters such as storms.[3] With the development of the modern insurance industry, new definitions of "risk" were introduced. In Merriam-Webster's Dictionary of Law, the definitions of "risk" include: (a) possibility of loss or injury (b) responsibility for loss or injury.[4] Similar understandings of the concept of risk are found in other disciplines

---

1 Ewald, F. (1991), Insurance and risk, in Burchell, G. Gordon, C. and Miller, P. (eds) The Foucault Effect: Studies in Govermentality, Chicago University Press.

2 Eckermann (2005), the Dialogue of Goethe.

3 Id 1.

4 Risk a: possibility of loss or injury; b: liability for loss or injury if it occurs <the risk of loss passes to the buyer when the goods are duly delivered to the carrier —Uniform Commercial Code> <the risk of personal injury and property damage should be placed with the manufacturer rather than the consumer —Case & Comment>. Merriam-Webster's Dictionary of Law, Merriam-Webster, Inc (1996).

such as statistics, actuarial science and insurance, where the "risk" is defined as the chance or probability of loss or injury to the subject. This can be summarized in the equation: (R)isk = (H)arm × (P)robability. Mary Douglas and Wildawoski, two anthropologists, give their definition of "risk" as the perception of a hazard by a group, and consider this ability to discern the hazardousness of an environment as one of inherent functions of social structure. In this vein, the definition of "risk" may be divided into two levels. Firstly, the chance of a disadvantageous outcome incurred either by human behavior or environmental factors; and secondly the cognition of the "risk" by the subject. It is this later which determines human behavior.

Legal Risk

In the legal field, the issue of risk is raised as a practical mater. In most cases, people's main concern is to discern and assess legal risk and to mitigate the downside; yet no clear definition of legal risk has been generally accepted.

Basel II gives us the explanation that legal risk involves penalties, punitive damages and private settlements incurred by administrative conduct.[5]

According to International Bar Association publications, legal risk is a risk of loss to an institution caused primarily by: (a) a defective transaction; or (b) a claim (including a defense to a claim or a counterclaim) being made or some other event occurring which results in a liability for the institution or other loss (for example, as a result of the termination of a contract) or; (c) failing to take appropriate measures to protect assets (for example, intellectual property) owned by the institution; or (d) a change in the law.[6]

In China's current legal environment, a party does not typically regard a legal channel as a potential protective measure for its own good, but sees the legal framework as an external restriction imposed upon its will. Essentially, the motivation for giving heed to legal risk is to avoid potential charges for inadvertent conduct in violation of laws and regulations. In one sense, legal risk is the risk incurred by the functions of law on the person(s) at dispute. *The Reminding Letter of Legal Risks in Civil Litigation*, issued by the Supreme People's Court of China, also prescribed that legal risks are procedural, incurred as a result of the violation of procedural laws.

In Lovell's 2005 publication, *Legal Risk of Top 100 Chinese Enterprises*, Legal Risk is defined as a commercial risk involving the perils or economic losses incurred by the violation of related laws and regulations, breach of contract, tort (intellectual infringement), or delay in performing corporation rights. It embraces the following categories: operational risks (income or profit loss, cost or

---

5 Basel II: International Convergence of Capital Measurement and Capital Standards: a Revised Framework.

6 IBA Working Party on Legal Risk.

responsibility increase, etc.), civil claims, judgments or judicial opinions (attorney fees and settlement expenses), administrative or criminal penalties or punishment, losses of enterprises' assets, reputational damage etc. The reasons for the above injury or loss include: violation of related regulations, tortious acts to a third party, nonfeasance of legitimate rights or taking positive measures to obtain or protect legal rights.

In conclusion, we can say that legal risk can be interpreted as the assumption of possible responsibility or unfavorable results incurred by the conflicts in legal rules per se or between the subject's behavior and legal rules. Considering that the legal codes of different states contain different legal risks, the analysis in this book will confine itself to the unique legal risks embedded in Chinese legal system.

1.1.2 Types of Legal Risks Embedded in Chinese Legal System

In this book, the legal risks embedded in the Chinese legal system are divided into two categories: institutional risks and behavioral risks.

Institutional Risks

First and foremost, legal institutional risks are not merely the risks generated by the provisions of legal papers or specific regulations, because the occurrence of unlawful results or legal risk can be avoided if the party performs in accordance with the law and the law provides clear instructions and anticipates results. If a party acts against unambiguous regulations, there is clearly a behavioral risk.

Institutional risk implies risk due to equivocal provisions of laws and regulations, lack of specific regulation, institutional change or other legal institutional blankness. Institutional risk can be broken down as follows:

Ambiguity in the Law. The principal function of the law is to provide instructions as to acceptable human behavior. There may be some ambiguous provisions arising from China's imperfect legislation other than multi-vocal legal expression. These ambiguities constitute a legal risk. Furthermore, the conflict and overlapping of different legal rules, which is a characteristic of China's legal system, are problematic, as there is a lack of conflict law.

Blankness in the Law. In an unceasingly changing world, the written law cannot keep step in all corners of society. Theoretically, one's civil action may be justified unless it contravenes expressly prohibitive provisions in private law. Legal risk does not co-exist with the unrestrictive nature of human behavior. The case in China is different. Conduct is permitted only if there exists detailed legal provisions permitting it. To take the example of the take-over of a listed company, "*Company Law*" and "*Securities Law*" both provide general rules, but in reality a party cannot take substantial steps to realize the proposed take-over before relevant provisions regarding compulsory disclosure of information are issued. Unfortunately, China's laws and regulations often lack the detailed rules of implementation as support. Legal risks are therefore incurred as business proceeds where there are merely general principles established, without detailed implementation rules. In addition, under some extreme circumstances, one will came cross the legal risk due to the lack of both general principles and implementation rules.

Change in the Law. As a social measure to guard against conflict of interest, the law is required to be stable and concrete. Most international organizations take legal stability into account when assessing the level of investment risk in a country. Legal risk is maximized in a transition country like China because of the unstable legal environment.

Behavioral Risks

Logic suggests that all legal risks are behavioral risks; that is to say, there is no legal risk without action. All legal risk is incurred by human behavior.

From the point of view of legal risk, human behavior can be divided into two parts: normative behavior and non-normative behavior. The latter (which does not necessarily constitute an illegal act) includes any action in violation of the law or covered under ambiguous, nonexistent or changeable laws. Based on the definition of legal risk, we can say non-normative behavior is the root of all legal risks.

1.1.3 Legal Risks for Foreign Investment in China

Having defined legal risk, we can extend this and say that legal risk in foreign investment is the possible liability or unfavorable results incurred by the conflicts in the foreign investment legal system per se or between the behavior of foreign investors and related legal institutions.

In addition to economic behavior, foreign investment is also a complicated legal activity. The legal risks lie dormant behind a set of legal institutions, with which foreign participants interact with in the course of investment activities.

Although China's current legal system governing foreign investment[7] provides a set of basic rules for investors, the underdevelopment and imperfections in this code may bring about certain legal risks. Luc Laeven and Christopher Woodruff's studies demonstrate that the quality of the legal system has a significant effect on the size of investing firms. Based on their research, a standardized one point improvement in the quality of the legal system increases the average firm size by

---

7 Legal institutions of foreign investment does not equal to the laws related to Three Forms of Foreign Investment Enterprises, also include all of laws and regulations concerning foreign investments, such as "*Civil Law General Principles*", "*Company Law*", "*Securities Law*", etc.

about 10-15 percent.[8] The low-quality of China's legal system is causing it to act, to some extent, as a legal-risk-maker.

As to the subjective behavior in foreign investments, it contains not only the foreign investor, but also the guest country and host country (also including central and local governments and their ministries), the employees of foreign firms, their partners, their executive officers and competitors in different levels. For each of subjects, its behaviors that may incur legal risks such as government's renege, improper control of join-venture partners, the counterfeits by rivals and so forth are often found in foreign investment.

1.2 Macro-analysis of Legal Risks in Investment Institutions

1.2.1 Macro-analysis of the Legislation Regarding Foreign Investment and Its Risk

Foreign investment legislation has been developing for more than 25 years since China's Open-up Policy was constituted, and has faired relatively well during this time. This framework is comprised of the *Constitution*, as its base; separate laws and regulations related to foreign investment, forming the core of the legislation; plus other economic laws. Some negative factors such as ambiguities, conflict between laws and the legal hiatus should also be taken into consideration.

First of all, because the legislation is "problem-oriented" all regulations are drafted as keys to specific problems. Hence, the coherence of the legal system is ignored, and there are frequently conflicts which not only serve to perplex people, but also debase or even negate the value of the law. This debasement has considerably obstructed the normal process of foreign investments. In identifying what constitutes a "foreign investor" for example, there are consistently two standards – the nationality of the legal entity and considerations of capital control. According to "*Company Law*" and other commercial registration procedures, foreign investment firms are supposed to be Chinese entities. Yet in contradiction to this fact, they fall under *Interim Provision on Re-investment within China by Foreign-invested Enterprises* as foreign entities while re-investments in China.

Secondly, the ambiguity of words in legislation may account for legal risks. For instance, property rights are an equivocal concept as constituted in some laws and regulations for foreign-funded mergers and acquisitions (see "*Reorganization of State-Owed Enterprises by Foreign Financing Tentative Provisions*"). These rights are effectively an economic concept rather than a legal one. So far, we have not considered whether we are discussing a proprietorship, a creditor's right, a

8 Luc Laeven and Christopher Woodruff, The Quality of the Legal System, Firm Ownership, and Firm Size, download on the official website of Word Bank, last visit in Oct. 2005.

share ownership or only a property right owned by a legal entity, and many rule-drafters have an imperfect understanding of this issue themselves. A similar problem arises in a book titled "*The Guidance of the transfer of State-owned Property Right*" issued by the State-Owned Assets Supervision and Administration Commission of the State Council (SASAC). It defines "state-owned property right" as "a summation of every property right owned by the State". The transaction with regard to state-owned property right is "a transaction between two or more parties pertinent to the transfer of all or parts of property right … or parts of property right without change of the proprietor's title". Here it adopts a concept of "a cluster of rights" that property right is a cluster of congregated rights, as typical definition in economics. Contrarily, in another regulation of SASAC, it provides that the state-owned property rights are the investment incomes and interests in all kinds owned by the state, state holding or state-owned companies, and other rights and interests owned by the State under law. In fact, the term is translated from the conception of "ownership" used in accounting.[9] Since there is lack of certain and uniform definition of property right in writing, the risks concerning property right transactions would sharply increase in practice. To be worse, most of legal drafters only have economics backgrounds rather than legal ones, which implies recent laws and regulations regarding foreign investment have been transplanted into over-abundant economic terms. Consequently, this becomes a main reason for the growing legal risks in foreign investments.[10]

Furthermore, the problem of legal hiatus looms large in foreign investment, even though there are plenty of related laws and regulations. The rapidly expanding, newly-enacted laws cannot meet the needs of social and economic development. On the one hand, there is still a lack of general principles and of laws at the supreme level; on the other hand, the guidance rules and regulations at the second or third level still fall short. Some have commented that "China's laws and regulations are too simple to be used." Unfortunately, most of the rules that govern foreign investment are administrative regulations, at a lower level than the law or code. Searching China's law database on the Website of Peking University (www.chinalawinfo.com), there are only 20 administrative regulations but 754 administrative rules. In judicial practice, the administrative rules are deemed to be a legal resource that "could be referred to" in accordance with *Administrative Procedure Law*. Also, in "*Several Issues Concerning Application of the 'Contract Law' Interpretation (1)* " issued by the Supreme Court, it is provided that the court shall be entitled to invalidate a contract in accordance with the laws constituted by the National People's Congress and its Standing Committee, and the regulations of the State Council; not under local regulations or administrative rules. By this token, there is no real foreign investment "law" in China. (in a narrow sense; in a broad sense, the law includes law, regulation and administrative rules).

---

9 See Article 2, Section 3 of "Tentative Provision of Transfer of Property Right".

10 Zhang Ya (2005), The Legal Dilemma of Property Right Transaction, The Report of State-owned Enterprises Reforms Vol. 2.

1.2.2 China's Commercial Law and Its Legal Risks for Foreign Investment

The commercial law is a set of outstanding rules regarding merchants and business organizations, guided by civil law principles in a specific historical and business context. It is equivalent to civil or criminal law which is a separate body of laws and regulations. In China, there is no uniform code as is the case in Germany or France, but a literal system consisting of commercial laws and rules such as "*Company Law*", "*Securities Law*", "*Insurance Law*", "*Maritime Law*", "*Trust Law*", "*Investment Fund Law*", etc. Foreign investment is by its nature a commercial activity. Thus, the quality of commercial laws is crucial to the success of foreign investments. We now examine the negative characteristics of China's commercial law in detail, so as to give a clearer picture of the legal risks involved.

Abnormal Characteristics of China's Commercial Law and Their Legal Risks

Anti-mercantilism. Traditional commercial law originated in the middle ages in Europe. It broke the shackles of feudal law, patrician law and church law; being both convenient and flexible it greatly boosted the prosperity of Mediterranean cities during the Middle ages. By contrast, China's commercial law seems to revive the specter of the Dark Ages, with inflexible institutions and unnecessary and burdensome procedures.

In a survey of business registration procedures in 85 nations and areas in the world; LaPorta and Shleifer of Harvard University, Lopez. De. Silanes of Yale University and Djankov of the World Bank, collected data regarding registration formalities and average application days and fees. Including Chinese Taiwan, Hong Kong and Macao, China ranks similarly with Italy (mainly influenced by Mafia) where the commercial environment is hardest in the world for foreign investors.[11] This depressing result is mainly caused by the fact that the setting-up of a corporation in China proceeds under the registration-by-approval, rather than registration-by-recording principle prevalent in the rest of world. In addition, the Statutory Capital System (embracing Three Principles "Capital Ascertained, Capital Sustainable and Capital Unchangeable") may be taken into account for the badness of commercial environment that was adopted in drafting the Company Law of China.[12] On October 27, 2005, the Chinese legislature made

---

[11] Chen Zhiwu (2002), Who obstructs our business? New Fortune, December Issue.

[12] As the basic doctrine, Statutory Capital System principle has been preserved apparently and coherently along the whole process of law from legislation to adjudication. The functions of this principle are extraordinarily exaggerated up as the mythology of Capital Credit. A series of institutions deriving from it accordingly clamp down the passion of

critical adjustments to the capital system in the new Company Law, but the Statutory Capital System (with amendments) was retained. The Authorized Capital System adopted by most states was passed-over again.[13]

Discrimination by Ownership. Most commercial laws and regulations are constituted to serve state-owned enterprises centered on economic reforms. Consequently, they inevitably provide many favorable treatments and priorities for the interests of state-owned enterprises and their employees. On the other hand, non-state enterprises may be unequally scrutinized. Even though it tries to blur the legal distinction of ownership status, the continued existence of solely state-owned companies in the newly amended *Company Law* implies the ongoing differentiation of legal status and treatment by nature of ownership. This discrimination against non-state owned enterprises is often rooted between the lines of the written law.

China's tradition that one's fate is decided by class and origin has great influence on the legislation of commercial law. By the nature of ownership, enterprises are classified into the following types: state-owned, collectives, foreign-invested, and privately-owned. There are a number of biases for state-owned collective and foreign-invested enterprises. The later in particular enjoy preferential taxation (the actual rate of tax paid by foreign-invested enterprises is 10%-15%, a far cry from the 33% nominal rate; domestic enterprises pay 25%). In this classification, domestic privately-owned enterprises come in at the bottom of the pile. According to statistics collated by the Investment Institute of the State Planning Commission (predecessor of the National Development and Reform Commission), there are a large number of barriers to entry for privately-owned enterprises in nearly 30 industries. In particular: infrastructure, heavy manufacturing, financial and insurance services, telecommunications, education, culture, public sanitation and tourism

investments and new businesses, including minimum registration capital requirement (0.1 million for limited liability corporation, 10 million for joint stock limited corporation), payment in-a-lump of registered capital, legalization of forms of capital contribution (limited in cash, intellectual property, tangible property, land use right, non-patented property), maximum of capital contribution by intangible property, prohibition of withdrawal, limitation of shareholder's reinvestments (less than 50% of new assets), prohibition of discounted offering, redemption and mortgage of shares, rigid procedures for reduction of contributions, etc. "The obsession with it becomes the shackle of the advancement and innovation of China's company law. We created it but at last were lagged by it.", said Professor Zhao Xudong, as assistant director of Drafting Team of Company Law. In any case, we are baffled with the conditions provided by ourselves.

[13] The newly amended Company Law made considerable adjustments such as lowering the maximum of capital contribution, allowing capital contribution in installment, extended forms of contribution and limited withdrawal and redemption of shares and canceling the limits of foreign holding shares. However, by my perspective, current commercial law circumstances are not completely changed since the belief of anti-mercantilism is still haunting in most legislators' minds.

as well as any transactions involving state-owned property. This discriminatory treatment highlights the unbalanced structure of investment in China.[14] Although some efforts have been made to change the situation, the newly amended Company and Securities Law still remains somewhat conservative and inexorable in some areas.

Excessive Governmental Control. As is the case in many transition countries, China's government would like involve itself in all aspects of society. From the very beginning, legislators set out with the principle that conduct should be prohibited unless expressly permitted by law. The system is therefore more vulnerable to a breakdown in public law than if laws were drafted to prohibit rather than permit behavior. As a typical example in "*Insurance Law*", it is provided that "[t]he basic insurance clauses and insurance premium rates for major categories of commercial insurance shall be formulated by financial supervision and administration departments." Some optimists observed that, as a part of political reform, the central government has recently begun clearing up 4159 overstepping examinations and verifications interfered by governments, 800 of which will be called off; however, the authorities in the rest ones may be of much influence to the civil life.

In contrast to Adam Smith's "invisible hand", the hand of the Chinese government is busy in its attempts to promote the social good, an endeavor in which it has ultimately proved to be ineffectual. Government involvement remains all pervasive in China, and its institutions are accustomed to acting as a broker for the distribution of foreign investment. Most participants in the market may count on official favors and judgments over economic values. The commercial law does not restrain public power from interfering in civil life, but rather sidesteps it with legal justifications. In addition, the lack of independent commerce guilds or organizations, which hurdles by governmental restriction on the right of constituting an association, may explain the fact that government can at will intervene civil society. Actually, the existed guilds or organizations at every level usually function as authoritative intermediaries or mufflers for harsh official voice. Free-will sits at the core of business, and is the origin of market forces. In this sense, an ignorance of market forces and economic freedoms will cost China dearly.

Warlordism in Commercial Law. A Taiwanese Scholar has expressed the view that oriental culture, especially Chinese culture, is a form of warlordism. It can be compared to the social structure in the ant world with the "queen" living on supplies from the lower-status "workers", even though the she cannot materially con-

[14] By a survey, even in the city of Dongguan, Gong Dong province, where there is less than governmental regulation, only 41 areas into which private capital funds may be allowed to enter in the contrast with 81 areas open to foreign investors. In Jiang Su province, the loan for private economy just takes 5.2% of the whole bank loans in 2000. Similarly in Zhe Jiang province, the proportion of bank loans flowed to township and village enterprises is only 6.5%.

trol the "workers". It is the same in China's traditional political culture. The supreme authority is worshiped by its subordinates but cannot effectively govern these subjects. Subordinates come to be the material authority in their own kingdom as long as they serve their superiors well. Similarly, in commercial law, some so-called implementation rules from local authorities have trespassed into a higher level without correction mechanisms or effective conflict law. China's governments at every level also like to constitute specific rules in the investors' favor outside the laws prescribed by the National People's Congress and its Standing Committee. For example, Beijing Municipal Bureau of Industry and Commerce once created some institutional innovations such as "limited partnership", capital contribution in installments and the removal of limits on the scope of business; all contravening the "*Company Law*" of the time. All kinds of governmental rules, orders and documents form the main body of China's commercial law; these are the warlords of the commercial law world. Since separate rules represent the interests of different departments, conflicts inevitably occur, not to mention the impact of under-the-table rules. Some local authorities have taken erratic measures such as prohibiting the set-up of limited companies held by a husband and wife. In some provisions, the majority shareholder cannot contribute more than 85% of the share capital, while the minority shall contribute more than 15% of the share capital. Again, this chaos in commercial law inevitably leads to confusion among investors.

Blankness of Credit Legislation and Credit Crisis. In Chinese tradition, **"Benevolence, Justice, Courtesy, Wisdom, Faith"** ("Ren, Yi, Li, Zhi and Xin") are the basic doctrines for people's behaviors. However, in modern China, there is an unprecedented credit crisis. Dwight Perkins, director of the Harvard Institute for International Development, has observed that it takes a long time to get to know a partner in China's current legal climate, before actually getting down to business. Time is needed to ascertain who the partner is, what his goal is and whether or not he is trustworthy. The traditional Chinese method is rooted in assumptions about people's morality, and is probably not ready to deal with complex modern challenges. It is totally different in Western developed countries, in which there is a set of advanced institutions regarding commercial credit bolstered by related laws and regulations. One of the functions of a credit record system is to reduce the cost of transaction. Credit investigation, according to research from the World Bank, decreases the default rate of big banks by 41%, and of small banks by 78%. This credit checking capability, backed up by legal institutions, allows banks to be flexible and provide loans without a mortgage, in sharp contrast with the loan operations of China's banks. Most lines of credit are built up through personal or family connections which can prove stifling and somewhat fragile. It cannot accommodate the needs of the modern economy.

The legislation concerning commercial credit just sets off its way out in China. According to a study by Professor Justin Yifu Lin, Director of the China Economic Research Institute of Peking University, the inefficient distribution of credit costs China 585.5 billion RMB, equal to 37% of total government revenue and representing 2 percentage points of lost GDP growth. Put plainly this credit issue has become a crucial problem in the development of China's economy. More alarmingly still, the traditional credit system is on the verge of collapsing, particularly during the transition period.

Commercial Law Booming and Its Legal Risks

It is no bluff to say that there has been a great revolution in China over recent years. The commercial law in the transition of Chinese society from the mode of planned economy to the market-oriented one mostly features provisionally. Old laws act more as a roadblock for economic prosperity than a proper mechanism for advancing social welfare. Recent events illustrate a legislation boom ongoing in the field of commercial law.

Company Law. Company law is one of the basic legal pillars in a modern market-oriented economy. In a sense, it is the legal expression of intrinsic economic rules. A good institutional framework composed of advanced legal principles provided by company law can have a great influence on the protection of market participants, forms of capital investment, property security, and business transactions. The first "*Company Law of PRC*" was adopted at the Fifth Session of the Standing Committee of the Eighth National People's Congress on December 29, 1993, effective on July 1, 1994, and contained 11 chapters and 230 articles. It was amended for the first time at the thirteenth session of the Standing Committee of the Ninth People's Congress on December 25, 1999, adding supervisory committees for solely state-owned companies and loosening the requirements for public offerings for high-tech companies. In early 2004, the Office of Legislative Affairs of the State Council initiated a new revision process and completed the first draft for public consultation in July, 2005. At the 18th session of the Standing Committee of the Tenth National People's Congress on October 27, 2005, the new revised Company Law was adopted with a large number of amendments.

Some important amendments include: new provisions for single shareholder limited liability companies, independent boards of directors, cancellation of outward investment restrictions, the lowering of standards for public offering, reinforcement of controlling shareholders' responsibilities and loosening the restrictions on share redemption. More details are given in Table 1.1.

Securities Law. The first modern *Securities Law of the PRC* was born at the Sixth Session of the Ninth National People's Congress Standing Committee on 29 December 1998, effective on July 1, 1999. Before this, only related administrative regulations had existed for some 12 years. The promulgation of *Securities Law* was a reaction to the challenges of the Asian financial crisis in 1999. Thus, there are many prohibitions and privatives under stringent finance policies in such special period. Needless to say, many terms and clauses were not of a mature and deliberate

Table 1.1. Changes in Revised Company Law[15]

Areas of Amendments	Before Revision	After Revision
"To Pierce the Corporate Veil"	None	Article 20 Paragraph 3
Cumulative Voting System	None except for some provisions of CSRC	Article 106
Minimum Registered Capital down to 30,000 RMB in installments for Limited Liability Companies	Article 23 (separately 100,000, 300,000, 500,000 RMB for different forms of company)	Article 26
Minimum of Registered Capital down to 500 million RMB for Joint Stock Companies	Article 78 Paragraph 2 (Minimum of Registered Capital is 10 million RMB)	Article 81 Paragraph 3
Forms and Structure of Capital Contribution	Article 24 (limited to cash, industrial property rights, non-patented technology or land use rights)	Article 27 (added "non-monetary properties that may be assessed on the basis of currency and may be transferred in accordance with the law")
Removal of the compulsory ratio of outward investment to net assets	Article 12 Paragraph 2 (cumulative sum no more than 50% of net assets)	None
Enhancing the institution of derivative litigation and shareholder's litigation	Article 111 ("[i]f the resolutions of a meeting of shareholders or the board of directors have violated the law, administrative decrees or encroached upon the legitimate rights of shareholders, the shareholders concerned have the rights to sue at the people's courts …")	Article 20 Paragraph (resolution abolishment lawsuit); Article 75 Paragraph 2 (lawsuit regarding the compensation for dissenting shareholders); Article 152, 153 (managers and board of directors liability lawsuit)
Clarification of shareholder's rights regarding accessing to financial and account statements	Article 32	Article 34

15 Particular thanks contributed to the article of Zhang Yabo regarding the amendments to Securities Law and Company Law for its very helpful references.

Table 1.1 (continued)

Areas of Amendments	Before Revision	After Revision
Right of withdrawal for minority shareholders of limited liability companies in specific circumstances	None	Article 75
Independent Board of Directors	None except for some provisions of CSRC	Article 123 (to set up an independent board of directors in listed companies; the State Council constitutes the implementation measures)
Strict regulation of related-party transactions	None except for some provisions of CSRC	Article 21, Article 125, Article 217 Item (4)
Removal of provisions for statutory reserve funds	Article 177 Paragraph 1 ("… set aside 10 percent of the profits for the company's statutory reserve fund and 5 to 10 percent as the company's statutory public welfare fund.")	Article 167 (the statutory reserve fund for the welfare company employees.)
Securing independence of accounting firms	None except some provisions of Securities Regulatory Commission	Article 170, Article 171
Shareholder's rights of application for the judicial dissolution of company under certain conditions	None	Article 183 ("[w]here any company meets any serious difficulty in its operations or management so that the interests of the shareholders will face heavy loss if it continues to exist and it cannot be solved by any other means, the shareholders who hold ten percent or more of the voting rights of all the shareholders of the company may plead the people's court to dissolve the company")
Emphasis of social responsibilities	None	Article 5 Paragraph 1
Equipping sole shareholder limited liability companies with risk prevention mechanisms	None	Article 58 Paragraph 2, Article 59 – Article64

Table 1.1 (continued)

Areas of Amendments	Before Revision	After Revision
One-third requirement for shareholders' representatives in the supervisory committee	Article 52 Paragraph 2, Article 124 Paragraph 2	Article 52 Paragraph 2, Article 118 Paragraph 2
Specification of the responsibilities of intermediary institutions	None except some provisions of Article 63 of Securities Law	Article 208 Paragraph 3 (Where the appraisal result or proof of asset verification or certificate verification as provided by any institution that undertakes the appraisal or verification of assets or the verification of certificates is proved to be untrue, which has caused any loss to the creditors of the company, it shall bear the compensation liabilities within the sum which is found to be untrue, unless it can prove that it is not at fault in the incurrence of the loss.)
Employees' redemptive rights under dissolution and liquidation	Article 195 Paragraph 2, Paragraph 3	Article 187 Paragraph 2 (The residual properties that result from paying off the liquidation expenses, wages of employees, social insurance premiums and legal indemnification premiums, the outstanding taxes and the debts of the company with the properties of the company may, in the case of a limited liability company, be distributed according to the proportion of capital contribution of the shareholders or, in the case of a joint stock limited company, distributed according to the proportion of stocks held by the shareholders.)
Permitting the redemption of shares to award company employees	None	Article 143 Paragraph 1 Item (4)

nature. Even the rather technical term "T+1" (Today + One day), for instance, was adopted in the text. In addition, "[s]tate-owned enterprises and enterprises with controlling stakes purchased with state-owned assets may not speculate in stocks being traded on the market."[16] The meaning of "speculate" is equivocal. Similarly, there are no specific interpretations of the term "in violation of regulations".[17] Today, the booming investment market requires a new securities law to accommodate its development. To this end, a revised Securities Law was passed at the 18th Meeting of the Standing Committee of the 10th National People's Congress on October 27, 2005. Main Changes are presented in following chart.

Table 1.2. Changes in New Revised Securities Law

Areas of Amendments	Before Revision	After Revision
Loosening of financial regulation	Article 6	Article 6 ("[t]he regulatory mode by industry shall be applied to the industries of securities, banking, trusts and insurance. The securities companies and the business organs of banks, trusts, and insurance companies shall be separately established, unless it is otherwise provided for by the state.")
Broaden the channels for financing	Article 32	Article 39 ("Any stocks, corporate bonds or any other securities that have been publicly issued according to the law shall be listed on a stock exchange as legally established or in any other securities trading system as approved by the State Council.")
Enhancing the structure of investments & funds	Article 76 ("[s]tate-owned enterprises and enterprises holding stocks purchased with state-owned assets may not speculate in stocks being traded on the market."); Article 133 Paragraph 1 ("[b]anks are prohibited from putting funds in the stock market in violation of regulations.")	Article 81 ("[t]he channel for capital to enter into the stock market shall be broadened according to law. It's prohibited for any unqualified capital to go into the stock market."); Article 83 ("[t]he state-owned enterprises and state-controlled enterprises that engage in any trading of listed stocks shall observe the relevant provisions of the state.")

16 See Article 76, "Securities Law" of 1999.

17 See in Article 133, Id.

Table 1.2 (continued)

Areas of Amendments	Before Revision	After Revision
Fundamental reform of transaction systems	Article 33 ("[t]he method of open and centralized price bidding shall be adopted for trading of stocks in stock exchanges. The principle of price and time preference shall be practiced in centralized price bidding in stock trading."); Article 35 ("[t]he spot transaction method shall be implemented in stock transactions."); Article 36 ("[s]ecurities companies shall not engage in stock trading activities to raise capital or stocks from clients."); Article 106 ("[t]he securities companies, either entrusted or self-operating, shall not sell securities on the same day that they are purchased.")	Article 40 ("[t]he means of public and centralized trading or any other means as approval by the securities regulatory authority under the State Council shall be adopted for the listed trading of securities in stock exchanges."); Article 41 ("[t]he securities as purchased or sold by the parties involved in securities trading may be in paper form or in any other form as approval by the securities regulatory authority under the State Council."); Article 142 ("[w]here a securities company provides any service of securities financing through securities trading for its client, it shall meet the provisions of the State Council and shall be subject to the approval of the securities regulatory authority under the State Council.")
To adopt the supervisory mode by the scope of business on securities company	Article 119, Article 121, Article 122	Article 125, Article 127
Reinforcing the regulation of securities companies as majority shareholders	None except for some provisions of CSRC	Article 124 Item (2) ("… [t]he major shareholders having the ability to make profits continuously, enjoying good credit standing, and having no irregular or rule-breaking record over the last 3 years, and its net assets being no less than 0.2 billion yuan …"); Article 129 Paragraph 1 ("[w]here a securities company … alters its shareholders who hold more than 5% of its stock rights or the actual controller … it shall be subject to the approval of the securities regulatory authority under the State Council.");

Table 1.2 (continued)

Areas of Amendments	Before Revision	After Revision
		Article 130 Paragraph 2 ("[a] securities company shall not provide any financing or guaranty for its shareholders or any related person thereof."); Article 151 ("[w]here a shareholder of a securities company makes any fake capital contribution or removes registered capital, the securities regulatory authority under the State Council shall order them to correct this irregularity within a prescribed period and may order them to transfer the stock rights of the securities company they hold. Before a shareholder as prescribed in the preceding paragraph herein corrects the irregularity and transfers the stock right of the securities company they hold according to the relevant requirements, the securities regulatory authority under the State Council may restrict the shareholders' rights thereof.")
Strengthening the continual supervisory institutions based on net capital & establishing and improving internal supervision	Article 123, Article 124 ("[a] securities company's total external debt must not exceed the prescribed multiple amount of its net assets; its floating debt must not exceed the prescribed percentage of its floating assets. The State Council's securities regulatory body will provide regulations on the specific multiple amount, percentage, and management procedures."), Article 132 Paragraph 2	Article 129, Article 130 Paragraph 1 ("[t]he securities regulatory authority under the State Council shall formulate provisions on the risk control indicators of a securities company such as net capital, the ratio between net capital and liabilities, the ratio between net capital and net assets, the ratio between net capital and operational scale of self-operation, underwriting and asset management, the ratio between liabilities and net asset, as well as the ratio between current assets and current liabilities."), Article 139, Article 150

Table 1.2 (continued)

Areas of Amendments	Before Revision	After Revision
Specification of the institution of withdrawal of securities companies	None	Article 153 ("[w]here any illegal operation of a securities company or any major risk thereof seriously disturbs the order of the securities market or injures the interests of the relevant investors, the securities regulatory authority under the State Council may take such supervisory measures as suspending its business for rectification, designating any other institution for trusteeship, take-over or cancellation.")
Setting up of investor protection fund	None	Article 134 ("[t]he state shall establish a securities investor protection fund. The securities investor protection fund shall be composed of the capital paid by securities companies and any other capital lawfully raised. The specific measures for financing, administration and use of the foregoing fund shall be formulated by the State Council.")
Defining the meaning of public issuance	None except for some provisions of "*Securities Regulation*"	Article 10
Specification of recommending institutions and their duties	None	Article 11
Lowering of the standards for public offering	None except for Article 137 of "*Company Law*"	Article 13
Lowering of the standards for public listing	None except for Article 152 of "*Company Law*"	Article 50
Establishing the institution of pre-disclosure	None	Article 21 ("[w]here an issuer applies for an IPO of stocks, it shall, after submitting the application documents, disclose the relevant application documents in advance according to the provisions of the securities regulatory authority under the State Council.")

Table 1.2 (continued)

Areas of Amendments	Before Revision	After Revision
The failure of public issuance	None	Article 35 ("[a]s for a public offer of stocks through sale by proxy, when the term of sale by proxy expires and if the number of stocks fails to reach 70 % of the planned number in the public offering, it shall be deemed a failure. The relevant issuer shall refund the issuing price plus interest as calculated at the bank deposit rate for the relevant period of time to the subscribers of stocks.")
Improvement of the institution regarding profits from short-line transactions	Article 42	Article 47
Granting more supervisory authority to the stock exchange		Article 50 Paragraph 2, Article 55-56, Article 60-61
Redefining the scope of the term "major event"	Article 62	Article 67
Inclusion of recommenders, holding shareholders and actual controllers in the scope of subjects with responsibilities	None	Article 26, Article 69
Change from compulsory purchase offer to optional purchase offer	Article 81 ("[w]hen an investor, through trading on the stock exchange, possesses 30 percent of the stocks issued by a listed company and plans to make more purchases, he shall make a purchase offer to the company's stockholders as is required by law, except where such an offer is exempted by the securities regulatory body of the State Council.")	Article 88 ("[w]here an investor holds individually or with any other person 30% of the stocks as issued by a listed company by means of agreement or any other arrangement through securities trading on the stock exchange and continues to purchase, he shall issue a tender offer to all the shareholders of said listed company to purchase all or part of the shares of the listed company."), Article 96 Paragraph 1
New regulations regarding the withdrawal and transfer of shares of target companies after acquisition	Article 86-87, Article 92	Article 97-98

These revisions suggest the healthy development of *Securities Law*. However, such changes cannot be expected to solve all the problems of China's capital markets. The system of divided supervision and traditional management systems remain fully intact. More areas of the investment market need to be more deeply explored. Reformers' efforts in the stock and financial markets might be more fruitful in the context of fundamental reform of the whole economic system.

Bankruptcy Law. The new *Enterprise Bankruptcy Law of PRC* (the "Bankruptcy Law") was adopted on August 27, 2006 and will take effect on June 1, 2007, superseding the 1986-enacted *Enterprise Bankruptcy Law (Trial)* (the "1986 Law"), governing the bankruptcy of State-owned Enterprises ("SOEs"). The Bankruptcy Law offers for the first time a unified regime applicable to all types of enterprises in China and also provides a more robust and detailed regime for enforcement of creditors' claims.

The 1986 Law only applies to the bankruptcy of SOEs, while the Bankruptcy Law provides a unified bankruptcy system for all "enterprises with legal person status," covering both SOEs and privately-owed companies, including foreign investment enterprises ("FIEs"). Individual or partnership bankruptcy, however, is not covered by the Bankruptcy Law.

The 1986 Law allows a creditor to file a bankruptcy petition only when the debtor is unable generally to pay its debts as they fall due. Under the Bankruptcy Law, both the debtor and its creditors are allowed to file reorganization or bankruptcy petitions to the People's Court under certain circumstances (subject to special rules for financial institutions).

Under the 1986 Law, a corporate reorganization can only be petitioned for and carried out by the government authorities. The Bankruptcy Law, however, allows either the debtor or the creditor to apply to the People's Court for reorganization of the debtor. When a creditor petitions to bankrupt a debtor, the debtor, or its investors holding more than one third of the debtor's registered capital, may apply to the court for reorganization after the court has accepted the bankruptcy petition, but before the debtor is declared bankrupt.

A debtor may apply to the People's Court for conciliation of its debt after the court accepts the bankruptcy application. If the court approves the conciliation application, it will make a public announcement and convene a creditors' meeting to discuss the draft conciliation plan. Once the reconciliation is approved by the creditors' meeting and the court, the administrator shall transfer the business and assets to the debtor. To become effective, the plan must be approved by more than half of creditors present at the meeting holding more than two-thirds of the total amount of confirmed claims (excluding secured claims). If the conciliation plan is rejected, the court will declare the debtor bankrupt.

The Bankruptcy Law stipulates a scheme for claim payment priority. Unlike the 1986 Law, the Bankruptcy Law no longer gives higher priority to unpaid employee wages and social insurance premiums. Under Article 109, secured creditors have payment priority to the extent of the value of the secured properties, while the under secured portion is treated as a common claim. Payment of claims in a liquidation must be made according to the following order:(i) bankruptcy expenses and joint interest debts; (ii) unpaid employees' salaries and basic social insurance premiums; (iii) outstanding tax; and (iv) ordinary unsecured credits.

Until the enactment of the Bankruptcy Law, China did not have a unified bankruptcy law applicable to all enterprises. Historically bankruptcies of SOEs have often been driven by public policy concerns more than the interests of creditors out of concerns for large unemployment and social instability. Bankruptcies of other types of entities have been subject to relatively vague and general bankruptcy provisions of the Law of Civil Procedure and of Supreme Court interpretations. The Bankruptcy Law, with its detailed provisions governing a broad range of enterprise debtors, will bring sweeping changes to the administration of creditors' claims in the PRC. More streamlined procedures will help enhance the transparency of bankruptcy proceedings. New rules, including those providing for bankruptcy petitions, role of administrators, corporate reorganization, conciliation, role of creditors and priorities of claims, will bring China's enterprise bankruptcies closer to international standards.[18]

Unmooring Legislation regarding Commercial Credit. In the Third Session of the Sixteenth Central Committee of CPC, the Resolution of Several Issues regarding improving the Socialist Market-Oriented Economy System further stated that it was necessary to establish a social credit system, bolstered by socialist morality, centered on property rights and secured by legal institutions. This reform would involve: the fast-tracking of the development of credit services for enterprises and individuals, the set up of the institutions of credit checking and accreditation and the gradual opening of the credit service market by developing legal institutions, promoting the franchise system and enhancing professional services under modern business protocols.

The CPC's policy is to accelerate the legislation regarding commercial credit. At present, the People's Bank of China is drafting *the Administration of Credit Collection.* It covers several areas such as credit information collection and conservation, processing and sale to secure authenticity and completeness. Resolution of issues with respect to the supervision of credit information collection agencies and entry standards for foreign-related agencies are also on the agenda. With reference to other countries' models, the next few steps are expected as follows: firstly, to open a database of credit information based on compulsory disclosure, with penalties for non-compliance; secondly, to improve the security systems for confidential information. The scope of credit information and the means and time limits for its processing and release will be specified in detail. In addition, the

---

[18] New Law Ushers in Sweeping Changes to Bankruptcy Regime in China, from www.mofo.com.cn, the last visiting on October 4, 2006.

provider (including government departments and individuals) shall be charged for false disclosure. Accordingly, some current laws and regulations, such as "*Commercial Bank Law*", "*Contract Law*", "*General Rules of Bank Lending*", etc., will be revised in conformity with developed credit collection institutions.

In fact, this project of credit information collection was launched before relevant legislation was in place. On December 15 2004, it was announced that a uniform database of individual credit information was to be operational the next July, involving every wholly state-owned bank, joint stock commercial bank and municipal bank in seven cities (Beijing, Chongqing, Shenzhen, Xi'an, Nanning, Mianyang and Huzhou). In 2005, the database covered the whole nation. Following an integrated resource of individual credit records has been finally built up, after the database of enterprise credit records completed in 2002. With the advancement of the credit system, the Supreme People's Court has begun to construct a database concerning the execution of judgment. Some local judicial authorities go further. They have established databases of adjudication in their own jurisdictions. The Beijing government launched its municipal system of information regarding mischievous behavior, being the first database of its kind on the internet. Similarly, The Shanghai municipal government has its own collaborated system of individual credit information collection. In Guangzhou, the government uploads files of local enterprise credit information to a public network in three security levels. Shenzhen Municipal Council has passed *the Administration of Individual Collection and Credit Rating* as the basic regulation in its area. The rumblings of commercial credit information systems being constructed are radically shaking up the commercial environment.

In addition, the revision of the income tax law has been scheduled for the next session of National People's Congress. The Draft of the Anti-monopoly Law was passed on June 7, 2006 in the Standing Meeting of the State Council, and such a Draft was submitted to the National People's Congress the next day by the Office of Legal Affairs. A fully fledged framework for China's market economy is being born.

The recent boom in commercial legislation has fundamentally changed the commercial law environment in China, and the boom is not yet at an end. The legal space for foreign investors living has sharply changed after law revision or issuance. In general, with continuing changes and revisions, more legal risks will blossom beyond anyone's expectations. Foreign investors need to seek innovative living rules in the newly changed commercial environment. In particular, foreign investors must learn to adapt to the continuously evolving legal environment.

Table 1.3. Timetable of Commercial Legislation

Law	Legislation Progress	Range of Changes	Influences to Foreign Investors
Company Law	Effective on October 27, 2005	To amend more than 120 articles. Revisions and additions run to more than 400	Thoroughly changes the rules for company management and operation in China; great influence on foreign investors
Securities Law	Effective on October 27, 2005	Considerable changes broadening the channels of financing in the stock market	Since the entry of foreign investment is limited, the present effects do not seem as great as they do in the long term.
Bankruptcy Law	Effective on June 1, 2007.	The law completely shakes up current institutions	Greatly influential
Antitrust Law	Passed by the State Council, and has entered the legislation process.	Unprecedented legislation activity.	Great impact on foreign investors.
Income Tax Law	The reform is expedited on a tight schedule.	Predicted to enhance uniformity in both domestic and foreign-invested enterprises; the super-national treatment of the latter shall be cancelled in future.	Great impact
Credit Collection Law	A unifying law is expected to be released, integrating separate related rules.	To establish a system of business credit collection, to a great extent, it will change the rules of business operation.	Great impact

1.3 Macro-analysis of the Risks Arising from Foreign Investors Behavior

As Professor Chen An detailed in his article, the process of foreign investment can involve several legal entities and multiple legal relations.[19] The participants of foreign investment can be simply divided into two parts: government authorities and foreign investors (including foreign-invested enterprises).

---

[19] Chen An(1998), Discussion on Limitation, Integration and independence of the Subject of International Economic Law, Series of International Economic Law, China Law Press, Vol.1.

1.3.1 The Risks from the Authorities

Foreign investment protrudes its distinctions from other business behavior under strict governmental supervision. In China, the governmental influences are far greater. The reasons may be: (1) The idea that officials make all the decisions is deeply rooted in society. The authority is inclined to stretch its arms into private areas, particularly in foreign-related investments. (2)Like other transition countries, China's authorities can not promptly adapt their functions and roles to the new economy. Additionally, we need to differentiate between two kinds of governmental influences on foreign investors: central government and local authorities.

Risks Coming from Central Government Behaviors

When foreign investors began knocking at the doors of China's market, the nationalization of key industries was raised as one of the critical issues. Many worries of confiscation came from a misunderstanding of communism. Some cases of confiscation and expropriation of bureaucratic and private capital by "the CPC's government" without doubt aggravated this concern. As the investment environment has improved, the worry of nationalization has given way to concerns about the risks of volatile policies. Most of risks arise from the impacts by the central government making macro-economic policies. On July 20 2005, for example, the effects of *"Steel & Iron Industry Development Policy"* issued by the NDRC, was well known to aspiring and active foreign investors. It set up a number of standards defining qualified foreign investors including: ownership of proprietary intellectual property rights. The output of ordinary steel should be more than 10 million tons in the previous year; or 1 million tons for high alloy specialty steels. The majority share is not permitted to be held by the foreign investor in principal. New consolidated enterprises, individual enterprises and steel-making mills are not authorized to be solely built by foreigners. Once, for instance, Guang Gang Group planned to cooperate with JFE (a Japanese company, the latter being the controlling shareholder) on a joint venture for producing steel plate for vehicles. The issuance of new policy created great legal risks in the transaction. The "*Opinions on the Acceleration and Rejuvenation of the Equipment Manufacturing Industry*" issued by the State Council on June 16, 2006, explicitly closed the door for foreign investors to purchase controlling shares of the enterprises that play vital roles in the manufacture of technological equipment, which will remain under state control during their restructuring. Meanwhile, "*Opinions on the Regulation of Foreign Capital in the Real Estate Market and its Management*" issued on July 11, 2006 sharply improved the threshold of foreign capital entering into China's real estate market.

There are two characteristics of the risks which come from the central government's behavior: It is overwhelming over an entire range; and it is non-compensable. There is no redress or compensation under current laws for the victims.

Risks Arising from Local Authorities' Behaviors

Some experts consider the reforms that took place from 1978 to 1997 to have substantially transferred the centralized economy into many localized ones administered by local authorities. One kingdom has effectively transformed into many independent small kingdoms.[20] These small kingdoms are China's 32 provinces. At a local level, the quality of government is inevitably connected with the quantity of foreign investment. Since foreign capital rather than the needs of domestic consumers', is the major driver of economic growth (evaluated by GDP) the foreign investment aims towards short term results that are visible as most important achievements of local officials and leaders. Moreover, local interests sometimes drive local governments to scramble for foreign investments. The input of foreign investment is not only essential to local officials' political career, but also drives the scramble (it may lightly be called "run-to-bottom") for foreign investment between different areas. In this contest, many local governments are forced to implement extraordinarily favorable terms or provide other irrational benefits (out of legal restriction) such as governmental guaranty, tax returns or even free land use in impoverished areas. Legal risks will be incurred by such favorable treatment offered by local authorities.[21]

1.3.2 Risks Arising From Foreign Investors' Behaviors

The influence of foreign investors' behavior should not be ignored in the assessment of legal risks. In some cases, it even becomes the sole reason for the failure or loss of investments. The following case, created a huge stir throughout Chinese society.

DPC Case

> *As a subsidiary of Diagnostic Products Corporation (DPC) in California, USA, DPC (Tianjin) Limited Company (DPC (Tianjin)) offered bribes of $1.6 million to staff in three hospitals over a period of 11 years. According to the Department of Justice of US, most of bribes were personally handed in cash to the staff in charge of purchasing. The manager of DPC (Tianjin) personally approved the payments and recorded them as sales expenses. DPC investigated and reported to authorities in the United States two years ago. Jim Brill, CFO of DPC, disclosed to the press that they thought it (refers*

---

[20] Ping Xinqiao, Motive and Effect of Governmental Umbrella – Positivism Analysis, China Center for Economic Research (CCER) at Peking University Discussion Paper (No. C200332).

[21] See the detailed analysis of legal risks arising from the local authorities' behaviors in Chapter 5.

to the reporting) was right; "as an American company, we just could not do business in such way". In any event, DPC did violate anti-bribery provisions under the Foreign Corrupt Practices Act of 1977 by bribing, as an American firm, foreign recipients. Under the settlement, DPC agreed to pay penalties of $2 million and $2.4 million separately to the Department of Justice and the Securities Exchange Commission, in addition to a $0.75 million pre-trial fee; a total of over $4.8 million. More details will be disclosed with further criminal and civil investigations.

—— Chen Mohan, International Herald Leader, San Diego.

In fact, ever since the publication of Ethan Gutmann's "*Losing the New China: A Story of American Commerce, Desire and Betrayal*", many multinational companies have faced increasing criticisms of losing sight of their principles and their bottom lines in China. This book describes how Microsoft had bragged that it once bribed officials to enter China's market in an under the table agreement, how managers of Asia Global Crossing destroyed financial documents to conceal deficits, and how some foreign enterprises in China had offered five star hotels and sexual services to officials for dealing with the supervisory officials. From Gutmann's radical perspective, China bears the blame for these scandals because of its "wild west" business environment.

It is unfair to jump to the conclusion that China's environment is unjust. American companies have not proved themselves saintly over the years. Bribery was once common in the western world, and this triggered the "*Foreign Corrupt Practices Act*" of 1977.[22] Indeed, many foreign adventurers came to China looking for their "golden nuggets" thanks to indulgent regulatory authorities and a lack of related laws and administration. Because of this, foreign enterprises used to provide low-grade products to Chinese consumers. Since 2005, more cases have been filed in China's courts regarding product liability such as harmful ingredients found in the fried food of KFC, skincare products of P&G, Shanghai Johnson-Johnson, Unilever, Nestle milk powder, etc. The frequency of these cases implies non-normative conduct and double-standards at multinational companies. The speculators' ends in the U.S. are totally different, because there is a more precise and firm regulatory mechanism complete with punitive measures. Their conduct is different, and their multiple faces switch in different situations. As for redress and compensation in China, multinational firms often deal with claims of product liability by simply recalling defective products. Previously, without uniform implementation standards, adjudicators and officials were hesitant to rule in favor of the claimants. Increasingly, foreign enterprises will drag themselves into ceaseless litigations and claims with such conduct.

---

[22] See Partrik M. Norton (2004), The Foreign Corrupt Practices Act: A Minefield for US Companies in China, an O' Meleny& Meyers LLP Research Report, Download from the website of O' Meleny&Meyers LLP, the last visiting on Oct. 2005.

Part One:

Legal Risks of Foreign Capital Entry

Part One:

Legal Risks of Foreign Capital Entry

2 The Legal Risks of Green Field Foreign Investment

Do not do in China what you won't do in New York or London.

—— U.S. Department of Commerce[1]

2.1 Case Study: Legal Risks Behind the Curtain of Carley[2]

This appalling case originated from a joint venture, named Beijing Carley Ltd. In Sept. 1994, Beijing Second Commerce Group, Beijing Heye Real Estate Company, and the Hong Kong Carley Group reached an agreement to form the Beijing Carley Co. Ltd. to erect up Beijing Carley World Trade Center in Chaoyang District, Beijing. Their shares were 32%, 8% and 60% respectively. The joint venture was approved by the Beijing Municipal Bureau of Commerce in January 1995, with a $30 million total investmnet and $12 million registered capital. In March, the business license was obtained and they opened for business. The early capital Hong Kong Carley contributed was $12.25 million, plus $35 million for fund raising in the joint venture. Approximately $7.72 million, of the $12.25 million invested as registed capital, came in RMB via Gongdong Huitong Company and Foshan Huaqiang Company, which planted a fuse for latter troubles. In September 2001, the Beijing Second Commerce Group charged the Hong Kong Carley Group with defaulting on its obligation of capital contribution. They applied to change their foreign partner at the Beijing Municipal Bureau of Commerce, and reorganized the joint venture, named Bejing Meibang Real Estate Co. Ltd., with Beijing Anhua Company. Hong Kong Meibang Group replaced Hong Kong Carley. On September 27, Beijing Municipal Bureau of Commerce gave its official reply, transferring Hong Kong Carley Group's approximatly 60% share holding valued at 0.6 billion RMB to the Hong Kong Meibang Group. Three days later, Beijing Commerce Bureau issued a license to the newly-established joint venture. This

---

1 A warning advice provided by Commercial Service of US Department of Commerce in a material named The Growing China Market: *What It Means for Alaskan Exporters, downloaded from* www.stimson.org/exportcontrol/pdf/WalshUSCCTestimony-Jan02.pdf (last visited on Nov. 2005).

2 The facts of Carley case is mostly cited from reports in Phoenixtv Week, Issue 183.

switch of shareholders gave rise to the first case with the Ministry of Commerce of the PRC as defendant. Ultimately Carley failed to recoup its huge loss of invested capital.[3]

According to applicable laws, the contribution in cash by foreign investors in newly established enterprises shall only be made in convertible foreign exchange, except for contributions in RMB drawn from returns on investments made in China. In Article 25 of "*Implementation Rules for Law on Wholly Foreign-invested Enterprises of the PRC*", it is provided that

> "[t]he foreign investors may make their investments with freely exchangeable foreign currencies, or with machinery and equipment, with industrial property rights and proprietary technology by appraising their value.
>
> Upon approval by the examining and approving authority, foreign investors may also invest profits in RMB gained from any other enterprise that they have established in China."

Even though the document uses "may", not "must" or "shall", contribution with foreign currency is required in most cases. Exceptions arise where foreign investors meet the following conditions: (1) Investors must have investments in China. (2) The contribution in RMB is entirely taken from their investment return in RMB. (3) Investors need to apply for approval from the foreign exchange supervisory authority.[4] Under the Implementing Rules, the Carley case was triggered because of minor defects in their funding chain – the provisions prohibiting contributions in RMB were violated.

Similarly, in Article 7 of "*Administrative Regulations on the Capital Contribution by Parties to Sino-foreign Equity Joint Enterprises*",

---

3 In September 20, 2005, the China International Economic and Trade Arbitration Commission (CIETAC) made a final rule at Carley case: it affirmed the status of Hong Kong Carley Group as the shareholder of Beijing Carley Real Estate Ltd. by 60% of shares.

4 Related Policies have become lax latter. In terms of Article 10 of "*Interim Provisions on Restructuring State-owned Enterprises with Foreign Investment*", "[f]oreign investors shall pay for the prices of transferred property rights or make their contributions with freely convertible currencies remitted from beyond the territory or any other lawful property rights. They may also pay or make their contributions with the net profits of RMB obtained from their investment within the territory of China or with any other lawful property rights subject to the approval of the foreign exchange administration. The lawful property rights as mentioned above shall include: a. The properties obtained by foreign investors from the liquidation, transfer of equity, advance reclaim of investment or reduction of registered capital of any other foreign-funded enterprises established within the territory of China; b. The state-owned property rights or assets of any state-owned enterprise or company-based enterprises that consist of state-owned equity purchased by foreign investors; c. The credits of the creditors of any of the state-owned enterprises purchased by foreign investors; d. Any other contribution provided by any law or regulation."

> "[A] party in a joint venture will be regarded as in breach of contract if it has failed to put up or contribute fully its required capital according to the time schedule agreed in the joint venture contract. The other party in the joint venture having fulfilled the contribution obligation shall then inform and urge the breaching party to fulfill its obligation within a one-month period. If the breaching party still fails to fulfill its capital contribution obligations, the breaching party will be considered as "voluntarily withdrawing" from the joint venture and "voluntarily surrendering" all its rights to the joint venture. The remaining party shall then apply to the original examination and approval authority either to dissolve the joint venture or to find another partner to undertake the obligations and rights of the breaching party as provided in the original joint venture contract. The abiding party shall have the right to make claim for compensation as a result of the breaching party's failure to fulfill its capital contribution obligations."

In Article 2 of *"Instructive Opinions on Solving the Issue of Directors failing to attend Board of Directors Meeting"* promulgated by the Ministry of Foreign Trade and Economic Cooperation (later, the Ministry of Commerce) and the State Administration of Industry and Commerce,

> "... if a shareholder fails to fulfill or incompletely fulfill its obligations according to the agreed time schedule in the joint venture contract, other shareholders may directly request the authority previously permitting its registration to change shareholder or transfer shares under the provisions of *'Administrative Regulations on the Capital Contribution by Parties to Sino-foreign Equity Joint Enterprises' and 'Provisions for the Alteration of Investors' Equity in Foreign-funded Enterprises'."*

The administrative authority was thereby granted special powers to directly confirm the breaching party and alter its rights as a shareholder only by the other party's unilateral alleger.

Clearly the Hong Kong Carley Group made an illicit move in making its contribution in RMB. Nevertheless, the result of the administrative review by the Beijing Minicipal Bureau of Commerce repealing its shareholder status is vulnerable to attack. The Ministry of Foreign Trade and Economic Cooperation (MOFTEC) overruled the above-mentioned result taking the line that: The "defective" contribution of RMB by Hong Kong Carley was just marginally illicit. The decision of Beijing Minicipal Bureau of Commerce infringed Carley's lawful rights and interests. So Carley's shareholder status should be reinstated. The award of CIETAC also confirmed that a "defective" contribution should be distinguished from full failure to contribute. The investment of RMB equal to the agreed sum of foreign currency was not the real cause for the failure of the joint venture. It is unfair and unethical for the Chinese partners to have cut out Carley for only minor faults in fulfillment of contractual obligations and violation of official ordinances after running out of joint venture's funds.

The result seems to support the notion that a "defective" contribution will not definitely lead to deprivation of shareholder status. Even so, the legal risks should not be ignored. The arbitrary nature of authority may exaggerate any trivial defect in the process of a transaction. Some may make advantage of this, under the possible abuse of public execution, to nibble away their foreign partners' cake.

In December 2004, a similar case in Guiyang (the capital of Guizhou Province) drew public attention again. In its ruling, the Intermediary Court of Guiyang nullified the review decision (No.50, 2004) of the Ministry of Commerce of China. The central government agency lost its lawsuit as the defendant in a local court. It was released that: In February 2004, Guizhou Province Administration of Foreign Industry and Trade repealed registration certificate of jointly-funded hotel "Guizhou Hotel Co. Ltd." after its operation of over 10 years. Its Hong Kong partner, Hanshan Group was therefore disqualified for default in the contribution. MOFCOM was sued by China's shareholder for its nullification of notification of repealing registration certificate of Guizhou Hotel Co. Ltd. issued by Administration of Foreign Industry and Trade Guizhou Province.

To escape blame, the MOFCOM sent an official letter to the Office of Legal Affairs of the State Council on April 29, 2004, which gave a restrictive interpretation of Article 7 of "*Administrative Regulations on the Capital Contribution by the Parties to Sino-foreign Equity Joint Enterprises*". In the letter, it set out a preliminary procedure for officially determining whether or not a failure of contribution or full contribution has occurred. The examination and approval administration shall dissolve the joint venture or replace the original breaching party on the abiding party's request according to related arbitration or court judgment.[5] The reply of the Office of Legal Affairs of the State Council on January 20, 2005[6] was consistent with the interpretation of MOFCOM.

Reviewing the two cases, the abuse of public power was primarily to blame, but it just upgraded the minor defects. Consequently the roots of legal risks still come from imperfections in the practices of green field foreign investments. The initial

---

5 MOFCOM says: "In practice, it is very common that one party unilaterally claims as the abiding side. The administration shall not arbitrarily support their claims or has no authority to judge whether or not 'failed to put up or contribute fully its required capitals' and which side is the 'abiding party' or 'breaching party'. The examination and approval administration shall dissolve the joint venture or look for another joint venture partner to undertake the obligations and rights of the breaching party as provided in the original joint venture contract, on the abiding party's request, according to related effective arbitration ruling or court's judgment."

6 Since the official letter of MOFCOM sent on April 29, 2004 to the reply on January 20, 2005, eight and half months have elapsed!

contribution is the first and most important step in green field investment, and also the most likely to cause disputes. A high level of self scrutiny therefore, is advisable in this area filled with potential landmines.

2.2 The Risk in Partners Choosing

During the course of an annual inspection in 2001, the Tianjin municipal authorities found 637 foreign investment enterprises whose China's partners were disqualified or deceased, making up 11.11% of examined enterprises and 18.81% of current Sino-foreign equity and cooperative joint ventures. The reasons for this include: (1) Chinese partners losing their qualification to cooperate with foreigners after reforming. (2) Ignorance of regulations for business registration and failure to file registrations as required. (3) Loss of legal person status for the violation of regulations. (4) Discrepancies between business registration procedures for domestic and foreign-invested enterprises.[7]

There are various legal risks in the selection of cooperative partners, since laws and regulations only permit qualified Chinese entities to cooperate with foreign investors. Negligence in choosing a partner, will give rise to legal problems once the joint venture is established.

According to the *"Constitutional Law"*, "[t]he People's Republic of China permits foreign enterprises, other economic organizations and individual to invest in China and to enter into various forms of economic cooperation with Chinese enterprises and other Chinese economic organizations in accordance with laws and regulations of PRC." In this vein, "Law on Sino-foreign Equity Joint Venture of PRC" and "Law on Sino-foreign Cooperative Joint Venture of PRC" give similar definitions of Chinese partners and foreign investors. The former must be companies, enterprises or other economic organizations; whereas the scope of foreign investors may include companies, enterprises or other economic firms which shall be set up in accordance with foreign laws and certain registration formalities, as well as individuals who are entitled to launch joint ventures under their own names.

More detailed standards are furnished by the "Circular of Strict Examination of the Qualification of Chinese Entities in Sino-foreign Equity Joint Ventures" (hereafter, "the Circular"):

(1) Chinese Entities in a joint venture must fall under the definition of "Enterprise" in the provisions of Articles 36 to 49 of "*Civil Law General Principles*", or be another form of economic organization which has obtained legal person status.

7 Gao Zhanyun, Zhu Yaning (2003), Origins and Regulations of Disqualified or Deceased China's Investors in Sino-foreign Equity and Cooperative Joint Ventures, China Business Management Study, Issue 10.

(2) Political parties and governmental agencies at all levels, including political parties, administrative and military agencies, cross-industry, cross-area and national administrative organizations, associations, civil groups, academies, institutes, colleges and judicial departments, are not permitted to be Chinese cooperators in a signed contract or carry out negotiations with foreign investors if they fall short of the related provisions of *Civil Law General Principles* and are without legal person status.

(3) Cooperative enterprises involving military logistics, factories and farms affiliated with research institutes and cross-industry and cross-area firms, if registered and approved by the supervisory administration of industry and commerce, may individually sign legal documents such as contracts and Articles of association with foreigners.

(4) Town and village individual businesses (Ge Ti Hu), personal contractors for industry and commerce and individual partnerships, shall not independently carry out negotiation or sign contracts or Articles of association in joint ventures, without permits or licenses.

False Definition of "Other Economic Organization"

In the Circular, the Chinese cooperator must be an enterprise or other economic organization with legal person status. Furthermore, the Circular requires that the related authorities shall not accept and approve joint venture contracts or Articles of association with enterprises or other economic organizations without legal person status as a party. The other economic organization shall be an organization with legal person status as per the interpretation of the document. After the release of the Circular, the authorities in charge of approval of foreign investment projects and the administration of industry and commerce at all levels all hold that Chinese partners in joint ventures must have obtained legal person status, and if they do not, related documents will not be approved.[8] This book argues that the interpretation of this Circular is inappropriately narrow.

Under the provisions of "*Civil Law General Principles*", the civil subjects of civil law are classified into "citizens" and "legal persons". In Chapter II, "citizens" includes natural persons, individual businesses (Ge Ti Hu) and leaseholding farm households and individual partnerships. "Legal persons" embraces enterprises, official organs, institutions, social organizations and economic associations. In this sense, "other economic organizations" just means the entities cannot obtain the "legal person" status prescribed by *Civil Law General Principles* if they are not natural persons, individual businesses (Ge Ti Hu), leaseholding farm households or individual partnerships. In addition, article 40 of "*Supreme People's Court Provisions on the Rightful use of Civil Procedural Law*" and Article 49 of "*Civil Procedural Law*" define, "other organizations" as entities established in accordance with the law

---

8 Li Qiang, Reconstruction of Legal Institutions of Foreign-invested Enterprises, www.civillaw.com.cn, the lasting visiting on Oct 19, 2005.

which have not qualified for legal person status as prescribed by the law, and are in possession of necessary property or funds and departments. This includes: (1) private solely-owned enterprises and partnerships with business licenses; (2) associated businesses in partnership with business licenses; (3) Sino-foreign Cooperative joint ventures and foreign solely-owned enterprises with business licenses; (4) social groups approved and registered by the civil administration; (5) lawfully established branches of legal persons with business licenses; (6) branches of the People's Bank of China and other commercial banks; (7) branches of the People's Insurance Company of China; (8) town village and street enterprises with business licenses; (9) other organizations under the provisions of this article. Therefore, "other economic organizations" should be interpreted as entities that have business licenses but no legal person status, with the exception of social groups approved and registered by the civil administration. Thus the above-mentioned Circular definition of "other economic organizations" as organizations with legal person status is totally wrong. The Chinese industrial and commercial registration system does not distinguish "market subject" from "business subject".[9] An entity obtaining a business license without legal person status is virtually equal to "other economic organizations". By the same token, the expression "other economic organizations with legal person status" used in the Circular is an oxymoron.

"*Opinions of Improving Administration of Industry and Commerce to Boost Exercising Reform and Open-up Policy*" (No.163, 1992) issued by SAIC in 1992 provides that "... to support the cooperation of privately owned enterprises and individual businesses with foreign investors. It is allowed for private enterprises (solely-owned and partnerships) to set up Sino-foreign equity or cooperative joint ventures for processing businesses and trade." It is expressly provided that private solely-owned enterprises and partnerships without legal person status may engage in cooperation with foreign investors in the establishment of joint ventures. Such paradoxical provisions cause confusion. The selection of suitable partners thereby becomes a headache suffered by foreign investors in an environment of inconsistent rules and standards.

Doubt Exists About "Natural Person" Being Foreigners' Partner

Under the provisions of "*Constitutional Law*", "*Sino-foreign Equity Joint Venture Law*" and "*Sino-foreign Cooperative Joint Venture Law*", Chinese citizen or Chinese "natural persons" definitely cannot be one of the parties in Sino-foreign joint ventures. However, some local regulations provide different answers.

---

9 Some countries and districts distinguish "market subject" from "business status". In the U.K., the new enterprises must select the scope of business after setting up. Singapore government provides the issuance of registration certificate does not indicate that the applicant has met other legal requirements of business operation. In the typical case of Chinese Taiwan, the ascertainments of market subject and business status separately fall into two different approval authorities of administration. See the report "Thoughts about Registration Management Systems of Modern Foreign-invested Enterprises".

In Article 56 of "*Regulations on Zhong Guan Village Science Park*" promulgated on December 8, 2000 by the Standing Committee of Beijing People's Congress, it is provided that "[o]verseas economic organizations or individuals may establish new- and high-technology joint ventures and cooperative enterprises in Zhong Guan Village Science Park with domestic organizations or individuals." Similarly, in Article 24 of Chapter V (Individually Funded Equity or Cooperative High-Technology Joint Ventures) of "*Administrative Measures of the Registration of Enterprises in Zhong Guan Village Science Park*", it further specifies: "Chinese citizens may as natural persons contribute funds to establish Sino-foreign equity or cooperative high-technology joint ventures in conformity with laws and regulations of Sino-foreign equity or cooperative joint ventures,..." Latterly, the provisions of "Opinions on Reform of Market Entry Rules and Improving Economic Development Environment" (issued by Beijing Municipal Administration of Industry and Commerce on February 12, 2004) limitlessly broaden the applicable scope of the above-mentioned special provision. In its Article 7, it provides that a Chinese citizen may cooperate with foreign investors on joint ventures in the city of Beijing. Obviously, these Beijing municipal regulations constitute a contradiction with or even violation of the provisions of "*Constitutional Law*", "*Law on Sino-foreign Equity Joint Venture of PRC*" and "*Law on Sino-foreign Cooperative Joint Venture of PRC*". Beijing becomes a special legal zone over the issue of qualified Chinese parties of Sino-foreign joint ventures.

With further improvements in the foreign investment environment, minor adjustments have been made to some outdated provisions of the prohibition of Chinese citizens being one of the parties in Sino-foreign joint ventures. According to the provisions of "*Circular Reinforcing Administration of Registration, Foreign Exchange, Taxation of Foreign-invested Enterprise* " (No.575, 2002), after being approved, Chinese natural person shareholders who have kept their shareholder status for over one year may still act as Chinese investors in the newly-established foreign-invested enterprises after alteration. Under the "*Interim Regulations on Merger & Acquisition of Domestic Enterprises by Foreign Investors*", Chinese natural person shareholders may after approval become Chinese investors in the acquired company by way of share purchase. All the above provisions imply that previous rigid provisions turn out to be more flexible under specific conditions. Laws and regulations have relaxed the prohibition of Chinese citizens being shareholders of a foreign-invested enterprise. But the prohibition still applies to newly established Sino-foreign joint ventures in provinces other than Beijing. The risk of constitutionality review is all along connected with any action taken by Beijing municipal authority over the issue of Chinese citizens being Chinese investors in Sino-foreign joint ventures.

Constitutionality of Local Regulations

The "*Constitutional Law*" provides that: "[n]o laws or administrative or local regulations may contravene the Constitution." In Article 63 of "*Law on Legislation*", it specifies:

> "[t]he People's Congress of a province, autonomous region, or municipality directly under the Central Government and the Standing Committee thereof may, according to the specific circumstances and actual needs of the jurisdiction, enact local regulations provided that such enactment does not contravene any provision of the Constitution, laws or administrative regulations."

The lack of constitutionality and judicial review process in China allows the space for widely recognized "violation of constitution at goodwill" as the Beijing model shows in practice. The current situation may later change if the laws of the above level revise the contradicted provisions. As it stands, the 'Beijing model' introduces a high level of risk.

Judicial Assent

In Article 52 of "*Administrative Procedural Law*", it is provided that: "In handling administrative cases, the people's courts shall take laws, administrative regulations and local regulations as the criteria for their judgment. Local regulations shall only be applicable to administrative cases occurring in the corresponding administrative areas." Accordingly, as for the disputes filed over joint ventures where Chinese natural persons are one of the parties, the court will not be stranded if the case sheerly happens in Beijing administrative areas or other similar areas where there is "violation of constitution at goodwill" or even between them. The long arm of the Beijing courts does not reach into other jurisdictions where the violation at goodwill is not recognized even if the joint venture at dispute has been set up and registered in Beijing. The risks are usually aware for the unconstitutionality of local regulations per se.

2.3 Risks of Registered Capital Contribution

2.3.1 Legal Rules Regarding Registered Capital Contribution of Foreign-Invested Enterprises

Newly Issued Rules for Registration of Foreign-Invested Enterprises

On April 24, 2006, SAIC, MOFCOM"), GAC and SAFE jointly issued the Implementing Opinions on Certain Questions Concerning the Laws Applicable to the Administration of the Approval and Registration of Foreign-invested Companies (Gong Shang Wai Qi Zi [2006] No. 81) ("Implementing Opinions"). The Implementing Opinions restates a great deal of current laws but also attempts to clarify certain principles in China's foreign investment regime that overlap or conflict with the newly revised Company Law of PRC ("Company Law") and the Regulations of the Administration of Company Registration of PRC ("Company

Table 2.1. General Provisions for Registered Capital Contribution of Foreign-invested Enterprises

Forms of Contributions in Foreign-invested Enterprises	
Forms of Contributions	Cash (including loans), building, workshop, machine and equipment or other materials, industrial property rights, patent and right of land use, etc.
	Under the authorization of approval administration, foreign investors may contribute the profits of other joint ventures in China in the form of Renminbi.
Conditions of Contributions	The machines, equipments or materials as foreign investors' contributions shall be indispensable to the operation of joint ventures. The fixed prices of them shall not be more than the normal ones of their counterparts in international market at the time. Furthermore, they are required to meet the following conditions: (1) can considerably improve the performance, quality and efficiency of current products; (2) can considerably economize the usage of raw material, mineral and energy.
	Fixed prices for industrial property rights or patents shall be in accordance with the pricing principles commonly used in the world. The fixed prices shall not be more than 20% of the total sum of registered capital of the Foreign-Invested Enterprises. See Article 27, *Implementation Rules of Wholly Foreign-owned Enterprises Law.*
Prohibitions	No mortgage or other forms of guaranty shall be allowed to lay on the contribution or consideration of cooperation. Each of parties shall make its own property rights as the contributions or consideration of cooperation.
	No leased property is allowed to make the contribution.

General Provisions of Ratio of Registered Capital against Total Sum of Investment and Time Requirement for Contribution in Foreign-invested Enterprises			
The Total Sum of Investment (in 10 thousand US Dollar)		Minimum Ratio of Registered Capital against Total Sum of Investment(in 10 thousand US Dollar)	Time Requirement for Contribution
Below 300	Below 50	At least 70%	Within 1 year
	50-100		Within 1.5 years
	100-300		Within 2 years
300—1000		At least 50%, no less than 210	Within 3 years
1000—3000		At least 40%, no less than 500	Depending on the approval authority's discretion on specific conditions
Above 3000		At least 33.34%, no less than 1200	
Note: 1. Complete the contributions in a lump as agreed in the contract or the Articles of association within 6 months as of the issuance date of business license. 2. Fulfill the first contribution of no less than 15% of each share of contributions, if as agreed in the contract or the Articles of association; complete the contribution in arrears within 3 months as of the issuance date of business license. 3. The rate of added registered capitals by increased investments is executed in terms of this chart.			

Registration Regulations"), both of which came into effect on January 1, 2006. On May 26, 2006, SAIC issued a notice clarifying certain provisions under the Implementing Opinions ("SAIC Notice").

a) Time Limit for Paying Capital Contributions

Contributions of the registered capital of a foreign-invested limited liability company, such as an EJV, a CJV and a WFOE, must be made in full within six months or must be made in installments, with the first 15 percent (and no lower than the statutory minimum, i.e., RMB 100,000 for a Single Person WFOE and RMB 30,000 for other types of FIEs) be contributed within three months of the issuance of the business license and the balance be paid in within the time limitations set forth in the Company Law, the laws related to foreign investment and the Company Registration Regulations. Capital contributions to a FISC must comply with the relevant requirements in the Company Law.

b) In-Kind Contributions

Among other things, Capital may not be contributed in the form of labor, debt, the name of a natural person or goodwill. The value of the accepted forms of in-kind contributions of registered capital, including land use rights, buildings, machinery and equipment and intellectual property rights, must be appraised by an asset appraisal institution registered in China, and, in accordance with the Company Law, the value of cash contributions must be no less than 30 percent of the total amount of registered capital of the FIE.

c) Increases in Registered Capital

According to the *Implementing Opinions*, no less than 20 percent of the amount of an increase to the registered capital of an EJV, a CJV, a WFOE and certain FISCs must be paid in at the time when the application to amend the FIE's registration is filed. Contributions of the balance may be made in accordance with the time limitations set forth by the Company Law, the laws related to foreign investment and the Company Registration Regulations.

2.3.2 Some Special Risks with Contributions

Legal Risks of Complicated "Transferring Funds"

In June 7, 2003, A Company (thereafter, "A") and B Group Ltd. (thereafter, "B") reach an Agreement of Cooperation. Both agreed: they decided to set up C (Hong Kong) Group Ltd. (thereafter, "C") in Hong Kong by fifty-to-fifty shares rate. And C intended to set up its wholly-funded enterprise D named International Real Estate Ltd. (thereafter, "D"). Actually, C had not been established before D registered.

So both parties agreed to transfer $7 million funded by B to D as the registered capital via E company's account (substantially controlled by A). The routine is from B to E and then to D. On November 5, 2004, B purchased A's shares in C, so that it fully held shares of C and D. Being aware of this, A sued D for $7 million debt with the proof of account records of capital transfer, and filed the application for confiscating D's certificate of land use and freezing its bank accounts. As a result, D was stranded into ceaseless litigations.[10] (Refer to the illustration)

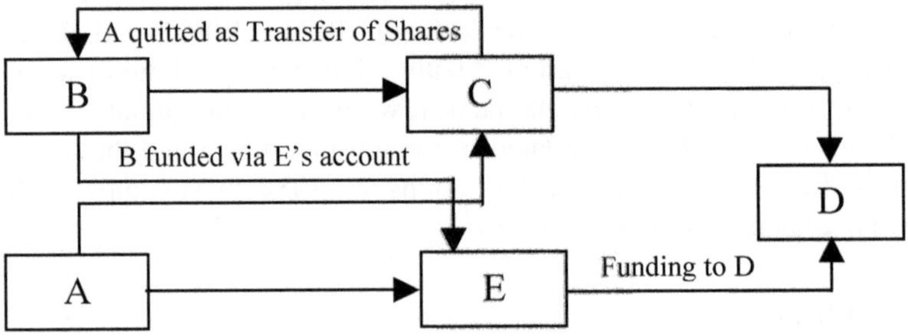

Legally, it seems that the funds through E's account, from C, the shareholder of D as well as the compulsory contributor, to D were virtually investor's contributions in nature not the loan. E acted as the coordinator and actual executor for this transfer of funds. There is no debt between E and D. Thus, E has no right to claim the said funds from D.

Nevertheless, under the theory of "who possess the cash who own it", there was ostensibly the loan from E to D since the funds were under E's account or "possessed" by E at the time even though substantially owned by B. If D countered that there was no such debt, it would constitute unjust enrichment. Therefore, A may claim the funds under the name of E as A withdrew from the joint venture when B fully purchased all shares. In addition, it was disadvantageous for D that both parties neither had an explicit agreement over this matter, nor properly kept the records of the capital transfer. B may have to pay off the "debt" then claim for the funds it contributed into E's account. But this option would entail a great amount of litigation fees and liability of insufficient or false contribution.

Risks with "Shell Account"

On November 15, 1999, International Trade Company of Canada (thereafter, "A"), Tiannan Pharmacy Ltd. (thereafter, "Tiannan") and Haikang Real Restate Ltd. (thereafter, "Haikang") entered into an agreement of establishing a Sino-foreign joint venture, Pacific Real Receivable Company (thereafter, "PRRC").

[10] Rewrite the facts of the case in which the author took representation.

PRRC then registered and obtained its temporary business license in registered capital of 200 million RMB. The ratios of contributions of each party are separately: A contributed 140 million RMB, taking 70% of the total; Tiannan contributed 40 million RMB, 20%; Haikang 20 million RMB, 10%. Mr. Deng, legal representative of A, took on the position of legal representative and general manager of PRRC. After the joint venture was registered, Mr. Deng asked a favor from Mr. Yang to transfer 140 million RMB for implementing its obligation of capital contribution, and the capital Mr. Yang transferred was just for completing the registered capital contribution verification certification which will return to him after verification. From November 20, 1999 to January 15, 2000, Mr. Yang separately transferred funds in draft or wirelessly in a congregated sum of 140 million RMB. By the assessment and examination based on invoices, records of capital transfer and proof of taxation, an accounting firm issued the registered capital contribution verification certificate asserting that till February 10, 2000, PRRC had received the pack-up capital of 140 million RMB contributed by A from its profits in other investments in China. After finishing a false statement of contribution, Mr. Deng returned the "borrowed money" to Mr. Yang's company. On March 20, 2000, PRRC submit the investment verification certificate and other related materials to authorities for obtaining business license.[11]

It is a very common way by which domestic companies complete their registrations, and so do foreign-invested enterprises in some cases. To be more specific, as demonstrated by the PRRC case, domestic companies usually possess the funds at the time of the investment verification and then promptly returned them, which are substantially borrowed or acquired from other lenders. In practice, domestic firms often set up an agency for funding resources, and foreign-invested enterprises used to make connected companies as the "cover' or intermediary.

Risks are apparent with such form of contributions. The funds will be converted into corporation assets once shareholders complete the contributions. Corporation assets in a legal person are absolutely independent from the possession of shareholders. Under Chinese legal circumstances, foreign investors of a Sino-foreign Cooperative Enterprise are allowed to take back investment before agreed cooperation period expires, if complying with certain procedures, even though fixed assets will finally belong to China's cooperators when the contract period expires. Yet, foreign investors should be prudent to withdraw the investments, when the joint venture is set up in the form of legal person who has independent status. The contributions of cooperators shall be separated from the assets of joint ventures. Both the above-mentioned transfer of contribution and mingling investors' properties with corporation assets will cause the civil charge of piercing the veil of corporation, or even administrative and criminal liabilities of illicit registered capital withdrawal. According to the Article 159 of "*Criminal Law of PRC*", Mr. Deng

[11] Xie Wangyuan etc. (2005), How to Judge the Case of Foreign Company Using the Loan to Make Contributions and Withdrawing them, People's Prosecution, Issue No. 1.

and his company would likely to be ruled liable for false contributions.[12] In judicial practice, the violators of false contribution often commit the crime of illicit registered capital withdrawal.

Traps with Contribution in Service

So far, there is no commonly accepted definition of "service". It might be explained as managerial service by abilities and experiences, or labor or knowledge or technical support. All of these explanations focus on the value the service in whichever form creates and then the corresponding return the contributors want.[13]

In theory, the appraised service may account for a contribution to the enterprise. In the Article 27 of "*Company Law of PRC*", "A shareholder may make capital contributions in currency, in kind or intellectual property rights, land use right or other non-monetary properties that may be appraised in currency and may be transferred according to laws and regulations, excluding the properties that shall not be used as capital contributions under any laws or administrative regulations."[14] However, it is generally known that service or labor is so inalienable as to be made as contribution.[15] But the laws of Sino-foreign equity or cooperative enterprises do not expressly impose rigid restrictions on it. In the Article 5 of "*Law on Sino-foreign Equity Joint Venture*", investors may contribute currency, properties, industrial property right. So there is no material legal obstacle for shareholders of foreign-invested enterprises to contribute by service.[16]

There is still risk with contribution in service because of the difficulty of the appraisal of the value of service and the wideness of its scope. A typical risk, just like what the following case illustrates, lies in the Chinese partners offering some rare sources as their capital contribution, such as the acquisition of land use right or specific distribution channels.

> In June, 2003, a foreign company A, under a political leader's introduction, made the acquaintance of Mr. B (a child of superior official of Communist Party of China). Both of them agreed to cooperate on a joint venture D of small goods wholesale. B used a shell company C (controlled by B) to sign a contract with A, containing that A con-

---

[12] Id. Refer to Views of Professor Xie Wangyuan.

[13] Tang Shumei (2003), Research on Capital Structure of Foreign-invested Limited Liability Company, Tianjin Social Science, Issue 5.

[14] The *Company Law* before the amendment provides that "shareholder shall only use currency, in kind or tangible properties, industrial property right, non-patented technology or land use right to make capital contributions".

[15] Jiang Ping, Zhao Xudong, Chen Su, Lecture Materials on the subject of Revision of Company Law and its Significance.

[16] It is inappropriate to adopt the form of foreign-invested limited liability company under current legal circumstances.

> tributed \$30 million and B contributed in the form of service that can help to acquire land use right of 1200 acres for D by his influence in political network. They split the shares of D by 50-to-50 rates. After the agreement was signed, A gave \$3 million to B as the preliminary funds for service. Later, B asked for extra \$1.5 million since he asserted that the more strict policy of land use right caused the increase of the costs of lobbying. Otherwise, he would like to change the shareholding rate. To avoid more loss, A had to agree to change C's shareholding rate to up to 55%, a controlling rate. Then, under B's manipulation, company E (controlled by B), C's creditor, filed a lawsuit of freezing C's shares in D, foreclosing C's shareholdings in E to D. As a result, D was completely controlled by B. Finally, because B could not obtain the approval of land use right, E filed to clear up D in the basis of Articles of corporation, and acquired majority of funds and properties A previously contributed to D.

Because the so called "resources or channels" exclusively offered by Chinese partners are imponderable, foreign investors lost their bargain power in the cooperation. Furthermore, it is burdensome to evaluate the complete performance of "service" of this kind. Particularly, since most cases involve onerous administrative procedures, Chinese partners commonly defend themselves by the excuse of "force majeure" which implying governmental renege. By offering such airy contribution, they can enjoy their shareholdings or even peculate the assets of the joint venture without paying a penny. Moreover, most of these lobbying "services" are supposed to start after the foreign investors have completed their contributions. Thus, Chinese investors have gained their own shareholdings from the very beginning of joint venture. Both the dependency on the special "resources" of joint ventures and the possible default in lobbying service suggests fragile relationship between them.

Managerial Rights During the Period of Contribution

In the provisions of *"Supplemented Rules for Several Administration Regulations on the Capital Contribution by the Parties to Sino-foreign Equity Joint Enterprises"* (promulgated on September 29, 1997 by the State Administration of Industry and Commerce and Ministry of Foreign Trade and Economic Cooperation) (thereafter, "Supplemented Rules"),

> "Investors shall at the same time fulfill their contributions under the agreed period and rate in the contract of joint venture. Except they can not make the contributions at the same time, as the previous approval authority approves, they shall distribute the profits by the rate of actual contributions. As for the controlling shareholder (including relative controlling) of joint venture, it shall neither obtain enter-

> prise decision-making rights, nor include their rights and interests into financial sheets under its category by consolidated financial reports. The present rules apply the same for parties to Sino-foreign cooperative joint venture and wholly foreign-invested enterprises. "

According to "Circular of Replies by the Office of Legislative Affairs for Implementation Questions of Contributions and Clear-up of Foreign-invested Enterprises by the Ministry of Commerce" (No.32, 2005), the enterprise decision-making rights means all the rights that could be enjoyed by contributors. In this sense, the breaching party of incomplete contribution shall not have enterprise decision-making rights without any specific agreement.

The purpose of the Supplemented Rules is to prevent "Chinese Strategy Phenomenon" reappearing,[17] which means foreign investors will fully make use of leverage tool to control the decision-making rights and then pledge the share or assets of the enterprises to collect money for contribution. But, too far the east is the west. For an instance, one foreign company A cooperates with a domestic enterprise B on a joint venture. They agree that A holds 70% of shares and both make the contributions in installment. In this case, according to the hyper-corrected provisions of *Supplemented Rules*, neither A nor B can obtain enterprise decision-making rights before they complete their obligations of contribution. There must be a gap when no one takes the managerial reign, further affecting the normal business operation. If A does not fulfill its obligation of contribution while B has finished, then B may have the right to control the company. However, it is irrational that a company with 30% shares hold one hundred per cent managerial authority. The unexpected results – no one hundred per cent managerial authority unless full contribution –apparently suggest the deviation from the tenet of related laws. Actually, only the prohibition of consolidation of financial sheets can prevent "Chinese Strategy Phenomenon" from reappearing. According to the Article 4

---

[17] In 1991, the event of "Chinese Strategy" did drop a bomb in China's capital market. The full name of Chinese Strategy Company is Hong Kong Chinese Strategy Investment Company, established in December, 1991. In April, 1992, it purchased a state-owned enterprise of Shanxi province – Taiyuan Rubber Factory. In May, it purchased all state-owned enterprises in Quanzhou of Fujian province. In September, it realized the "transplantation" with the entire industry under the authority of Dalian Municipal Bureau of Light Industry. Then it fastly extended its businesses in Hangzhou, Ningbo and Wuxi by the way of controlling shareholding in a total of 3 billion RMB. Since April, 1992, by setting up joint ventures of which Chinese Strategy held more than 51% of shares in over two years, it have restructured and integrated more than 100 state-owned enterprises into 35 Sino-foreign equity joint ventures in different areas and industries. After finishing the integration of domestic forces, it consolidated their financial statements into the sheets of its overseas subsidiaries, for financing in international stock market. In return, it gained more funds from international financing to invest in more target firms. The cunning usage of funds in installment and leverage tool feature its impelling action as "Chinese Strategy Phenomenon".

of "*Company Law*", shareholders have the rights to "enjoy the capital proceeds, participate in making important decisions, choose managers and enjoy other rights." Since there is no outstanding restriction on "other rights", the investors of joint ventures can make good use of this concept and make appropriate arrangements in their contracts and Articles of association for interim managerial authority.

Joint Liabilities in Defective Contribution

Seemingly, it does not involve any third person if the investors of the joint venture have fully and timely performed their rights and fulfilled their obligations in light of the contract and the articles of association. But, under modern company law, company takes on more social liabilities in addition to the accountability to its shareholders. For the sake of outside creditors, Article 31 of "*Company Law*" provides protective measures – "[a]fter the establishment of a limited liability company, if the actual value of the capital contributions in non-monetary properties is found to be apparently lower than that provided for in the articles of association of the company, the balance shall be supplemented by the shareholder who has offered them, and the other shareholders of the company who have established the company shall bear joint liabilities." And article 218 of the same law stipulates "[t]he limited liability companies and joint stock limited companies invested by foreign investors shall be governed by the present Law." Thus, the shareholders of joint venture may have the right of recourse against the debts to the other shareholders, but at the same time, they have to bear the cost and risk of exercising it when they supplement insufficient capital contributions.[18]

[18] Zhao Yumin, Wang Baojun (2002), Views to Management of Contributions in Foreign-invested Joint Ventures, Study on China Administration for Industry & Commerce, Issue 2.

3 The Legal Environment and Risks for M&A by Foreign Investors in China

Actually, the sole threat of litigation may often kill a merger.

—— Richard A·Posner[1]

The market is set for complex inbound acquisitions, but regulatory hurdles abound.

—— Yingxi Fu[2]

3.1 Macro-Analysis of Current Legal Environment for M&A by Foreign Investors in China

This chapter mainly provides analysis of the legal feasibility for mergers and acquisitions (M&A) by foreign investors under China's current legal environment in regards to the aspects of the legal rules and market access, and how M&A by foreign investors is circumscribed by the legal environment in China. Legal risks hidden in such an environment for M&A are also illustrated in this part.

3.1.1 Insight into the Macro Legal Environment for M&A by Foreign Investors from the Perspective of Legal Rules

Without a sound legal rule system, the success of foreign-funded M&A cannot be reached. The lack of explicit and necessary legal rules certainly brings great uncertainty to M&A by foreign investors. Eventually, the fear of risks incurred by the uncertainty of game rules may hold back the steps of foreign acquirers and investors into China. In this sense, it is crucial to set up a set of applicable laws and regulations for the decent legal environment of foreign-funded M&A activities. In fact, M&A is still unfamiliar for those in both academia and practice in China.

1 Richard A. Posner (2003), Anti-Trust Law, Sun Hongning Translated, China University of Political Science and Law Press, p. 138.

2 Yingxi Fu-Tomlinson is a partner resident in the Shanghai office of Kaye Scholer LLP. Yingxi Fu, Red tape casts shadow on cross-border M&A, International Financial Law Review, Supplement.

Fortunately, there has been a relatively complete legal system based on the "*Tentative Provisions on Merger with and Acquisition of Domestic Enterprises by Foreign Investors*" (thereafter, "*Tentative Provisions*"), which is substituted by "*Regulations Concerning the Merger and Acquisition of Domestic Enterprises by Foreign Investors*" (the "New M&A Regulations"), to offer necessary legal guide to foreign investors. To much extent, it provides basic guidelines and obviate the uncertainty in legal rules. The smooth progress of M&A initiated by foreign investors is no longer just an idea staying in someone's mind.

This chapter compiles more than 70 pieces of laws and regulations governing M&A by foreign investors, trying to illustrate a frame of M&A by foreign investors.

General Provisions

Basic Rules on Corporate Merger and Division – Chapter 9 of "Company Law"

Under Chapter 9, there are provisions involving primary issues in the merger or division of a company, and its increase or reduction of registered capital, debts assumption or alteration of titles. It provides basic rules for all kinds of companies as to the subject of merger or division.

Code of M&A by Foreign Investors—"New M&A Regulations"

On March 7, 2003, the Ministry of Foreign Trade and Economic Cooperation (the predecessor of "MOFCOM"), SAT, SAIC and SAFE jointly promulgated the "*Tentative Provisions*", to specify two main forms of M&A: share purchase and asset purchase – whatever form is taken would result in the creation of foreign-invested enterprise – and answer some basic questions thereof. The "*Tentative Rules*" applies to domestic enterprises in any kind of ownership and any constitutional form. It constitutes an embryo of code regarding M&A by Foreign Investors, at least to some tune. A comprehensive set of "*Regulations Concerning the Merger and Acquisition of Domestic Enterprises by Foreign Investors*" (the "*New M&A Regulations*") was promulgated by MOFCOM, SASAC, SAT, SAIC, CSRC and SAFE on 8 August 2006, to repeal the old provisional regulations of the predecessor as "*Tentative Rules*". There are some areas excluding the long arm of the "*New M&A Regulations*" such as M&A involving with insurance, securities and fund and other financial institutions which otherwise are governed by securities, banks and insurance industries' supervisory administrations. Furthermore, "[t]he existing laws, administrative regulations concerning foreign-invested enterprises and the '*Provisions for the Alteration of Investors' Equity interests in Foreign-invested Enterprises*' shall apply to equity acquisition of foreign-invested enterprises in China by foreign investors. Matters not covered therein shall be handled by reference to these in the New M&A Regulations"

Special Rules Regarding M&A by Foreign Investors

There are various special regulations prevailing in specific areas, divided by the nature of target companies. Except for the general laws and regulations, parties shall abide by special regulations.

Special Laws and Regulations for the Takeover of Listed Companies by Foreign Investors

In Chapter 4 of newly-amended "*Securities Law*", it provides fundamental rules for taking over of listed companies by domestic and foreign investors, including the procedures of a tender offer, purchase by agreement or other lawful ways, compulsory information disclosure, and trigger point for incurring general offers to all shareholders.

On September 28, 2002, CSRC issued "*Administration of Takeover of Listed Companies*" as a detailed supplementation to Chapter 9 of "*Securities Law*". The new "*Administration of Takeover of Listed Companies*" ("*New Takeover Rules*") was lifted on July 31, 2006, which will take effect on September 1, 2006. Pursuant to it, a purchaser may hereby conduct its offer by means of a tender offer, agreement, or on-market bidding to obtain substantial control of a target company.

On November 4, 2002, the "The Notice on Relevant Issues concerning the Transfer to Foreign Investors of Listed Company State-Owned Share and Legal Person Share"("Transfer Notice") was promulgated, permitting the transfer of state-owned shares and legal person shares in a listed company to foreign investors. It provides the principles, conditions and procedures concerning such transfers. This marks an unfastening of the 1995 Ban which restrained the acquisition of state-owned shares and legal person shares in a listed company by foreign investors.[3]

On the last day of 2005, the "Administrative Measures of Strategic Investments on Listed Companies by Foreign Investors" ("Strategic Investments Rules") was promulgated. Under the Strategic Investments Rules, foreign investors may acquire A-shares of listed companies directly on the Chinese stock market. Strategic acquisitions of A-shares of a listed company may be consummated through transfer by agreement, subscription of new issuance or "any other means as permitted by the national laws and regulations". Additionally, they may make investments in installments, in which the first part of investments shall be no less than 10% of its public offer, with the exception of approvals from the relevant supervisory authorities. They can also transfer their A-shares after holding them for more than

[3] It was well known in 1995 that for the purpose of refrainment from "eroding state-owned assets", the General Office of the State Council issued a Ban (No. 48, 1995) after Isuzu and Itochu purchased the shares of "Beijing Travel Automobile Ltd.". In terms of the Ban, "no firm or company is allowed to transfer state-owned shares and corporate shares to foreign investors, before relevant administrative regulations are promulgated."

3 years. From then on, investments by agreement or fundraising from targeted sources will signal a landmark in China's capital market that the door has been irreversibly open to international investors.

Special Regulations for Merger with or Acquisition of Unlisted State-Owned Enterprises and the Ones in Non-financial Industries by Foreign Investors

On November 8, 2002, the "*Tentative Provisions of Foreign-funded Restructuring of State-owned Enterprises*" was promulgated. It was elected to be the fundamental guidelines in the case of foreign investors restructuring state-owned enterprises, or companies with state-owned shares (except financial institutions and listed companies), into foreign-invested enterprises.

On December 31, 2004, MOF issued with SASAC the "*Provisional Measures of Administration on Transfer of State-owned Property Rights of Enterprises*". It applies to the case that state-owned assets regulatory authorities and the enterprises with state-owned shares lucratively transfer their state-owned property rights to domestic or overseas legal entities, natural persons or other organizations. The transfer of state-owned property rights in financial institutions and listed companies shall comply with other relevant provisions.

Special Regulation for Merger with or Acquisition of Financial Institutions by Foreign Investors

In consideration of the special status of financial institutions, China's administrative agencies differentiate financial institutions from other institutions in an administrative sense. The case remains the same with issues of M&A of financial institutions by foreign investors, for example, the above-mentioned rules like "*New M&A Regulations*", "*Tentative Provisions of Foreign-funded Restructuring of State-owned Enterprises*" and "*Provisional Measures of Administration on Transfer of State-owned Property Rights of Enterprises*" are all not applicable to M&A of financial institutions by foreign investors. Currently, relevant laws and regulations of M&A of financial institutions by foreign investors mainly include:

On October 26 2001, "*Tentative Provisions of Foreign Funds into Restructuring and Disposal of Financial Assets Management Companies*" was promulgated by, PBC, MOF and MOFCOM. It provides that asset management companies may absorb foreign funds to restructure and dispose of its own assets.

On June 1, 2002, CSRC promulgated two rules –the "Rules of the Set-up for Foreign-shared Securities Companies" and "Rules of the Set-up for Foreign Foreign-shared Fund Management Companies" (Note: it was invalidated by the 'Measures for the Administration of Securities Investment Fund Management Companies'), allowing overseas shareholders to purchase shares of domestic securities or fund-management companies, in order to alter its financial structure, or to purchase jointly with domestic shareholders to fund the setup of securities or fund-management companies.

Other regulations followed on December 8, 2003 – "Administrative Measures of the Investment and Shareholding in Chinese-funded Financial Institutions by Foreign Financial Institutions", embracing the investments into China's commercial banks, urban and rural credit cooperatives, trust investment companies, finance companies, financial lease companies and other Chinese financial institutions approved by CBRC. Securities companies and insurance companies are excluded, which are otherwise governed by specific regulations.

On September 16, 2004, CSRC promulgated the "*Measures for the Administration of Securities Investment Fund Management Companies*", which opened the door for foreign investors to co-establish securities investment fund-management companies with Chinese partners.

Special Rules for M&A of Foreign-Invested Enterprises by Foreign Investors

According to the "*New M&A Regulations*", "[t]he existing laws, administrative regulations concerning foreign-invested enterprises and the '*Provisions for the Alteration of Investors' Equity interests in Foreign-invested Enterprises*' shall apply to Merger and Equity Acquisition of foreign-invested enterprises in China by foreign investors. Matters not covered therein shall be handled by reference to these Provisions." Besides, we cannot overlook another regulation as basic rules governing M&A of Foreign-invested Enterprises by Foreign Investors– "*Regulations of Merging and Splitting of Foreign-invested enterprises*" (promulgated on November 22, 2001 by MOFTEC and SAIC).

Rules for Specific Legal Issues in M&A by Foreign Investors

In the wide cross-section of foreign-funded M&A, which is a very complex systematic structure, it involves various legal issues such as market access and entry, asset valuation, asset pricing, administration of foreign exchange, taxation, protection of creditors and safeguards for employees, land-use rights, market monopoly and financing etc. Laws and regulations governing those issues can be divided into ten categories, each of which provide essential legal support for the cruxes and roadblocks in practice.

3.1.2 Insight into Macro Legal Environment for M&A by Foreign Investors from the Perspective of Market Access

Market access is another crucial side of the macro legal environment for M&A by foreign investors. The issue of market access is parallel to the number of fields in China the foreign purchasers are considering to participate in. Market access sets the space for M&A by foreign investors, which stands in breach of proposed foreign investments in China. It primarily contains two facets: one is the restriction on the scope of targeted firms, the target limits; the other is industrial entry also known as market entry in a narrow sense. This section will elaborate on these two issues as follows.

Target Limits

By the nature of ownership, the possible target entities for M&A by foreign investors could be divided into four categories: state-owned enterprises, collective enterprises, privately-owned enterprises and foreign-invested enterprises. Most of the concerns of legislators focus on foreign investors' participation in mergers with and acquisitions of state-owned enterprises or state-owned factors. As for M&A by foreign investors of other kinds of targeted enterprises, except involving listed companies or financial institutions, it falls into the orbit of general foreign investments and rarely needs to take into consideration the specific administrative influences, and issues relating to market access and partner selection.[4] The foremost purpose of the present laws and regulations on foreign-funded M&A is to protect state-owned assets against erosion. Until recently, Carlyle Group proposed acquiring an 85% stake of Xuzhou Construction Machinery Group Co. Ltd. (XCMG), thus attracting attention of those who fear losing control of a vital industry due to M&A activities by foreign investors. In this sense, the book is to mainly narrow the issue of target limits to state-owned enterprises.

China's laws and regulations always encourage foreign capital to enter into reforming and restructuring unlisted & non-financial state-owned enterprises. Retrospective to September 14, 1998, SETC issued "*Tentative Provisions for Usage of Foreign Funds to Restructure State-owned Enterprises*" to encourage state-owned enterprises to utilize foreign funds to participate in mergers with and acquisitions of other domestic enterprises, reinforce their own current assets and to pay for outstanding debts.[5] According to the "*New M&A Regulations*", unlisted and non-financial state-owned enterprises are encouraged to use foreign funds to take part in the restructuring of state-owned companies. It seems that laws and regulations do not set special restrictions on M&A by foreign investors in which unlisted and non-financial state-owned enterprises are engaged.

---

4 The great majority of foreign investors still crave for quality enterprises or assets, most of which are, or involves, state-owned factors, particularly state-owned listed companies and state monopolies, whereas individual-owned and foreign-invested enterprises are exponentially growing in the state economy. In this sense, the focus in foreign-funded merger & acquisition is certainly on state-owned factors or enterprises.

5 The provisions do not exclude the application to stated-owned listed and stated-owned financial enterprises. Actually, it is of no significance to stated-owned listed companies because the Ban of 1995 had not been called off. Similarly, it was hardly enforced on financial firms without any specific official measures of financial regulatory authorities.

Under present laws and regulations, the intangible hands of regulatory authorities are observed in two main subjects: state-owned listed companies and state-owned financial institutions.

A Review of the Policy Regarding M&A by Foreign Investors over State-Owned Shares or Legal Shares in Listed Companies

It was well known in 1995 that for the purpose of preventing the "eroding (of) state-owned assets", the General Office of the State Council issued the Ban (No. 48, 1995) after Isuzu and Itochu purchased the shares of "Beijing Travel Automobile Ltd.". In terms of the Ban, "no firm or company is allowed to transfer state-owned shares and corporate shares to foreign investors, before relevant administrative regulations are promulgated. Since then, it has been 6 years that foreign investors have not been able to move into this area. (A-shares were prohibited to be targeted, as well as state shares of listed companies).

On November 1, 2002, the Ban was lifted as *the Notice on Relevant Issues concerning the "Transfer Notice*" was promulgated, providing the principles that allows state-owned corporate shares be transferred by means of free exchange of currency and open bidding process to foreign investors. Moreover, it also specifies relatively strict industrial policies and procedures for the administration of state-owned shares and foreign exchange. Since the issue of the "*Transfer Notice*", only a limited number of transactions of this type have been approved by the Chinese government. Among the most notable are Citibank's acquisition of a minority stake in Shanghai Pudong Development Bank in May 2003, Kodak's acquisition of a minority stake in China Lucky Film Corp. in Oct. 2003, and Newbridge Capital's acquisition of a minority stake in Shenzhen Development Bank in May 2004. The complex approval process partly is responsible for difficulties of M&A by foreign investors over listed companies. What is more important is that most listed companies in China are still controlled by corporate investors or the state itself, and their blocks of shares, which were owned prior to listing, and not tradable, are called "Legal Person Shares" or "State Owned Shares". Especially, "Legal Person Shares" or "State Owned Shares" commonly occupy the majority stake of most listed companies. Until recently, the reform of non-tradable shares initiated by CSRC drastically converted non-tradable "Legal Person Shares" and "State Owned Shares" into tradable ones. Such a reform makes it possible for investors to control a listed company by the acquisition of shares in it.

Until recently, foreign investors could only purchase tradable shares of Chinese companies which had issued B-shares or H-shares, but not A-shares. This situation was changed at the end of 2002 by the Chinese policy to permit so-called Qualified Foreign Institutional Investors (QFII) to invest in A-shares.

As a very important step for reform of the Chinese capital market, on December 31, 2005, MOFCOM, CSRC, SAT, SAIC, and SAFE, jointly issued "*Administrative Measures for Strategic Investments in Listed Companies by Foreign Investors,*" allowing foreign investors to purchase A-shares directly on China's domestic stock markets as strategic investments. Strategic acquisition of A-shares of a listed company may be consummated through transfer by agreement, subscription of new issuance or "any other means as permitted by national laws and regulations".

Restrictions on M&A by Foreign Investors over State-Owned Financial Institutions

By the different supervisory forms and institutions, state-owned financial institutions could be divided into commercial banks, urban and rural credit cooperatives, trust investment companies, finance companies, financial lease companies and other Chinese financial institutions approved by the CBRC, as well as securities companies (governed by CSRC) and insurance companies (governed by CIRC).

On June 1, 2002, CSRC promulgated two rules – "Rules for the Set-up for Foreign Capital in Shares of Securities Companies" and "Rules for the Set-up for Foreign Capital in Shares of Fund Management Companies" (Note: It was invalidated by the "Measures for the Administration of Securities Investment Fund Management Companies"), allowing overseas shareholders to transfer or purchase shares of domestic securities or fund-management companies to alter its financial structure, or jointly transfer or purchase shares with domestic shareholders to fund the establishment of securities or fund-management companies. With the open provisions, they set strict conditions for foreign-shared securities companies and fund-management companies.[6] On September 16, 2004, CSRC promulgated the "Measures for the Administration of Securities Investment Fund Management Companies", distinguishing majority shareholders and other shareholders by the line of 25% of shareholdings.

Similarly, as the promulgation of "Administrative Measures of the Investment and Shareholding in Chinese-funded Financial Institutions by Foreign Financial Institutions" on December 8, 2003, the market of investments into Chinese-funded financial institutions was gradually open with certain limited access.[7]

---

[6] Both foreign shareholders of foreign-shared securities companies and foreign-shared fund-management companies shall meet some conditions, and the shares held by foreign shareholders or the equity possessed by them (both directly and indirectly) in a foreign-shared securities company may not exceed one third of the total accumulatively. As for the latter, the paid-in capital shall be freely convertible currency equal to no less than RMB300,000,000 and the shares held by foreign shareholders or the equity possessed by them (both directly and indirectly) in a foreign-shared fund-management company may not exceed 33% of the total accumulatively, and the ratio may not exceed 49% in 3 years after China's entry into the WTO.

[7] "To invest or hold shares in a Chinese-funded financial institution, a foreign financial institution shall meet the following conditions:

1) For making an investment or holding shares in a Chinese-funded commercial bank, the total assets of the foreign financial institution at the end of the last year shall, as a general principle, be no less than 10 billion US dollars; for making an investment or

Industry Entry

The rules of industry entry apply to all foreign-invested enterprises of every kind. The "*Provisional Regulations on Direction Guide to Foreign Investment*", as an interim policy, was very instructional at the time. Then, it was repealed by the "*Circular on Questions of Implementation of New Foreign Industrial Policies by the State Administration of Industry and Commerce*" on April 30, 2002. At present, the government directs foreign investments in accordance with the "*Catalogue of Industries for Guiding Foreign Investment* (*Revised 2004*) "(thereafter, "the *Catalogue*"). By the *Catalogue*, the state pilots the direction of foreign investments into some fundamental fields such as agriculture, high-technology, basic industry, environmental protection and possessing-for-export. The opening-up of the service market is still limited. As the "*Catalogue*" was effective on the first day of 2005, it was observed that it involved three important adjustments compared with its predecessor:

(1) Compared with the previous one, it adds new catalogues of industries and products encouraged for foreign investment, such as key parts of large-screen multicolor projection displays, production of recordable CDs, electronic parts of cars, production of glycol, etc., to augment the extent of the opening-up of the Chinese market and absorbtion of advanced technologies.

---

holding shares in a Chinese-funded urban credit cooperative or rural credit cooperative, the total assets at the end of the last year shall be no less than 1 billion US dollars; for making an investment or holding shares in a Chinese-funded non-bank financial institution, the total assets at the end of the last year shall be no less than 1 billion US dollars;

2) The long-term credit ranking given by an international ranking institution recognized by CBRC for that foreign financial institution is good;

3) The foreign financial institution has been making profits for two consecutive fiscal years;

4) If the foreign financial institution is a commercial bank, the capital adequacy rate shall be no less than 8%; if it is a non-bank financial institution, the total amount of capital shall be no less than 10% of the total amount of the risk-weighted assets;

5) The foreign financial institution has a sound internal control system;

6) The place of registration of the foreign financial institution has a sound supervision and administration system;

7) The home country (region) of the foreign financial institution has satisfactory economic status; and

8) Other prudential conditions provided for by CBRC." See Article 7, *Administrative Measures for the Investment and Shareholding in Chinese-funded Financial Institutions by Foreign Financial Institutions*;

"The proportion of the investment or shareholding in a Chinese-funded financial institution by a single foreign financial institution may not exceed 20%." See Article 8, *Id.*

(2) It promotes the progress of the opening-up of the service market. The production and issuance of movies, television programs and radio broadcasts are firstly included in the areas targeted for opening-up.

(3) It reclassifies some catalogues of blindly-invested, or construction-of-low-level, industries into the catalogues of industries that are permitted for foreign investment but which are no longer encouraged for further investment. It also adjusts some over-heated catalogues such as the production of certain kinds of special steel and chemicals by raising the technological entry level.

Except for the "*Catalogue*", the Ministry of Commerce and other administrations also separately or collaboratively promulgated specific measures, some of which boldly step beyond the limitation of the "*Catalogue*". Particularly, China entered into *Closer Economic Partnership Arrangements* ("CEPA") with both Hong Kong and Macau in 2003, which are designed to be permissible regional free trade agreements under the WTO rules. More recently, a third batch of CEPA benefits for Hong Kong and Macau companies were introduced by agreements signed in June 2006. Among other things, these arrangements provide investment and trade access to qualified Hong Kong and Macau enterprises with terms more favorable in certain respects than the terms stipulated in China's WTO accession protocol, such as opening the payable telecommunication service to Hong Kong and Macau investors. Although these arrangements are designed primarily to benefit Hong Kong and Macau companies, they may also indirectly benefit multinational investors with significant subsidiaries already established in Hong Kong or Macau through their application to such subsidiaries. These ongoing arrangements may therefore provide additional options to multinational corporations planning to invest in certain restricted industries in China. By this, these two agreed important papers largely broaden the scope of foreign investments in the mainland.

In addition to the aforesaid general rules of industry entry, the ones regarding specific industries also deserve attention. The controversial case of Carlyle Group's proposed acquisition of an 85% stake in Xuzhou Construction Machinery Group Co. Ltd. (XCMG) catalyzed the birth of "*Opinions on Speed-up Rejuvenation Equipment Manufacturing Industry*" issued by the State Council on June 16, 2006. Such a newly born policy strictly limits foreign investors entering into the equipment-manufacturing industry, which embodies a new trend that prevents the Chinese state from losing control over some so-called vital industries or enterprises during the process of attracting foreign capital. Later transfers of controlling stakes in big-scale, backbone equipment-manufacturing enterprises shall seek the opinions of concerned ministries of the State Council. The enterprises that play vital roles in the fields of important technology equipment-manufacturing in the process of restructuring shall remain under state control. As a prelude to the trend of strengthening state control over some vital industries and enterprises, *the Steel and Iron Industry Development Policy* issued on July 8, 2005 by NDRC, in principle, does not permit foreign investors to obtain controlling status in the steel and iron industries.

Furthermore, the new atmosphere of opposing the sales of shares in Chinese enterprises to foreigners is spreading in China. In a surprise announcement on July 30, 2006, Shandong Chenming Paper, a listed company in Shenzhen Stock Exchange, said it had scrapped a May agreement under which CVC Asia Pacific (a Citigroup-backed private equity fund) would have become the Shenzhen-listed company's largest shareholder through a private placement. In a statement to the Shenzhen Stock Exchange, it cited differences over future policy and board membership. Financial Times commented that such a case illustrates the new trend of nationalism in the area of M&A by foreign investors.[8] Such a change deserves the close attention of foreign investors with the intention of entering China by M&A.

Investors shall note another new basic principle being introduced by the *New M&A Regulations* to safeguard economic security, which is the requirement to report to MOFCOM where:(i) a proposed M&A transaction will result in foreign investors acquiring actual control of, or will involve, important or priority industries, and the economic security of the State will or may thereby be jeopardized; or (ii) a proposed M&A transaction will result in foreign investors owning famous or well known PRC trademarks, or result in the transfer of actual control of PRC domestic enterprises which have a very old and established reputation.

In general, almost all territories of foreign investments are mapped in the "*Catalogue*". Accordingly, the range of industries open to foreign investments is relatively large, with some areas being limited or restricted to foreign investments.

3.2 Micro-analysis of Current Legal Environment of M&A by Foreign Investors in China

In this section, we discuss each subsystem of the legal systems of M&A by Foreign Investors. Then the analysis for each part eventually forms an opinion of the integrated legal system of M&A by Foreign Investors in China.

3.2.1 Industrial Policies for Market Access[9]

Conformity with industrial policies of market access is a basic principle in foreign M&A. In a broad sense, the policies of market entry include two parts: Firstly, it concerns whether a certain industry or area is permitted to be entered into; secondly, it involves the qualification requirements of foreign investors such as quality, size, etc. The rigid principles require the following: it is not permitted that foreign investors hold a majority, or all, of the shares in a prohibited-foreign-individually-

[8] Mure Dickie, Chenming scraps deal with foreign equity fund, Financial Times, July 31, 2006.

[9] Since it has been discussed in previous paragraphs, here is just a brief of specific procedures.

owned enterprise through the disguise of a merger or acquisition. The enterprise requires the Chinese-funded part to be the majority or holding shareholders shall not change its shareholding structure after the merger or acquisition. Foreign investors are not permitted to purchase or make an offer for an enterprise under the prohibited catalogues. Furthermore, there are detailed requirements for foreign investors.

3.2.2 Governmental Approval Procedures

Under current PRC law, transactions involving a transfer of the registered capital of an existing FIE or the conversion of a domestic LLC (or SOE) into an FIE via a direct equity transfer would require approval and registration, similar to the situation where a new FIE is formed. MOFCOM and/or its local counterparts have the power to examine and approve transactions involving foreign investments in domestic companies and FIEs, and would in most cases be the relevant approval authority for this purpose (unless otherwise specified by laws or administrative regulations, or where the target companies are in certain special industries). The SAIC and its local branches (AICs) are responsible for the administration of the registration procedures once the proposed transaction has been approved by the appropriate approval authority.[10] Moreover, there is one important difference between approval procedure of M&A by foreign investors and newly-setup FIEs: the former require s antitrust approval.

In addition, some special industries have their own specific approval authorities such as CSRC reserves the authority to approval foreign capital holding equities of securities companies and China Banking Regulatory Commission (CBRC) for foreign financial institutions funds into shares of Chinese-funded financial institutions.

Once the merger or acquisition involves state-owned enterprises, extra procedures should be taken into account. More details are presented as follows.

General Provisions

The approval procedures are mostly provided in "*Interim Measures for the Management of the Transfer of the State-owned Property Right of Enterprises*", which requires:

The transfer of the state-owned property right of the contributed enterprises shall be decided upon the state-owned assets supervision and regulation institutions. Where the transfer of the state-owned property right of an enterprise results in the State's loss of the controlling position, it shall be reported to the people's government of the same level for approval.[11]

---

[10] See Article 6, Tentative Provisions.

[11] Article 5. Also see the Article 24, *Interim Measures for the Supervision and Administration of State-Owned Assets of the Enterprises.*

The transfer of the state-owned property right of the subsidiary enterprise(s) of a contributed enterprise shall be decided by this contributed enterprise. The significant transfer of the state-owned property right of its important subsidiary cnterprise(s) shall be reported to the state-owned assets supervision and regulation institution of the same level in collaboration with the public finance department for approval. Where such a transfer relates to the social public regulation items subject to the examination and approval of the government, it shall be reported in advance to the relevant departments of the government for examination and approval.

Where the transfer of the state-owned property right of an enterprise relates to the change of the nature of the state-owned shares of a listed company or the change of the actual controlling power, it shall be in line with the laws and administrative regulations of the State and the rules of the pertinent regulatory departments. With regard to the regulation on the transfer of the state-owned property right of a non-listed joint-stock limited company, if it is otherwise provided for by the State, such provisions shall be followed.

As for groups of transfer of state-owned property rights of enterprises organized by the provincial governments, governments of autonomous regions and municipalities directly under the central government, it shall be submitted to the State Council for approval. Without performance of approval procedures, the trade shall not be continued until the approval procedures are performed. The governments of prefecture-level cities have no authority to organize the grouped trading of state-owned property rights.[12]

In the case of the sale of minor state-owned enterprises, the governments of county level shall file the proposal to the governments of prefecture level for approval, recorded in provincial governments. It shall not be sold if not approved by the provincial government. As far as the enterprises in prefecture-level cities, the sale plan shall be filed to the provincial government for approval. Only governments of prefecture level or above have the authority over the trading of state-owned property rights in their jurisdiction; none of organs, departments, institutions, enterprises or individuals have the right to decide the sale of enterprises.[13]

Specific Provisions for the Transfer of State-Owned Shares of Listed Companies

As for the transfer to foreign investors of state-owned shares and legal person shares of listed companies involving restructuring and industrial policies, the State Economic and Trade Commission (later incorporated into MOFCOM) shall be responsible for the approval and supervision process. The management of state-owned shares falls into the authority of the Ministry of Finance, except for impor-

[12] See the Article 1, Circular on the Enhancement of Administration of the Trade of State-owned Assets by the General Office of the State Council.

[13] See the Article 3, Circular on the Views of Several Questions of the Sale of Minor State-owned Enterprises.

tant matters, which shall be filed to the State Council for approval. Also, all filings of the transfer to foreign investors of state-owned shares and legal person shares shall comply with the rules of information disclosure issued by CSRC. Except for the above said organs, none of the departments or authorities have jurisdiction for the transfer.[14]

MOFCOM and SASAC have specified the approval procedures for the transfer of state-owned shares of listed companies held by non-financial enterprises to foreign investors and foreign-invested enterprises: If it is a local enterprise, state-owned share holders shall submit applications to the SASAC via the provincial administrations of state-owned assets supervision, carbon copied to the MOFCOM. If it is a central enterprise, its parent company or superior authority shall file it to the SASAC, carbon copied to the MOFCOM. Under the approval of SASAC, the listed company shall draft related legal documents pursuant to legal provisions and then file it to the MOFCOM as a transfer of shares and change of Articles of association. After the examination and approval from MOFCOM, the documents shall be carbon copied to the SASAC, SAIC and CSRC.

3.2.3 Asset Appraisal

Appraisal Requirements

The parties shall confirm the transaction price on the basis of valuation for the value of shares or assets intended to be transferred by appraisal institutions. For this, each transfer has to be connected with a result of a valuation, which establishes a compulsory system of valuation, regardless of the nature of ownership of the object for transfer.[15] In practice, there are usually specific regulations with regard to the valuation of state-owned assets, to which foreign investors should pay better attention towards. The difference in assessment methods for state-owned assets and non-state-owned assets determines, to some extent, the process of the transfer of state-owned shares. It is invalid if it has not been valuated or registered and affirmed as required in the merger with and acquisition of state-owned enterprises.[16] However, there is no specific regulation in regards to not making a valuation of the assets of non-state-owned enterprises.

---

[14] On the matter of a foreign-funded merger with, or acquisition of, listed companies, in accordance with the political reform of the State Council, the jurisdiction of each department and office has been rearranged. As to the usage of foreign investments, the MOFCOM has the responsibility. The SASAC shall be responsible for the transfer of state-owned shares in non-financial listed companies. The trade concerning financial institutions is under the authority of the Ministry of Finance, while CSRC are still in charge of information disclosure.

[15] In fact, the evaluation process functions as an anti-money-laundering mechanism, as well as protection against the erosion of state-owned assets.

[16] Refer to the *Article 10*, Detailed Provisions of Implementing *Tentative Provisions*.

Method of Appraisal

In the Chapter 4 of "*Rules on the Evaluation and Management of State Assets*", the methods of evaluation include: "(1) The method of current value of future profit; (2) The method of replacement costs; (3) The method of current market prices; (4) The method of clearing prices; (5) Other methods of evaluation of assets prescribed by administrative departments in charge of the management of state assets under the State Council." "[R]evaluation of the value of state assets shall be carried out according to factors such as their original value, net value, degree of newness, replacement costs, and profitability and methods of asset evaluation stipulated in these Rules."[17] The appraisal institution shall select the methods of appraisal, and decide to use one method or more according to different evaluated aims and targets. In the case which more than one method is adopted, they shall recalculate and readjust it to reach a rational value of assets by comparison of results based on different methods.[18] In recent regulations, international commonly-used methods have become more popular. The Article 14 of "*New M&A Regulations*" prescribed that the valuation shall be conducted with international commonly-used methods.

For the sake of anti-erosion of state assets, more evaluations are conducted on the basis of book value, which implies the use of replacement costs prevailing in practice. To pursue the reason, it is because related incumbents have to take on political or legal responsibilities for erosion of state assets that are inculpated by the cause of sale prices less than book values. Whether it constitutes an erosion of state assets depends on the account of book values. It is affirmed in the "*Interim Measures for the Administration of Assessment of State-owned Assets of Enterprises*" promulgated by the SASAC on August 25, 2005, which places "[t]he difference between the book value of assets and the assessment result" as important items in the supervision and examination of the evaluation of state assets. Because the method of current values of incomes may lead to various results, it somewhat not welcomed in practice, even though it is more likely to account for real values and more popular worldwide.

To the appraisal of Non-State-owned Assets, the owners or proprietors of assets or evaluation departments retained by each or both parties have the right to select the method of valuation.

Confirmation of Valuation Results

According to the "*Working Views on Supervision and Administration of Evaluation of State-owned Assets*" on December 31, 2001, it changed the systems of application and examination, managed by the departments responsible for admin-

---

[17] See the Article 22, *Rules on the Evaluation and Management of State Assets.*

[18] See the Article 37, Detailed Provisions of *Rules on the Evaluation and Management of State Assets.*

istering the evaluation of state assets (prescribed in the "*Rules on the Evaluation and Management of State Assets*"), to the systems of approval and recording. Without approval and recording, the result of evaluation has no effect.

3.2.4 Transaction Pricing for State Assets Transfer

Theoretically, the pricing of transfers is subject to the parties' discretions. To avoid the illegal transfer of capital abroad under a legitimate cover, the parties shall fix a price on the basis of evaluation for the shares or assets planning to be targeted. It is prohibited to transfer or sell the assets at obviously lower prices than assessed ones. These provisions actually cap or leave few spaces for negotiation by both parties, which apply to all kinds of enterprises.[19] There are some specific regulations in the cases regarding state-owned enterprises. The following will brief the pricing principles of foreign-funded transfers of state-owned assets.

Pricing Basis

Commonly, it deems the assessed price by the authoritative department of administration of state assets as the base price of the transfer or pricing basis.[20] Other factors such as the state of debts and assets, employees of acquired enterprises, supply and demand of property right market, counterpart prices, application of technology, etc., shall be taken into consideration.[21]

Price Floating

In the Article 12 of "*Regulation of Several Questions of Administration of Evaluation of State Assets*", the holding organ of assets shall conduct economic behaviors related to asset appraisal with the reference of evaluated prices. It shall report the causes of difference to finance authorities or group companies at the same level by a written statement, provided that actual prices are different from evaluated ones by more than a 10% margin. In the provisions of "*Interim Measures for the Management of the Transfer of the State-owned Property Right of Enterprises*", "[i]n the course of a property right transfer transaction, if the transaction price is lower than 90% of the valuation result, the transaction shall be stopped for the time being, which may not be resumed until it is approved by the relevant authoritative institution for the transfer of property rights." Thus, less than a 10% range is required for

---

19 See the Article 8, Tentative Provisions.

20 See the Article 33, Detailed Provisions of *Rules on the Evaluation and Management of State Assets.*

21 See the Article 7, Interim Provisions on Finance Questions of Merger with Enterprises; the Article 6, Views on the Regulation of Reorganization and Reform of State-owned Enterprises.

actual prices to be floated. As for state-owned shares of listed companies, according to "*Views on the Regulation of Reorganization and Reform of State-owned Enterprises*", the price of transfer shall not be less than the net asset per share. Also, the capability of earning profits and market performance shall be considered.

Official Examination of Pricing

The acquiring price shall be examined and approved by the administration of state assets in the course of M&A. According to "*Interim Provisions on Finance Questions of Merger with Enterprises*", the prices of property rights of targeted enterprises shall be affirmed by the authority of administration of finance and state-assets. If acquiring prices are lower than base prices, it shall be examined and approved by those authorities. Therefore, the parties do not have the final say of pricing, which falls in the administration of related authorities.

3.2.5 Forms of Payment

As one form of foreign investment, foreign investors may "take the form of cash belonging to the joint equity parties, material objects, industrial property rights, proprietary technology, etc.," to pay for transferred objects pursuant to "*Several Administration Regulations on the Capital Contribution by the Parties to Sino-foreign Equity Joint Enterprises*".[22]

Under certain circumstances, foreign investors may use RMB to make the payment of M&A under the following conditions: (1) They must be foreign investors who have made their investments in the territory of China; (2) The contribution in RMB is only from the profits of investments in China; (3) They have obtained the approval of foreign exchange authorities.[23]

"Takeover of the listed companies may be conducted through payment by cash, by lawfully transferable securities, or by other means prescribed by laws, or rules and regulations." See *Article 6, Regulations on the Takeover of Listed Companies* (promulgated on Sep. 28, 2002, by CSRC).

Using shares swap to conduct a M&A transaction is defined in the New M&A Regulations as an arrangement whereby a foreign company or its shareholders use(s) the shares of that foreign company as consideration to pay the acquisition price for purchasing the equity or for subscribing for new equity of a PRC domestic company. The New M&A Regulations is the first piece of legislation to lay down specifically the pre-requisite conditions which must be fulfilled before foreign investors are permitted to use the shares of a foreign company to pay the price for an Equity Acquisition or Asset Acquisition. Although cross-border shares swaps were not

[22] See Article 2, *Provisions for the Contribution of Capital by Parties to Joint Ventures Using Chinese and Foreign Investment.*

[23] See Article 7, *Transfer Notice.*

prohibited under PRC law, the rules for carrying out a M&A transaction using shares swaps and the criteria for obtaining the requisite approvals from MOFCOM and SAFE had, prior to promulgation of the New M&A Regulations, never been made public. The New M&A Regulations therefore represent a major legislative development which will, hopefully, facilitate cross-border share swaps in future.

3.2.6 Time Limits of Payment

Foreign investors who establish a new FIE through the acquisition of equity in or assets of a PRC domestic company should pay the acquisition price in full within 3 months from the date of issuance of the business license of the FIE. If the approval authorities have agreed to grant an extension of time for the payment of the acquisition price, then at least 60% of the acquisition price should be paid within 6 months, and the remaining 40% should be settled within 1 year, from the date of issuance of the business license.

For an Equity Acquisition which involves the subscription for new equity in the target company, or which involves the promotion of a new company limited by shares, the shareholders are required to pay not less than 20% of the subscription price for the new equity at the same time when the application for the business license is submitted, and the remaining balance of such a subscription price can be paid in accordance with the time period which complies with the "PRC Company Law" and the "Regulations of the PRC on the Administration of Company Registration" (effective as from 1 January 2006). Hence, if a FIE is formed as a result of a subscription for new equity by foreign investors in a PRC company, then foreign investors have to pay at least 20% of the subscription price for the new equity before the issuance of the business license of the FIE.

If foreign investors intend to establish a FIE through an Asset Acquisition, the time for capital contribution shall be determined in accordance with the provisions of the joint venture contract and articles of association of the FIE. If foreign investors were to establish a FIE for the purpose of purchasing and operating assets acquired from PRC domestic companies, an amount of capital contribution which is equivalent to the price of those assets to be acquired shall be paid within the time period for the payment of acquisition price set out in sub-clauses above. The remainder of the capital contribution may be paid within a time period which complies with the regulations governing capital contributions in FIEs (i.e. within 6 months if capital is to be contributed in one lump sum, or by installments with the first installment being not less than 15% of the capital subscription and to be paid within 3 months after date of issuance of the business license).

When foreign investors establish a FIE through a M&A transaction and if the equity interest of such foreign investors is less than 25% of the target company's registered capital, the foreign investors' capital contribution should be made within 3 months from the date of issuance of the new business license where capital is to be contributed in cash, or within 6 months from the date of issuance of the new business license if capital is to be contributed in the form of non-cash assets or industrial property rights.

3.2.7 Anti-trust Approval

According to an early rule named "*Regulations of Merging and Splitting of Foreign-invested enterprises*",

> "In case the merging with other companies are to be examined and approved by the MOFTEC, and that the MOFTEC considers that the merging will have a trend of industry monopoly or will possibly form a market-controlling status of some of the specific commodities or services that may hinder fair competition, it may call, after the receipt of the documents prescribed in the previous Clause, a public hearing of the companies to be merged, which is attended by the departments and institutions concerned, and may organize an investigation on the companies and the relevant market. In such situations, the period for examination and approval as prescribed in the preceding Clause may be extended to 180 days."[24]

The above said provisions only apply to the splitting and merger between foreign-invested enterprises and domestic enterprises or other foreign-invested enterprises. In this sense, it does not play as a typical anti-trust regulation.

As in the case of the old regulàtions, the New M&A Regulations expressly confer powers on MOFCOM and SAIC to review each M&A transaction, whether to be conducted onshore or offshore, to determine whether there is any breach of the anti-monopoly rules set out in these Regulations.

Onshore Acquisitions

The investors in a proposed M&A transaction are required to report to MOFCOM and SAIC if a foreign investor's proposed acquisition of a PRC domestic enterprise falls within one of the following categories:(i) the business turnover of any one party to the proposed M&A transaction in the China market exceeds RMB1.5 billion in the year of completing the proposed M&A transaction; (ii) the foreign investor has already acquired more than 10 PRC domestic companies engaging in the same or related businesses as the target company during the past one year;(iii)the market share in China of any one party to the proposed M&A transaction has reached 20%; or (iv) the proposed M&A transaction would result in the market share in China of any one party reaching 25%.

The reference to any one party to a proposed M&A transaction includes the affiliates of the foreign investor.

After considering such issues as market competition, over-concentration and the economic security of the State, MOFCOM and SAIC will decide whether to grant approval for the proposed M&A transaction within 90 days after the date of receipt of the acquisition plan and relevant application materials.

---

24 See Article 26, *Regulations of Merging and Splitting of Foreign-funded Enterprises.*

Offshore Acquisitions

If an offshore acquisition of one foreign company by another foreign company to be conducted outside China is characterized by any of the following circumstances, then the acquiring party in such offshore transactions is required to submit the acquisition plan to MOFCOM and SAIC before it makes any public announcement of such acquisition plans, or at the same time when it submits such acquisition plans to the competition authority in its home country for approval:(i)any party to the offshore acquisition already owns assets in China with a value exceeding RMB3 billion;(ii) the business turnover in the Chinese market of any party to the offshore acquisition exceeds RMB1.5 billion in the year of completing the offshore acquisition;(iii) the market share in China of any party to the offshore acquisition and its affiliates has reached 20%; (iv) the offshore acquisition would result in the market share in China of any party to the offshore acquisition and its affiliates reaching 25%; or (v) the offshore acquisition would result in any party to the offshore acquisition having directly or indirectly an equity interest in more than 15 FIEs engaging in the same or related businesses.

Waiver

Parties to a proposed M&A transaction can apply to MOFCOM and SAIC for a waiver of the requirement to submit a report or acquisition plan as prescribed in sub-clauses (a) and (b) above if any of the following circumstances exist in relation to the proposed transaction:(i) such a M&A transaction is capable of enhancing fair competition in the market place; (ii) such a M&A transaction will restructure a loss-making enterprise and can safeguard the employment of employeeat that enterprise; (iii) such a M&A transaction will attract advanced technology and management talent, and can enhance international competitiveness of PRC enterprises; or (iv) such a M&A transaction can improve the environment.

3.2.8 Labor Issue

Employees' Rights Protection

As for M&A among domestic enterprises, laws and regulations commonly require the acquiring party to take over the entire payroll of target enterprises.[25] However, as far as M&A by foreign investors is concerned, such a rule does not mechanically apply. Both parties shall take on the responsibilities of employee arrangement in a "two-way selection" principle. Article 8 (2) of "*Tentative Provisions of Foreign-funded Restructuring of State-owned Enterprises*" provides:

---

[25] See Article 9, Tentative Provisions; Article 9, Circular on the Views of Several Questions of the Sale of Minor State-owned Enterprises.

> "If, after restructuring, the control of the enterprise is shifted or all or the major part of the management assets of the enterprise is sold to a foreign investor, the restructuring party and the restructured enterprise shall formulate plans for proper replacement of the employees, which shall be subject to adoption by the employee meeting upon deliberation. The restructured enterprise shall clear off the various expenses such as the defaulted salaries of the employees, the outstanding funds raised, and the due social security premiums, etc. with the existing assets. The restructured enterprise and the employees shall be entitled to select each other. If any of the employees are to be retained, labor contracts shall be concluded anew or be altered. For those employees whose labor contracts are dissolved, economic indemnities shall be made thereto, and for the employees that are transferred to social security institutions, the social security premiums thereof shall be paid lump sum and in full amount according to laws and regulations, with the money required being deducted from the net assets of the restructured enterprise before the restructuring is made or being paid in priority from the earnings of the holder of the state-owned property rights incurred from the transfer of state-owned assets."

In general, such legal protective provisions are set up for employees of state-owned enterprises acquired by foreign investors. Mostly, the issue may be annoying to the foreign acquirers.

The Control Power of Employees to a M&A by Foreign Investors

On December 15, 2003, SASAC issued the "*Views on Regulation of Restructuring of State-owned Enterprises*", in which specific protection is provided for employees' lawful rights and interests. According to related provisions, any plan of restructuring of state-owned enterprises, or enterprises substantially held by the state, to non-state-owned enterprises shall be submitted to the employee meeting for deliberate discussion and opinions collection. In this case, the arrangement plan of employees carried out shall be passed in the employee meeting. Some comments said that provisions offering the strongest voting rights for employees, at least to some extent, have provided maximum protection for employees in recent times. Nevertheless, the employees are not able to control the whole or part process of M&A in practice. Before the capital forces, they merely have nominal rights to discuss in a rather narrow range.

Special Compensation for Management Staffs

Sometimes, the management of acquired enterprises may seek certain compensation in M&A agreements for their actual controlling authority in the target company. But it only concerns the bargaining power in the balance for M&A. No compulsory compensation is required by law for management staff because there is no division between managers and regular employees in current labor law. Compared with foreign laws with respect to compensation provisions, China's present regulations seem to provide a more useful environment for foreign acquirers.

3.3 The Legal Risks of Foreign-Funded M&A

It is a long way to improving China's legal environment for M&A by foreign investors. Those man-made impediments and obstructions bring various legal risks for M&A by foreign investors. The risks are mainly dormant in the following areas:

3.3.1 Institution Risks

Institutional risks are behind the weakness of present legal regulation as follows. (1) Most rules are administrative regulations subordinate to laws and codes passed by the People's Congress and its standing committee. (2) The problem of scattered, conflicted and inconsistent laws and regulations has not been solved. (3) Some regulations are "thin" such that they have no supporting implementing rules.[26] The key to those problems is almost all legal rules regarding M&A by foreign investors are problem-oriented. It means all rules center on practical problems, which ignores the consistency and systematization inside the lines of more than 70 related laws and regulations. Not only outsiders, for example, foreign investors, but also administration officials are baffled. Moreover, the conflicts of laws and regulations may result in downgrading assuredness and authority of law. In this vein, foreign investors may encounter more risks beyond their expectation.[27]

Frequent legal risks include lots of policies lacking in clarity. They are volatile, unstable and incomplete. In a dualistic administrative system, the inconsistencies between central government and local ones, or between the various laws, rules and administrative regulations, seem certainly unavoidable. Thus, legal risks turn out to be hardly predictable and preventable.

Especially, the *New M&A Regulations* set the requirement to report to MOFCOM to safeguard economic security where:(i) a proposed M&A transaction will result in foreign investors acquiring actual control of, or will involve, important or priority industries, and the economic security of the State will or may thereby be jeopardized; or (ii) a proposed M&A transaction will result in foreign investors owning famous or well known PRC trademarks, or result in the transfer of actual control of PRC domestic enterprises which have a very old and established reputa-

---

[26] Dexter Roberts, Joyce Barnathan, Robert J. Dowling (1998), *Now, It's Reform or Busting Beijing*, Business week, April 6.

[27] Franc Kaiser, Swimming among Sharks, Shanghai Report "M&A in China", By University of Applied Sciences Solothurn Northwestern Switzerland In cooperation with Fiducia Management Consultants Shanghai, January 2003.

tion. If no report is made by the relevant parties in the above situations, MOFCOM may, jointly with other PRC government departments, require the relevant parties to terminate the M&A transaction or to adopt and implement effective measures (such as the transfer of shares or assets) in order to eliminate the adverse impact on the economic security of the State. Hence, MOFCOM and other government departments may stop a M&A transaction involving the transfer of famous or well known PRC trademarks, or well known and established PRC domestic enterprises in sensitive industries, by citing concerns over economic security. Such uncertain provisions hide a dangerous legal risk for foreign-funded M&A.

3.3.2 Risks with Property Rights Transfer

The risk primarily exists with the legal status of assets and properties of targeted enterprises. Usually, it is unclear whether there are some burdens or limits upon the target, such as: Is the land being possessed by the target enterprises state-owned or collective organizations-owned? Is the title of the land being used guaranteed to be free from any claims for ownership or administrative fees? Has intellectual property been acquired lawfully? Has it been paid by the licensee?

Particularly, some risks lie deeply dormant inside the chain of proprietary rights. For example, according to the provisions of China's guarantee law, the object of pledge shall be real estate. But in practice, in order to revive bad assets, the State Administration of Industry and Commerce issues related administrative measures for mortgage on machines. Some specific current assets such as machines may be used as mortgages. Therefore, in legal practice, some current assets of target enterprises may be pledged but this is totally unknown to foreign investors and their consultants, who have no idea on such special legal issues. The huge risk here cannot be ascertainable. Risks of this kind often occur in the area of land-use rights.

3.3.3 Operational Risks

There are various levels of risks rooted in operational processes in regards to M&A by foreign investors.[28] This section will discuss some major obstructions facing the operation of M&A by foreign investors that will put them into risky situations.

---

[28] The "To Boost Multinational Companies Investments in China" Team held the symposium on various fields concerning the legal subjects of foreign-funded M&A, with foreign-funded enterprises, domestic enterprises, governments, accounting firms and law firms. Based on the discussion, legal blanks and handicaps were mainly present in the following respects: 1. more approval authorities and procedures, less practical measures; 2. the impracticability of some provisions; 3. the problems in employees arrangement and debts disposal; 4. more restrictions, less encouraging provisions; 5. Inconvenience of current regulations of foreign exchange. See The "To Boost Multinational Companies Investments in China" Team (2001), *Multinational Companies Investments by M&A in China: Meaning, Trend and Reactive Tactics*, Management World, Issue 3, pp 16-26.

Complicated Approval Procedures for State-Owned Assets Transfer

Up to now, good enterprises in China are mostly state-owned enterprises, especially listed state-owned ones. Therefore, the administrative approval procedures are rather decisive to the success of M&A regarding state-owned assets. Nowadays, it is the complicated approval systems creating the roadblock to undertaking a M&A by foreign investors. Firstly, as for the administration of state assets, it involves the SASAC, local organs of state-owned assets supervision and local government, the Ministry of Finance and its subordinate organs in every province.[29] The condition of multiple regulatory organs irks foreign investors as they have to choose the correct authority to deal with.[30] Secondly, in regards to approval procedures, besides the excessively complicated rules for transferring state-owned shares of listed companies specified by the SASAC and MOFCOM, there is no other specific procedure for other types of state-owned enterprises.[31] Even though the "*New M&A Regulations*" provide basic rules, the administrative organs may arbitrarily handle the applications for shares transfer due to a lack of practical standards or detailed measures. Thus, the risks seem to be inevitable.

Valuation and Pricing

For the sake of avoiding the erosion of state-owned assets, it is popular to adopt the method of replacement costs in the appraisal of assets, even though the "*New M&A Regulations*" otherwise require the acceptance of international routines methods. Generally, foreign investors take the method of current value of future profit for its popularity internationally. Hereby, there is a huge distinction between results based on the two foresaid methods. Many failures in the transfer of state-owned assets is due to the crux of this matter being unsolvable. Furthermore, the "*Detailed Provisions of Rules on the Evaluation and Management of State-owned Assets*" place some restrictions on the qualification of appraisal institutions, which makes the crux of the problem even more insurmountable. In the same provisions,

---

29 Even if the administration of state assets is included into a general centralized system, since the SASAC was established, the whole system is virtually divided into different sectors such as SASAC and local administrations in the role of contributors of non-financial assets and the Ministry of Finance enjoying the proprietorship of financial assets.

30 Michael Pennington (2000), *M&A in China – Where, how and which onion not to buy!* Lehman Brown, Shanghai, Issue 5.

31 In general, there are several gates foreign acquirers may need to pass – the MOFCOM for transfer of identification of acquired enterprises and anti-trust issues with the State Administration of Industry and Commerce; the SASAC for transfer of state shares, the NDRC for the conformity with industrial policies. And if the case involves listed companies, China Securities Regulatory Commission takes the responsibilities of examination for information disclosure. Obviously, the whole approval procedures are rather complex.

pricing is restricted to a narrow range.[32] At the same time, the examination and approval authority of pricing are granted to the administration. Thus, free-trade is hampered, and the principles of market economy may be easily violated.

Forms and Time Limits of Payment

Under current circumstances, cash (including convertible foreign currencies and RMB), tangible and intangible property, securities, credit and other properties or property rights are allowed. At present, payment by foreign currency is the norm, and even a "share swap" is permitted in the *New M&A Regulations*. The method of "share swap" has a long way to cover to realize because it faces against the "wall" of foreign exchange administration. Just only this point may considerably limit M&A by foreign investors happening in large quantities. In addition, it is required to pay for purchase prices within 3 months, with the exception that the acquirer shall pay more than 60% of totals within 6 months and the arrears within 1 year, if approved by the authority. Actually, the provisions can be hardly executed in practice. To avoid the case of "Chinese Strategy" reoccurring, Chinese laws and regulations provide that foreign investors cannot enjoy decision-making rights of enterprise and consolidate the incomes and assets of the enterprise into the acquirer's financial sheet before clearing off the total purchase prices if the controlling shares in the acquisition of the state-owned enterprises then restructure to a newly-setup foreign-invested enterprise. In this case, they may lose their decision-making rights in a certain time, and what is worse is that the enterprise will face the situation of having nobody possessing the controlling power over it, which causes management troubles during the transition period. In all, they are constantly impracticable.[33]

Employee Arrangement

It is particularly troublesome for foreign investors to face the issue of employee arrangement and lay-offs of a newly-acquired state-owned enterprise. At the same time, they also need to deal with the insurance, pension and compensation for retired and disabled employees. The cost of this matter is most uncertain or immeasurable in foreign investors' budget proposal of the proposed M&A.[34] Based

---

[32] According to the provisions of "*Interim Measures for the Supervision and Administration of State-Owned Assets of the Enterprises*" promulgated on December 31, 2003 by the SASAC and MOFCOM, the trade shall be suspended if receivable prices are less than 90% of the evaluation; it can be resumed if approved by related authority for transfer of property rights. Therefore, except with special approval, the minimum prices for transfer of state assets shall not be less than 90% of assessed values.

[33] John P. Karalis (1992), International Joint Ventures: A Practical Guide, St. Paul, Minn. West Publishing Co., pp.138.

[34] Wu, Zhipan (2003), Legal Issues in Foreign-funded Purchase of State Shares, CASS Journal of Law, 6:83.

on rigid principles in China's laws and regulations, the employee arrangement is extremely crucial to a merger or acquisition. However, those principles are not equipped with appropriate, explicit and practical measures. When foreign investors plan their offers, they must take quite many unpredictable factors such as the cost of arrangement into account, in addition to trade prices and other necessary expenses. In the end, it is most possible for them to largely increase their actual costs, outstanding, impending and latent, more than transfer prices.

Furthermore, redundant employees may be "hot potato" to foreign acquirers, including the issues of reemployment, compensation, economic remedy and social insurance indemnity. Under present policies, in the case that the majority of assets or controlling rights of an enterprise are transferred to foreign investors, in principle, all of unpaid salaries, economic remedies, returnable public reserve funds in arrears and social insurance indemnities for un-arranged employees shall be paid at the expense of assets of acquired enterprise.

Since there have been incomplete advancement of social insurance for a long time, many enterprises have paid prices for their short-sightedness by neglecting this issue. Assuredly, this may significantly impact on the process of foreign investments, given that foreign investors cannot hammer out to solve problems associated with the issue. In this case of "Butterfly Effect", even one trivial unsettled thing may trigger a group event like a mass protest by silent sitting, which is currently very serious in China's society. For this reason, local governments are inclined to precede social stability over the interests of foreign investors by compromising with the protestors at the expense of foreign investors.

3.3.4 Risks Arising from Change of Enterprise Ownership

In China, the risks arising from the changing of enterprise ownership are usually observed from the aspect of whole political and economic institutions. Even if the model of a market-oriented economy has prevailed for years, the state still hold control over the management of state-owned enterprises. It is mostly because governments are unwilling to give up their way in the areas of finance and taxation. More losses of authority in finance and taxation means more losses for those engaged in rent-seeking activity. Therefore, foreign investors may have to deal with the challenges of administrative and political impediments. In addition, owing to the relative independence of the local economy historically, various favorable treatments, for example, subsidies, to local state-owned enterprises may possibly be cancelled once they are acquired by foreign investors. In this sense, it is essential to foreign investors to know well in advance about the attitude of local government and the favorable treatments the target company may continue to enjoy after the acquisition.[35]

---

[35] Yu Wen, Risks with Foreign-funded M&A and Responsive Measures against It, Webpages of Shanghai Securities News.

Attacks by third parties may also call grab the attention of foreign investors. Since old relationships around the acquired enterprise are broken with a M&A, the newly-setup enterprise is likely to be a target of criticisms and claims from the administration, court and employees associated with the enterprise's compensation or debts. For instance, local government, who previously offered some favorable treatments on the ground of its state-owned nature, may pull back its offers. Even worse, the new enterprise may have to pay more taxes, fees, and bills for water, power, gas or telephone defaulted by the previous enterprise who were exempted from payment due to its state-owned nature. Even the costs not included in the account are imposed upon the credits of the newly-setup enterprise.

3.3.5 Other Risks

Other risks include the costs of taxation, environment protection and potential litigation. The risks with taxation refers to the costs or penalties imposed for tax evasion, tax dodging, tax violation and tax arrears, or other cancelled favorable treatments. The risks associated with environmental protection primarily refer to new enterprise bearing liabilities for the violation of environmental protection committed by the previous enterprise. In current legal conditions of environmental protection, quite a few enterprises omit or are unwilling to invest in this area at their short-term expense. In some cases, they unlawfully avoided supervision or liabilities because of a cover provided by the local administration. All defaults may be uncovered with the M&A, which are followed by payouts transferred to the bills of the new enterprise. Similarly, the risks of litigation including outstanding and impending lawsuits or even unpredictable ones, also irks foreign investors. Any slacks and flaws in the management or funding chain of reciprocal or multiple guarantees among the enterprises may result in costly expenses.[36]

[36] Id.

Appendix: Laws and Regulations Regarding M&A by Foreign Investors in China

Type	Name	Effective Date	Provisions related to M&A	Remarks
Basic Rules	Interim Provisions on the Management of the Issuing and Trading of Stocks	Apr.22, 1993	Chapter 4 "Acquisition of Listed Companies", providing basic regulations.	Related Provisions are valid unless contradicted with provisions of Securities Law
	Company Law	Jan.1, 2006	Provisions in Chapter 9 "Merger and Split-up of Company"	Revised on Oct. 27, 2005
	Securities Law	Jan.1, 2006	Chapter 9 "Acquisition of Listed Companies", providing the methods for a tender offer or agreement-based acquisition and the conditions and exemptions of a compulsory offer.	Revised on Oct. 27, 2005
Rules Regarding Domestic M&A	Interim Measures of Merger with and Acquisition of Enterprises	Feb.19, 1989	To specify primary issues such as the conception, principles, direction, methods, and procedures of merger with and acquisition of enterprises, evaluation of assets, transfer pricing, fund resources, proprietorship, employee arrangement, and taxation and finance.	It is the first regulation pertinent to a merger with and acquisition of enterprises.
	Circular on the Views of Several Questions of the Sale of Minor State-owned Enterprises	Feb.11, 1999	To prevent trend of auctioning state-owned enterprises, it provides the approval, procedures, transfer pricing, protection for creditors and employee protection, as well as supervisory measures such as audit for leaving posts.	Legal Responses to the policy of "Controlling in Fundamental Areas whereas Loosing in Minor Areas", to regulate the sale of state-owned enterprises.
	Circular on Regulation of Major Purchase or Sale of Listed Companies (invalid)	Jun.26, 2000	To specify the conditions, procedures and compulsory information disclosure regarding major purchase or sale of listed companies.	
	Circular on Enforcing Regulation of Agreement-based Transfer of Non-transferable Shares of Listed Companies	Sep.30, 2001	To prohibit any of OTC trading on nontransferable shares of listed companies, and to emphasize that Shanghai and Shenzhen Stock Exchanges are the only two legal places for the trading of non-transferable shares of listed companies.	

Type	Name	Effective Date	Provisions related to M&A	Remarks
Rules Regarding Domestic M&A	Regulations on the Takeover of Listed Companies	Dec.1, 2002; Amended on July 31, 2006	To provide the means of acquiring listed companies (agreement-based or tender offer), the procedures, information disclosure, etc. and details on exemptions of tender offer and applicable protective measures of target companies.	It is the first regulation for the acquisition of listed companies in a wide range.
	Views on Regulation of Restructuring of State-owned Enterprises	Dec.15, 2003	Specifies provisions on approval, clear-up and examination, audit, evaluation, trade administration, pricing management, payments supervision, protection for creditors and employees in restructuring state-owned enterprises.	It is the first general regulation after the foundation of SASAC.
	Interim Measures for the Management of the Transfer of the State-owned Property Right of Enterprises	Feb.1, 2004	Complete Provisions on the areas of approval, procedures, methods, evaluation of assets, payment, and protection for employees, creditors of transfer of state shares and properties, and the conditions of invalid transfer.	The updated provisions are completely offered for domestic transfer and the deal to foreign investors.
Rules Regarding M&A by Foreign Investors	Interim Provisions on State-Owned Enterprises' Utilizing of Foreign Investment for Reshuffling	Sep.14, 1998	To provide practicable procedures of merger with and acquisition of other domestic enterprises, supplement current assets and payment for debts by state-owned enterprises using foreign funds.	The so-called "foreign transplantation" method of using foreign investments in reforms of state-owned enterprises
	Interim Provisions on Drawing Foreign Capital into the Asset Restructuring and Disposal by Financial Asset Management Companies	Oct.26, 2001	Asset management companies may restructure and dispose of their own assets by using foreign investment.	
	Notice of Relevant Issues concerning the Transfer of State-Owned Shares and Corporate Shares of Listed Companies to Foreign Investors	Nov.4, 2002	To completely reactivate the suspended process of foreign-funded acquisitions of listed companies by allowing transfer of state and corporate shares of listed companies, and providing its principles, conditions and procedures.	It signals that the Ban of 1995 has been nullified, spurring future foreign-funded acquisitions of domestic companies.
	Administration of Qualified Foreign Institutional Investors Engaging in Domestic Investments on Securities	Dec.1, 2002	To allow qualified foreign investors to invest in A-shares market via a trust bank.	The A-shares market has been open to foreign institutional investors.

Type	Name	Effective Date	Provisions related to M&A	Remarks
Rules Regarding M&A by Foreign Investors	Tentative Provisions of Foreign-funded Restructuring of State-owned Enterprises	Jan.1, 2003	To regulate relevant policies relating to transfers of state-owned shares, assets, properties, and credits of state-owned enterprises (except financial firms and listed companies), or the restructuring of foreign-invested enterprises via receipts of foreign investments.	These two regulations inaugurate an era of complete legal systems concerning M&A by foreign investors. They made a number of breakthroughs in comparison with previous laws
	Regulations Concerning the Merger and Acquisition of Domestic Enterprises by Foreign Investors	Aug. 8, 2006	Including the principles, procedures, and approval of M&A by foreign investors.	
	The Notice on Relevant Issues concerning the Transfer to Foreign Investors of Listed Company State-Owned Share and Legal Person Share	Jan.21, 2004	To specify the application procedures for transfer of state shares of listed companies held by non-financial enterprises to foreign investors and firms.	
	Measures for the Administration of Strategic Investment in Listed Companies by Foreign Investors	Dec.31, 2005	Includes: foreign investors may acquire A-shares of listed companies by agreement-based transfer, targeted offers or other means prescribed by law; the investments may be made in installments if the first contribution shall be no less than 10% of shares publicly offered, and the exceptions are otherwise provided for special industries or by the approval of relevant authorities; the acquired A-shares of listed company may be allowed to transfer after 3 years.	It signals that the domestic capital market gate has irreversibly been open to foreign investors
Foreign Investments Rules	Provisional Regulation of the Establishment of Companies Limited by Shares with Foreign Investment	Jan.10, 2005	To regulate the conditions and procedures of increasing offers, or subscription of capital, to foreign investors, or transferring shares held by foreign investors.	
	Provisions for the Alteration of Investors' Equities in Foreign-invested enterprises	May 28, 1997	Including approval, conditions and practical procedures of transfer between foreign investors based on the agreement, transfer to associated enterprises or other recipients, and the successor who has rights to take entire shares of previous investors after the merger or split-up.	It provides specific legal guidelines for such activities.

Type	Name	Effective Date	Provisions related to M&A	Remarks
Foreign Invest-ments Rules	Supplementary provisions regard-ing investment contributions by parties to a Sino-foreign equity joint venture	Sep.29, 1997	Foreign investors who set up FIEs by acquiring assets or shares of domestic enterprises shall, within three months of issuing business licenses of these FIEs, pay the full amount of purchase funds. Should special circumstances warrant an extension of the payment date, with the approval of the examining and approving authorities, within six months upon issue of business licenses, pay over 60% of the aggre-gate purchase amount and, within one year, pay the full amount of the purchase funds and distribute yields according to the percentages of actually paid-in investment. Before paying the full amount of the pur-chase funds, investors with a con-trolling interest shall not incorporate their rights, interests and assets into their own financial statements in the form of a consolidated statement.	
	Provisional Regu-lation of Domestic Investments of Foreign-invested enterprises	Jul.25, 2000	Specifies the conditions and proce-dures of the purchase of other enter-prises by Sino-foreign equity or cooperative joint venture and exclu-sively foreign-owned enterprises and foreign-funded limited corporation.	
	Some Opinions Relevant to For-eign Investment in Listed Companies	Oct.8, 2001	Provides the principles for allowing foreign-funded limited corporations to offer A or B shares and to receive non-transferable shares of listed companies.	Tentative prohi-bition for foreign investment com-panies to receive non-transferable shares of listed companies
	Regulations of Merger and Split up of Foreign-invested enter-prises	Nov.22, 2001	Provides the conditions and proce-dures of the merger or split-up between Sino-foreign equity or cooperative joint ventures that qualify for the status of "legal per-son" or exclusively foreign-invested enterprises and foreign-funded limited corporations or with Chi-nese-funded enterprises	Anti-trust hearing is firstly pre-scribed for the merger with enterprises.
	Provisions on the Establishment of Foreign-funded Investment Com-panies	Jul.20, 2003	Under relevant provisions, invest-ment companies are allowed to hold unlisted corporate shares of another domestic foreign-funded share limited company; the companies of over $30 million dollars of regis-tered capital may acquire the shares of shareholders in Chinese-funded companies in the territory of China.	The regulations congregated the previous four regulations and replaced them.

Type	Name	Effective Date	Provisions related to M&A	Remarks
Foreign Invest-ments Rules	Provisions on the Establishment of Foreign-funded Investment Com-panies	Mar.15, 2004	Extends the business range of for-eign investment companies. A few revisions are made for other issues.	
	Provisions on Guiding the Orien-tation of Foreign Investment	Apr.1, 2002	Revises old provisions; foreign-funded projects fall into 4 catego-ries, namely encouraged, permitted, restricted and prohibited ones.	Basic Regula-tions for Indus-trial Policies
	Catalogue of Industries for Guiding Foreign Investment	Nov.30, 2004	According to the new edition of this catalogue, China has realized the state of complete openness, with many areas unrestricted.	
	Catalogue of En-couraged Hi-tech Products for For-eign Investment	Jun.2, 2003	Expands the business range of foreign-invested enterprises to any, and every, present enterprises in air transportation	
	Measures for the Administration of the Investment and Shareholding in Chinese-funded Financial Institu-tions by Foreign Financial Institu-tions	Dec.13, 2003	Allows foreign financial institutions to contribute investments to Chi-nese-funded financial institutions legally established, and provides the limitations of contribution.	Inapplicable to qualified foreign institutions acquiring trans-ferable shares of Chinese-funded listed financial companies.
	Catalogue of Priority Industries for Foreign In-vestment in the Central-Western Region	Jul.23, 2004	The projects falling into the cata-logue also enjoy various favorable policies for encouraged programs of "*Provisions on Guiding the Orienta-tion of Foreign Investment*".	
Rules Regard-ing Ad-ministra-tion of State-owned Assets	Circular on En-forcement of Regulation of Property Trade of State-owned Enterprises	Apr.25, 1994	The trading in groups of provincial range shall be approved by the State Council; none of the trade organized by the cities below prefecture-level is allowed. The businesses of markets and trading institutions on enterprise property rights shall be suspended.	Curb the trend of state-owned enterprises sold in block by local governments
	Tentative Provi-sions of Administration of State-owned Shares of Share Limited Com-panies	Nov.3, 1994	Defines the definitions of "state share" and "corporate share" and exchange ratio in restructuring; provides the subjective matter and means of state shares and approval, and supervision of their transfer.	Directs the re-forms of state-owned enter-prises, prelimi-nary definitions are provided of "state share" and "corporate share".

Type	Name	Effective Date	Provisions related to M&A	Remarks
	Rules on the Management of Property Right Registration of the State Assets of Enterprises	Jan.25, 1996	The registration of property rights of enterprises' State assets is a behavior of registering carried out by State assets management departments on behalf of the Government in relation to the assets, liabilities, proprietary rights and interests, and other matters concerning the property rights of various enterprises occupying state-owned assets and confirming the relationship of imputation of these property rights in accordance with law.	
	Circular on Printing and Distributing Interim Measures on the Management of State Capital and Financial Affairs in Enterprises	Apr.28, 2001	Regulates the investment, operation, management of income of state assets; approval and practical procedures of outside investments, merger, split-up, transfer and restructuring in the form of corporation.	Relevant provisions replace the ones in "Interim Measures on the Management of State Capital and Financial Affairs in Enterprises"
	Interim Measures on the Management of State Capital and Financial Affairs in Enterprises	May 13 2000	The state assets of enterprises are owned by the state. The State Council and the people's government of local levels separately represent the State to be contributors, who enjoy the ownership with relevant responsibilities and the management in assets with the authorization in personnel and labor. It authorizes SASAC to be in charge of the duties of contributor, under the principle of separation of the ownership from the managerial rights. The SASAC does not directly step into the areas of private enterprises.	It establishes the new administrative systems of state-owned assets. It does not apply to financial institutions
Valuation & Pricing	Rules on the Evaluation and Management of State Assets	Nov.16, 1991	Provides that institutions occupying state-owned assets shall make the assessment, its methods and procedures.	
	Implementing Detailed Rules of Measures of Valuation and Management of State Assets	Jul.28, 1992	Specifies the items that shall be evaluated, and provides specific practical procedures.	
	Interim Provisions of Finance in the Merger of Enterprises	Jul.25, 2000	Confirms the definition, practical formalities, asset evaluation, transfer pricing, ownership of income, payment periods, and asset transfer.	

Type	Name	Effective Date	Provisions related to M&A	Remarks
Valuation & Pricing	Provisions of Several Issues on Evaluation and Management of State Assets	Jan.1, 2002	To enumerate the conditions in which the institution occupying state assets shall make an evaluation; it shall make a written statement of reasons for the difference between actual trading prices and assessed prices if more than 10%, to the Department of Finance at the same level.	
Foreign Exchange Control Rules	Regulation of Foreign Exchange System	Jan.29, 1996	Provides the administration of foreign exchange in current account, capital account and personal use.	Basic regulation for administration of foreign exchange in China
	Notice concerning the Relevant Issues on Strengthening the Approval, Registration, Foreign Exchange Control and Taxation Administration of Foreign-invested enterprises	Jan.1, 2003	Includes: taxation treatment and administration for foreign-invested enterprises in which foreign shares are below 25%; contribution time limits, administration of approval, registration and foreign exchange; the Chinese natural person shareholder of an original domestic company has the status as a shareholder for one year or more, who may, upon approval, continue to be the Chinese investor of the foreign-invested enterprise established after the modification.	Temporarily not allow Chinese natural person to set up Foreign-invested enterprises by means of a new establishment or purchase.
	Circular on the Relevant Issues concerning the Improvement of Foreign Exchange Administration of Direct Investments by Foreign Investors	Mar.3, 2003	Includes: where a foreign investor does not establish a foreign-invested enterprise but engages in direct investments or activities related to direct investments inside the territory of China, it may apply to the foreign exchange bureau at the locality of the investment project to open a special foreign exchange account for the foreign investor in its own name; Expansion of contribution methods; clarify administrative procedures of foreign exchange in M&A by foreign investors.	
Taxation Rules	Interim Provisions of Income Tax in Restructuring Businesses of Foreign-invested enterprises including Merger, Split-up, Equity restructuring, asset transfer	Apr.28, 1997	Provides: tax issues relating to favorable treatment, business continuity, asset pricing and balance, and transfer of deficits in the restructuring of foreign-funded enterprises such as merger, split-up, equity restructuring and asset transfer.	

Type	Name	Effective Date	Provisions related to M&A	Remarks
Taxation Rules	Circular on Income Taxation Issues of Merge and Split-up of Enterprises	Jun.21, 2000	Income Tax issue concerning each party in merger and split-up of enterprises	
	Reply to The Issue of Exemption from Business Tax of Enterprises that Transfer Property Right	Feb.21, 2002	The transfer of property rights of enterprises does not fall into the range of imposition of business tax.	
	Circular on Taxation Issues of Equities of Domestic Enterprises Purchased by Foreign Investors	Jan.1, 2003	After the merger or acquisition, foreign investors shall be taxed according to relevant laws applicable for foreign-invested enterprises, if their shares are more than 25% in newly-established enterprise.	
	Circular on Taxation Issue for Foreign-invested enterprises where Foreign Investors' Shares are below 25%	Apr.18, 2003	It shall apply tax system and registration of domestic enterprises to foreign-invested enterprises in which foreign shares are below 25%, without specific favorable tax treatments for foreign-invested enterprises, unless otherwise provided for by the State Council.	To clarify the taxation treatment to enterprises with foreign shares below 25%
	Circular on Taxation Policies of Restructuring & Reorganization of Enterprises	Aug.20, 2003	Under certain conditions, the enterprise is exempted from deed tax in corporation reconstruction, equity restructuring, merger, split-up, sale and debt-for-share.	
M&A Financing Rules	Provisions of Administration of Enterprises Bonds	Aug.2,1993	The total par value of bonds offered by the enterprise shall be not more than the net value of its own assets. The funds raised in the offering shall not be used for any venture of investments unrelated to the business of enterprise such as real estate, stock and futures.	
	General Principles of Loan	Aug.1, 1996	Borrower shall not use the loan for the investment of equity capital, except otherwise provided for by the State.	
	Interim Measure of Administration of Convertible Bonds	Mar.25, 1997	One of the offering conditions: the accumulative balance of bond offerings shall be no more than 40% of corporation's net assets.	
	Circular on Conditions of Additional New Offerings	Jul.25, 2000	The sum of funds in additional new common share offerings shall be not more than non-audited net assets of last year.	

Type	Name	Effective Date	Provisions related to M&A	Remarks
M&A Financing Rules	Measures of Convertible Bonds Offered by Listed Companies (Repealed)	Apr.26, 2001	The issuer shall sign the guarantee contract of the entire amount with the guarantor by any means of guarantee, mortgage or hypothecation. Where the guarantee is taken, it shall be the guarantee of joint and separate liability. The range of guarantee shall include the principal and its interests of convertible bonds, default fine, compensation for default loss and fees for the fulfillment of debts.	Relevant regulations of guarantee exemption by CSRC shall apply if otherwise provided for.
Land Use Right Rules	Interim Provisions of Administrative Transfer of Land Use Right in the Reforms of State-owned Enterprises	Feb.17, 1998	The administration of land use rights of the government's allocation regarding the reforms in organization of enterprise group, corporation reconstruction of state-owned enterprises, equity cooperative restructuring, lease operation and sale, merger, acquisition and bankruptcy.	
	Reply to How to Handle the Approval of Collective Land Use in Merging of Other Enterprises by Sino-foreign Equity Joint Ventures	Jan.3, 2000	Where the Sino-foreign equity joint venture intends to acquire the collective land occupied by the target enterprise, it is required to be confiscated as the land owned by the State, then its right-of-land use transferred to the acquirer by means of sale or lease. Foreign investors in general cannot acquire the collective land in a direct way.	
Information Disclosure Rules	Detailed Rules of Information Disclosure of Public Offering (Tentative Implementation)	Jun.10, 1993	Includes: conditions, contents, requirements and procedures of interim reports of M&A.	
	Measures for the Administration of Disclosure of Shareholder Equity Changes of Listed Companies	Dec.1, 2002	Provides disclosure requirements of changes or possible changes on the number of shares of a listed company possessed or controlled by the investor	It formulates the conception of "… group as a person that is" *See Article 6*
	Contents and Formats for Information Disclosures by Companies That Offer Securities to the Public Guidelines (No. 15)——The Report of Changes of Investors Equities of Listed Companies	Dec.1, 2002	More detailed practical rules for "*Measures for the Administration of Disclosure of Shareholder Equity Changes of Listed Companies*"	

Type	Name	Effective Date	Provisions related to M&A	Remarks
Information Disclosure Rules	Contents and Formats for Information Disclosures by Companies That Offer Securities to the Public Guidelines (No. 16)——The Report of Acquisition of Listed Companies	Dec.1, 2002	The purchasers shall formulate and disclose the reports of acquisition according to the Guidelines, where they obtain or possibly obtain actual control of targeted listed companies.	It places the minimum disclosure requirement for acquisition activity.
	Contents and Formats for Information Disclosures by Companies That Offer Securities to the Public Guidelines (No. 17)——The Report of Tender Offer	Dec.1, 2002	The purchasers shall formulate the reports of tender offer according to the Guidelines, where they increase their shareholdings of acquired listed companies by tender offer.	Also, it places the minimum disclosure requirement for acquisition activity.
	Contents and Formats for Information Disclosures by Companies That Offer Securities to the Public Guidelines (No. 18)——The Report of Board of Directors of Acquired Companies	Dec.1, 2002	The board of directors of acquired listed companies shall formulate the report according to the Guidelines with respect to acquisition.	It places the minimum disclosure requirement of acquisition activity for the Board of Directors of acquired companies.
	Contents and Formats for Information Disclosures by Companies That Offer Securities to the Public Guidelines (No. 19)——Application Documents for Exempted Tender Offer	Dec.1, 2002	Pursuant to "*Measures for the Administration of Disclosure of Shareholder Equity Changes of Listed Companies*", the purchasers, who shall increase their shareholdings by tender offer but fall into the exemptions of tender offer, shall formulate the application documents for the exemption of tender offer to the CSRC according to the Guidelines.	This is the minimum disclosure requirement for application for the exemption of tender offer.
Creditors Protection Rules	Circular on Reinforcing the Administration of Financial Debts in Restructuring Small and Mid-size State-owned Enterprises and Collective Enterprises	Jun.5, 1998	The enterprise shall fully respect the opinions of financial institutions over the preservation of financial debts and ascertain them by law. Where the enterprise to be restructured does not confirm its financial debts, relevant authorities shall not approve its application and registration for restructuring and shall issue the new business license after alteration.	

Type	Name	Effective Date	Provisions related to M&A	Remarks
	Circular of Implementing the "*Circular on Reinforcing the Administration of Financial Debts in Restructuring Small and Mid-size State-owned Enterprises and Collective Enterprises*"	Nov.26, 1998	Related authorities shall require the enterprise to submit documents of financial debts preservation issued by financial institutions, when they handle the alteration of titles, business registration and taxation registration.	
Employee Protection Rules	Proposals for Several Issues in Implementing Labor Law	Aug.4, 1995	Under actual conditions, the employer in merger or split-up may alter the employment contract with employees of the previous employer under the principles of equality, voluntaries and agreement of negotiation.	
	Proposals for Application of Law in Cases regarding Labor Disputes	Apr.30, 2003	The employer shall pay for remuneration, economic compensation, as well as damages, where it forces the employee to terminate employment contract.	
Disputes Resolution Rules	Regulation of the Supreme People's Court on Several Issues of Civil Cases regarding Restructuring of Enterprises	Feb.1, 2003	Provides the resolutions for relevant legal disputes and application of laws in the restructuring of enterprises including the transfer of equity rights.	It does not apply to foreign funded acquisition of domestic enterprises.
Local Regulations	Proposals On Merger & Acquisition of State-owned Enterprises By Foreign Investors in Shanghai	Apr.4, 2002	Provides measures for such concrete issues such as procedures, asset evaluation, employee settlement and payment of M&A by Shanghai municipal government.	Promulgation before several laws and regulations of M&A by foreign investors prescribed by the State.
	Detailed Rules for Proposals On Merger & Acquisition of State-owned Enterprises By Foreign Investors in Shanghai	Aug.4, 2003	Provides practical rules for the "Proposals On Merger & Acquisition of State-owned Enterprises By Foreign Investors in Shanghai".	The securities may be taken as a method of payment by foreign investors.
	Interim Measures of Merging and Acquisition of State-owned Enterprises by Foreign Investors or Domestic Non-public Economic Organizations	Apr.4, 2002	Provides measures for such concrete issues such as procedures, asset evaluation, land use, employee settlement and asset separation of M&A by foreign investors or the private capital holders by Beijing municipal government.	

4 Modes and Risks for Foreign Investments in Restricted Industries

Despite its entry into the WTO, China still presents challenges to foreign investors hoping to enter the Chinese financial market.

—— David Liu of Jun He Law Offices

4.1 Industry Entry Rules for Foreign Capital

It is a basic principle to comply with industry entry policies for foreign investments in China. The main policies include: 1. Basic Rules, referred to in "*Provisional Regulations on Direction Guide to Foreign Investment*" (thereafter, "the Provisional Regulations") and "*Catalogue for the Guidance of Foreign Investment Industries*" (thereafter, "the Catalogue"), the Catalogue in particular enumerates restricted industries and restrictive manners. 2. Detailed provisions regarding specific industry commonly co-formulated by each authority in charge of the specific industry with MOFCOM. 3. Special Arrangement: formed between the Mainland of China and Hong Kong Special Administrative Region and Macao Special Administrative Region.

4.1.1 Basic Regulations

In regards to related industry policies of entry for foreign investments in China constituted, there have been legislative efforts in the years from the 1990s. We have made several timely adjustments to specific changes in China's development. As to the Provisional Regulations and the Catalogue, the first versions were constituted in 1995. In 1997, they were revised.

On Feb.11, 2002, the State Council promulgated new *Provisional Regulations*, followed by a new version of the *Catalogue*. The old versions were repealed; the two regulations were revised significantly. Again, at the end of 2004, NDRC and MOFCOM promulgated the latest *Catalogue* for foreign investment industries, effective on Jan.1, 2005. There are three main revisions.[1]

The *Provisional Regulations* and the *Catalogue* exert their legal force compulsorily upon all foreign investors, even though in the name of "the Guidelines".

---

1 See related part of Chapter Three.

There is exception for the foreign investor intending sole operation in the case that full-control of shares is not allowed. Similarly, it is restrictive in shareholding or majority holding of foreign investors if the law requires. Foreign investors cannot enter into the prohibited areas prescribed by law.

4.1.2 Rules of Entry to Specific Industries by Foreign Investors

Besides the Provisional Regulations and the Catalogue, there are quite a few specific regulations for foreign capital entry into specific industries. The function of some regulations is the implementation of the Provisional Regulations and the Catalogue; the function of some is to break the limitations of the Provisional Regulations and the Catalogue in the entry by extending the scope of foreign-invested businesses.

Table 4.1. Rules for Industry Entry of Foreign Investment (Partially)

Name	Date of Issuance	Provisions for the Entry of Foreign investments
Rules for the Establishment of Foreign-shared Securities Companies	2002-06-01	Domestic shareholders may receive or subscribe equities of the domestic securities company or Sino-foreign jointly contributed securities company., in which case the proportion of shares of abovementioned companies held (directly or indirectly) by foreign shareholders cannot be more than one-third.
Rules on the Establishment of Foreign-shared Fund Management Companies	2002-06-01	Domestic shareholders may receive or subscribe the equities of the domestic fund management company or Sino-foreign jointly contributed fund management company, in which case the proportion of shares of the abovementioned companies held (directly or indirectly) by foreign shareholders cannot be more than 33%, then 49% in three years after China's entry into WTO.
The Provisions on Foreign Investment in Civil Aviation	2002-06-21	Where foreign investors invest in civil airports, the Chinese party shall take the relative holding position. Where foreign investors invest in public air transport enterprises, the Chinese party shall take the holding position, and the proportion of investment made by one foreign investor (including its associate enterprises) may not exceed 25%. Where foreign investors invest in the general aviation enterprises engaging in business flight, air sight-seeing or that serving the industry, the Chinese party shall take the holding position; where they invest in the general aviation enterprises engaging in agriculture, forestry or fishery operations, the proportion of foreign investment shall be determined by both the Chinese and foreign parties through negotiation.

Table 4.1 (continued)

Name	Date of Issuance	Provisions for the Entry of Foreign investments
Circular on the Relevant Issues concerning the Experimental Establishment of Logistics Enterprises with Foreign Investment	2002-06-20	In Jiangsu Province, Zhejiang Province, Guangdong Province, Beijing Municipality, Tianjin Municipality, Chongqing Municipality, Shanghai Municipality and Shenzhen Municipality, upon approval, foreign investors may invest in the international circulation logistics and third-party logistics businesses. For a foreign-invested logistics enterprise engaging in the international circulation logistics business, the proportion of the shares held by the investors from the outside of the territory shall not exceed 50%
Provisions on the Administration of Foreign-invested Construction and Engineering Design Enterprises	2002-09-27	The total contribution of the Chinese party to a Sino-foreign equity joint construction engineering design enterprise or a Sino-foreign contractual joint construction engineering design enterprise shall not be any lower than 25% of the registered capital.
Circular on Further Opening the Investment Field of Road Transport to Foreign Investors	2002-11-28	From December 1, 2002, upon the approval for projects by the Ministry of Communications, companies, enterprises, other economic organizations or individuals of foreign countries, and those of Hong Kong, Macao and Taiwan areas (hereinafter referred to as foreign investors) will be allowed to, jointly with companies, enterprises or other economic organizations of China, establish Sino-foreign equity joint road transport enterprises, in which the foreign investors are in the holding position, in the road transport fields such as road goods transport, road goods convey, loading and unloading, road goods storage and other auxiliary services and vehicle maintenance etc that relate to road transport, by taking the form of Sino-foreign equity joint ventures, among which the ratio of foreign investment may reach 75%.
Measures for the Administration of Foreign-invested International Freight Forwarding Enterprises	2002-12-11	Foreign investors may establish foreign-invested international freight forwarding enterprises within the territory of China in the form of Sino-foreign equity joint venture or Sino-foreign contractual joint venture. Wholly foreign-invested international freight forwarding enterprises are allowed to be established as of December 11, 2005. Foreign investors may purchase the established foreign-invested international freight forwarding enterprises by purchasing their stock equity thereof, however, the equity ratio and investors' qualification shall meet the requirements as prescribed in these Measures, and where state-owned assets are involved, the relevant laws and regulations shall be followed.

Table 4.1 (continued)

Name	Date of Issuance	Provisions for the Entry of Foreign investments
Interim Measures Governing the Establishment of Sino-foreign Equity Joint Foreign Trade Corporations	2003-01-31	The Sino-foreign cooperation shall be in the form of equity joint venture. Before December 11, 2003, the application for the establishment of an equity joint foreign trade corporation, in which the registered capital provided by the Chinese investor is less than 51%, shall not be accepted for the time being.
Interim Provisions on the Establishment of Foreign-Controlled and Wholly Foreign-invested Travel Agencies	2003-6-21	Any overseas investor who meets the conditions may, upon approval of the State Council, establish a foreign-controlled or wholly foreign-invested travel agency in a national tourist resort, or in Beijing, Shanghai, Guangzhou, Shenzhen, or Xi'an.
Mainland and Hong Kong Closer Economic Partnership Arrangements	2003-06-29	In some essential fields such as telecommunication, Hong Kong investors are permitted to set up equity joint enterprises in the Mainland first. They are also provided with several favorable treatments other than the investors from other countries or areas.
Interim Provisions Concerning the Management of Sino-foreign Joint Job Intermediary Agencies	2003-09-04	The contribution made by the foreign investor shall not be less than 25%, whereas that by the Chinese investor shall not be less than 51%. No wholly foreign-owned job intermediary agency may be established.
Mainland and Macao Closer Economic Partnership Arrangements	2003-10-17	There are the same provisions as formulated in the Arrangement between the Mainland and Hong Kong.
Provisional Regulation on Investment in Cinemas by Foreign Investors	2003-121-25	With respect to Sino-foreign equity joint cinemas, the proportion of the investment made by the Chinese party in the registered capital shall account for no less than 51%; with respect to Sino-foreign equity joint cinemas established in such pilot cities as Beijing, Shanghai, Guangzhou, Chengdu, Xi'an, Wuhan, and Nanjing, the proportion of the investment made by the foreign party in the registered capital may not exceed 75% at the most; foreign investors may not establish any solely-owned cinemas or form any film network companies.

Table 4.1 (continued)

Name	Date of Issuance	Provisions for the Entry of Foreign investments
Supplemented Provisions of Measures for the Administration of Foreign-invested International Freight Forwarding Enterprises	2003-12-07	As of January 1, 2004, Hong Kong and Macao suppliers may set up international cargo transportation agency enterprises in the forms of equity, collaborative or solely-funded joint venture.
Supplemented provisions of Interim Measures Governing the Establishment of Sino-foreign Equity Joint Foreign Trade Corporations	2003-12-07	As of January 1, 2004, Hong Kong and Macao suppliers may set up foreign trade companies in forms of equity, collaborative or solely-funded joint venture.
Measures for the Administration of Sino-foreign Cooperative Audio-video Product Distribution Enterprises	2003-12-08	The interests of Chinese cooperators cannot be less than 51% in the collaborative joint enterprise of audio-video product upon approval.
Measures for the Administration of the Investment and Shareholding in Chinese-funded Financial Institutions by Foreign Financial Institutions	2003-12-08	The proportion of contributions to the Chinese-funded financial institution by sole foreign financial institution cannot be more than 20%.
Provisions on the Administration of Foreign-invested Construction Enterprises	2003-12-19	Where a construction enterprise established by a Hong Kong service provider or Macao service provider in the Mainland undertakes Sino-foreign construction projects, it shall not be subject to the restrictions on Chinese and foreign investment percentages.

Table 4.1 (continued)

Name	Date of Issuance	Provisions for the Entry of Foreign investments
Supplemented Provisions of the Provisions on the Administration of Foreign-invested Urban Planning Service Enterprises	2003-12-19	As of January 1, 2004, Hong Kong and Macao suppliers may establish urban planning service enterprises in the form of a solely-funded joint venture.
Supplementary Provisions on the Administration of Foreign Investment in the Road Transport Sector	2003-12-31	As of January 1, 2004, Hong Kong service suppliers and Macao service suppliers are allowed to set up solely-funded enterprises to provide road passenger transport services in the western areas of the mainland of China, road cargo transport services in the mainland of China and "non-stop" cargo transport services from Hong Kong, Macao to the provinces, municipalities, and autonomous regions of the mainland of China.
Provisions on Administration of Foreign Investment in International Maritime Transportation	2004-02-25	With the approval of the Ministry of Communications and the Ministry of Commerce, a foreign investor may invest in and operate international maritime transportation in the following forms: (1) to establish a Sino-foreign equity joint venture or a Sino-foreign contractual joint venture to engage in international shipping services, international shipping agency services, international ship management services, loading and unloading of international shipments and international maritime container freight station and container yard services; (2) to establish a Sino-foreign equity joint venture, a Sino-foreign contractual joint venture or a wholly foreign-owned enterprise to engage in international maritime cargo warehousing services; (3) to establish a Sino-foreign equity joint venture, a Sino-foreign contractual joint venture or a wholly foreign-owned enterprise to offer routine services for the vessels owned or operated by the investor. As for a foreign-invested international shipping agency enterprise, the proportion of investment made by foreign investors shall not exceed 49%.
Administrative Provisions on Foreign Investment in Advertisement Industry	2004-03-02	Foreign investors are allowed to hold majority equity as of the promulgation date of the present Provisions, which shall not exceed 70% of the total equity. Foreign investors are allowed to establish foreign-invested advertising enterprises as of December 10, 2005. As of January 1, 2004, Hong Kong service providers and Macao service providers are allowed to establish wholly-funded advertising enterprises.

4.1.3 Other Specific Arrangements

Needless to say, the State Council separately reached two important agreements with the governments of Hong Kong and Macao: the Mainland and Hong Kong Closer Economic Partnership Arrangement and Mainland and Macao Closer Economic Partnership Arrangement. According to the Arrangement, Hong Kong and Macao investors may largely broaden their range of investments in the mainland, particularly in some essential areas such as telecommunication (i.e. value-added telecommunication services).

4.2 Dancer in Shackles: Modes of Foreign Investment in Restricted Industries

4.2.1 Case Study: Shanda's Contractual Control Mode

PRC regulations currently limit foreign ownership of companies that provide services concerning internet content including the operation of online games to 50%. In addition, foreign and foreign invested enterprises are currently not able to apply for the licenses required to operate online games in China.

Shanda Interactive Entertainment Limited. (a listed company in NASTAQ, hereinafter "Shanda") is a foreign or foreign-invested enterprise under PRC law and accordingly is ineligible to apply for a license to operate online games. In order to comply with foreign ownership restrictions, Shanda operates an online game business in China through Shanda Networking Co. Ltd. (hereinafter "Shanda Networking"), a company wholly owned by Tianqiao Chen and Danian Chen, both of whom are PRC citizens. In order to comply with PRC regulations, Shanda Networking holds the licenses and approvals that are required to operate online game businesses in China. Shanda has entered into a series of contractual arrangements with Shanda Networking and its shareholders, including contracts relating to the transfer of assets, the provision of services, software licenses and equipment, and certain shareholder rights and corporate governance matters. As a result of these contractual arrangements, which provide Shanda with substantial control over Shanda Networking, Tianqiao Chen and his teams are considered the primary beneficiary of Shanda Networking and accordingly Shanda consolidates Shanda Networking's operation results in their financial statements.

Pursuant to its contractual arrangements with Shanda Networking, Shengqu Information Technology (Shanghai) Co. Ltd. (thereafter, "Shengqu") provides services, software licenses and equipment to Shanda Networking in exchange for fees. The principal service, software license and equipment lease agreements that it has entered into with Shanda Networking includes:

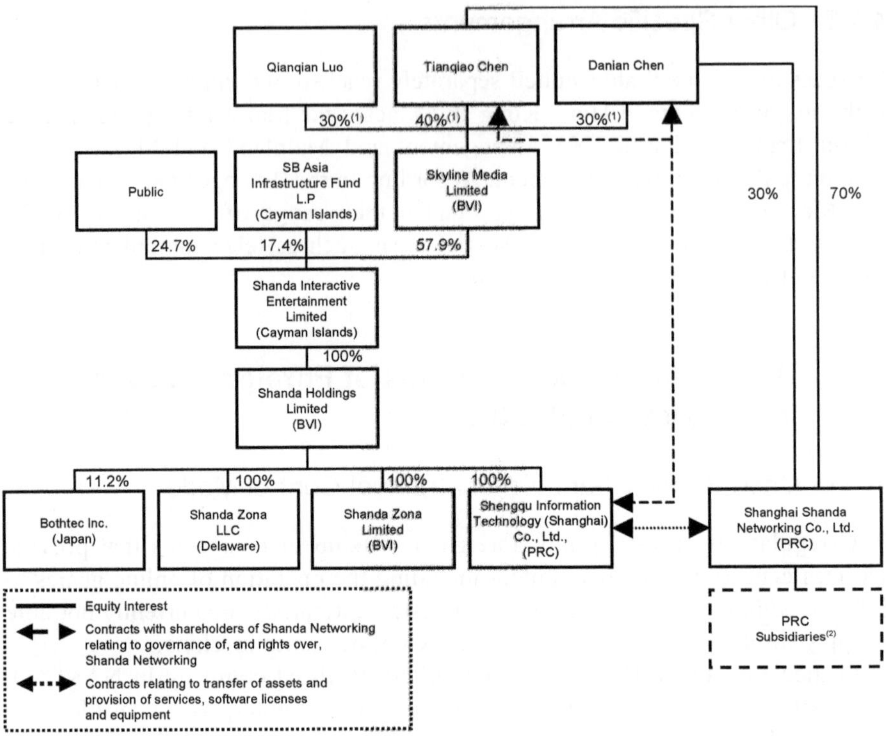

Chart 4.1. Corporate and Ownership Structure Chart of Shanda (Referred to IPO prospectus provided by Shanda to SEC of US)

(a) an amended and restated equipment leasing agreement, pursuant to which Shanda Networking leases a substantial majority of its operating assets from Shengqu;

(b) an amended and restated technical support agreement, pursuant to which Shengqu provides technical support for Shanda Networking's operations;

(c) an amended and restated technology licensing agreement, pursuant to which Shengqu licenses certain billing technology to Shanda Networking Co. Ltd.;

(d) software license agreements, pursuant to which Shengqu licenses certain software to Shanda Networking; and

(e) an amended and restated strategic consulting agreement, pursuant to which Shengqu provides strategic consulting services to Shanda Networking Co. Ltd.

In addition to this agreement, Shanda has entered into agreements with Shanda Networking and its shareholders that provide Shanda with the *Substantial Ability to Control* Shanda Networking. Pursuant to these contractual arrangements:

(a) the shareholders of Shanda Networking have granted an irrevocable proxy to individuals designated by Shengqu to exercise the right to appoint directors, the general manager and other senior management of Shanda Networking;

(b) Shanda Networking will not enter into any transaction that may materially affect its assets, liabilities, equity or operations without our prior written consent;

(c) Shanda Networking will not distribute any dividends;

(d) Shengqu may purchase the entire equity interest in, or all of the assets of Shanda Networking for a purchase price of the lower of RMB10 million or the lowest price permitted under PRC law when and if such purchase is permitted by PRC law or the current shareholders of Shanda Networking cease to be directors or employees of Shanda Networking;

(e) the shareholders of Shanda Networking have pledged their equity interest in Shanda Networking to Shengqu to secure the payment obligations of Shanda Networking under all of the agreements between Shanda Networking and Shengqu; and

(f) the shareholders of Shanda Networking will not transfer, sell, pledge, dispose of or create any encumbrance on their equity interest in Shanda Networking without the prior written consent of Shengqu.

(g) each of Shengqu's contractual arrangements with Shanda Networking and its shareholders may only be amended with the approval of our audit committee or another independent body of our board of directors.

Shengda Interactive Entertainment Ltd. just acquired the substantial ability to control Shanda Networking via the intermediary of Shengqu by a series of agreements. At the same time, Shengda Interactive Entertainment Ltd., being a foreign enterprise (registered in Cayman Island), finally initiated its investments in the domestic online game industry. The Shanda case proffers a typical mode of contractual control investment in restricted industries for foreign investors.

4.2.2 Modes for Foreign Investments in Restricted Industries

In practice, foreign investors innovatively invented many ways to invest in restricted industries in China. The contractual control mode of Shanda is a typical one. In addition, there are other modes either in theory or practice. Foreign investors may reach their destination in a roundabout way.

Contractual Control Mode

As demonstrated in the Shanda case, Shanda Interactive Entertainment Ltd. takes substantial control of Shangda Networking by contractual control. Thus,

Shanda Interactive Entertainment Ltd., a foreign enterprise constituted in Cayman Islands, may enter into the online game industry, a restricted industry set by the *Catalogue*.

Characters of the mode include: (1) to establish or find a domestic company that may have a right to engage in restricted industries; (2) to reach a series of key agreements for substantial control between foreign investors and domestic companies; (3) to consolidate domestic results of operations in financial statements of foreign investors. Because "substantial control" is generally deemed as a sole standard to achieve consolidation under international accounting rules, the foreign investor may reach its aim this way. For example, for U.S. accounting purposes, the affiliated Chinese entity may be classified as a variable interest entity ("VIE") in accordance with Financial Accounting Standards Board ("FASB") Interpretation No. 46, *Consolidation of Variable Interest Entities*. Under the FASB rule, since the equity owners of such an affiliated Chinese entity do not have the characteristics of a controlling financial interest or do not have sufficient equity at risk for the entity to finance its activities without additional subordinated financial support from other parties, a VIE's financial statements are consolidated in the financial statements of its "primary beneficiary," the Cayman Company.[2] The normal routine is that foreign investors consolidate results of target companies operations into their own financial statements to indirectly achieve substantial control in restricted industries of China.

Based on the contractual mode, the agreements which are usually of key or substantial influence to domestic enterprise operations include: equipment lease, product purchase, targeted sale, technology licensing, brand franchise, targeted service and reserved acquisition, etc. There is a different emphasis for different targets – technology licensing or technical service is appropriate for software enterprises; supply agreement or sale agreement is suitable for distribution enterprises.

Proxy Mode

There are two means for voting in shareholder meetings or meetings of the board of directors: one way is to vote personally in presence of the meeting, another way is by proxy vote. The latter is prevailing in western companies. The proxy is a written proof on which the person authorized by the shareholders or directors exercise their surrogate voting rights. For the shareholder or director who has a right to vote, it may do so in person or authorize other persons to vote by written letter of attorney. The authorized persons may vote on shareholder meetings or meetings of the board of directors or for a particular question. In related provisions of "*Company Law*":

---

2 Fred Greguras, Carol Li, *Investment and Operating in Restricted Industries in Chin, download from the website of* Fenwick & west LLP.

> "[a] shareholder may entrust an agent to attend a shareholders' meeting. The agent shall present a proxy issued by the shareholder to the company and shall exercise his voting rights within the authorization scope."
>
> "The meetings of the board of directors shall be attended by the directors in person. Where any director is unable to attend the meeting for a certain reason, he may, by issuing a written proxy, entrust another director to attend the meeting on his behalf, and the proxy shall state the scope of authorization."[3]

Under some conditions, proxy voting may become a feasible way for foreign investors intending to enter into such restricted businesses. In the case of shareholder proxy voting, for example, it may occur this way: foreign investors are able to pay for all or part of the shareholders who have voting rights, accordingly, the latter transfer their voting rights to foreign investors by proxy. It may be possible for foreign investors to take substantial control of such a company, provided that authorized votes exceed the agreed ratio prescribed by articles of association to pass certain resolutions. Similarly, as substantial control taken on the board of directors by proxy, thus foreign investor may consolidate results of acquired companies operations into their own company's financial statements in accordance with international accounting rules. As a result, they realize the objective in finance.

Sino-Sino-foreign Mode

The Sino-Sino-foreign mode is as follows: one foreign enterprise with the shareholders of domestic targeted enterprise firstly establishing an equity joint enterprise and then takes substantial control of such an enterprise. They use the name of the equity joint enterprise to pursue an agreement of cooperation with a target enterprise on sole business, to finally share huge profits from investments in the restricted industry. By this, foreign enterprises may indirectly invest in those restricted fields. A good example is seen in the initiation of China Unicom.

> [For the chances in China's telecommunication market, most foreign investors' method of entry is slow but steady. Usually they establish a form of strategic partnership with some suppliers, and then reorganize it to form an equity joint corporation. In the end, they often acquire the substantial control of the joint corporation. China Unicom craved for funding in its initiation. The capital base sums up to 1.34 billion RMB contributed by the Ministry of Electronics, Ministry of Railways, CITIC Group and other majority shareholders is utterly inadequate to satisfy the enormous need for investments. As an alternative, China Unicom took the Sino-Sino-foreign method

[3] See *Article 107, Article 113, Company Law.*

by instructing an affiliated enterprise to set up a joint venture with foreign enterprises. The joint corporation and China Unicom then signed a contract of program cooperation for the usual period of 15 years. In such a contract, the joint corporation offers funding to jointly built telecommunication networks in certain areas that are later operated by China Unicom after establishment. Both parties share cash flow from the investments according to a promissory ratio. From April, 1995 to December, 1997, China Unicom reached contracts of cooperation in 46 programs with 32 foreign counterparts from 11 countries and areas in a Sino-Sino-foreign manner. Their cooperative projects are mainly set up on a GSM service, as well as for urban ground telephone, long distance telephone and CDMA. Based on some statistics, the total investments included 61.8 billion RMB, with actual financing totaling more than 1 billion US dollars.]

Later, because the right of finance is often controlled by foreign companies, there is no connection between most of the cash and profits of joint ventures and China Unicom. Therefore, the authority called off the cooperation mode in 1998. China Unicom had to pay around 4 billion RMB for compensation and return over 10 billion RMB capital base to foreign investors. The China Unicom case demonstrates a feasible way even though it was terminated by the authority. If relevant legal risks are evaded, it is still of applicability to some extent.

Dormant Investment Mode

Dormant investment is cooperation where one party virtually makes a contribution but the contributor or partner is registered in the name of other person(s) in the articles of association, register of shareholders or other business registration documents. In practice, foreign investors generally sign the contracts with a domestic partner (natural person or legal entity), providing that the domestic partner engage in operation and investment in restricted industries on the foreign investor's request; the latter provides funding and technology to be the actual controlling shareholder or proprietor of the invested enterprise. Indeed, it is a trust relation in nature. According to the provisions of "*Trust Law*", if the relationship is to "serve a legitimate purpose of trust", foreign investors may make their investments in those restricted industries by acquiring substantial control and equities in legal documents such as the equity trust agreement or surrogate shareholding agreement.

This mode is prevalent in investments from Taiwan investors. The main reason is in order to evade from several restrictions (to prohibit a large integrate circuit industry from entering the Mainland) set by Taiwanese authority to block the investors' steps to the Chinese Mainland. To avoid the approval of the Investment Commission of Economic Department of Taiwan, some investors sneak their ways by doing dormant investments. Furthermore, because there is no protocol related to taxation, Taiwan investors may have motivation to engage in dormant investments under others' name for the consideration of double taxation if they comply with administrative formalities of the Investment Commission of Taiwan.

Convertible Debt Mode

The so-called Convertible Debt Mode is deduced from the case of Pacific Century Insurance Holdings Ltd. buying convertible notes in the life insurance industry. The PCCW case is presented as follows to help us understand more about this mode:

On June 6, 2005, Pacific Century Insurance Holdings Limited (thereafter, "PCIHL" or the "Company") affiliated to PCCW Ltd. held by Li Tzar Kai made an announcement that Noblenew, a wholly-owed subsidiary of PCIHL, decided to subscribe 508.302 million HK dollars of convertible notes at maturity of eighty years issued by Praise Idea. According to their agreements, Noblenew may exercise its right of conversion by taking over 13.25% and 8.84% shares of Sino-Life Insurance separately held by Wuhan Wuxin Industry Ltd. (thereafter, "Wuxin") and Beijing Fengli Investment Ltd. (thereafter, "Fengli"). At the same time, Praise Idea consented to designate the representatives of Noblenew to be one supervisor and its secretary by August 3, 2005, or no later than October 3, 2005. Acoording to the agreement, the representatives of Noblenew would replace all present directors of Wuxin and Fengli and three Directors of Sino-Life Insurance to attend the boards of Directors of Wuxin, Fengli and Sino-Life Insurance, as well as all supervisors of Wuxin and Fengli and one supervisors of Sino-Life Insurance and its secretary. If they succeeded to close the deal, the Company would take 22.09% shares of Sino-Life Insurance, which broke the 20% limit of maximum proportion of shareholdings. (referred to "*Administrative Provisions on Insurance Companies*" effective on June 15, 2004: "No individual legal person enterprise or other organization (including the associated parties thereof), except for an insurance holding company or insurance company approved by the CIRC, that invests in any insurance company may hold as much as 20% of the total shares of the insurance company." And "[t]he shares held by all foreign shareholders shall be less than 25% of the total shares of the insurance company.") Besides, two subsidiaries – Tokio Marine and Fire Insurance Co., Ltd and Millea (Asia) Ltd. held by the Millea Holdings Ltd., the largest insurance group in Japan, separately subscribed 12.45% of shares of Sino-Life Insurance (the total proportion is 24.9% by Millea Holdings Ltd.) Referred to the following chart:[4]

---

4 Chen Yuqiang, Questions about Li Tzar Kai (2005), *Steps Across the Lines to Insurance Industry in the Mainland,* Stock Market Weekly, June 13.

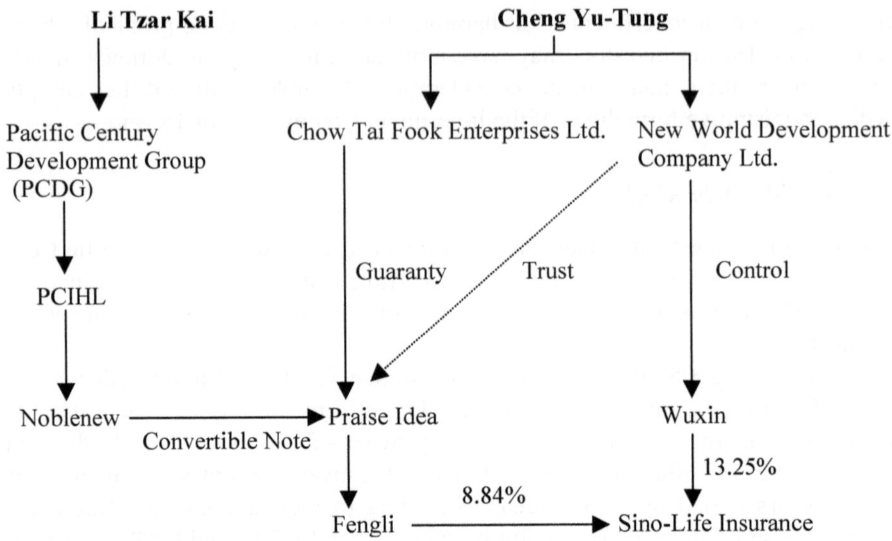

Chart 4.2. The Route of PCIHL Offers for Sino-Life Insurance

Accordingly, the mode is to use a special legal structure designed for foreign companies intending to enter into restricted industries. It is carried out by the following steps: (1) Directed Financing; (2) Financing by the arrangement where the representative of the foreign acquirer is usually designated to be the directors of the target company; (3) Reserved Transfer of Shares: it may be doable for foreign investors to directly hold the target company by taking over the shares unless restricted in legal circumstances by the Mainland. The mode features as follows: (1) The director is designated directly by the foreign investor rather than by proxy voting in an indirect way; (2) The reserved transfer of shares provide the option for investors to straightforwardly hold shares, in order to have substantial control in connection with other agreements; (3) It is executed step by step. The step to chairs in the board of directors often precedes direct holding of shares until the conditions mature.

4.3 The Legal Risk of the Modes for Foreign Investment in Restricted Industries

All above-mentioned modes are just used to bypass restricted provisions of the Provisional Regulations and the Catalogue. In essence, it is a conduct of legal evasion. There may be enormous risks beneath the surface where overt contradiction to or breach of related restricted regulations occurs. In conclusion, there are the following types of legal risks:

4.3.1 Risks with Effectiveness of Contracts

The life of the agreement-backed investment mode completely relies on the bolster of a series of agreements. Upon the same theory, the proxy voting mode does run based on a letter of attorney or agreement of authorization. In the Sino-Sino-foreign mode, the transfer of profits is often arranged by the agreement. Similarly, the trust agreement is generally applied to the relationship between dormant partners and nominal partners under the dormant investment mode. For example, the convertible debt agreement per se in the PCIHL case is a specific contract.

Therefore, the foremost legal risk is connected with the effectiveness of contract and legal protection contingent to it. Just like the warning of Shanda in its prospectus: "If the PRC government finds that the agreements establishing the structure for operating Chinese business do not comply with PRC government restrictions on foreign investment in the online games industry, we could be subject to severe penalties."

All agreements under the contractual control mode are stipulated for the sake of evasion from legal obligations or restrictions. Under current legal circumstances in China, most provisions are compulsory for investors even if the Provisional Regulations or Catalogue is named "Direction or Guideline". Thus, each agreement used by the modes of foreign investment in a restricted industry inevitably falls into the regulation of "*Contract Law*" on the basis of "[a]n illegitimate purpose concealed under the guise of legitimate acts;" or "[v]iolating the compulsory provisions of the laws and administrative regulations."[5] When the disputes are filed in front of judges, the effectiveness of contract is usually ruled in a discreet manner. The court is likely to affirm the effectiveness unless there is flagrant opposite evidences of illegal purpose and facts. However, the investors may not be served a positive judgment over the agreement if there are facts of evasion based on the contract itself. To avoid the term of nullification or invalidity, judges always rule that "according to the agreement, there is no such said legal relationship between the said parties, in which case the said parties are not entitled to claim for … (legal protection)". As a result, foreign investors are exposed to the risk of the domestic company's default. In case the domestic company breaches the contract, foreign investors not only cannot resort to the court for legal protection, but may also suffer large amounts of property loss.

For other specific modes, there are risks of other kinds. In dormant investments, agreement in the form of trust between the dormant partner and nominal partner may be ruled invalid on the basis of illegal purpose of trust. In practice, the trust of equity (trust of equity?) commonly is not registered in the administration of industry and commerce. So it lacks support due to public credibility, particularly in the case of the trustee defaulting. If ruled to be illegal, it shall fall in the provisions of "*Contract Law*" related to effectiveness of contract, in which case the equities shall be confiscated once any impairment of state interests occurs. In the end, investors may lose everything including the investments and any possible profits.

5 See *Article 52 (3) & (5), Contract Law of PRC.*

4.3.2 Risks in the Administration of Foreign Exchange

At present, China still exerts strict regulation on foreign exchange of capital accounts, but (somewhat open up in current account?). Especially, much stringency is imposed in the administration of foreign exchange, for making appropriate reactions to speculative money rush quick money movements? and relieving pressures of further gains in the RMB. In the case, foreign investors who make investments in alternative ways necessarily come across relatively high risks of foreign exchange regulation.

Legal Obstruction in Funding Flows

In China, strict regulation is carried out throughout the whole process of the funding chain. Thus, provided that the legal funding chain foreign currency cannot be bridged, the inflow of foreign investments may be obstructed to some extent, as well as the issue of outflow being an insurmountable thing under current systems even though considerable profits are earned from the investment in an indirect way. This becomes the largest consideration among foreign investors for their investments in restricted industries.

Irrealizable Consolidation of Financial Sheets

Pursuant to the provisions of "*Interim Regulation on Consolidation of Accounting Sheets*" issued by China's MOF, the coverage of consolidation includes the enterprise of which the parent company possess more than half of the lucrative capital or take substantial control in other means. International commonly-used accounting routines generally place emphasis upon who holds substantial control of the acquired enterprise to assess the possibility of consolidation. For this reason, foreign investors just acquire substantial control of domestic targeted companies by means of "agreement-based control", "proxy voting" or "assigned director", etc., to consolidate the results of operation of the target company into the financial sheets of foreign investors themselves. However, the attempt of consolidation by taking substantial control may be nipped. The scope of consolidation excludes "the foreign subsidiary under the regulation of foreign exchange and other regulations of the domicile country where the transfer of funding is restricted ..."[6] In this vein, the goal of investment can hardly be realized due to legal restrictions for consolidation, in whichever alternative means the investor may take.

Taxation Risks

The target enterprise in restricted industries of the *Catalogue* still retains its nature of domestic entity after obtaining foreign capital. In this sense, it cannot enjoy

[6] See *Article 3 Section 6, Interim Regulation on Consolidation of Accounting Sheets.*

favorable taxation treatment for foreign investors as they should be. On the contrary, the burden of taxation will otherwise largely increase. For example, in the import entry, the imported equipment in this case can not obtain the treatment of tax-free. Moreover, it may be challenged by the charge of taxation authorities on the basis of intentional tax evasion by some agreements or methods as the following case shows.

Suzhou Nike, established in 1996, is a fully-owed subsidiary of Nike International registered in China. The connection between them is an "Agreement of Industrial Property License and Exclusive Distribution". (hereinafter the "Agreement") In the Agreement, 6% of the sale of Suzhou Nike will be paid to Nike International as the licensing fee trademark of Nike. However, the disharmony happened in 2003 over the dispute of the accusation of tax evasion by Taichang Customs against Nike International. The 6% of sales was deemed by Customs to be taxed, because the indirectly transferred payments should be considered levied duties as a composition of trade prices under related WTO accords. The administrative fines were finally imposed upon it.

Risks of Assuming Joint and Several Liabilities

Because of substantial control, the connection between foreign investors and their domestic target companies, the creditors of target companies may base the theory of "piercing the corporate veil" or "negation of independence of legal entity" to claim for excessive control or improper manipulation liabilities against them. It has been written down in the new revised Company Law. In its Article 20, Section 3,

> "Where any of the shareholders of a company evades the payment of its debts by abusing the independent status of legal persons or the shareholder's limited liabilities, if it seriously injures the interests of any creditor, it shall bear several and joint liabilities for the debts of the company."

Related responsibilities of controlling shareholder or substantial controller are also specified. In Article 21,

> "Neither the controlling shareholder, nor the actual controller, nor any of the directors, supervisors or senior management of the company may injure the interests of the company by taking advantage of its connection relationship. Anyone who causes any loss to the company due to violating the preceding paragraph shall be liable for the compensation. "

Obviously, foreign investors, as substantial controllers, may not be exempted from the joint liabilities in some circumstances, even though they are the nominal shareholders.

Special Risks for Dormant Investment

There are a large number of risks in the mode of dormant investment. Undoubtedly, it runs like a time bomb. Any imprudence in the chain may trigger the failure of investments.

> Caisheng, a Taiwan businessman, found an opportunity to open a KTV nightclub in the Mainland. It is hardly approved to invest in this restricted area for foreign investors. Thus, Caisheng found a way to register the KTV under the name of one of his friends, Liang. During negotiations, they discreetly reached an agreement that Caisheng held the ownership of the KTV business and they should be separately liable for their own debts. The business went well for years until Liang lost in a lawsuit filed by his creditors in another investment program that was in closedown due to bad management. In the court forcible execution, the assets of said program cannot clear up the entire debt amount. Therefore, from the investigation, the assets of the KTV business under Liang's name were held in seizure, even if Caisheng was its substantial operator and investor.

In general, dormant investments mainly include the following risks, as Doctor Shi Jiansan and Shi Yubing said:

(a) Under the current legal system, the theory of Registration is adopted that nominal shareholders actually grip the right of use in the dormant investment. In this vein, the nominal partner may cause the failure of the dormant investor by transferring his equity in the investment without the dormant shareholder's approval.

(b) Because there is lack of specific protection for the dormant investor under present laws, they are exposed to the risk of being kicked off after the nominal shareholder is getting stronger in the partnership. The dummy becomes a real player in the management. The dormant investor may accordingly lose its control.

(c) It is unavoidably happens that some discredited nominal partners deceive the dormant investor's trust. They may take advantage of their nominal status to misappropriate the assets of dormant investments by setting a mortgage on the assets or other means to make feigned debts falling on the dormant investor.

(d) The dormant investor may not exercise his management right as a substantial contributor under the structure of co-management, in which cases there are inevitably conflicts in investment planning, business management, employment or other areas between dormant investors and their nominal partners. Thus, the dormant investor may give up his rights of final decision and substantial control.

(e) As demonstrated in the above case, the creditor of the nominal partner may bring about the risk of encroachment on the investment of the dormant investor for unsettled debts.

Besides, from my perspective, the following risks shall be considered into account:

(a) The legal validity of the agreement between dormant and nominal partners may be challenged. For the goal of investment, they also reach a contract of joint venture. The latter is approved and registered by the authority. As a result, any provision of the agreement in contradiction with the contract may be deemed invalid. In addition, without the registration, the agreement cannot come into effect under current laws.

(b) For transferring the ownership, the dormant shareholder cannot or hardly make the investment by any means other than cash.

(c) The dormant investor cannot enjoy the favorable treatment of taxation. Instead, the burden of tax will increase in the import of equipments.

(d) The profits in the dormant investment cannot be transferred overseas.

(e) Provided that the dormant investment was not based on a written agreement, the agreement in itself, a form of factual trust between dormant and nominal shareholders, may not acquire legal protection under the provisions of "*Trust Law*". In the terms of "*Trust Law*", a trust shall contain "certain trust properties lawfully owned by the trustor", "written form" (such as written contracts, wills, etc.) and trust registration according to provisions of related laws.[7]

4.4 The Outline of Anti-risk Measures for Foreign Investment in Restricted Industries

Foreign investors may always think over the question of how to walk away from legal risks associated with investing in restricted industries. Essentially, it is more or less unavoidable. In an alternative perspective, the risk may be regarded as an indirect necessary cost of the investment. Some risk may inherently exist in specific laws and regulations pertinent to risk evasion, whereas some may be resolved by artful legislative drafts. In any way, at least, the possibility of risks or harmful results occurring can be lowered by some legal arrangement.

[7] See the *Article 7, 8, 10, Trust Law*.

4.4.1 Draft the Contracts to Be Perfect

Since every mode foreign investors may take in investing in restricted industries is generally related to some contractual arrangements, the contracts drafting, as the preliminary stage, is fundamental to the success of the investment. In the dormant investment, for example, the agreement of dormant investment, as the core of transaction documents, shall be complete, specific and detailed. By this, the risk is resolved as much as possible; the investors may protect their interests from the beginning. According to the thoughts of Doctor Shi Jiansan and Shi Yubing, an agreement of dormant investment shall include the following terms:

(a) The time, amount, form of the investor's contributions, to prove its status as an actual contributor.

(b) The brief of nominal shareholders, to ascertain who the nominal shareholder is.

(c) The method of management and operation in the cooperation, to prevent any disputes in the upcoming cooperation.

(d) Specific responsibilities and rights of dormant and nominal shareholders.

(e) Warranties of the nominal shareholder, such as none of transfer of shares approved without the dormant investor consent.

(f) Property or credit guaranties by the nominal shareholder in case of any default in his fulfillment of the agreement.

(g) The most important term: the method of profit distribution. In a general arrangement, the dormant investor enjoys the shareholder's rights, while the nominal shareholder obtains its certain remunerations. In the case that both parties may take precautious arrangement for any potential litigation under some restrictive provisions in market entry, it can be specified as: the return of the dormant investor deemed as the creditor's right, in the sum equal to or in some specified proportion of the dividend.

(h) Specify the rights and liabilities of both parties in case the dispute concerning the third party occurs. Pre-wariness is necessary in this case.

4.4.2 Risk Evasion by an Offshore Company

In some cases, foreign investors cannot but face the joint and several liabilities in connection with their target enterprises for the reason of failures in the areas of management and operations. To escape from these risks, it is feasible to set up a form of firewall – the system of offshore company – between the foreign investor and domestic target company.

The offshore company is a special form of company commonly registered in some open areas such as British Virgin Islands (BVI), Cayman Islands and Bermuda. It does not indeed run its businesses in the foresaid registration land, and is exempted from any tax other than business license and maintenance fees. It is highly useful to be an effective tool to evade the risks in investment in restricted industries. Usually, the investor initially sets up an offshore company, and then makes the offshore company to invest. The investors may be immune from the jurisdiction of host countries being invested in because of its independence. In this sense, the offshore company may succeed to finalize the goal of evasion or law selection. By this, the foreign investor can walk away from the liability where they set a "protective cover" – the offshore company that vicariously participates in the investments, transactions and M&As in other countries take on legal responsibilities and management risks as an independent entity.

4.4.3 Reversion Clause

In addition to resolving legal risks in advance by all kinds of means, the protection of investors' interests should be taken into account in case the risk eventuates. We must consider how to lower the loss therein. There is a risk of the validity of the agreement in a roundabout way being challenged. The reversion clause is hereby formulated so that investors can retrieve their investments to some extent or in full, in which case the agreement is legally nullified. I specify this kind of clause "reversion clause" as follows: if the agreement was invalidated for its violation of Chinese laws and regulations or other causes, the investor has a right to retrieve the residue of its original investments; the investment acquirer or recipient takes on the duty of returning the said residue. Reversion clause may be stipulated as a separate agreement or included in the general agreement. As for the latter, it should specify that "the clause is independent from other clauses in the present agreement; the fact that if other clauses in the present agreement are invalid does not affect the clause being valid". In any means, the court is likely to adopt a reversion clause if it is in accordance with specific conditions and laws. For this, the investor at least regains part of the resource put into its investments.

Part Two:

Legal Risks in Operation of Foreign-Invested Enterprises

5 Changeable Government: Political Risks for Foreign Investment

Keeping up with changes in rules and interpretations is a real challenge.

—— Hubert Lem[1]

It is hard to avoid the political risk in a country like China which is currently moving towards a market economy., The intelligent investor should keep a close eye on policy changes and use them to their advantage. In short, if you want to make money, you must acclimatize yourself to China rather than expect China to change to accommodate you.

—— Rong International(China), CEO, Sun Hongwei

5.1 Nationalization and Expropriation

5.1.1 History of Nationalization and Expropriation

Nationalization is one of the major risks facing international investment. It started to become a critical concern to multinational companies investing abroad in the middle of the twentieth century, when a large number of Latin American and Middle Eastern countries began to nationalize subsidiaries of large multinational companies.[2]

During the initial years of China's opening-up policy launched by Deng Xiaoping in 1978, nationalization was regarded as a particular risk by foreign investors due to the lack of a legal framework to complement the political changes. In an effort to dispel such concerns, the 1982 Chinese Constitution provided as follows:

---

1 Executive director in the law division of Morgan Stanley in Hong Kong talks to IFLR's Siew-Fong Leung about the challenges facing foreign investors in China in the International Financial Law Review Supplement: The IFLR Guide to China 2005.

2 From the 1950s to the 1970s, almost half of developing countries carried out nationalization policies. There are a total of 1,954 examples over this period: 412 cases in the 1950s, 406 in the 1960s, and a sharp increase to 1,136 cases in the 1970s. In terms of geographic distribution, 219 cases occurred in Asia, 464 in the Middle East, 826 in Africa and 454 in Latin America. See Yao Meizhen (1993), Comparative Foreign Investment Law, Wuhan University Press, p.764.

> "[t]he People's Republic of China permits foreign enterprises, other foreign economic organizations and individuals to invest in China and to enter into various forms of economic cooperation with Chinese enterprises and other Chinese economic organizations in accordance with the law of PRC.
>
> All foreign enterprises, other foreign economic organizations as well as Sino-foreign joint enterprises within Chinese territory shall abide by the law of PRC. Their lawful right and interests shall be protected by the law of PRC."

However, apart from these general provisions protecting foreign investors' lawful rights, the Constitution contained nothing about nationalization per se. According to *the Charter of Economic Rights and Duties of States*, Article 2, "Every State has the right: ... to nationalize, expropriate or transfer ownership of foreign properties, in which case appropriate compensation should be paid by the State adopting such measures ...". This right is recognized by some developed countries such as the United Kingdom and United States of America. In a note handed to Iran by the British on June 19, 1951, the British acknowledged the legitimacy of the Iranian government's actions in nationalizing the oil industry. Also, in a joint statement regarding the nationalization after the 1956 Suez Crisis, France, the U.K. and U.S, gave up their opposition to the nationalization policy of the Egyptian government as a sign of Egypt's full and permanent sovereignty.

In an effort to attract foreign investment, Article 2 of the "*Sino-foreign Equity Joint Venture Law of PRC*" passed in July 1, 1979, states

> "[t]he Chinese government shall protect, in accordance with the law, the investment by a foreign party in a joint venture and the profits due to it pursuant to the agreements, contracts and articles of association authorized by the Chinese government as well as its other lawful rights and interests.
>
> A joint venture shall observe the laws and regulations of PRC in all its activities.
>
> The state shall not nationalize or expropriate joint ventures. Under special circumstances, in accordance with the public interest, a joint venture may be expropriated according to the procedure prescribed by law, in which case appropriate compensation shall be given."

Article 5 of the "*Wholly Foreign-owned Enterprise Law of PRC*" passed on April 2, 1986, reemphasizes that:

> "[t]he State shall not nationalize or expropriate wholly foreign-owned enterprises.
>
> Under special circumstances, where necessary for the public interest, a wholly foreign-owned enterprise may be expropriated in accordance with legal procedures, and appropriate compensation paid."

However, the provisions of the "*Sino-foreign Co-operative Joint Venture Law of PRC*" passed on April 13, 1988 do not contain any express provisions about nationalization and expropriation and merely provide that the State shall protect the lawful rights of joint-venture investors and joint-venture enterprises.

It is clear that the State does not seek to nationalize or expropriate foreign investment enterprises unless in exceptional circumstances, and only as prescribed by law with appropriate compensation to be paid. In 1938, Cordell Hull, the then U.S. Secretary of State, addressed the question of compensation by stating that it be paid in a "full, timely and effective" way. In terms of the standard of "appropriate" compensation adopted by China, another interpretation was provided by the Sino-US Agreement in 1979, whereby China agreed to compensate the U.S. with 80.5 million dollars for their assets that were nationalized during the early years of the establishment of the People's Republic. This amounted to just 41% of the total value of those assets.[3]

Attempts are presently being made to demarcate property law rights in China. In the draft *Property Law*, there are three articles relating to property expropriation. In Article 49, "... in the public interest, local people's governments above-county level may requisition or expropriate real property or chattels belonging to individuals or collective organizations in accordance with the procedures and limits prescribed by law, in which case compensation shall be given as provided by the regulations, or reasonable compensation shall be given." In Article 67, "[t]he State shall protect private savings, investments and profits. The right of inheritance and other lawful rights shall be protected by the State." In Article 68, "[t]he State shall protect individual ownership. It is prohibited for the State to illegally change the title of private property by confiscation or expropriation, in which case compensation shall be given pursuant to related regulations, or reasonable compensation be given, and it shall be ensured the expropriation was properly settled. Civil and administrative liability, or criminal liability in some cases, shall be incurred for any damage or injury to private property."[4]

It should be noted that the term "public interest" in Article 49 has no fixed definition, even under the U.S. legal system. Indeed, a recent judgment of the U.S. Supreme Court gave it a very broad interpretation. In 2000, the city of New London approved a development plan that, in the words of the Supreme Court of Connecticut, was "projected to create in excess of 1,000 jobs, to increase tax and other revenues, and to revitalize an economically distressed city, including its downtown and waterfront areas.[5] To obtain the land needed for this project, the city's development agent purchased property from willing sellers and proposed to use the power of eminent domain to acquire the remainder of the property from unwilling owners in exchange for just compensation.[6] The principal issue in this case

---

3 Yao, Meizhen (1993), Comparative Foreign Investment Law, Wuhan University Press, pp 803- 804.

4 Expert Opinion on Draft Property Law.

5 268 Conn.1, 5, 843 A. 2d 500, 507 (2004).

6 "KELO V. NEW LONDON" 545 US (2005).

was whether this violated the words for "public use" in the Takings Clause of the Fifth Amendment[7]. Justice Stevens delivered the opinion of the court which held that the exercise of the power of eminent domain qualified "as a public use within the meaning of the Takings Clause of the Fifth Amendment to the Constitution."[8] Justice O'Connor and three other Justices all dissented. In China, the power of eminent domain is commonly exercised by the government in the furtherance of "public interest". Most interpretations of "public interest or use" relate to such matters involving public transportation, public hygiene, disaster prevention, scientific and cultural pursuits, environmental protection, conservation of historical sites and preservation of relics, riverhead and forest conservation, as prescribed by law. Takings may not be used for commercial purposes unless the government and the seller enter into a binding agreement.[9]

Although the term "public interest" is deliberately left undefined, the opportunity it affords for a broad interpretation means an increased risk of abuse of the law in this area. As the legislation grants substantial powers of interpretation to the judiciary and executive, the outcome of specific cases is very much dependant on the exercise of their discretion. This is a matter of some concern given that the competence and professionalism of many such judges and officials have come under criticism in recent years.

5.1.2 Nationalization

The Case of China Water Company Limited (Hereinafter "China Water Ltd.")[10]

> In 1999, the city of Changchun in Jilin province reached an agreement with the China Water Ltd to jointly invest in the construction of a water distribution factory. In 2000, they contracted as to this investment when the city of Changchun issued a municipal regulation (hereinafter "the Regulation") that the sewage fee should be collected by the water company, transferred to the sewage company via a specific account, and then eventually paid to the joint venture. The payment process was running smoothly until the sewage company defaulted on payment of sewage fees to the joint venture in mid 2002. As a result, the joint venture encountered financing and operational difficulties. Since March 2003, the sewage company owed the joint venture a total of 97 million RMB. To resolve the dispute, the joint venture invited the Bureau of Foreign-invested Commerce of Jilin province to mediate this dispute. At the mediation, China Water

---

7 "Nor shall private property be taken for public use, without just compensation.".

8 Id.

9 Zheng Chuankun, Tang Zhongmin, (2005) the Improvement of the Institutions of Expropriation, Legal Forum.

10 Published in China Industry and Commerce News, December 25, 2003.

> Ltd. held that the city of Changchun had unilaterally repealed the Regulation which had the effect of destroying their investment base. The city of Changchun asserted that the agreement reached by both parties was created on an unequal basis with regard to the sharing of profits and debts. The city also countered that there were some bottom clauses in the contract based on the Regulation to evade China's laws which prohibit the establishment of "fixed return" investment projects. Thus, the Regulation should be abolished. Having failed to reach a settlement after several mediations, China Water Ltd. finally initiated an administrative lawsuit. The construction of the water plant in the investment plan was put on hold due to the pending lawsuit. The shut-down was followed by a huge penalty for environmental damage and then a dramatically forcible take-over by the government using the pretext of protecting citizens' interests.

Although large scale nationalization will not occur in China unless the institutions of government undergo a fundamental political change, nevertheless, as an alternative to expropriation, foreign investments, especially infrastructural investments, have frequently become subject to forcible take-overs in the name of "public interest". According to Article 18 of the *Administration of Municipal Public Utilities Franchising*, "the organs in charge shall terminate the franchise, revoke the license and exercise a temporary take-over if the franchisee enterprise engages in the following acts: (1) to transfer or lend the franchise without approval; (2) to deposit or mortgage the property without approval; (3) to cause a serious manufacturing accident involving injury, death and serious consequences or quality issues due to inappropriate management; (4) to halt, shut down the business without approval thus seriously affecting public interest and security; (5) other acts prohibited by the law and regulations." The broad scope of terms such as "public interest and security" leaves the judiciary and officials with wide discretion in interpretation thus increasing the risk of temporary take-overs and a disadvantageous outcome for a foreign investor.

"Take-over" refers to special government action taken for a specific purpose. It is not the same as nationalization or expropriation because there is no substantial transfer of property title but instead the enterprise being taken over is subject to the government's 'temporary supervision'. In China, there are currently no laws or regulations governing this area. The methods of compensation for damages or losses during the course of a take-over include: administrative proceedings against the trespassing government if the take-over constitutes an actionable claim and civil action in the event that the government's actions violate procedural regulations. Nevertheless, regardless of which course of action is initiated, neither can escape the bureaucracy and influence of a large powerful government.[11] Cases in which the government is acting as a party will rarely be decided purely on their merits and such judicial bias is ultimately damaging to the enterprise being taken over.

---

[11] The financing of local level courts in China and nomination of judges is controlled by local government.

Typically, enterprises most vulnerable to take-overs are investments in municipal facilities, public infrastructure and education deemed to concern the public interest. Similarly, investments with a Chinese partner, particularly enterprises that support the local economy, are likely targets for take-over by local government.[12] Given the serious consequences of a take-over for an enterprise, foreign investors should be put on notice of these risks.

The Risk of Indirect and Slow Nationalization

Under international pressure to liberalize its economy, a government may switch from direct and overt acts of nationalization to more indirect and gradual methods which ultimately have the same effect, such as tax increases or rejecting applications for renewal of permits for investment ventures. For example, because an agreement could not be reached regarding a dispute over highway tolls, Thailand's regulatory body once forced a Japanese enterprise, which had shares in a highway joint-venture, to sell its 65% shareholding to Thai investors. This aggressive action almost led to the complete withdrawal from Thailand of all Japanese enterprises involved in infrastructure construction. In another instance, the Canadian government once amended its foreign investment policy to restrict foreign investment in its natural resources. A year later, a series of actions by the government such as tax increases and buy-out of foreign investors' shares eventually resulted in the cancellation of an energy project involving over 100 billion US dollars and suspension of another 50 billion US dollar project. The above actions are in fact a form of indirect and gradual nationalization. Another form of indirect nationalization is the establishment of a government sponsored agency to profit from agents fees as done with mineral products in some African countries such as Zaire and Zimbabwe.[13]

At one time, China's government took measures resulting in a "dilution of interests" which achieved the same effect as nationalization. The following case may help in understanding this method.

> *The Case of Fujian Bridge*[14] In 1997, Xiu Ming Company (held by China Travel Service (Holdings) HK Ltd.) invested in bridge construction together with the Municipal and Suburbs Construction Development Company of Fuzhou. They set up a joint-venture by entering into a franchise contract whereby Xiu Ming company held 70% of the shares by investing 0.84 billion RMB. According to the franchise contract, the city of Fuzhou guaranteed a certain amount of traffic through tolling stations in which Xiu Ming Company

---

[12] See the case of the city of San Shui, Guangdong, taking over the assets of a subsidiary of Jianlibao.

[13] Peng, Xuefeng, Xu, Yongqian, Recognition and Management of the Risks of BOT Financing, www.dclf.com.cn.

[14] Modified from the original article "Foreign Investor Sues the City of Fuzhou for Failure to Pay Compensation of 0.9 billion RMB", Beijing Youth, July 14, 2004.

could hold a stake during the franchise period. However, a new expressway was built by the Fuzhou Municipal Government in breach of the franchise contract and Xiu Ming Company suffered a huge loss of income as a result of a drastic reduction in traffic. Monthly profits dropped by 70%, falling from 8 million to 2 million RMB and more than 150 employees had to be laid off. Xiu Ming Company was also running out of funds to make its loan repayments and eventually decided to file a lawsuit against the city of Fuzhou.

5.2 The Risk of Changes to Economic Policies

5.2.1 Huang Qiao Case[15]

In 1994, to solve the problem of power shortages, the city of Taixing in Jiangsu Province, absorbed investment from Australia Asia-Pacific Electricity and Bulb Limited (thereafter "Asia-Pacific Electricity") to set up a joint venture "Tai Xing Huang Qiao Pacific Electric Power Limited" (thereafter "Huang Qiao Electricity"). According to the contract, the foreign investor held the majority of shares (51%) by investing 8.5 million US dollars, with the remainder of the shares going to the Chinese partner who leased equipment and land to the foreign investor without reward. They agreed that the Chinese partner would be responsible for the construction, management and operation of the joint venture which would pay a fixed return of 21 million RMB to Asia-Pacific Electricity for its total investment. After Asia-Pacific Electricity had recouped its total investment, the remaining profits would be shared between both parties in the proportion to their shareholding. This was like a build-operate-transfer (BOT) project in terms of the project financing and fixed returns, however, the difference being that in the BOT investment mode it is normally the foreign investor who is responsible for the construction, operation and management of the venture. The contract also stipulated the amount of electric power and price per KWH, with a guarantee of 50 million RMB provided by the Taixing Branch of the Construction Bank. At the same time, another Chinese investment company provided a whole package of surety. In these circumstances, Asia-Pacific Electricity was assured of no risk except for exchange rate risk and inflation.

However this seemingly flawless business plan later disintegrated in the face of major policy changes by the Chinese government in the energy sector. In 1998, there was a sudden change in *policy which injected lots of state-debt funds into the infrastructure with the result that general product performance no longer provided joint ventures with a competitive edge.*[16] As a consequence, like many BOT projects, the

[15] "Huang Qiao Case", Southern Weekly, Jan. 29, 2003.

[16] Please note the italicized parts which denote the risks to foreign investment from changes in economic policies.

Huang Qiao project ran aground. The Chinese government fully defaulted on its financial guarantee with the joint venture obtaining only 10 million RMB in 2000.

Pricing power reverted to the hands of the Jiangsu provincial authority who replaced the favorable policies of the municipal governmental with a competitive pricing policy. As a result, the purchase price of Huang Qiao dropped from 0.57 Yuan/kwh to 0.45 Yuan/kwh, causing a huge loss of 1.8 million RMB to Huang Qiao Electricity.

Moreover, Huang Qiao Electricity had paid value-added tax of 5-6 million RMB in light of the *newly issued tax regulation* that repealed previous favorable tax-free treatments over a 20-year term. Employees' salaries and other compensation plans also increased threefold according to related policies. Therefore, both parties added an annex to the original contract which reduced the return to 8.5 million RMB per year over a period of 10 years, followed by 250 thousand US dollars per month for 4 years after that period. However, a few weeks later, the joint venture was indirectly affected by *strict implementation of China's coal policy* which resulted in a sharp rise in coal prices. The growing cost of raw material increased their losses and the amended part of the contract became void.

In September 10, 2002, the State Council issued "*Notice on Relevant Issues concerning the Appropriate Handling of Existing Foreign Invested Projects Guaranteeing Fixed Return*" (abbr. No. 43 Document) which expressly set the end of 2002 as the deadline for every provincial government to renegotiate the Fixed Return clause. Unfortunately, the non-retroactivity of No. 43 Document means that the fixed return in the original contract cannot be retrieved.

In China, political reform lags behind economic reform meaning that foreign investors who have already realized their investment in economic terms have to wait for the execution of related policy changes before they can be truly assured of these gains. As the above six changes of policies (see the italicized parts ①-⑥) in the Huang Qiao case) demonstrate, foreign investors may be blind to this type of risk when dealing with the rule makers.

5.2.2 Types of Change in Government Policy

Changes to Macro-Policies. In transition from a centrally planned economy to a market-oriented one, at present China's economy can be called a "governmental economy" or "economy regulated by the government" as the hand of government continues to play a visible role in the development of the economic process. In comparison with China's legal regime which has developed at a fairly steady pace, policy volatility can have a more immediate effect on the economy. For example the discontinuation of favorable policies or the impending adoption of materially unfavorable policies may adversely impact investment by destroying its institutional foundation.

An Example of Frequent Changes to Political or Economic Policies in China

Table 5.1. Schedule of Macroeconomic Management in 2004

Date	**Issuer**	**Name**	**Content**
2004/04/26	State Council	Notice of Liquidation of Fixed Assets Investment Project	The required capital ratio of several over-developed industries relating to steel, cement and real estate is raised to 35% or 40%.
2004/04/29	State Council	Urgent Notice of the Regulation and Management of Land Market	To carry out complete regulation and management of the land market and suspend the transfer of farming land for other non-farming purposes. All related approvals fall within the authority of the State Council in order to strictly implement the general plan of land use and balance farming and non-farming institutions.
2004/04/30	NDRC, PBC, CBRC	Notice of Industrial Policy Corresponding to Loan Policy & Catalogue for Curbing Low-level Repeated Construction in Industries	To require the clean-up within a certain timeframe of restricted category industries such as steel, petroleum and chemical, in the areas of industrial safety, heavy pollution, low quality and high energy cost; to stop construction of, eliminate, close down and refuse approval of enterprises falling under the banned category.
2004/07/16	State Council	Decision Concerning the Reform of Investment Institutions & Catalogue of Investment Projects approved by the Government	To clearly change governmental functions, establish the status of enterprise as investor, improve the investment system, regulate governmental investment, enhance and improve macro-economic management, and finally set up a new investment system embracing market-oriented investment, various financing conduits, efficient government and good intermediary services.
2004/08/06	NDRC & SAEP	Interim Measures for the Examination of Clean Production	Four key principals:(1) it is the responsibility of the enterprise to clean up production; (2) voluntary and compulsory examination, the former applies to enterprises that have satisfied emission requirements and the latter to enterprises whose emissions exceed the standard; (3) internal and external examination; (4) adjustments to be made following the application of the measures in specific circumstances

Table 5.1 (continued)

Date	Issuer	Name	Content
200409/05	NDRC	Interim Measures for the Approval of Investment Projects	To require enterprises responsible for applying for approval to deliver the application for approval to the relevant authority; to enhance the enforcement and regulation of approval procedures; to specify the standards to be used by the approval authorities. The approval authorities include the NDRC and corresponding or subordinate authorities at local level.
2004/04/25	ETCZJ[17]		To prevent overheating investment in the cement industry, ETCZJ raised the entry standards for investors. It said it would close the door to projects whose output is below 4000 tons / day, and shut down four projects where the construction process was delayed due to lack of accessorial conditions. So far, nine projects have been suspended.

Changes to Industrial Policies. In the 1970s, the term "industrial policy" was first used at a conference of OECD Industrial Commission under the heading of "Japanese Industrial Policy". In the late 80s and early 90s, the concept of a "market-oriented economy driven by industrial policy" was prevalent throughout all levels of government in China. From central government to local authorities, some fundamental enterprises and industries were given favorable treatment and support by the government.[18]

Industrial policy is made up of two parts: one relates to the overall arrangement of industries such as the supply of general infrastructure to the industry (including industrial land, roads, ports, water and electricity), favorable treatment (e.g. subsidies for technical development, tax exemptions or tax-free treatment and loans with low interest rates) and more importantly, long-term financing in developing countries. The other concerns organizational behavior including vertical management strategy, in other words, the policies from top to bottom in an industrial organization (e.g. industrial organization, allocation, rate of substantive operation and layout of national industry), and horizontal management policy involving a variety of sectors.[19]

---

[17] The Economy and Trade Commission of Zhejiang Province.

[18] Yang Peng (2002), A Official's Experience – The State of Industrial Policy in China, Strategy and Management, Second Issue: p. 54.

[19] Why the Policy Failed in China—economic analysis of automobile industrial policy in China, 2004, the Anthology of Annual Economics Symposium.

In 1988, the National Planning Commission set up a specific organ called the Department of Industrial Policy to deal with related issues and followed this with the paper "Guidelines of China Industrial Policy" in February 14, 1989. In "Decision regarding Points of Present Industrial Policy", it specified a list of restricted industries and industries that enjoyed government support.[20] In 1994, a more detailed compendium was issued to enhance backbone industries and support developing sectors.[21] Later, both the State Council and National Development and Reform Commission (formerly, the National Planning Commission) separately issued several policies for specific industrial sectors. Not only are these policies relevant to the specific industry but also to foreign investment.

In July 2005, the new industrial policy for the steel industry came into effect which in principle does not allow foreign steel mills to hold controlling stakes in China's steel enterprises. The consequences can be seen in the Chinavalin case where the steel giant Mittal Steel decreased its holding from the agreed 37.17% to 36.67% thus losing its position as majority shareholder. This change was directly governed by the official reply of the NDRC.[22] Furthermore, the policy also had a direct impact on the transaction between Arcelon (the second largest steel mill trust in the world) and Laigang Group. Arcelon's attempt at an early entry into China's market was encumbered by the shareholding requirement, unexpectedly resulting in a 50-50 shareholding ratio.[23]

In 2006, "*Opinions on the Accelerated Development of the Equipment Manufacturing Industry*" issued by the State Council on June 16, dealt a heavy blow to the Carlyle Group's proposed acquisition of an 85% stake of Xuzhou Construction Machinery Group Co., Ltd. (XCMG). This industrial policy strictly limits foreign inves-

---

20 In the Decision, the principles of drafting policy are stated as "... guided by the industrial policy, to fortify Macroeconomic management, instruct the development of the market and make concerted arrangements". Also, it specifies "... to constitute correct policy, pinpoint pillar industries and categorize the supported and restricted sectors ...". It is divided into three parts: the principles of drafting policy, the development of industrial layout and safeguard policy and implementation rules.

21 Article 3 of the "Compendium of National Industrial Policy in the 90s", passed in the 16th session of the State Council Standing Committee, states "... to make efforts to develop pillar industries including mechanical and electronic, petroleum and chemical, automobile and architecture industries." "The State shall set up general policies, enact corresponding laws and regulations, improve the financing systems for supported enterprises, increase the size of stock and bond offerings for IPOs and other financing of those enterprises, support their technical development, authorize a few large-scale enterprises to be entitled to direct overseas financing and guaranteed rights and provide timely and appropriate protection for some immature products of pillar enterprises in accordance with certain international agreements or clauses".

22 The New Policy Curbs the Intent of Foreign-Holdings in Steel Industry, Nanfang Daily, July 21, 2005.

23 Laigang Case—Preliminary Agreement by Arcelon and Laigang Group, Economic Observation, October 9, 2005.

tors' entry into the equipment manufacturing industry, and stipulates that the relevant ministries of the State Council must be consulted about the later transfer of a controlling stake in large-scale and backbone equipment manufacturing enterprises. In addition, enterprises that play a vital role in the manufacture of critical technological equipment shall remain under state control when undergoing restructuring.

Table 5.2. Overview of Chinese Industrial Policies

Policy Name	Time of Issuance	Excerpt of Content
Opinions on the Accelerated Development of the Equipment Manufacturing Industry	2006/06/16	1. Relevant ministries of the State Council shall be consulted about the transfer of controlling stakes in large-scale and backbone equipment manufacturing enterprises 2. Enterprises that play a vital role in the manufacture of critical technological equipment shall remain under state control when undergoing restructuring.
Opinions on the Reform and Development of the Insurance Industry	2006/06/15	1. Enhancing the full understanding of accelerated reform and development of the insurance industry; 2. Development of agriculture insurance; 3. Widening the channels of insurance capital utilization.
Opinions on Foreign Capital Entering the Cultural Sector	2005/08/04	1. Foreign enterprises are allowed to set up enterprises involving packaging and upholstery, distribution of publications, production of recordable disks, artwork businesses, etc in the form of exclusive investment, joint venture or cooperative businesses. Foreign investors are allowed to set up enterprises engaging in publishing and recordable disk production only in the form of joint-venture or cooperative businesses, in which case the Chinese partner shall take more than 50% shares or a majority shareholding. Without prejudice to national censorship, foreign enterprises are allowed to set up enterprises engaging in entertainment product distribution (except movies) in the form of a joint venture or cooperative where the Chinese partner is the majority shareholder. 2. Foreign enterprises are allowed to invest in entertainment places, theaters, brokerage agencies, cinematic technology and shareholding reforms of state-owed enterprises engaged in publishing and entertainment products in the form of a joint venture or cooperative where the Chinese partner holds more than 51% or is a majority shareholder. 3. Foreign investors are prohibited from participating in the businesses of news agencies, radio, television, public broadcasting networks, the making and broadcasting of radio and television programs, movies, internet, art

Table 5.2 (continued)

Policy Name	Time of Issuance	Excerpt of Content
		performance groups, the export and distribution of movies, videotape display companies, the publishing and importing of books, audio & video products and electronic publications, internet entertainment programs and news websites, and internet publishing. In addition, they are restricted to enter into the channel, frequency, flat media, edition and publishing under the disguise form by engaging in distribution, advertisement, broadcasting and publishing.
Steel& Iron Industry Development Policy	2005/07/20	1. In principle, the setting up of new iron & steel enterprises is prohibited. Restructuring and expansion must be achieved by merger & acquisition of already existing enterprises and by moving to areas abundant in water and raw materials and which have good transportation and market access. 2. For foreign investment projects, industry policy requires the production of 10 million tons of normal steel per year or 1 million tons of special steel per year.
Opinions on Promoting the Development of the Commercial Circulation Industry	2005/06/09	It is necessary to develop a number of large internationally competitive enterprises that own well-known brands and exclusive intellectual property rights. These enterprises are invited to expand and strengthen through share transfer, shareholding, contracting, merger and acquisition, trust and franchising.
Opinions on Promoting the Development of the Coal Industry	2005/06/07	Starting from 2005, 3-5 years will be used to set up a regulated environment for the exploitation of coal and the ultimate goal of coal production on a large scale shall be visible with the construction of large size coal enterprises and corporations producing billions of tons of coal. The safety of coal mines shall be improved and the use of colliery gas shall be effectively controlled to curb the occurrence of serious accidents and environmental damage. Another 5-years will be needed to establish 5 systems: a system of supervision for the exploitation of resources with strong emphasis on reasonable safeguards and economizing, a system for the supply of coal revolving around large scale coal mines and coal enterprises and corporations, a system of safeguards for safe production based on strong management and investment supported by advanced technology, a system for a cyclic economy with coal processing, consolidated use of resources and environmental management of mines as its core and a system of rules and regulations based on the "PRC Coal Law" and "PRC Mineral Resources Law".

Table 5.2 (continued)

Policy Name	Time of Issuance	Excerpt of Content
Automobile Industry Development Policy	2004/05/20	1. The State encourages international cooperation in the automobile and motorcycle industries, and supports the merger of large domestic enterprises with foreign auto syndicates. 2. Enterprises that sell their products only in the domestic market shall establish their own brands and sale and service systems. 3. The relevant provincial government organs shall report registered projects to the NRDC for registration. For special vehicle projects, the investment regulatory organs in the provincial government shall report to NDRC; for newly-established automobile projects the NRDC shall report directly to the State Council. 4. For joint ventures concerning automobiles, special vehicles, agricultural vehicles and motorcycles, the Chinese partner must not have less than a 50% share; when shares are sold, the Chinese partner shall be the majority shareholder. Foreign enterprises may build no more than two factories for automobile products, unless jointly acquiring other auto enterprises with their Chinese partners.
Decision on the Accelerated Development of the Forestry Industry	2003/06/25	To further open the forestry industry, it is necessary to take advantage of both of domestic and overseas markets and resources and accelerate its development. Furthermore, it is essential to obtain advanced technology, management experience, funds and good seeds. Foreign investment is supported to flow into forestation and forestry processing.
Decision on Promoting the Development of Professional Education	2002/09/25	To encourage foreign organizations and individuals with the required legal qualifications to invest in professional education; they are allowed to cooperate with domestic organizations and institutions to explore the market for professional training and promote graduate employment.
Opinions on Promoting the Development of the Sewage Disposal & Waste Industry	2002/09/12	The goals of sewage industrialization are as follows: to reform pricing and management systems; to promote various forms of investment and financing institutions to satisfy the needs of a market-oriented economy which requires the waste disposal industry to embrace multiple investors, market-oriented management and open operation.
Development Policies for the Software & Integrated Circuit Industry	2000/06/24	The state imposes value-added tax at a fixed rate of 17% on taxable entities that develop their own software before 2010 in order to boost related enterprises in the domestic market. The tax paid over 3% which is returned as soon as it levied is required for use in technological research and software development.

Table 5.2 (continued)

Policy Name	Time of Issuance	Excerpt of Content
Policy for the Development of Water Facilities Industry	1997/09/04	1. The state shall preferentially develop the water resources industry by encouraging a broad scope of investment in a variety of ways and channels in order to boost the industrialization of water resources. It shall adopt overall plans for industrial use and residential use, and for the preservation and exploitation of resources. 2. The state encourages the use of barren mountains, valleys, hills, sandy wasteland and other areas of soil erosion by lease, auction, cooperation by share and contracting for a 50-year term. During the specified period, the owners or proprietors by contract, lease or shareholding shall be entitled to transfer or inherit the land prescribed by law. The owner by purchase has right to transfer, inherit, mortgage or dispose of by share the cooperative management of the land. The construction and operation of many different types of small scale irrigation schemes shall be encouraged.

Changes to Specific Policies. In 2002, changes in local policy concerning pharmaceutical retail were a great shock for retailers in Guangdong. The issuance of the new policy "Guangdong Province, Interim Regulation for Allocation of Pharmaceutical Retail" in March 2002 attracted a throng of retailers to the Guangdong market. However, to their surprise, some local administrations put into force unreasonable registration procedures, which included restrictions on pharmacies opening within 500 meters of each other, requirements for retailers to submit their residence registration book, marriage certificate, and certificate of [no] criminal record and a 24-hour business guarantee. This resulted in some investors suffering great losses.[24]

It is common in China for the government to manipulate the economy at the expense of investors and unexpected policy changes mean that well-prepared business drafts have little use except as scrap paper. In such circumstances the failure of investments seems unavoidable.

(a) On July 11, 2006, six ministries jointly issued the "*Opinions on the Regulation of Access to Foreign Capital in the Real Estate Market and its Management*", which raised the ratio of registered capital in relation to the total investment amount, and required foreign investors to pay the full price of acquired shares in an existing domestic real estate company.[25]

---

[24] Zhao Daibo, Deng Juan (2002), Investment Traps, Shangjie, October Issue.

[25] See Article 1 (5) and (9) of *Opinions on the Regulation of Access to Foreign Capital in the Real Estate Market and its Management.*

(b) On September 15, 2002, the "*Implementing Provisions for Medicine Management*" were issued at the same time that the seventh edition of the new "*Administration of Management of Medicine Registration*" was drafted. The new regulation specified a 5-year supervision period during which only one category of medicine would be permitted to enter the market. Following this new rule, domestic enterprises with lower research costs as their medicines are contemporaneous imitations of foreign counterparts look set to lose their market niches since foreign medicine providers commonly are not able to bring out their new medicines over such a short term.

(c) In accordance with the new standard of 65% energy efficiency in residential construction, since October 2005, the construction committee of the city of Zhengzhou in Henan province, is required to check all ongoing or planned construction as the first procedure in obtaining a certificate of construction. In reality, few structures under construction before this rule came about in this jurisdiction can meet this standard, meaning that they are unable to obtain the requisite approval for construction.[26]

Shortly after China's admission to WTO, there followed a special transition period in which China amended, implemented and adjusted a large number of laws and regulations in accordance with WTO rules and entry requirements. After this, there was a period of enormous adjustment and amendment of the legal regime at the time of the Sixth Plenum of the 15th Central Committee of the Chinese Communist Party. Some investment projects which had been reaping the rewards of favorable policies may have found themselves in an awkward predicament if they were unwilling to make any changes, lessen their dependence on the policies or even retreat from the area.

5.2.3 Suggestions for Combating Political Risks

Taking an optimistic view, the most effective way to combat the political risks is to learn as much as possible about government policies, rules and instructions and correctly anticipate the trend of social and industrial development, from which an analysis and judgment of the profitability and feasibility of an investment can be made. Mr. Kaifu Lee, CEO of Google (China), pointed out in his article "Making it in China" that "knowing the rules and developing the right relationship" is the first of the six challenges foreign investors must face.[27] In China, a decent relationship with government means a great deal to investors and entrepreneurs. Establishing government contacts and maintaining that relationship is an important first step before investing. The government or government institutions (including state-owned enterprises) is not only a valuable client, but also a rule-maker and supervisor of

[26] No 65%, No Construction, www.xinhua.net, (last visited on Oct. 24, 2005).

[27] Kaifu Lee, "Making it in China", www.kaifulee.com (last visited on Oct. 2005).

businesses. In the event that a company is treated as friend of government, it will gain many advantages over its competitors such as access to crucial inside information. Without this knowledge, it could one day find that its products and services are to be downgraded or even excluded from the specific market in China. It is absolutely essential not to oppose the government even if in compliance with all the rules and regulations. Furthermore, it is necessary to develop a good relationship with the government at all levels, since China has a centralized political system that runs directly from central to local government. The government at a higher level makes the rules while the local government implements and even adapts them to suit the local economy. Multinational companies that do not enjoy an extensive relationship with government cannot carry out their investment plans effectively. As mentioned above, "knowing the rules and developing the right relationship" is a crucial step to investing successfully in China.

To succeed in the long-term, it is necessary to avoid excessive dependence on favorable policies. At the end of the day, the entire investment environment and future development of the local market are much more important.[28]

5.3 The Risks Coming from Local Government

5.3.1 Localized Policy when Inviting Foreign Investment

In the current mode of an investment driven economy, foreign investors are warmly welcomed by local governments. There are two things local governments have commonly done to attract investors: one is to improve the local investment environment and the other is to provide favorable policies. They are likely to choose the latter because the former takes a longer time to realize. To attract more investment, local governments take all kinds of measures such as selling land at an extremely low price or even giving it away, ignoring environmental protection and exempting enterprises from their environmental responsibilities, tax and fee reductions or exemptions, providing governmental guarantees for large loans, or underground direct financing of enterprises.[29] Lax execution of rules, severe competition and insufficient funds are the basic reasons as to why underdeveloped areas recklessly increase the subsidies offered without too much concern for the quality of investing enterprises. The poorer the area is, the more subsidies are offered. In China's western regions, some local governments provide full subsidies to investments of 5-years or more and half subsidies for 10-year investments. Some even offer land for a nominal sum to factories that are under construction or re-

---

[28] Zhao Daibo, Deng Juan (2002), Traps in Investment, Shangjie, October Issue.

[29] Xu Changsheng, Local Governments Are Missing in the Tricks of Invitation of Investments, www.dajun.com.cn (last visited on Oct. 2005).

structuring which then rent this out to investors for a low price.[30] The most popular way to reward investors is the transfer of land to them at an extraordinarily low price. This has become so prevalent across China that the government has to pay for it by substantial and expensive debt issuance.[31] Below are two examples of such favorable land policies:

(a) Yanshan county in Hebei province took startling measures to attract investment. It announced that it would offer 50 acres of land for free to projects with a 10 million RMB investment, 100 acres for 20 million RMB investments, 150 acres for 30 million RMB investments and so on. In terms of local policy, the county government agreed to completely support the use of land for industrial and investment purposes, and ensure there a sufficient quota of land to meet demand. It is also responsible for handling the approval procedures for land that is given away. As for land used for new construction or technical reconstruction projects where investment is below 10 million RMB, the approval procedures are applicable after the construction and investors may also be exempt from having to pay the usual occupancy fee.[32]

(b) Zhengning county in Gansu province issued a policy that included "zero rental" for a qualified projects with 1 million to 5 million RMB investment and free transfer of land for investments of more than 5 million RMB (inclusive). In addition, the county will handle the land fee for the whole undertaking.[33]

5.3.2 The Legal Risks of Localized Policy

Untrustworthy Government Promises

When trying to attract foreign investment, local governments often make dazzling promises of favorable and long-term policies to foreign investors. However, after the first great influx of foreign investment, the government often changes its tone and the risk for foreign investors is when they realize that their investment and high expectations are founded purely on an oral promise by a local official as opposed to a rational decision based on professional analysis and assessment of local conditions. When local government is short of funds and capital, both parties are more likely to reach an agreement where the high rate of return promised has little basis in reality. The transfer and reelection of officials provides further uncertainties

---

30 Hu Xiangting, Traps in Local Favorable Polices for Inviting Investment, the Essay of China's Economics Annual Meeting of 2004.

31 MLR Official: Government at Local Level is Involved in Violation of Land Law, www.xinhuanet.com, (last visited on August 27, 2004).

32 Western Times, August 10, 2005.

33 Some Strange Phenomena in Inviting Investment, www.people.com.cn (last visited on Oct.7, 2005).

and concerns for investors, especially in the case of long term projects. Newly-elected governors may alter their predecessors' policies, causing an adverse effect on investment.

Illegitimacy of Localized Rules

The fact is that some local governments are overstepping the limit of their authority by creating rules and policies to suit local interests. For instance, detailed rules regarding tax reductions and exemptions already exist in the "Administration of Tax Reductions and Exemptions (for Trial Implementation)", separately issued by the State Administration of Taxation on August 3, 2005 as a supplement to the "Law of Administration of Tax Collection". It requires taxation organs to exercise vertical administration meaning that governmental arms below provincial level cannot exercise administrative powers except in the area of surtaxes. Thus, the promises of long term localized tax-free policies are often hollow words.

Moreover, land policy tends to be a closely policed area because of the strict stance taken by the central government in an effort to meet China's growing industrial and residential development needs. In the "Decision of Further Reforms and Strict Administration of Land" of 2004, the extraordinarily low price policy was prohibited and criminal liability may be incurred for serious breaches of the regulation. In addition, any state functionary who engages in tampering with the general plan for land use shall be subject to serious administrative penalties imposed by superior or supervisory organs. On October 13, 2005, with the approval of the State Council, MOF, Ministry of Land and Resources, National Audit Office and Ministry of Supervision cooperated in carrying out a special investigation concerning compensation for land used for construction and which covered the registration and approval of newly-added land and the imposition and collection of a land use fee over the period of January 1, 1999 to June 30, 2005. The investigation (in the period of the first half of 2006) was coordinated with the self-examination (in the period of October 1, 2005 to December 31, 20005) of local governments regarding this issue.[34] Foreign investors found to have engaged in construction in violation of the law are not only subject to a large number of penalties, but are also required to reconstruct within a certain time limit. Enterprises facing these charges may suffer from a grave shortage of funds as a result, perhaps causing the failure of the whole project.

As far as these various favorable "sweeteners" are concerned, foreign investors are well advised not to forget to take political change into account and to be wary of oral promises by officials regardless of how legitimate they appear to be. All these local policies run the risk of conflicting with the laws and regulations promulgated by central government, and the impetuous investor who ignores this danger will suffer the consequences.

---

[34] Land Use Fee, focused by Related Ministries in The Great Investigiation, New Jing Daily, October 14, 2005.

6 Corporate Governance Troubles in Sino-foreign Joint Ventures[1]

It is easy to combine capitals but not easy to combine minds, which is the biggest hurt Chinese joint ventures face. After 20 year development, conformity is still the main problem in joint ventures.

—— Science & Technology Brain Power Issue 8, 2005

The management performance of about 37-70% joint ventures in the world is unsatisfactory.

—— Geringer, J.M. and L. Herbert[2]

6.1 Difficulties in Managing Legal Entities Shown in the Upsurge of Foreign-Invested Enterprises

Foreign investors normally establish foreign-invested enterprises in China in the following three modes: Sino-foreign Equity Joint Venture (EJV), Sino-foreign Co-operative Joint Venture (CJV) and Wholly Foreign-owned Enterprises (WOFE). At the beginning of China's reform and openness to the world market, foreign capital entered China mainly in the mode of EJV and CJV and the capital was mainly from Hong Kong, Macao and Taiwan. However, WOFEs have developed rapidly and the foreign investors have requested more shareholder rights since 1992. In 1997, the

---

[1] Concerning the management structure, EJVs generally adopt the general manager responsibility mechanism under the guidance of board of directors. CJVs normally adopt one of the following three managing methods: (1) The general manager responsibility mechanism under the guidance of board of directors, applicable to companies with limited liabilities and legal entity qualification. (2) Joint management, applicable to cooperatives without legal entities established. (3)Entrusted management, applicable to legal entity or non legal entity cooperatives. There are two ways of entrusted management. One is full authority entrust by the cooperative for one party's management, another is full authority entrust by the cooperative for a third party's management. The management modes of WOFEs and joint ventures are similar. The author mainly discusses management problems of Equity Joint Ventures in this article, but these problems also exist in enterprises of the other two types in certain degree.

[2] Geringer, J.M. and L. Herbert (1991), Measuring Performance of International Joint Venture, Journal of International Business studies, 19:365-388.

Table 6.1. Foreign Investment Mode Variation

Year / Mode	1988-1994	1995	1996	1997	1998	1999	2000	2001	2002
Total	100	100	100	100	100	100	100	100	100
EJV	47.64	43.54	43.50	43.08	40.36	39.26	35.23	33.57	28.42
CJV	22.32	19.51	19.51	19.73	21.38	20.47	16.20	13.25	9.59
WOFE	36.15	36.87	36.59	35.78	36.22	38.55	47.31	50.93	60.15
Others	3.89	0.08	0.40	1.43	2.04	1.72	1.26	2.25	1.84

(Resource: Foreign Enterprises Statistics on the website of the Ministry of Commerce.)

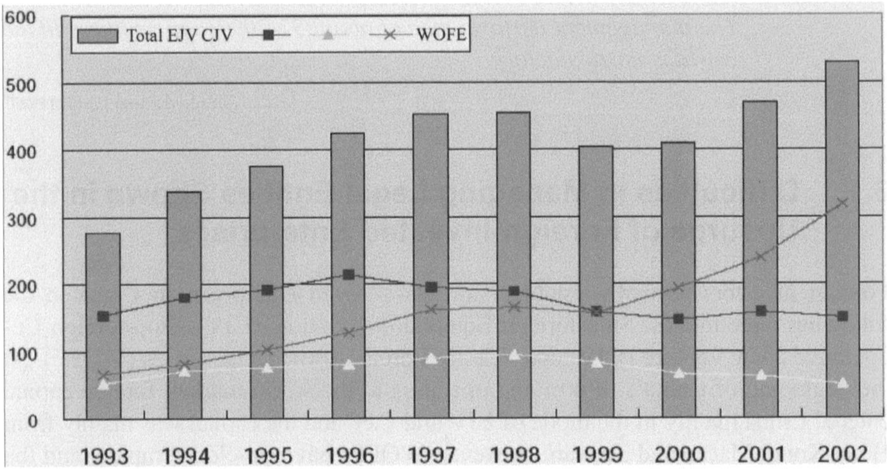

Chart 6.1. China's Utilization of FDI From 1993 to 2002 (Variation in China's FDI entrance mode structure from 1993 to 2002)

number of WOFE projects exceeded that of joint ventures for the first time. WOFEs are becoming the 'fashion' in foreign capital's entrance into China.

Since the end of the 20th century, the newly entered foreign capital has not only generally adopted the foreign-invested method but also had an important tendency, that is, foreign capital is increasing their capital contribution in exchange for more control in China's foreign-invested enterprises. Increasing capital has turned to be an essential mode for China's utilization of foreign capitals. The above facts show that the tendency of being wholly foreign owned enterprises has appeared in the development of joint ventures in China. Wholly Foreign-owned Enterprises would be the main choice of foreign capital's investment in China.

Why did foreign investors adopt the mode of EJV and CJV at the beginning of its reform and opening but have changed the mode into WOFE or taken the way of increasing capital to obtain the controlling status in recent years? One of the main reasons is more and more legal problems have occurred in managing joint venture legal entities. The joint venture mode is losing its advantages in the new legal environment. The WOFE mode, due to the high consistency of ownership and managing power, has no corporate governance problems and turns to be the favorite of foreign investors.

In joint ventures, especially those with only two shareholders, the directors usually consider issues based on the interest of the shareholder which they represent instead of that of the joint venture enterprise. When one shareholder holds majority shares, it would misuse its controlling power for its own benefits while damaging the joint venture and other shareholders. When the shares are equally allocated between the two partners, the shareholders may have common control over the joint venture, which may easily lead to 'deadlock of the board of directors' and negatively effects operation of the joint venture. Besides, EJVs or CJVs, in their nature, are not stable corporate structures. The joint venture parties or cooperative parties have no symmetrical information and knowledge. They may diverge in corporate governance and culture during their cooperation, which may directly negatively influence the performance of the joint venture's operation and management. Even worse, some joint ventures without internal cooperation may have bad investment effects.

> Unilever's entrance into the Chinese market is a typical case. Unilever is one of the world's most famous companies entering the Chinese market at the early stage. It sets up the first daily chemical equity joint venture in Shanghai. However, the joint venture, due to its nature of property rights in common and common control in governance, could only reach decisions through consensus of the parties, which is hard to realize, so the operational performance of the enterprise is unsatisfactory. Finding no other resolution, the enterprise moved to an independent new factory in 1995, after which the conflicts between the parties are solved.[3]

Under such a background, foreign capital may enter China through the way of setting up wholly foreign owned companies or obtaining controlling shares so as to avoid disputes. Such enterprises may better realize the strategic intents of the parent company and fully combine the production and investment chain in China into the global system of the parent company. This method is also helpful for prevention of technology divulgence and may meet the needs of internalization of technology and market of multinationals.

[3] The Multinationals in China-Winners and Losers by the [Great Britain] Economist Intelligence Union (EIU) , published by the Xinhua Publishing House in 2001, 1st Edition.

Since the 1990's, the operational performance of Chinese joint ventures is commonly low. Actually, it is not a problem only in China. According to the research by Geringer and Herbert in 1991, about 37% to 70% joint ventures in the world do not have satisfactory performance.[4] Unstableness exists in joint ventures. At least two parent companies from China and abroad share the property rights of a joint venture and manage it together. Since the cooperating parties have different aims and expectations as well as different commercial practical experiences, the social cultural tradition divergence leads to difficulties in realizing and maintaining harmony and consolidation inside the joint venture. The Chinese government formerly insisted on the strategy of 'exchange market for technology', so it encouraged joint ventures by multinationals and Chinese enterprises in legislation. In fact, this is not the best resource deployment, but achieves the outcome of catering for social and political needs.[5] When policies are changed, internal legal risks are more and more exposed in such manners as pre-arranged marriage.

6.2 General Situation of Corporate Governance Modes of Joint Ventures

6.2.1 Corporate Governance of Joint Ventures Review

Basic Modes of Corporate Governance

Different nations have varied property right structures, financing modes and resource markets due to diversified social traditions, legal systems, political systems and economic systems, which lead to varied corporate governance modes. The core of corporate governance is the expression form of ownership and control power. With this as a reference, the different corporate governance structure modes of various nations may be divided into the following four types:[6]

Market-Oriented Mode. The most outstanding feature of this mode is decentralized ownership. The separation of ownership and management right in modern companies causes decentralized shareholders unable to supervise the managing level's behaviors effectively, which is called the 'weak shareholder with strong

[4] Geringer, J.M. and L. Herbert (1991), Measuring Performance of International Joint Venture, Journal of International Business studies 19:365-388.

[5] Deng Jin (2005), The Twenty Years of Multinationals: We Need New Foreign Affair Strategies, *the Southern Weekend* on 8 September.

[6] Masahiko Aoki and Qian Yingyi (1996), View the Corporate Governance in Transition Economy, China Economy Publishing House, pp213; Zhang Weiying (1995), the Entrepreneurs in Enterprises-Contract Theories, Shanghai Sanlian Bookstore and Shanghai People's Publishing House; Zhang Weiying (1999), the Enterprise Theories and Reform on Chinese Enterprises, Beijing University Publishing House, pp 122.

managing level' situation. Therefore, the agency problem arises. Solving this problem mainly relies on maintaining arm's length financing and a market for corporate control as well as an external mechanism of bankruptcy and court system. Two main features of such a mode are: first, only the board of directors are set under the shareholders' meeting while no supervisors' meeting is set; second, the board of directors' has numerous and detailed management functions. The board of directors under the company's shareholders' meeting is the regular management decision body of the company while various committees are set under the board of directors as the regular concrete deciding bodies of the board of directors. The concrete operation of the company is executed by the officers of the company authorized by the board of directors. These officers are engaged by the board of directors while the main ones are appointed from among the directors. America, England, Canada, Australia, etc. typical use the market oriented mode.

Bank-Centered Mode. The feature of the bank-centered mode is centralized shareholder rights and a greater role of the bank in financing and corporate management. The heart of the bank-centered corporate governance mode, mainly used by Japan companies, is the firm's main bank. A firm's main bank is a large shareholder that provides the firm with loans and diverse financial services. It helps the firm access capital markets, sometimes by providing financial guarantees and underwriting the firm's securities. It monitors the firm's management and intervenes at times of poor performance. The main bank typically sends directors to the firm's board in periods of distress to help the firm improve its performance. At times, it acts like a management consultant, providing information and advice to management. While the influence of main banks may have fallen over the last twenty years, it is still large enough to sharply distinguish the Japanese corporate governance from that of Anglo-Saxon countries.

Family Control Mode. In most East Asia and Latin America nations, shares are centralized under family control while the controlling families generally participate in the company's operation and management. Therefore, the core of the family control corporate governance model shifts from interest conflict between the management team and shareholders to interest conflict among controlling major shareholders, managing level and minority shareholders which are referred to as strong family majority shareholders, managing level and weak minority shareholders.

Transitional Economy Mode. The former Soviet Union and other middle and east European nations in the transitional economy share some common features such as having lots of large scale state-owned enterprises needing restructuring and inherit the formerly disordered legal system. Therefore, in transitional economy nations, the biggest problem in company management is insider control which refers to management's strong and effective control of the enterprise by making use of the vacuum left after the disaggregation of the planned economy under the situation of an absence of a legal system with weak enforcement power. to a certain degree, the managing level turns to be the actual owner of the enterprise.

Table 6.2. Main Characteristics of Various Corporate Governance Modes

Management Mode	Key Issues in Company Management
Market-Oriented Mode	Strong Management, Weak Shareholders
Bank-Centered Mode	Bank has Decisive Influence on Corporate
Family Control Mode	Strong Family Majority Shareholders, Management and Minority Shareholders
Transitional Economy Mode	Insider Control

Taking developed nations' successful experiences in reforming the company system as a reference and considering the situation of China, the corporate governance and organizational structure set up in *the Company Law of PRC* have the following features:

Concerning the allocation and balance of company powers, the common mode of power division and balance in the continental law system nations is adopted. Three specific company organs with power and work division are set up to form the organizational structure. The Shareholders' meeting is the power and decision-making organ of the company. The Board of directors and managers are the implementation and daily operational organ of the company. The Supervisors' meeting is the supervision organ of the company. Such an organizational system belongs to the duality or double level corporate governance model adopted in Germany and Japan, with special similarities with the Japanese parallel duality system. Mutual binding and balancing principle is set up in the internal relation of organization structure. Since company managers are the implementation organ under control of the board of directors while being the legally comparatively independent company management and operational organ of the company, Chinese corporate governance model is also referred to as the triplex party system formed by the board of directors, managers and supervisors' meeting under the shareholders' meeting. Compared with other nations, the authority of shareholders' meeting under the *Company Law of PRC* is much greater, not only including the decision making power concerning major issues such as mergers, separation, dismissal or liquidation of the company, modification of articles of association, and appointment and removal of directors or supervisors, but also including the final decision making power of important proceedings in company management such as operational policy and investment plans of the company, annual financial budget plans and final accounts of the company, etc. However, the various power of shareholders' meeting empowered by law could not be fully and effectively realized due to the system features of the shareholders' meeting. Legal status of the board of directors and supervisors' meeting in China is also different from that in America, Germany and Japan. According to *Company Law of PRC*, members of the board of directors shall be appointed and removed by shareholders' meeting. The Board of directors is the operational implementation organ of the company, being responsible for shareholders' meetings, and has the decision making power concerning management issues beyond the authority of shareholders' meetings, including operational plans and investment projects of the company, setup of internal management organs of the company and so on. The Chairman is the actual core of the board of directors and even the company since he or she is the legal representative of the company and may act on the board of directors' behalf for part of its authority during the closing meeting period of board of directors. The manager is set as the executive organ of the board of directors, being responsible for the daily operation and management of the company, and constitutes the operational management team together with the board of directors in the organizational system of Chinese companies. Supervisors' meeting is the supervision organ of a company. Its members are appointed and removed by the board of directors. The Supervisors' meeting, with parallel relations with the board of directors, is in charge of supervising whether accomplishment of corporate duties by directors and managers violate laws or articles of association of the company, and is entitled to inspect company's finance. Furthermore, directors, managers and financial officers are not allowed to act as supervisors so as to ensure the independence of supervisors' meeting in supervision.

Legal Provisions on Corporate Governance of Joint Venture Legal Persons in China

Corporate Governance of foreign-invested enterprises in many countries is the same as that of ordinary domestic companies while no different treatment exists. However, obvious difference exists in China. It is stipulated in Article 18 of *the Company Law of PRC* that 'The Law applies to limited liability companies with foreign investment. Where the laws on Sino-foreign equity joint venture enterprises, Sino-foreign cooperative joint venture enterprises and wholly foreign-owned enterprises otherwise provide, the provisions of such laws apply', under which Sino-foreign joint ventures or cooperatives and wholly foreign-owned enterprises with legal person status are all limited liability companies and shall be established according to *Company Law* with the exception that special provisions in laws on foreign-invested enterprises shall apply in priority. The legal person corporate governance of Sino-foreign joint ventures under *the Law on Sino-foreign Equity Joint Venture Enterprises* is much different from the general provision on corporate governance under *Company Law*.

The organizing form of Sino-foreign equity joint ventures is commonly a company with limited liability, but joint ventures are different from common companies whose management structure is formed according to the Company Law. Joint ventures do not have the 'shareholders-board of directors-supervisors' meeting' setting with division and balance of power in the typical sense. No shareholders' meeting or board of directors is set up and the general manager liability under the guidance of board of directors system is adopted. Board of directors is the organ with highest authority, combining double functions of shareholders' meeting and

Table 6.3. Comparison of Corporate Governance Design under *Company Law* and *the Law on Equity Joint Venture Enterprises*

Stipulations of the Company Law	Shareholders' meeting enjoys the highest authority. Board of directors is the execution organ. Supervisors' meeting is the supervision organ. Shareholders share the right to vote according to the contribution proportions.	Board of directors appoint or remove general managers and vice general managers.
Stipulations of the Joint Venture Law	Board of directors enjoys highest and sole authority, which is agreed by shareholders under the principal of equality and mutual benefits.	Parties to the venture appoint general managers and vice general managers.

supervisors' meeting. The authority of directors' meeting is stipulated in the articles of association of joint ventures, containing the decision making power on all important issues of joint ventures such as enterprise development plan, production and operation activity plan, income and expenses budget, profit distribution, labor wage plan, shutout, appointment, removal, authority and treatment of general manager, vice general manager, chief engineer, chief accountant and auditor, etc. To fully protect Chinese and foreign investors' legal rights and benefits, *the Law on Sino-foreign Equity Joint Venture Enterprise* also requests issues concerning major alteration of enterprises such as modification of articles of association, increase and transfer of registered capital, mergers, break down and dismissal of enterprise, etc. be approved unanimously by directors presenting board meeting and through decision, which allows parties with less contribution effectively participate in decisions concerning company operation through exercising veto for directorate decision.

Directors are appointed by parties to the joint venture while the chairman of the board is the legal representative of the joint venture. If one venture party acts as the board chairman, the other parties may act as the vice chairmen. Due to lack of shareholders' meeting, the board of directors could not come into being through election by shareholders' meeting. Directors of joint ventures are appointed through negotiation of Chinese and foreign parties, and the proportion of director allocation for each party is up to the stock right structure of the company. The directors appointed by the parties form the board of directors. Chairman of the board is also determined by the parties in joint venture negotiation, but need confirmation by the board of directors. Therefore, board of directors of joint venture actually comes into existence under double-track system. The process for forming board of directors of joint ventures is shown in the following chart:

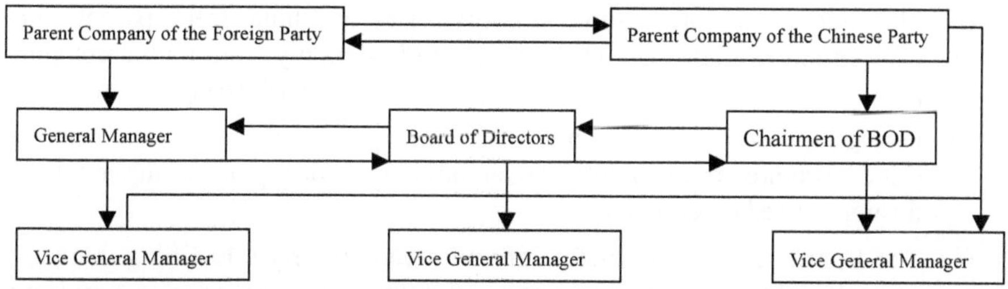

Chart 6.2. The process for forming board of directors of joint ventures
(Resource: Research on Management Mechanism of Foreign-invested Enterprises Set by Multinationals in China by Li Wei'an, in the Frontline of Company Management Theories and Practices compiled by Li Wei'an, published by China Finance and Economy Publishing House in 2003, pp3 – 25.)

Sino-foreign joint ventures set up management organ under the guidance of the board of directors to take charge of the daily operation of enterprises. The General Manager, vice general managers and other senior management personnel constitute the management organ. Members of the management organ are retained and dismissed by the board of directors, being either Chinese citizens or foreign citizens. The Board Chairman or directors may also be such members. Generally, venture parties act as general manager and vice general manager or factory director and vice director respectively. Within authorization by the board of directors, the general manager could represent the joint venture externally, appoint and remove affiliating personnel internally, and exercise other authority as authorized by the board of directors.

But it is needed to be said here, unlike JVs or WFOEs, the governing structure of a Foreign-invested Stock Company ("FISC") consists of the shareholders' meeting, the board of management (BOM), and the general director (who is the executive manager). An FISC is governed by a board of directors which is subordinate to the shareholders. In addition, a board of supervision consisting of representatives of the shareholders and employees is required for certain companies. The shareholding of the investors in a FISC is in the form of issued shares, which essentially is a blend between an EJV and a Western stock company or public company. Therefore some troubles existing in a normal Sino-foreign joint venture as following discussion will disappear in a FISC. So the following analysis is not totally applicable to FISC.

6.2.2 Survey of Sino-foreign Joint Venture Corporate Governance

China Corporate Governance Research Center of Nankai University issued the first Survey Report on Problems in Management of Foreign-invested Enterprises in China, analyzing current status of Sino-foreign joint venture legal person management structure through investigation of 200 foreign-invested enterprises set up by multinationals in Tianjin Developing Zone and concluding as follows:

(a) Management of foreign-invested enterprises in China is the parent company oriented mode. The company control is mainly from the parent company while the internal management takes on a subordinating status.
(b) Foreign investors of these enterprises emphasize controlling share rights in share structure arrangements with an obvious tendency of turning to wholly foreign owned enterprises.
(c) The Board of directors of foreign-invested enterprises in China is mainly controlled by the parent company. For the convenience of supervision, board chairman and general manager are appointed separately. the Board chairman of joint ventures is eviscerated to some degree while the real power is still in the hand of the general manager. The General manager is generally appointed by the foreign party of the venture while the Chinese party acts as the board chairman.
(d) The main form for multinational's control of enterprises in China is to directly appoint general manager, supervise and control finance and directly appoint managers of key departments.
(e) Incentives of management by foreign-invested enterprises in China are mainly with basic salaries along with considerable consumption in active service. The Annual salary of foreign party managers is rather high while the annual salary of Chinese party managers must be distributed again under the state regulations and is finally a little bit higher than that of persons in the same level positions in state-owned enterprises. Some Chinese party managers resign under the lure of high salary and bring their personal relations into the foreign party.
(f) Localization tendency of foreign-invested enterprises in China is obvious. Most managing staff are from the local talent market while the proportion of Chinese in senior management positions increases rapidly.
(g) Interested parties include employees, trade unions, creditors and governments do not play apparent role in management of foreign-invested enterprises.

Sino-foreign joint ventures, though existing as independent legal entities, have no independent management structure. The Board of directors of a joint venture is controlled by the parent company and has no full authority while senior managers are appointed by the parent company with a vague agency relation. The parent company makes standards for assessment of managing staff and the internal supervision is secondary. The specific corporate governance existing in Sino-foreign joint ventures is referred to as 'parent company oriented mode' legal person management structure.[7]

---

[7] Li Wei'an and Wu Xianming (2002), The Analysis of Sino-foreign Joint Venture Parent Company Guiding Type Company Management Mode, World Economy and Politics, Issue 5.

6.3 Review of Legal Risks Arising from Sino-foreign Joint Venture Corporate Governance

6.3.1 Risks of Existence Reliance: Review from the Aspect of Imbalance Between the Control Right and Residual Claim Right

The Key issue in corporate governance is how to distribute the enterprise residual claim right and control right among various enterprise participants, for which economists have concluded as follows: first and most basic, residual claim right and control right shall be as balanced as possible which means persons with residual claim right and bearing risks shall have control right or persons with control right shall bear risks.[8] The problem of residual claim right and control right imbalance is quite serious in Sino-foreign joint venture enterprises, which is mainly caused by the unbalanced power of venture parties. The Residual claim right is distributed according to capital contribution proportion, but the control right is up to each party's advantages, which means capital contribution proportion has not decisive power. Under traditional enterprise theories, capital and management skill are the main resources of control right. However, it is shown in the operational practice of Sino-foreign joint ventures that technology resource advantage and market advantage are also main resources of the control right while the former is a power resource that may make capital, management and market resource right impractical.[9] In practice, foreign parties generally take control right of joint ventures relying on capital, management, technology advantages. Sometimes, Chinese parties may also take certain control right relying on monopoly of sales channel. However, joint ventures are generally controlled by foreign parties since the base for sales control still rest with good products by joint ventures. Under such a situation, serious imbalance of the residual claim right and control right is unavoidable unless the foreign investor's share in a Sino-foreign joint venture happened to be equal to its advantages and control right. Unfortunately, foreign investors with obvious advantages and ability to control Sino-foreign joint ventures cannot subscript majority registered capital when investing in some restricted industries.

In Sino-foreign joint ventures, if one shareholder's material control power arising from advantages other than share ratio is powerful enough to make the joint venture rely on the party while the party may not obtain the balanced residual claim right due to relatively less proportion of capital contribution, the shareholder is then activated to use control power to obtain return beyond profit distribution,

[8] Zhang Weiying (2005), The Property Rights, Incentives and Company Management, the Economy and Science Publishing House, pp. 2-3.

[9] Lu Changcong, Zhen Wenquan, Li Zhongguang (2004), The Property Right Variation and Proceeds Dispute in Sino-foreign Joint Ventures, the China Industry Economy in Issue 11.

Table 6.3. Forms of Foreign Parties' Control of Joint Ventures

Measures	Proportion(%)
Right to appoint general manager	80.2
Right to directly appoint managers of key departments	30.4
Control right based on technology advantage	20.6
Control of product sales or raw material supply	10.3
Finance supervision	40.8
Other appointment authority of board chairman	10.1
others	9

(Resource: Li Wei'an(2003), the Research on Management Mechanism of Foreign-invested Enterprises Set by Multinationals in China, in Li Wei'an (eds) the Frontline of Company Management Theories and Practices, China Finance and Economy Publishing House, pp3-25.)

realizing unification of material control power and residual claim right.[10] When the return brought by such 'abuse' of control power is larger than the profit realized through the normal profit distribution according to share proportion under efforts to realize maximum enterprise value, the best choice for the shareholder is no longer realization of maximum enterprise value with efforts but return through abusing material control power. Thus, the shareholder's profit-making mode is no longer normal enterprise profit multiplied by profit distribution proportion but return through abuse of material control power derived from its ability to provide technology or other resources needed by the existence of the joint venture. Under such a situation, shareholders of joint ventures are in the status of 'zero-sum game', realization of one party's interest is totally at the cost of erosion of other shareholders' interests which would otherwise belong to it. The smaller registered capital contribution proportion which the shareholder taking material control right have, the more serious imbalanced degree of control power and residual claim right, the more active for the shareholder to abuse the material control power, on

[10] Multinationals mainly realize matching or unifying of material control right and monopolized proceeds right through the strategy of 'conspired losses'. The concrete operation route is:(1)transfer profits and assets of joint ventures with all kinds of methods, causing loss and asset outflow of joint ventures; (2)increase capital input and enlarge share holding proportion till share control or even wholly foreign owned using the chance of Chinese parties' inability to make up losses. Main methods of turning joint ventures into loss by multinationals are: (2)raise price of using key resources including technology and transfer profits to wholly owned subsidies within Chinese territory; (2)transfer profits to subsidies abroad with 'high purchase price and low selling price, and two endings abroad'; (3)implement market expansion strategy and increase market input; (4)increase numbers of joint ventures and divide sales districts. See Lu Changcong, Zhen Wenquan, Li Zhongguang (2004), the Property Right Variation and Proceeds Dispute in Sino-foreign Joint Ventures, the China Industry Economy, Issue 11.

the contrary, if the shareholder with material control power have majority capital contribution proportion, it is more likely to avoid abuse of the control power. When the shareholder with the material control right has 100% share or registered capital in an enterprise, there is no motivation to abuse the control right. And obviously such an enterprise is just a wholly foreign owned enterprise. Such deduction could explain the surge of wholly foreign owned enterprises well. However, in practice, shareholders of one joint venture obtaining return at the cost of other shareholders' interest caused by imbalance of control right and residual claim right due to the joint venture's existence reliance on the former shareholders is also the main reason for disputes in Sino-foreign joint venture operation.

> In December 2003, Chinese Company A and Japanese Company B signed a joint venture contract for establishment of Beijing Creative Science Technology Co., Ltd. (hereinafter referred to as Company C or Joint Venture) researching and developing, producing and selling notebook computers. The joint venture sells notebook computers bearing brand of Company B, relying on the low price of bare bone computers for large amount purchase advantage of Company B and domestic sales network of Company A. In the joint venture, Company A holds 80% capital contribution while Company B holds 20%. However, Company B may actually control Company C since Company C severely relies on Company B's purchase advantage and trademark license. On 6 January 2004, Company C came into existence. In July 2004, Suzhou Factory of the Joint Venture started to have production ability. But Company B delayed to include the Joint Venture's raw material purchase order into the unified purchase plan of Company B and insisted to supply outdated material left in B's warehouse in the previous year to the Joint Venture. Furthermore, Company B maliciously sold bare machines with bad quality purchase from Taiwan to the Joint Venture (those with good quality were used in Japan while Company B claimed large amount quality compensation from the Taiwan seller), which lead to quality problems in raw material, that is, bare machines of notebook computers, and high price, causing the Joint Venture long in abnormal losses. Meanwhile, Company B got large amount of trademark license fees through the trademark license contract, at the same while, avoided huge losses through dumping the outdated materials to C. In 2006, A filed a claim against B in CIETAC.

The above case is a typical example of foreign shareholder's damage of joint venture's benefits and other shareholders' benefits through control of the purchase channel. In Company C, though Company B does not have the control in share, it may actually fully control Company C since the foreign party takes absolute control of the two existent living lines of the Joint Venture, that is, raw material purchasing and trademark license. In deed, Company B's control of Company C is 100%. However, Company B's profit distribution proportion is only 30% since profits are distributed according to capital contribution proportions. Thus, severe unbalance of control right and residual claim right occurs. Under such situation, the best choice for B is to rely on control of raw material purchasing and trademark license to transfer capital to its own company through offering of expensive outdated raw material on one hand and obtain return through collection of trademark license fee on the other hand. The foreign party, though losing initial capital investment (sometimes such investment is not actually made), may make up loss and get remarkable profits through the above ways. The Chinese party, through control of the sales channel may get extra return through the same way in the sales process, could not start up the route since there are no qualified products for selling. So it may only look to erosion of capital investment hopelessly.

In fact, under the arrangement of capital contribution proportions and power structure in the above case, the Japanese party gets 'profits' as transferred income (plus mitigated loss of disposing overstock and compensation from a Taiwanese seller) deducted by actual investment through capital transfer with 'raw material purchasing' and 'trademark license'. If such 'profits' are higher than profits through distribution according to share proportion via normal operation (losses arising out of not disposing overstock shall be deducted), the best choice for the Japanese party is to transfer capital instead of realizing maximum enterprise value.

This conclusion is well approved in Chinese automobile joint ventures. In the Tokyo International Automobile Exposition in October 2003, Mr. Carlos Gohsn, the President of Nissan said that Chinese cooperative partners generally hold 50% share capital in joint ventures co-established with foreign automobile manufacturers, which is the expense of foreign companies like Nissan to enter the rapidly developing automobile market of China. The purpose for foreign automobile manufacturers providing products and special technology is to 'add value' to factories jointly established with the Chinese party. On the contrary, the Chinese partner contributes almost nothing to the actual operation and management except providing low-cost labor force and sales channels.[11] In many automobile joint venture enterprises, though the Chinese and foreign party each hold 50% share capital, the joint venture severely relies on the foreign party for its existence since the foreign party has monopoly advantage in products, technology and management. Multinationals actually have taken an actual control right over intellectual property right, brand, product technology resources, management, distribution network and after-sale service, in which Chinese parties have done little work and made little achievement.[12] Under such a situation, transferring profits in various ways (or transferring capital if no profit) becomes the best and unavoidable choice

[11] Wang Xiaoling (2004), The Carrying on Joint Venture by Chinese Automobile Companies to the End?, Commerce Weekly, Issue 2-3.

[12] Wang Xiaoling, How Far Could Chinese Automobile Joint Venture Go? South Weekend on 2 February 2004.

of foreign parties. The State Development and Reform Commission ("SDRC") publicized the economic operation situation information in the first half year of 2005, showing profits in Chinese automobile industry lowered 48.8% than the same period in the previous year. However, statistics from China Automobile Industry Consultation Development Company show that the total number of automobiles produced in China in the first half of the year is 1.8517 million, 3.28% higher than the same period in the previous year; the sales amount is 1.843 million, 10.55% higher than the same period in the previous year. Profits in the Chinese Automobile industry are decreasing along with the increase of sales. Survey shows that it is related with foreign capital profit transfer in automobile joint venture enterprises.[13]

Most real cases are about foreign shareholders' infringement of the Chinese parties' interest, on which people usually make moral criticism from the level of national sentiment but omits essential problems. The main drive for abuse of the material control right lies with foreign parties since foreign parties have advantages over Chinese parties in taking control rights such as technology, intellectual property right and management skill advantages. When joint ventures could only exist relying on foreign parties while foreign parties could not obtain all profits, foreign parties, as reasonable economic participants, have a natural impulse of abusing the control right. If Chinese parties have an absolute advantage in joint ventures, abuse of the control right by Chinese parties may occur as well. Abuse of the material control right is opportunism caused by the governmental administration system of Sino-foreign joint ventures, which means parties concerned with Sino-foreign joint venture may still face such risks.

6.3.2 System Risks in Contorted Sino-foreign Joint Venture Management Structure

Parent Company Oriented Board of Directors with Incomplete Functions

Shareholders of joint ventures are normally two kinds of investment companies of multinationals and hosting nations. Sino-foreign joint ventures, except for Foreign-invested Stock Enterprises, have no shareholders' meetings and the members of board of directors are generally appointed through negotiation of parent companies of investing parties, which means approvals by parent companies are necessary for making and implementating joint ventures' strategies. Some important decisions including investment on developing new product projects, increase of registered capital, appointment of senior leaders and determination of product sales markets are basically decided by parent companies while directors of joint ventures is largely the representative of the parent company appointing them in fact.

13 Li Zhijun, Is Decrease in Automobile Joint Venture Profits Value Return or Transfer? Economy Observance on 6 August 2005.

Appointment of Senior Managers by Parent Companies with Vague Delegation Relations

In Sino-foreign joint ventures, division and unification of ownership and, management power of enterprises are contradictory. For example, parent companies not only directly appointed by general managers and vice general managers but also appointed managers of key departments since investing parties all intend to influence and control joint ventures to higher degree, which may easily lead to distortions in joint venture senior managers' activities and make them keep certain interests in relation to parent companies, leading to decentralization of joint venture management power.

Managers' Evaluation Standard Made by Parent Companies and Secondary Position of Joint Ventures' Internal Supervision

Concerning the supervision mechanism, joint ventures generally set up no supervisors meeting. Thus, parent companies of investing parties are in the oriented position of joint ventures' management. In general limited companies, important decisions of contradiction may finally be decided or coordinated by authority of shareholders' meeting and board of directors. However, in joint ventures, since contributors are only parent companies of investing parties while parent companies of investing parties have similar capital contribution proportions, conflicts or problems may be long left unsettled or be more and more severe under no highest authority or organ to settle them when parent companies have opposite opinions. Due to shortcomings in joint venture corporate governance, parent companies of investing parties are in dominant position of joint venture governance. Parent companies' incomplete and untimely understanding of joint venture management decisions increases risks in management decisions and may intensify investing parties' conflicts.

Meanwhile, lack of supervision urges one shareholder's abuse of the material control right to no small degree. In other words, no rational check mechanism exists for control of such abuses. This shortcoming in corporate governance not only encourages one party's abuse of the material control right but also leads to a passive situation of joint venture and other shareholders with doomed fate.

The joint venture law only stipulates board of directors as the internal organ of company, which is different from the 'three carriages' stipulated in *company law*. That is, shareholders meeting, board of directors and supervisors meeting. Thus, board of directors of joint ventures has no power to limit and balance and may be easily controlled by controlling shareholders and be their tools for infringement of the other party's interest. Meanwhile, the general manager and vice general managers are generally nominated by joint venture parties through their appointing directors, which makes the general manager always consider the interest of the party nominating him only but omit the other party's rational interest and overall benefits of the joint venture. Once moral risks occur in the management team or if the general manager is controlled by the other party through bribery, he may be a tool for infringement of his own party's interest. In practice, many Chinese enterprises turn into dependency of foreign investors after joint ventures. It may be concluded that the single Sino-foreign joint venture management structure is the foundation of interest unilateralism (in most cases, interest unilaterally flows to the foreign party).[14]

However, it should be noticed that limitations in joint venture management rules under the joint venture law only encourages or fails to prevent abuse of the material control right or could not stop abuse after it occurs. The original motivation for abuse of the control right is imbalance in the control right and residual claim right instead of institution flaw itself while the reason for such imbalance is imbalanced power and proportion of capital contribution in joint venture shareholders.

6.4 Can Sino-foreign Joint Ventures Tend Towards Harmony?

6.4.1 Failure in Dong Feng Nissan Joint Venture and Born of the Fundamental Law of Dong Feng Nissan[15]

Dong Feng Nissan is described as a combination of elites from Feng Shen, Nissan and Dong Feng. Before joint venture, main leaders of Feng Shen Company are gathering of young backbones of old Dong Feng Company and elites from Taiwan Yu Long and social employment. Mr. Ghosn, CEO of Nissan entrusted two standing officers of the company—Katsumi Nakamura and Mitsuyuki Tsuji to manipulate.

In joint ventures, foreign parties are generally at advantageous positions, being dominant in management, so is Dong Feng Nissan. Besides the general manager Miao Wei, the Japanese party appoints head of two important departments, that is, chief of business department and chief of manufacture department. As to work division, Miao Wei takes charge of sales while Ren Yong is in charge of production. It is now looked upon as failure in Dong Feng Nissan plan in 2004, making Chinese personnel understanding Chinese market best take in charge of production and quality control they are not good at but letting Japanese personnel following plans face rapidly changing Chinese automobile market. Japanese market staff's stiff attitude towards price fixing put Dong Feng Nissan in passive position in Chinese market much sensitive to price. After the 'honey moon period' in 2003, Dong Feng Nissan's sales amount in 2004 is

---

14 Luan Jianqi (2003), Discussion on Problems in Transfer of Trademark Rights in Foreign-invested Enterprises, Contemporary Law, Issue 3.

15 Cases quoted in this article and the five principles of dong Feng Nissan Basic Rules is from the From Joint Venture to Harmony by Yang Yunlong and Fu Qiang (2005), published in the Science and Technology Brainpower, issue 8.

> 6.6% lower than the previous year, making it falling outside 'top ten' in passengers' car market. Its market share of 2.6% is even lower than local car maker Cherry's market share of 3.7%.

After bearing serious loss, Chinese and Japanese management team of Dong Feng Nissan calms down and looks for a new conformity way. The two parties do not dispute on concrete issues but turn back to the starting point of their cooperation to determine mutual benefits and common value. On such bases, new enterprise central value sense is established through the way of making 'basic law' of Dong Feng Nissan after careful self-criticism and repeated communication, on which concrete management and market activity rules are determined.

The Dong Feng Nissan Basic Law emphasizes much on five principles for making of the Law in the general principles: (a) principle of accurate orientation: the passengers' car company is an enterprise affiliated to Dong Feng Co., Ltd., achieving business aims and shoulder business responsibilities within its business scope, so the basic rules shall be in accordance with the overall strategic requests, value standard and exemplification system of Dong Feng Co., Ltd. (b) principle of maximum joint venture interest: no matter where he or she comes from, he or she must regard the passengers' car company's interest as the sole struggling objective as staff of the company; leaders, departments, managing personnel and employees of the passengers' car company must be concerned about the service subject's interest all the time. (c) principle of market competition subject: all business and management activities of the passengers' car company must circle the core aim of the market; success or failure in the market is the sole standard for examination of efficiency and effect of business activities; in the process of facing passengers' car market and consumers, the passengers' car company must compete with other passengers' car manufacturers, which decides that the passengers' car company be an independent market competitive unit, so it must have corresponding abilities to integrate and allocate resources as well as self-decision power in business decision-making. (d) principle of culture consolidation: as a joint venture, it must realize that common interest of the joint venture decides different cultures will finally be integrated into the unified culture of the joint venture though employees from different parties bear clear mark of their parent companies; the joint venture could not be divided but should be in complete harmony with one faith, one group and one voice. (e) principle of respecting market environment. The passengers' car company is the result of strategic cooperation between Dong Feng and Nissan as well as the starting point for creation of a win-win situation in the Chinese market. Under the precondition of respecting the international usual practice, the enterprise must rely on the Chinese market for its operation and respect the specific civilization's environment in the Chinese market including the political structure, cultural ideas, economic situation, regional difference, consumers' conception and so on. The Chinese passengers' car market in the rapid development phase has features of great potential, fast change, fierce competition, continuous adjustment in product structure and gradual maturity and rationality of consumers which are environmental features which must be correctly realized and fully considered. The five principles must be obeyed in making *the Dong Feng Nissan Basis Law* which shows features of Dong Feng Nissan as a joint venture and considers both parties' mutual benefit and culture.

The Dong Feng Nissan Basis Law is a landmark case as well. It creates a new way of solving conformity problems in Sino-foreign joint ventures with core value. Conformity problems have existed in joint ventures for dozens of years for which no good solution has been found. Dong Feng Nissan offers a train of thought for reference. The sales volume of the company is over 200% higher than the same period in the previous year in the first half of 2005 when the whole industry's increased rate is only 9.35%. Such a result proves the preliminary success in integration of the company.

6.4.2 Way for Joint Ventures to Go Toward Harmony as Shown in the Dong Feng Nissan Basic Law

Professor Peng Jianfeng who participated in the draft of *Huawei Fundamental Law* thinks that the way of integrating joint venture parties with core value under *the Dong Feng Nissan Fundamental Law* is another landmark of enterprise culture in the joint venture management field following that of the *Huawei Fundamental Law*.

Enterprise culture may actually lead Dong Feng Nissan Joint Venture to harmony and solve difficult problems in management of Sino-foreign joint ventures. But it should be noticed that the successful way in this case may not be general since its success is under the limitation of one basic condition, that is, the two parties have strength of little disparity and basically balanced comparison of power and capital contribution proportion.

Nissan has advanced production methods, manufacture technology and cost control ability. Dong Feng, established in 1969, is a flag of China's national industry. Its self-owned development and research, manufacture and management abilities are equal to the world standard. Dong Feng also has good public relations and sufficient human resources. Feng Shen has a sensitive, condense and efficient market operation system. All parties have their unique advantages while no party has the overwhelming one. The joint venture does not rely on any shareholder for its existence. Furthermore, the share proportion and strength of joint parties are almost in balance, which means there is no serious imbalance of the control right and residual claim right existing inside Dong Feng Nissan Passengers' Car Company. The problem of the company lies in two aspects, one is different culture and behavior style,[16] another is disturbance of allocation of business management authority, that is, allocation of Chinese personnel having best knowledge of the Chi-

---

[16] First, different interest subjects in Dong Feng Nissan have different value orientation. The Chinese party wants large scale business while the Japanese party has pure market idea emphasizing benefit most. Second, Chinese party and Japanese party have different cultural basis and may adopt different working style and method in dealing with the same issue. Third, they have different management ideas and ways. The Japanese party emphasizes plans and enforceability in management but the Chinese party emphasizes emotion, flexibility, speed and efficiency.

nese market to take charge of production and quality control which they are not good at and allocation of Japanese personnel emphasizing plans to face rapidly changing the Chinese automobile market. Under such a situation, mutually accepted rules may be formed through integration of enterprise cultures for adjustment of business management authority allocation, which, if enforced appropriately, may lead the enterprise to harmony.

The case of *the Dong Feng Nissan Basic Law* shows that a joint venture which does not rely on any party shareholder for its existence, that is, joint venture parties have approximately balanced share proportions and strength, may solve joint venture governance problems through reasonable allocation of enterprise management authority and integration of enterprise culture. On the contrary, if a joint venture with seriously imbalanced control right and residual claim right and severe reliance on one party with too low share proportion, the corporate governance problem could not be solved only through integration of the enterprise culture.

6.4.3 Political Policy Being the Essential Reason for Joint Venture Governance Troubles

Under a deeper analysis, the basic reason for many Sino-foreign joint venture corporate governance troubles is a great difference from imbalance of residual claim right and control right. With further discussion, it may be found that the existence of the joint venture governance puzzle is essentially related with China's political policy of attracting foreign capital. China has long regarded attraction of foreign capital as an important strategy in a developing economy for absorbing foreign capital as well as learning foreign parties' advanced management experience and technology through joint venture, which means Sino-foreign joint ventures are taken as a platform for transfer of management experience and technology. Chinese parties participate in joint ventures with student identity, bearing strategic task of learning advanced management experience and technology. In other words, Sino-foreign joint ventures are political arrangements rather than the result of commercial consideration under many situations. Foreign parties lot on China's market capacity and cheap labor force when investing in China while a joint venture is not the sole way to obtain these resources. Foreign parties need no participation of Chinese parties as students except reliance on the latter for handling of relevant procedures and familiarization of market surroundings at the preliminary stage. However, the government sets limitations on certain industries for joint venture of share proportion in game rules for implementation of the market exchanging for technology strategy. Chinese parties are pushed to foreign parties through legislation under policy while Sino-foreign joint ventures turn to be products of political policy. However, policy may define joint venture as necessary or limit share proportion, but could not change the power balance structure of the parties. Chinese parties could only be a puppet emperor with no real control right though they formally take control (majority shares) after paying large amount of tuition (capital input) for entry into joint ventures. On the contrary, foreign parties naturally take control of joint ventures' real control right and become the real king behind the puppet emperor since joint ventures rely on foreign parties' technology and management for their survival and development.

When foreign parties with the material control right could not realize maximum interest through normal distribution of profits according to the share rate, abuse of control right is almost unavoidable. Once abuse of control right occurs, the Sino-foreign joint venture management system under China's joint venture laws could not plan the role of supervision or prevention. Therefore, invalidation of the Sino-foreign enterprise management is foreordination in a sociology sense. It is proved in practice that a joint venture would be the doll of a foreign party if it controls one or two key departments such as the purchasing department and technology department of the joint venture with control of the finance department in addition (it is commonly shown in practice, see the following table).

Table 6.4. Departments with Heads Commonly Appointed by Foreign Parties

Department	Percentage (%)
Human Resource	38
Technology	94.2
Sales	56.4
Finance	92.8
Administration	76
Public Relation	41.7

(Resource: Li Wei'an(2003), the Research on Management Mechanism of Foreign-invested Enterprises Set by Multinationals in China, in Li Wei'an (eds) the Frontline of Company Management Theories and Practices, China Finance and Economy Publishing House, pp3-25.)

For Chinese parties, calculation of interest is no longer profit allocation but whether they could exchange their loss with management experience and advanced technology and whether it is appropriate to use the lossed amount as a technology and experience transfer fee. From the current situation, this counting frame of Chinese parties turns to failure.[17]

[17] See latest discussion on policy of exchanging market with technology and self-innovation. Wang Xiaoling (2004),The Re-thinking of FDI Strategy, Commerce Weekly, Issue,3; Lu Feng, Feng Kaidong(2004), the Foundation for Failure in Automobile Industry, the Internal Reference of Reform, Issue 13,; Zhang Jingping (2005), the Chinese Strategic Orientation of Self Independence, the Economic Observance on 17 October.

7 Tax Risks Under the New Tax Law Environment

Foreign capital 'occupies market, avoid tax, takes profits and leaves GDP' in China.

——Anonymous Online Comment[1]

Risks in China's tax environment are the biggest and most challenging in Asia-pacific Region.

——Investigation Report of PricewaterhouseCoopers[2]

7.1 Introduction

Ms. Wang Cuiping, a partner of PricewaterhouseCoopers in charge of China Tax Department, said that the most frequent words of heads of multinationals are, "I could not fall asleep due to China's tax issues."[3] Tax is always one of the struggling points between Chinese government and multinationals. Steady increases of foreign investment do not bring continuously increasing revenues, but digs a huge tax black hole. In 2005, tax evasion continually increased. Almost all multinational companies list transfer pricing as one the biggest tax concerns. Meanwhile, the unification of income taxes of domestic and foreign-invested enterprises are moving ahead quickly under fierce controversy. Great changes in the taxation area cause foreign investors to repeatedly evaluate the increasing tax risks in China …

7.2 Cat and Mouse Game Between Tax Evasion and Anti-tax Evasion

7.2.1 Black Hole in Foreign-Invested Enterprises' Tax

Large amounts of foreign capital have rushed into China and the number of foreign-invested enterprises has increased much since China's reform and opening.

1 Quoted from the Re-evaluation of China's Foreign Economic Policy and Prevent Further Loss of State Assets, published in the China's Entrepreneurs in November 2005.

2 Quote Pricewatercoopers's Report: "2005 Global Annual Review", Download from www.pwc.com (the last visiting in Oct. 2005).

3 Id.

However, foreign-invested enterprises' tax evasion problem is more and more serious. Some foreign investors take various secret measures to evade large amounts of tax, causing great loss in China's foreign-related revenue and turning into a non-valuable black hole.[4]

According to the statistics of MOFCOM, 494,025 foreign-invested enterprises have been approved for establishment till the end of August 2004 while the actual utilized foreign capital is USD545,029 million. Within the over 490,000 foreign-invested enterprises, more than half are making losses.[5] SAT deems that quite a number of multinationals are in manmade loss for evasion of tax and China loses over RMB30 billion of tax income each year due to multinationals evading tax. Since individual income tax, business tax and other taxes are not counted therein, the actual tax evasion amount is far beyond the above figure. In fact, according to some local tax officers' evaluations, the figure may be as big as RMB127 billion. It is an open secret in the business circle that tax evasion is quite common for foreign-invested enterprises. The so-called tax evasion is enterprises' plan to reduce tax for individuals or groups by studying differences among tax laws of various nations in order to evade tax to maximize profits and tax.

7.2.2 Road Map for Tax Evasion by Foreign Investors

At present, foreign-invested enterprises in China often adopt the following ways of tax evasion:

Transfer Pricing. Multinational affiliated enterprises, when trading among each other, may sometimes artificially raise or lower trade prices or charge standard fixed prices and distribute expenses for the purposes of group interest or operations instead of obeying market principles with independent competition and market-determined trade prices. This causes one affiliated enterprise's profits to shift

---

4 According to the statistic result announced by the State Statistic Bureau on 23 May 2005, profits realized by industrial enterprises above medium scale level (all state-owned enterprises and non-state-owned enterprises with annual product sales income of more than RMB 5 million yuan) from January to April are RMB398.3 billion yuan, 15.6% higher than the same period in the previous year, among which profits realized by state-owned and state controlling enterprises are RMB200.1 billion yuan, 14.1% higher than the same period in the previous year; profits realized by collective enterprises are RMB13.7 billion yuan, 26.9% higher than the same period in the previous year; profits realized by stock enterprises are RMB201.5 billion yuan, 24.2% higher than the same period in the previous year; profits realized by private enterprises are RMB40.1 billion yuan, 28.8% higher than same period in the previous year. Only profits of enterprises invested by foreign investors and Hong Kong, Macao and Taiwan investors (with investment at RMB107.5 billion yuan) decrease 3.5%. Resource: Website of the State Statistic Bureau (the last visiting in September 2005).

5 Data show the loss of foreign invested-enterprises is 35% ~ 40% from 1988 to 1993, increases to 50%~ 60% from 1994 to 1995, and reaches 60%~ 65% from 1996 to 2000.

into the account of another. Such activity is referred to as transfer pricing. The occurrence of tax evasion is closely related to the specific features of multinationals. As stated above, multinationals consist of a parent company and subsidiaries with high internal centralization. In multinational enterprise groups with unified management, the parent company and subsidies are closely related through internal controls, each shouldering certain tasks and playing certain roles for common strategic purposes without regard to their different legal forms. In brief, a parent company and its subsidiaries have control relations, management relations, finance relations and investment relations. Although subsidiaries of multinationals are independent legal persons enjoying independent production and management rights, their board of directors are actually the parent company's representatives under the control of the parent company, following and implementing the parent company's instructions and policies. Such relationships allow the parent company to shift profits of enterprises in high-tax rate nations to entities in low-tax rate nations in order to avoid the higher taxes in high-tax rate nations and to cut the gross tax burden of multinationals. The concrete measures are: (a) lower price of goods and services supplied from high-tax rate nations to low-tax rate nations; (b) raise price of goods and services supplied from low-tax rate nations to high-tax rate nations; (c) combine the aforementioned measures to gain double tax benefits, that is, one parent company or subsidiary in a high-tax rate nation sells to another in a low-tax rate nation at a low price, then the latter re-sells to the one in the high-tax rate nation at a high price.[6]

Thin Capitalization. Thin capitalization is also known as capital conceal, share conceal, or proceeds drawing out, under which investors of an enterprise lowers a proportion of share capital and raises the proportion of loans in capital invested in the enterprise, replacing contributions with loans for investment or financing for the purpose of reducing tax or other. Companies, especially multinational-affiliated ones, weaken capital, increase interest payout and transfer income by increasing debt and decreasing contributions, while income-source nations adopt different policies for different income types when collecting tax from non-residents. Interest income bears a lower tax rate than operation profits. Since some nations lack control of interest income from abroad, therefore many multinational enterprises convert profits into interest of interested parties for tax evasion purposes.[7]

To ensure foreign-invested enterprises' capital credit and to avoid listing too much interest as cost, China's laws clearly specify the proportion to be maintained

---

6 See "Transfer Pricing in China", download from the website of Pricewaterhousecoopers, www.pwccn.com.

7 For example, American Enron Company makes use of two companies located at the Province of Nova Scotia, Canada to transfer large amount of fees paid by Quebec Sawmill into interest through loan and share trade. Canada has the provision that capital payout could not be deducted while interest income could. Enron cheated tax payment of about 93 million Canada Dollars from the Canadian government in this way.

for foreign-invested enterprises' total investment and registered capital. However, in real situations, foreign investors or Sino-foreign cooperative parties intentionally lower total investment to achieve the required legal proportion of total investment and registered capital so as to obtain approval for invested projects in the examination and approval phase. If approval authorities fail to find errors in feasibility reports or contracts, or intentionally omit the errors after finding out for seek of quantity of foreign capital attracted and approve the projects, the huge capital gap in the actual operation of foreign-invested enterprises would be solved solely with domestic bank loans. Thus, large amounts of loan interest are listed in the expenses of the same period justifiably, lowering enterprise profits and income, and leading to the realization of tax evasion.

The Law on Sino-foreign Cooperative Enterprises of PRC stipulates that the fixed assets of a cooperative joint venture enterprise shall all belong to the Chinese party upon the termination of the cooperation contract while the foreign party may take back its investment in different ways within the cooperation term. It is common practice that the foreign party of some enterprise bearing the name of a Sino-foreign cooperative only draws out fixed amounts of income, under the name of taking back investment in advance, for each year within the contract term without participating in enterprise management or assuming enterprise losses. This actually turns loans by the foreign party into nominal 'cooperative investment' or 'cooperative enterprise' for which the Chinese party pays back principal and interest in installments. Some 'cooperatives' even pay the foreign party principal and interest within a fixed time period as well as fixed profits to the foreign party. These foreign parties do not actually make direct investments and should not enjoy tax preferentials for foreign-invested enterprises, but they nevertheless receive the benefits of exemptions from customs duty and turnover tax for imported equipments and materials, as well as enterprise income taxes.

Utilization of Tax Havens[8]. Tax havens generally refer to nations and districts not collecting income and property taxes, or only collect with low or zero tax rates. Such nations and districts normally are politically stable in a certain degree, have convenient international air transport and communication services, have loose foreign currency control and low government interference, and legal systems strictly protecting commercial and bank secrets. Multinationals transfer income and property out of tax havens to accounts of base companies in order to avoid tax by setting up a base company, which is a company set up in a tax haven under the control of foreign shareholders and operated mainly or wholly out of tax havens. Nations and districts such as British Virgin Islands, Cayman Islands, Hong Kong, Bahama, Panama etc. are listed as tax havens by tax agencies of many nations.

---

[8] Zhang Shiwei, Li Shoushuang (2004), the Offshore Company Law, China Law Press.

(a) Transfer of Income Through 'Pipe Company'

If Company A has continual business with American Company C and obtains certain operation income and profits, Company A pays tax to local governments according to the operation income and profit obtained. If Company A connects with offshore Company B at British Virgin Islands (actually A and B are controlled by the same one) and Company B sells goods to American Company C, Company A's tax burden may be greatly alleviated as only a small portion of operation income and profit are reflected in Company A, while most income and profit are reflected in Company B, which as an offshore company, need not pay tax. This is a typical method of tax evasion through the use of a 'pipe company'. Company B is a 'pipe company' in nature. Company A's operation income is transferred to the registration place of Company B, where company B enjoys exemption from tax, hence Company A's heavy tax burden is avoided. Meanwhile, no legal provision is violated by Company B since it has no operation in its registered country.

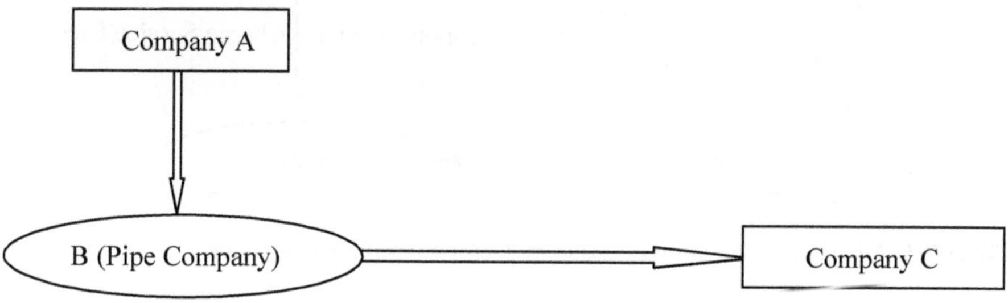

Chart 7.1. Transfer of Income through Pipe Company

(b) Tax Evasion through Employment of Senior Staff by Offshore Company

Many multinational companies hire foreign employees through offshore companies so as to lower individual tax, as the following example shows.

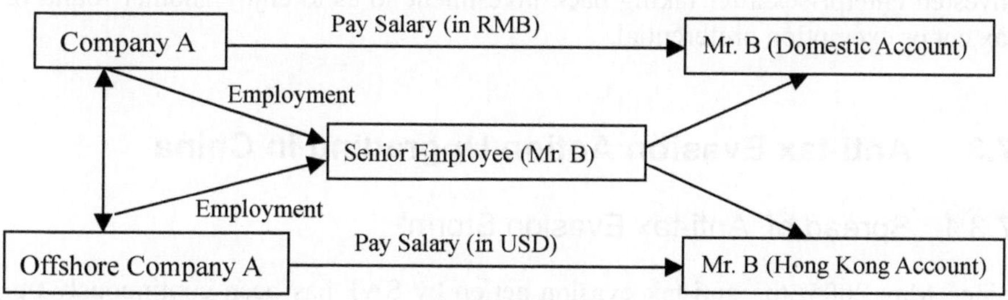

Chart 7.2. Tax Evasion through Employment by Offshore Company

(c) Agencies' Utilization of Offshore Companies for Tax Evasion

Such a model operates like this: First, the domestic agency registers an offshore company abroad then offers services to overseas clients under the name of the offshore company that also collects the fees. Thus, the service fees are income of the offshore company instead of the domestic agency. Meanwhile, the lowering of tax is realized due to the income tax preferential of the nation the offshore company is located in. This method is simple and easy to carry out because the core service is the provision of intelligence and expertise, which have no geographical work limitations. Even if the service is provided domestically, the tax plan purpose may also be achieved if the service is provided and the service fee is collected under the name of the offshore company.

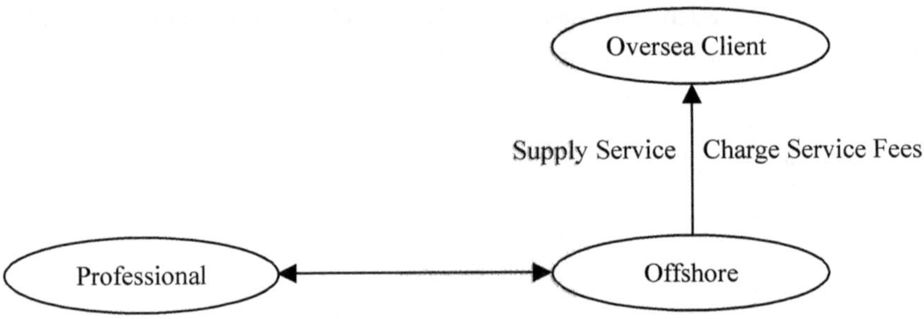

Chart 7.3. Agencies' Utilization of Offshore Companies for Tax Evasion

Tax Evasion with Tax Cut or Exemption Preferential. China allows 'two years exemption and three years half cut' tax preferential for the initial five years' profits of productive foreign-invested enterprises with an operating period of over 10 years. That is, tax exemption for the first 2 years and tax cuts for the following 3 years from the first profit year. Some foreign-invested enterprises gain profits in the tax cut or exemption term, but make little profit or losses at or near the end of the term, or even announce dissolution of enterprises and set up new foreign-invested enterprises after taking back investment so as to enjoy another round of tax cut or exemption preferential.

7.3 Anti-tax Evasion Action Upgrading in China

7.3.1 Spread of 'Anti-tax Evasion Storm'

Since May 2005, the anti-tax evasion action by SAT has been continuously upgraded and finally formed an 'anti-tax evasion storm' which makes many multinationals frightened since it is systemizing anti-tax evasion action and causing reform on China's tax system.

(a) On 12 April 2005, SAT issued *the Opinion on Various Issues Concerning Strengthening of Administration of Enterprise Income Tax,* requesting local tax authorities to carry out classified administration of different types of enterprises and strengthen tax collection and administration.

(b) In May 2005, SAT issued *the Notice on Further Strengthening Anti Tax Evasion Work,* which emphasizes 'international cooperation', 'foreign-investment tax', 'international tax administration departments' and so on. Anti-tax evasion against foreign-invested enterprises has been the most important part of SAT's work in that year. Concerning the existence of long-term loss in large amount of foreign- invested enterprises, the Notice clearly states that the tax authorities shall mainly investigate enterprises with long-term losses or tiny profits who have continually enlarged operation scales, and those with leaping profits. The object is focused on foreign-invested enterprises 'at loss'. According to the latest notices from SAT to local tax authorities, emphasis of anti-tax evasion work is on multinationals with continuous account losses who have continually enlarged production and operation scales and those with frequent affiliated trade.

(c) On 1 September 2005, SAT issued *the Work Plan on Making Clear and Standardizing Tax Order* for Year 2005 to 2007, setting anti-tax evasion as a long-term task. It points out that the struggle against tax dodging, evasion and cheating would exist for a long time and may even be fierce in certain periods; it should be realized that work on making clear and standardizing the tax order is important, hard and continuous; tax administration and standardization work should be carried out with focus; strikes on criminal activities involving tax issues shall be strengthened, and tax dodging, evasion and cheating behaviors shall be punished severely.

The sword of anti-tax evasion specially points at three types of enterprises: first, enterprises with continuous losses; second, enterprises with leaping profits or losses; third, enterprises with much affiliated trade relating to tax evasion during operation.

7.3.2 APA Limits Transfer Pricing

Transfer pricing is a common method of tax evasion adopted by multinationals. According to a survey, over 90% of multinationals with investment in China carry out transfer pricing in a certain manner. In its current phase, the center of the anti-tax evasion storm is focusing on transfer pricing activities. The introduction of the advance pricing rule makes anti-tax evasion activities go on the path of systemization and rule by law.

On 4 October 2004, *the Advance Pricing Agreements for Trade among Affiliated Enterprises* (APA) was promulgated by SAT after over one year of discussion. APA contains eight chapters covering thirty-three articles, which includes, general rules, preparation meetings, formal application, examination and evaluation, negotiation, execution of arrangement, supervision of performance and supplementary articles. Introduction of 'advance pricing' is one of the important breakthroughs of the new

Detailed Rules for Implementation of Tax Law. Implementation of APA rules allows enterprises to pay income tax for trade among affiliated enterprises by way of advance pricing. Enterprises and tax authorities may discuss and debate on the sales profit rates on which income tax is to be paid. China is the second Asian nation adopting APA.[9] It indicates that China's advance pricing is moving onto the path of the legal system and more legal guarantee is being provided.

In fact, former legislation also involves this issue. The transfer pricing issue is first referred to in *the Law on Income Tax of Foreign-invested Enterprises and Foreign Enterprises* adopted by the People's Congress in April 1991. *The Detailed Rules for Implementation of the Law on Income Tax of Foreign-invested Enterprises and Foreign Enterprises* issued by the State Council in June 1991 also deals with it. *The Implementation Measures for Tax Administration of Trade among Affiliated Enterprises* made by SAT in 1992 stipulates the standard for defining affiliated enterprises. *The Detailed Rules for Implementation of the Law on Income Tax of Foreign-invested Enterprises and Foreign Enterprises* amended in 2002 clearly states the legal basis for advance pricing. It is provided in Article 53 of *the Detailed Rules* that the tax payer may submit the pricing principal and calculation measure of trade among affiliated enterprises to the tax authority in charge for examination and approval, after which the authority and taxpayer make an advance agreement on relevant pricing issues and the authority supervises the taxpayer's performance. In practice, Xiamen Municipal Bureau of National Tax signed an advance pricing agreement with a Taiwan invested company back in 1998, which is the earliest one in China's advance pricing anti-tax evasion. In 2001, Shenzhen Municipal Bureau of Local Tax signed the first advance pricing agreement with a Japanese enterprise.

> **Enterprise agrees to pay RMB 6 million of evaded tax per year through negotiation with tax authority:** X is a wholly foreign-owned enterprise set up by Hong Kong Y International Co. Ltd. in Guangzhou city with total investment of USD 35 million. From 1998 to 2003, the company continuously increased registered capital and enlarged production scale, on the contrary, the company's on account losses were quite serious, the total loss being RMB62.92 million. The Guangzhou Municipal Bureau of National Tax, through analysis of operation quantity of the two affiliated enterprises, found Company X exported with low prices and shifted profits to its affiliated company in Hong Kong. The tax authority and the enterprise agreed through negotiation that the profits for re-sale abroad shall be reasonably distributed between Company X and Company Y in the ratio of 4:6 while the re-sale profit rate is fixed accordingly to calculate the normal price. Accordingly, Company X's sales income from 1998 to 2003 were adjusted to RMB 0.12 billion as the basis for

[9] Spencer Chong, Glenn DeSouza, China Transfer Pricing 2005 – Important and New Developments, Download from http://www.pwccn.com/home/eng/tp_china_developments2005.html, the last visiting on Dec. 12, 2005.

tax collection. The enterprise enters into profits from year 2000 after making up losses in previous years. It should pay enterprise income tax evaded for 2003 totaling RMB 6 million.

Implementation of APA rules, although not necessarily eradicating transfer pricing activities, but will undoubtedly increase the legal risks for multinationals' transfer activities. Facing the high pressure line set by anti-tax evasion laws, the probability for transfer pricing to 'get an electric shock' is much enhanced.[10]

7.3.3 Prevention of Weakening Capital Started by the Enterprise Income Tax Law (Draft)

The Enterprise Income Tax Law (Draft) has been accomplished and submitted to the State Council for discussion. The new law introduces the successful experience of developed nations in tax systems, mainly in the contents of anti-tax evasion. Concerning tax evasion and anti-tax evasion, the new enterprise income tax law sets a special chapter. The new law would limit Chinese enterprises setting up nominal foreign-invested institutions to transfer income and profits, and avoid tax. Control measures are especially specified against weakening capital, the secret tax evasion method.

The new enterprise income tax law would set limitations on multinationals' tax evasion strategies through weakening capital. The International Economy and Cooperation Organization (OECD) insists that ratio between enterprise self-owned capital and credit capital shall be 1:1. When the former is less than the later, capital is weakened. Prevention of weakening capital is for ensuring the creditor's interests and avoiding social financial risks. In other words, when enterprises face operation risks, self-owned capital shall co-exist with enterprise risks. Under the precondition of sufficient share capital, debt capital may be guaranteed when enterprises face operation risks.

However, the real situation in China is that foreign-invested enterprises always manage to borrow more debt capital instead of putting in more share capital for the purposes of obtaining more profits and lowering share capital risks in operation. If the rate of debt against assets is too high, large amounts of bad loans may occur once the enterprise closes down. Weakening capital not only increases enterprise operation risks, bank risks and social financial risks, but also is used for tax evasion since loan interest paid by the enterprise need to be deducted from the enterprise's total income. Many nations have already taken tax measures to control weakening capital tendency, but China has taken no limiting measure up to now.

It would be stated in the new enterprise income law that if the self-owned capital ratio of an enterprise is lower than a certain percentage, the loaned capital (mainly bank loans) interest to be paid by the enterprise shall not be deducted pre-tax, which is actually controlling weakening capital with tax measures.

[10] See "Transfer Pricing in China", download from the website of Pricewaterhousecoopers, www.pwccn.com.

7.4 Unification of Income Tax and Its Risks for Foreign Investment

7.4.1 Income Tax Reform Coming

China carries out one major taxation system reform almost every ten years. Historical tax system reforms took place in 1953, 1963, 1973, 1983 and 1994. Establishment of each taxation system is closely related to the macro economic situation. In 2004, the largest taxation system reform in ten years occured with the trial transition of a value added tax in northeast China old industry bases. All social circles pay great attention to this new round of taxation system reform since it would not only re-adjust the parties' interests in the re-allocation circle but also is taken by China's new administration as an important measure for settlement of major conflicts in the economic area. It has a direct influence on the prospects of social development. In the reform, the great change in the unification of domestic and foreign-invested enterprises' income taxes would directly change China's taxation environment and is essential to foreign investors' interests.

The biggest problem in the current Chinese enterprise income tax system is the sharp difference between income tax laws for domestic and foreign-invested enterprises, which leads to a heavy unfair tax burden. The current income tax rate for domestic enterprises is 33% while that for foreign-invested enterprises is 15% . Considering large amounts of tax preferential policies, actual domestic enterprises' average tax burden rate is about 23% while foreign-invested enterprises' average tax burden rate is about 13% . That is to say, the income tax rate of foreign-invested enterprises is half of that of domestic enterprises, which seriously breach the principle of neutral taxation.

7.4.2 Games on Unification of Income Tax Reform

At the early stage of reform and opening, China pushes forward many tax preferential policies favorable to foreign enterprises to attract foreign capital. However, the current economic situation is totally different and variation in tax may cause lose or win in competition among enterprises. Unfair tax burden also leads to domestic enterprises' continuous tax dodging and evasion and intentional establishment of nominal Sino-foreign joint ventures with foreign shell companies in BVI or Cayman Islands. After China's entry into WTO, current tax system is not in accordance with the neutral taxation principle of WTO rules as well as free trade and equal competition principles promoted by WTO. It is more important that the purposes of favorable tax treatment have not been realized. Studies show that common policies for encouragement of foreign investment are not the main stimulation for multinationals' investment while on the contrary unexpected results may exist. In most cases, common measures such as tax exemption term, subsidized financing, free land have no substantial influence on the investment amount, but reduce value may originally be created by investment projects. These policies directly lead to increase of financial and administrative costs and decrease of productivity. The Brazilian government's encouragement policy for car industry has caused over investment and decrease of productivity utilization rate and production rate. Similarly, import barriers and investment measures related to trade such as domestic production request and joint venture request fail to bring about obvious active effect, but limit competition and lower production rate. Consumption electric industry in India has lower consumption and production than that of China due to limitation of competition by high import custom duties. Under most circumstances, these policies do not realize the proposed purposes but lead to great cost.[11] Tax preferential policies do not play a decisive role in attracting foreign capital. Since nations, especially the United States, do not accept the tax sparing system, hosting nations' favorable treatment for foreign investment may be counteracted if there is no tax sparing agreement between capital outflow nation and hosting nation, which turns favorable tax treatment into a channel of tax transfer and cannot offer actual benefits to foreign investors.[12]

Therefore, suggestions have been made by experts since the middle of 1990s on unification of income taxes of domestic and foreign-invested enterprises. After China's entry into WTO, the unification falls with general course of development under the WTO principle of national treatment for all enterprises. In January 2005, just before the convening of the People's Congress annual Delegation General Meeting Meetings, the issue of unification of income taxes of domestic and foreign-invested enterprises attracted great attention and hot debates.

Facing great challenge to be occurred in China's tax law, 54 famous multinationals with vast amounts of investment in China prepared a joint report to be submitted to the Office of Legal Affairs of the State Council, stating possible influence of unification of income taxes of domestic and foreign-invested enterprises on multinationals, and applying for a five to ten year transitional period for canceling favorable policy for foreign-invested enterprises at the beginning of 2005. This report may also be submitted to MOF, MOFCOM and SAT simultaneously.[13]

Meanwhile, MOFCOM and SAT are intensely debating on the unification of income taxes for domestic and foreign-invested enterprises. SAT insists on unification of income taxes for realization of fair tax burden while MOFCOM points out that the unification would influence foreign investment surroundings of China and influence attraction of foreign capital thereby calling calls for careful consideration. The result of such game among different parties is unclear prospect for unification of income taxes for domestic and foreign-invested enterprises.

---

[11] Mckinsey Global Research Institute: New Horizon-Multinationals' Investment in Developing Nations (published in October 2003), from the website of Mckinsey.

[12] Zhao Jingxia (1995), The Micro Comparison of Investment Laws for Chinese and Foreign Capital and Revelation, International Economic Cooperation, Issue 4.

[13] See relevant report in the All China Industry and Commerce Times on 13 January 2005.

7.4.3 Unification of Income Taxes Moving Ahead Under Debating

From the response of various circles, the unification of income taxes for domestic and foreign-invested enterprises is imperative under the situation considering the existing problems in China's enterprise income tax laws. Common sense has been basically reached on the importance and feasibility of unification of domestic and foreign-invested enterprises' income taxes. A Income Tax Law uniformly applicable to domestic and foreign-invested enterprises of PRC which both complies with WTO rules and meets the development needs of socialist market economy in China need to be promulgated and implemented to terminate the situation of applying different tax laws and rules on domestic and foreign-invested enterprises. According to the actual tax burden of Chinese enterprises, the uniform enterprise income tax rate should be a little lower than the middle level. A tax rate of 24-28% may be appropriate. West developing districts may still enjoy favorable tax rate of 15% but should be no less while other favorable tax rates shall be canceled and preferential policies shall be regulated. Tax exemption and cut policy shall be adjusted under the principle of 'mainly for industry preferential with district favor as supplementary'.[14]

Unification of enterprise income tax should be carried out under the principle of integrating tax laws and realizing fair tax burden, changing current different tax treatment for domestic and foreign capital and offering tax environment for fair competition among various market economy subjects. The main contents include:

(a) Unification of tax laws and promulgation of the Enterprise Income Law meeting needs in social economy development and enterprise system reform.

(b) Lowering enterprise income tax rate. Enterprise income tax rate should be appropriately lowered in the uniform tax laws based on current actual tax burden of domestic and foreign-invested enterprises in China, taking international experience in reform on enterprise income tax as reference and coordinating with adjustment of enterprise income tax preferential policies.

(c) Unified regulation of enterprise income tax base. Pre-tax deduction scope and standard should be regulated and pre-tax deduction items for domestic and foreign-invested enterprises shall be unified to make scientific and standard tax base definition in accordance with international practice.

(d) Adjustment and regulation of enterprise income tax preferential policies. Tax preferential policies shall be adjusted and tax preferential measures shall be optimized for implementation of national strategy of strengthening the nation with science and education, strategy of continuous development and policy of basic industry, in which China's situation of unbalanced economic development in different districts is to be considered. Current policy

---

[14] Wang Zheng and Wang Jianxin (2005), The Influence of Enterprise Income Tax Unification on Economy, China Chief Accountants, November Issue.

orientation of making tax preferential policies according to investment sources or districts is to be changed.

(e) Maintenance of policies' continuity. Relevant measures shall be taken in the process of integrating tax laws and adjusting tax preferential policies to maintain continuity of tax policies for better promotion of investment surroundings so as to mitigate influence of policy change on enterprise investment and guarantee promises already made by Chinese government.[15]

After unification of income tax rates for domestic and foreign-invested enterprises, China will adjust tax preferential policies from the current 'mainly for district preferential' to 'mainly for industry preferential with district favor as supplementary'. The favorable treatment is to be 'mainly indirect tax cut and exemption with direct tax cut and exemption as supplementary'. District preferential policies are to be canceled except those for a few areas in West China. Through adjustment of income tax preferential policies, many favorable treatments for foreign investors may be canceled, including 'two years exemption and three years tax cut', 40% tax return for re-investment, tax cut and exemption for advanced technology enterprises, preferential for exporting enterprises and so on. Meanwhile, industries of whose development is encouraged and investment is promoted may enjoy corresponding industry preferential policies without limitation on district or enterprise ownership according to the state industry policy. Final tax rate for enterprise income tax after unification is not settled down yet.[16] However, the gross tax burden of Chinese enterprises would be lower since income tax paid by domestic enterprises is absolutely higher than that by foreign-invested enterprises. On the other hand, foreign-invested enterprises' gross tax burden will unavoidably rise up after unification.

Appendix I: Tax Law Applicable to Foreign-Invested Enterprises

According to the Decision on Application of Provisional Regulations on Value-added Tax, Consumption tax, Business tax, etc. on Foreign-Invested Enterprises and Foreign Enterprises of the Standing Commission of the People's Congress, tax laws and rules applicable to foreign-invested enterprises and foreign enterprises not only include the Provisional Regulations on Value-added Tax of PRC, the Provisional Regulations on Consumption tax of PRC, the Provisional Regulations on Business tax of PRC and the Law on Income Tax of Foreign-invested Enter-

[15] See the website of SAT http://www.chinatax.gov.cn/view.jsp?code=200404221051272361 (the last visiting on 20 September 2005.

[16] In discussion of enterprise income tax rate after unification, social circles intend to fix it at 24%.

prises and Foreign Enterprises of PRC, but also include the following provisional regulations:

- ✧ The provisional Regulations on Land Value-added Tax of PRC issued by the State Council on 13 December 1993;
- ✧ The Provisional Regulations on Resource Tax of PRC issued by the State Council on 25 December 1993;
- ✧ The Provisional Regulations on Stamp Tax of PRC issued by the State Council on 6 August 1988;
- ✧ The Provisional Regulations on Butcher Tax issued by the Government Affair Office of the Central Government on 19 December 1950;
- ✧ The Provisional Regulations on City Real Estate Tax issued by the Government Affair Office of the Central Government on 8 August 1951;
- ✧ The Provisional Regulations on Vehicle and Ship License Tax issued by the Government Affair Office of the Central Government on 13 September 1951;
- ✧ The Provisional Regulations on Deed tax issued by the Government Affair Office of the Central Government on 3 April 1950.

I. Enterprise Income Tax

As stated above.

II. Value-Added Tax (VAT)

Units and individuals sell goods or offer processing, repairing and supplying replacements service or import goods within the territory of PRC are tax payers for value-added tax.

Tax rate for value-added tax:

(a) tax rate for tax payers' selling or importing goods is 17% except the following item 2 and item 3;

(b) tax rate for tax payers' selling or importing the following goods is 13%: food, edible vegetable oil, water, central heating, air conditioning, hot water, gas, oil fluidified gas, natural gas, marsh gas, coal products for civilian use, books, newspaper, magazines, feed, chemical fertilizer, pesticide, farming equipment, farming film and other goods stipulated by the State Council;

(c) tax rate for tax payers' exporting goods is zero, unless otherwise stipulated by the State Council;

(d) tax rate for tax payers' supply of processing, repairing and replacement service (hereinafter referred to as taxable service) is 17%.

If common tax payers sell self developed and produced computer software products, tax may be collected according to the legal tax rate of 17% with immediate return of the part the actual tax burden exceeding 6%. For small scale tax payers belonging to production enterprises, the tax rate for value added tax of producing and selling computer software is 6%. For small scale tax payers belonging to commercial enterprises, the tax rate for value added tax of selling computer software is 4%. Tax departments issue different value added tax invoices for each tax rate respectively.

Foreign-invested enterprises may enjoy tax returns within the approved total investment with tax return for using equipment made in China if purchasing and using China made equipments.

III. Tax Return or Exemption for Export

Tax administration measures of tax exemption, deduction and return is generally applied to foreign-invested enterprises engaged in self-supporting goods exportation approved to be established after 1994, unless otherwise stipulated. Tax exemption refers to exemption of value added tax in production and sale process for production enterprises' self-made goods for self-supporting export. Tax deduction refers to deduction of tax paid for raw materials and spare parts used for enterprises' self-made goods for self-supporting export from taxable amount for domestically sold goods. Tax return refers to return of tax not fully deducted due to larger deduction amount than taxable amount within a quarter under approval of tax authority in charge of export tax return when production enterprises' self-made goods for self-supporting export account for over 50% of the total goods sale.

Export tax return rate: rate for coal and agricultural products is 3%; rate for industry products processed with agricultural product as raw material and other goods bearing value added tax rate of 13% is 6%; rate for other goods bearing value added tax rate of 17% is 9%; Rate for exporting enterprises engaged in production of weaving raw material and products is 11% or 6% according to goods purchase ways from common tax payers of value added tax or small scale tax payers.

For products listed in Directory of Chinese Advanced and New Technology Commodities Export of the Ministry of Science and Technology and the Ministry of Foreign Economy and Trade, the tax return may be made for exported products according to tax collection rate and current export tax return administration regulations under the approval of SAT if the export tax return rate fails to reach tax collection rate.

IV. Sales Tax

For tax payers' supply of taxable service, transfer of invisible assets or sale of real property, the taxable amount shall be calculated according to the turnover and stipulated tax rate. The formula for calculation of taxable amount is turnover multiplied by tax rate.

Table A.1. Tax items and tax rates for sales tax

Tax item	Tax rate
1. Transportation industry: land transport, water transport, air transport, transport administration, loading, unloading and conveyance	3%
2. Construction industry: construction, installation, repair, decoration and other work	3%
3. Finance and insurance industry	5%
4. Post and telecommunication industry	3%
5. Culture and sport industry	3%
6. Entertainment industry: singing hall, dancing hall, Karaoke dancing and singing hall, music tea house, billiards, golf, bowling and games	10%
7. Service industry: agency industry, travel industry, food industry, storage industry, lease industry, advertisement industry and other service industries	5%
8. Transfer of invisible assets: transfer of land use rights, patents, non-patent technology, trademark rights, copyright and commercial fame	5%
9. Sale of real property: sale of buildings and other attachments to land	5%

Incomes of units and individuals, including foreign-invested enterprises, research and development centers set up with foreign capital, foreign enterprises and foreign citizens from technology transfer, technology development or related technology consultation and technology service are exempted of sales tax.

V. Individual Income Tax

Tax Payer: Individuals with residence in China or without residence but living inside the territory for over one year shall pay individual income tax for incomes from within and outside China. Individuals without residence in China and not living in China or living in China for less than a year shall pay individual income tax for incomes from within China.

Individual income tax shall be paid for the following individual incomes: wage and salary income, production and operation income of individual industrial and commercial operators, operation income for contracting or leasing enterprises, labor remuneration income, author's remuneration income, license use fee income, interest, dividend and bonus income, property rental income, property transfer income, incidental income and other taxable incomes specified by the finance department of the State Council.

Individual income tax rate: rate for wage and salary income is 5-45% not including surplus progressive taxation; rate for production and operation income of individual industrial and commercial operators and operation income for contracting or leasing enterprises is 5-35% not including surplus progressive taxation; rate for author's remuneration income is 20% with proportional taxation and 30% of the taxable amount is to be reduced; rate for labor remuneration income is 20% with proportional taxation; for excessively high labor remuneration in one time, in addition taxation may be madc according to the concrete measures specified by the State Council; rate for license use fee income, interest, dividend and bonus income, property rental income, property transfer income, incidental income and other incomes is 20% with proportional taxation.

VI. Consumption Tax

Units and individuals producing, entrusting processing or importing the following consumables within the territory of PRC are tax payers of consumption tax under the obligation of paying consumption tax.

Taxable amount for consumption tax is assessed according to the selling price or quantity. Formula for calculation of taxable amount is: taxable amount with assessment according to selling price = sales × tax rate, taxable amount with assessment according to selling quantity = selling quantity × tax amount per unit.

Table A.2. Tax items and Tax Rate for Consumption Tax

Tax item	Taxation scope	Calculation unit	Tax rate (tax amount)
I. Tobacco			
1. Grade A cigarettes 2. Grade B cigarettes 3. cigar 4. cut tobacco	Including various imported tobacco		45% 40% 40% 30%
II. Alcoholic Drinks and Alcohol			
1. white spirits made from cereal 2. white spirits made from potatoes 3. yellow spirits 4. beer 5. other alcoholic drinks 6. alcohol		ton	40% 15% 240 yuan 220yuan 10% 5%
III. Cosmetics	Including cosmetics sets		30%
IV. Skin care and hair care products			17%
V. Precious Jewelry	Including all kinds of gold, silver, bijouterie, jade and precious stone ornaments		10%

Table A.2 (continued)

Tax item	Taxation scope	Calculation unit	Tax rate (tax amount)
VI. Fire crackers and fire works			15%
VII. Gasoline		liter	0.20yuan
VIII. Diesel oil		liter	0.10yuan
IX. Automobile tyres			10%
X. Motorcycles			
XI. Motor Cars			
1. sedan	Those with a car cylinder capacity (i.e. emission capacity) of more than 2200ml (including 2200 ml)		8%
	Those with a cylinder capacity of 1000—2200ml (including 1000ml)		5%
	Those with a cylinder capacity of less than 100 ml		3%
2. Cross-country Vehicles (four-wheel drive)	Those with a cylinder capacity of more than 2400ml(including 2400ml)		5%
	Those with a cylinder capacity of less than 2400ml		3%
3. Minibuses and vans with less than 22 seats	Those with a cylinder capacity of more than 2000ml(including 2000ml)		5%
	Those with a cylinder capacity of less than 2000ml		3%

VII. Land Value Added Tax

Units and individuals transferring state-owned land use rights, ground buildings and attachments and having incomes are tax payers of land value added tax under the obligation of paying land value added tax. Land value added tax is calculated according to value added amount tax payers obtained for transfer of real estate and the following tax rates.

Four levels of surplus progressive tax rate are applied to land value added tax: tax rate for the part of value added amount not exceeding 50% of the project amount is 30%; tax rate for the part exceeding 50% but not exceeding 100% of the project amount is 40%; tax rate for the part exceeding 100% but not exceeding 200% is 50%; tax rate for the part exceeding 200% is 60%.

VIII. Deed Tax

Units and individuals transferring land and house ownership within the territory of PRC are tax payers of deed tax under obligation of paying deed tax.

Taxation scope: transfer of state-owned land use right, transfer of land use right, including sale, grant and exchange, house trade, grant and exchange.

Tax base: bargaining price for transfer of state-owned land use right, land use right and house trade; price ratified by tax authority according to market price of land use right sale and house trade for grant of land use right and houses; price margin of exchanged land use rights and houses for land use right or house exchange.

Tax rate: 3—5%

IX. House Property Tax

The tax base is the remaining amount of enterprise self-owned house property's account value deducted by 30% at one time. The annual tax rate is 1.2% and the rental income tax rate is 12%. If foreign-invested enterprises have difficulty in paying house property tax, they may apply to local tax authority for approval after which house property tax may be exempted for 1-3 years.

X. Vehicle and Ship License Tax

Foreign-invested enterprises are exempted of vehicle and ship license tax.

XI. City Maintenance and Construction Tax and Education Expense Affixed

Foreign-invested enterprises are exempted of city maintenance and construction tax and education expense affixed.

XII. Stamp Tax

Units and individuals issuing or accepting following documents within the territory of PRC are tax payers of stamp tax under the obligation of paying stamp tax.

Taxable certificates: purchase and sale, processing and contracting, construction project contracting, property leasing, goods transportation, storage, loan, property insurance and technology contracts or documents with contractual nature; property right transfer documents, business account books, right and license certificates and other taxable documents specified by the Ministry of Finance.

Tax amount for stamp tax is 0.5/10000, 3/10000, 5/10000 or 10/10000 of the contract amount for different tax items.

XIII. Preferential Custom Duty for Imported Equipments and Value Added Tax for Importing Process

For foreign investment projects falling within encouragement type or grade B limitation type under the Directory of Foreign Investment Industry Guidance with technology transfer, custom duties and value added tax for importing process are exempted for self use equipments imported within the total investment except those listed in the Catalog of No Tax Exemption Imported Commodities for Foreign Investment Projects.

For technology reconstruction with self-owned capital beyond the total investment by foreign-invested enterprises, foreign-invested research and development center, foreign-invested enterprises with already established advanced technology and product export orientation of encouragement type or grade B limitation type, import custom duties and import process tax may be exempted according to the Notice on Adjustment of Import Equipment Tax Policy of the State Council (Guofa [1997]No. 37) for importing self use equipment or matching technology, fittings and spare parts which could not be produced in China or those produced in China could not meet the originally approved needs within the production and operation scope.

Import custom duties and import process tax may be exempted for import of self use equipment or matching technology, fittings and spare parts which could not be produced in China or those produced in China could not meet the need by research and development center set up with foreign investment within the total investment under the Notice on Adjustment of Import Equipment Tax Policy of the State Council (Guofa[1997] No. 37).

Custom duties and value added tax for import process are exempted from overseas payment of software fees according to contract by foreign-invested enterprises for the production of advanced technology listed in the Catalog of State-owned Advanced and New Technology Products.

Appendix II: Current Chinese Foreign-Invested Enterprise Income Tax System

The Law on Income Tax of Foreign-invested Enterprises and Foreign Enterprises of PRC was promulgated in 1991 while the *Provisional Regulations on Enterprise Income Tax of PRC* was issued in 1993. The two laws set foreign-invested enterprise income tax collection rules and establish different income tax systems for domestic and foreign-invested enterprises. If a foreign-invested enterprise sets its headquarter in China, it should pay tax for incomes from within China and outside China. The taxable income of organizations or sites engaged in production and operation set up by foreign-invested enterprises in China shall be the total income of each tax year deducted by cost, expenses and losses. Foreign-invested enterprise income tax rate shall be 30% calculated on income amount for tax while the local income tax rate shall be 3% calculated on income amount for tax with lots of exemption or preferential treatment as follows:

I. General Preferential Policy

(a) For productive foreign-invested enterprises with operation term of over ten years, enterprise income tax shall be exempted for the first and second years starting from the first profiting year while enterprise tax shall be cut half from the third to the eighth years. Local income tax is exempted.

(b) Annual loss of organizations or sites engaged in production and operation set up by foreign-invested enterprises and foreign enterprises in China may be made up with income of next tax year. If the income of next tax year is not sufficient, continuous making up may be made in following years which should be no longer than five years.

(c) Enterprises with products exported invested by foreign capital, after expiration of period for enterprise income tax exemption or cut, may enjoy half cut of enterprise income tax according to tax rate fixed by the Tax law if the export product value of a year is more than 70% of the product value of the year.

(d) Advanced technology enterprises set up with foreign investment may enjoy extension of three years for half cut of enterprise income tax according to tax rate fixed by the Tax Law if remaining as advanced technology enterprises after expiration of enterprise income tax exemption or cut under the Tax Law.

(e) If the foreign investor of a foreign-invested enterprise reinvest profits from the enterprise into it to increase registered capital or invest the profits as capital for establishment of other foreign-invested enterprises with operation term no less than five years, 40% income tax of the re-invested part may be returned upon application by the investor and approval by tax authority.

(f) If the technology development expense of a foreign-invested enterprise increases no less than 10%, 50% of the actual amount of technology development expense may be deducted from the taxable income after approval by tax authority.

(g) Foreign-invested enterprises and foreign enterprises' donation for non-affiliated scientific research institutions and universities' research and development may be fully deducted from the enterprises' taxable income in calculation with the tax treatment measure concerning donation in the Law on Income Tax of Foreign-invested Enterprises and Foreign Enterprises of PRC as reference.

II. Industry Preferential Policy

(a) Productive foreign-invested enterprises engaged in energy and transport fundamental facilities projects may pay enterprise tax income at the tax rate of 15% after approval by SAT.

(b) Foreign-invested enterprises engaged in agriculture, forestry and stock raising development and operation with operation term of over 15 years may be exempted of income tax in the first to fifth year starting from the first profiting year, pay half income tax from the sixth to tenth year, and pay income tax at the rate of 15-30% in the following ten years.

(c) Enterprises with investment in technology enhancement projects in accordance with national industry policy in Chinese territory, 40% of the China made equipment investment needed in the projects may be deducted from the newly increased enterprise income tax of the year such equipments are purchased compared with the previous year.

(d) Sino-foreign joint ventures engaged in ports and docks may enjoy favorable tax rate of 15%. For those with operation term of over 15 years, five years' exemption and five years' tax cut are applied. Productive foreign-invested enterprises engaged in energy, transportation and other fundamental facility projects may enjoy favorable tax rate of 15% (exercised since the second half of 1999).

(e) For industries and projects encouraging foreign investment, people's governments of provinces, autonomous regions and municipals directly under the central government may cut or exempt local income tax according to real situation.

III. Regional Preferential Policy

(a) Income tax preferential for foreign-invested enterprises in special economic zones.[17] Foreign-invested enterprises in special economic zones and foreign enterprises setting up organizations or sites for production and operation in special economic zones enjoy favorable income tax rate of 15%. Productive foreign enterprises established in the old city districts of cities where special economic zones locate enjoy favorable income tax rate of 24%. Technology centered and intelligence centered projects, projects with over USD 30 million foreign investment and long return term, energy, transportation, harbor and dock projects and other projects encouraged by the nation enjoy favorable income tax rate of 15% Enterprises set up in

[17] The application scope of this tax preferential policy is Shenzhen, Zhuhai, Xiamen, Shantou and Hainan Economic Special Zones and Xiamen Taiwan Merchants Investment Zone.

special economic zones, engaging in service trade, with over USD 5 million foreign investment and over 10 year operation term enjoy favorable income tax treatment of 'one year exemption and two year half cut'. Foreign banks, joint venture banks and other financial institutions set up in special economic zones with over USD 10 million investment or operation capital allocated from headquarter to branch and over 10 year operation term enjoy favorable income tax rate of 15%.

(b) Favorable tax policies for foreign-invested enterprises in seaside opening cities, seaside economic opening districts and economy and technology development zones.[18] Foreign-invested enterprises set up in economy and technology development zones enjoy favorable income tax rate of 15%. Productive foreign-invested enterprises set up in old city area of seaside opening cities, seaside economic opening districts, economy and technology development zones and urban districts enjoy favorable income tax rate of 24%. Technology centered and intelligence centered projects in the above areas, projects with over USD 30 million foreign investment and long return term and energy, transportation and harbor construction projects enjoy favorable income tax rate of 15%.

(c) Favorable tax policy for foreign-invested enterprises in free trade zones. Productive enterprises engaged in processing and exporting in free trade zones enjoy favorable income tax rate of 15%.

(d) Favorable tax policy in Shanghai Pudong New District. Productive foreign-invested enterprises set up in Pudong New District and foreign-invested enterprises with projects and engaging in fundamental facility construction on patches of land enjoy favorable income tax rate of 15%. Foreign-invested enterprises set up in Pudong New District engaging in airport, harbor, railway, power station and other energy transportation construction projects with over 15 year operation term enjoy five year exemption and five year half cut of income tax. Preferential income tax treatment for financial institutions is the same as that for those in special zones.

Favorable tax polity for foreign-invested enterprises in remote areas and middle and west districts. Foreign-invested enterprises set up in undeveloped remote areas, after expiration of tax exemption and cut under general provisions, continuously enjoy favorable income tax rate of 15-30% in the following ten years.

---

[18] This tax preferential policy is applicable to 14 seaside opening cities, Shantou, Zhuhai, Xiamen(not including city area outside special economic zone), Weihai City, Fuzhou Mawei Taiwan Merchants Investment Zone, provincial cities not included in seaside economi opening districts, territory side and riverside opening cities, Chang Jiang River Delta, South Fujian Xiamen Zhangquan Delta, East Liaoning Byland, other urban areas of opening cities in other seaside districts, urban areas of major counties, advanced and new technology development zones approved by the state, and Suzhou industrial park.

Foreign-invested enterprises set up in middle and west districts engaged in encouraged or permitted projects under the Directory of Foreign Investment Industries enjoy favorable income tax rate of 15% within three years after expiration of general tax exemption or cut term. During the period, enterprises with admitted advanced technology or product exportation value accounting for over 70% of gross product value of the year enjoy further half cut of income tax, but the final tax rate shall be no less than 10%.[19]

---

[19] This stipulation is implemented as from 1 January 2000.

8 Land Use Right Risks in Foreign Investment

China's real estate market is neither a foreign investor's paradise nor hell.

—— Xiaoyang Zhang[1]

8.1 Introduction

A county government, for the purpose of revitalizing local tourism market, decided to build villas for vacations with the land of the county so as to attract tourists from cities. Since the County Economic Cooperation and the county government are the same staff with two different titles, the county government attracted investment from outside under the name of the County Economic Cooperation. In September of the same year, a foreign investor signed *the Agreement on Sino-foreign Joint Development of Tourist Places* which stated that the name of the Sino-foreign joint venture established is Hualong Co. Ltd. for which the Chinese party contributed with 60 mu[2] construction area and the foreign investor contribute all the construction capital. The contract term is 15 years. The profit allocation proportion is 1:4. The property right of the tourist places shall belong to the Chinese party after the termination of the contract. After the tourist places were built, they gained local fame since Hualong made increasing profits with good management. Three years later, the joint venture was sued by a village collective organization of the county which alleged that the land used by the joint venture belong to the collectivity of villagers and claimed for allocation of large amount of profits. The court, after hearing, deemed that the 60 mu land belonged to the collectivity of villagers and should be operated and managed by the villagers' commission or the collective economic organization of the village while the county economic cooperation had no right to represent the villagers' commission to dispose the 60

---

1 Xiaoyang Zhang is a scholar in The Open University of Hong Kong. The sentence quoted in a paper wrote by Xiaoyang Zhang named Real Estate Investment in China – Legal Review and Analysis of Foreign Investors' Participation, downloaded from http://www.murdoch.edu.au/elaw/issues/v6n2/zhang62_text.html.

2 A Chinese unit of area.

mu land. The court decided that the contract was void and the parties shall deal with problems there from within the specified period.

The focus of this case, in its essence, is whether land use privileges obtained by foreign-invested enterprises are effective. In this case, the joint venture obtained the land use right through the Chinese investor's contribution of collectively owned land use right as the cooperation condition, which falls within the situation of obtaining land use right through transfer. Two problems exist in obtaining the land use right: first, the Chinese party signing *the Agreement on Sino-foreign Joint Development of Tourist Places* is not a qualified legal subject, the County Economic Cooperation is not the owner of the land collectively owned by farmers and cannot represent the villagers' commission to contribute with the collective land use right for establishment of enterprise jointly with foreign investors for the construction and operation of the tourist place; second, the procedure of the agreement conclusion is not in accordance with legal provisions, collective land use right cannot be directly used in real estate development, collectively owned land can only be supplied to foreign investors for use with payment after being requisitioned as state owned land. Though the tourist location is profitable, the foreign investor finds himself in an unfavorable passive dilemma due to the difficulty of obtaining land use right. Country land use rights are collectively owned. Under the principal of 'house going with land', the foreign investor is faced with the reality of losing his/her capital and buildings with little cost taking back since the Chinese party, though bearing main responsibilities for the void contract and compensating the foreign investor therefore, only compensates according to the construction cost.

Foreign-invested projects generally involve the use of land or land use right. Obtaining land use right is one of the essential legal issues in production and operation of factories established with foreign investment. For foreign-invested production enterprises, it directly influences the amount of investment cost and future profit of the whole project. The legal risks concerning the effect of obtaining land use right may even lead to the abortion of the formerly ideal investment project, so great attention should be paid to the land related legal risks in foreign investment.

8.2 Legal Issues in Foreign-Invested Enterprises' Use of Land

8.2.1 Policies Change

Foreign-invested enterprises' use of land is the first one of which compensated use is applied to in China. *The Law on Sino-foreign Equity Joint Venture Enterprise* promulgated in 1979 clearly states that the Chinese cooperating party may invest with land use right and stipulates that 'If the right to use a site is not a part of the investment by a Chinese party, the joint venture shall pay a fee for its use'. *The Regulations for Implementation of Sino-foreign Equity Joint Venture Enterprise* issued in 1983 further clarifies that the land used by a joint venture shall be obtained through the way specified in the land use contract signed between the joint venture and relevant land administration authorities, specifying the purpose, term and fee for the use of the land. Similar stipulations may be found in following *Law on Sino-foreign Corporative Joint Venture Enterprise*, *Law on Wholly Foreign Owned Enterprise* and the relevant detailed rules for implementation. Along with the expanding of land use system reform in China, the above mentioned laws allow foreign-invested enterprises to obtain land use right according to other Chinese rules besides the means of paying site use fees. It is stated in Article 85 of the new *Land Administration Law* of 1998 that 'This Law shall be applicable to the use of land by Sino-foreign joint ventures, Sino-foreign cooperative joint ventures and enterprises wholly owned by foreign capital; where laws have separate provisions, those provisions shall prevail'.

After the issue of *the Provisional Regulations on Land Use Tax in Cities and Towns* in 1988, MOF issued a notice in 1988, stating that the *Provisional Regulations* is not applicable to foreign-invested enterprises, which means that they are not obliged to pay land use tax but shall continue to pay site use fees. After the issue of *Interim Regulations Concerning Assignment and Transfer of the Right to the Use of the State-owned Land in the Urban Areas* (No.55 Decree) and *Interim Measures for the Administration of the foreign–invested Development of Tracts of Land* (No.56 Decree) notices in 1990, many foreign-invested enterprises have obtained land use right through the way of assignment. However, MOF later issued another notice, stating that foreign-invested enterprises shall still pay site use fees after obtaining land through the way of assignment, which was strongly objected by foreign-invested enterprises. Therefore, the Guobanfa [1999] No. 73 Order named *Opinions on Further Promotion of Foreign Investment* in August 1999 to clearly stipulate that foreign-invested enterprises were not obliged to pay site use fees after obtaining land use right through the way of assignment.

According to the above stipulations, compensation use is adopted in all land use by foreign-invested enterprises. Before the issue of the No. 55 and No. 56 Decrees by the State Council in 1990, foreign-invested enterprises generally obtained the land with compensation through signing land use right assignment contracts and paying land use fees. China was formerly accustomed to adopting different land use policies according to the different identities of land users. For example, state-owned enterprises may obtain lands within the scope of allocation lands through allocation while foreign-invested enterprises and privately owned enterprises may only use land with full compensation, which is obviously not in accordance with National Treatment principles of WTO. The Ministry of Land and Resources (MOLR) pays close attention to the adjustment of relevant administration modes, adopting different land use policies according to the industries and purposes instead of the ownership structures. In July 1999, MOLR made clear in a *Reply to China Petroleum and Natural Gas Group (Guotuzihan1999 [1999] No. 307)* that if land used by Sino-foreign cooperative exploitation of petroleum on land, should fall within the catalog of allocated land, may still be obtained through allocation.

The Various Opinions on Strengthening Land Asset Administration for Promoting Reform and Development of State-owned Enterprises issued in November 1999 (Guotuzifa [1999] No. 433) clarifies that land used by joint ventures or cooperatives of state-owned enterprises and foreign investors, qualifying within the catalog of allocated land, may be obtained through allocation after approval by authorities. *The Catalog of Allocated Land* issued in 2001 (No. 9 Minister Order of MOLR) further states that all construction project sites, complying with the catalog, may be obtained through allocation under approval in no regard of the land users' identities. Therefore, foreign-invested enterprises have enjoyed the same land use policy as other land users.

8.2.2 Ways for Foreign-Invested Enterprises' to Obtain Land Use Right

According to the current land use policy of China, foreign-invested enterprises may obtain land use right in the following ways:

Assignment (出让). It refers to obtaining right of using state-owned land from government land administration departments in mode of auction, bidding or agreement. Foreign-invested enterprises may obtain land use right through assignment. Within the assignment term, the assigned land use right may be transferred, leased or mortgaged. This method is most suitable for enterprises with large amount of investment, long repayment period and continuous operation.

Transfer. Land needed by foreign-invested enterprises may also be obtained from other land users through transfer of land use rights within specified term according to relevant stipulations. The so-called transfer refers to purchase of land use rights from the original land users in the secondary land market, which is an action of re-transferring land use right. The use term of the land use right obtained in this way is the term of the assigned land deducted by the time the land has already been used. If the original land users are allowed to unconditionally transfer land use rights, speculation of land may appear. Therefore, it is stipulated in relevant laws that the land cannot be transferred if the original land user fails to invest and develop the land according to the assignment contract. If the land is used for a construction project, 25% of the total investment shall be accomplished. If the land is for tract development, 'three connections and one leveling' shall be achieved, that is, the connections of water, electricity and heat, and the leveling of sites, so as to accomplish the industry of construction land use conditions. If foreign-invested enterprises obtain land use rights in this way, they shall pay land use fees to local land administrations according to the area and level of the land as well as other relevant expenses for land acquisition, removal and fundamental facility construction.

Leasing (including the way of paying site use fees). Foreign-invested enterprises may obtain right of using the leased land through the way of leasing. Under this way, foreign-invested enterprises obtain land use rights of certain term on the cost of paying rent. Similarly, to avoid disguised speculation of land, foreign-invested enterprises can only transfer, sublease or mortgage right of using the leased land under the contract or as approved by the land administration authorities after accomplishing development and construction within the leasing period. The rent standard takes reference of local normal land price. If the leaser pays relevant expenses for land acquisition and removal when obtaining the land use right, the rent standard shall be calculated as the price of land deducting relevant expenses.

Land Use Right Contribution. Contribution or equity participation with land use right as investment after evaluation. The state may evaluate land use rights of certain term as contribution or equity to co-establish enterprises with foreign investment. The land use rights are held by joint ventures and may be legally transferred, leased or mortgaged within the use term. Chinese enterprises may evaluate land use rights originally held by them as shares or cooperation conditions to form joint ventures or cooperatives within foreign investors under approval. The Chinese enterprise shall hold the land use certificates before evaluating the land use rights held by them as shares or cooperation conditions and shall accomplish relevant development and construction investment according to the assignment contracts. If the original land use rights are obtained through administrative allocation, Chinese enterprises shall handle the procedure of transferring state-owned land or pay land use fees according to relevant stipulations.

Administrative Allocation. MOLR issued *the Catalog of Allocated Land* on October 18 2000, changing the former policy of dividing land use ways according to land users' identities to dividing according to industries and purposes. According to relevant stipulations in *the Land Administration Law* and *the City Real Estate Administration Law of China*, foreign-invested enterprises may also obtain land through allocation if the land falls within *the Catalog of Allocated Land* and the allocation is approved by the land administration authority. Foreign-invested enterprises, if obtained land use right in this way, shall pay land development expenses including compensation and allocation expenses and land use fees. The land development expenses should be fully paid in one time according to the actual amount and be collected by local land administration authority under local standard if the land has already been developed. Such means is mainly suitable for non-profitable investment such as libraries or museums and only for fundamental facility sites including energies, transportation and water conservancy in profitable industry. For most foreign-invested enterprises, the costs are too high yielding little realistic significance.

Other. Along with the use of state-owned land, country collective economic organizations may co-establish enterprises, operational village commonweal enterprises or fundamental facility construction projects with other organizations or individuals including foreign-invested enterprises by way of equity participation or joint operation through contribution of land use right under the new *Land Administration Law*, which represents foreign-invested enterprises co-established by foreign investors and rural collective economic organizations contributing land use right as share capital or through joint management may use collectively owned land. However, foreign-invested real estate development projects can only use state-owned land.

8.2.3 Fee for Land Use Right

Foreign-invested enterprises shall pay fees for land use rights according to Chinese laws, rules and relevant contracts. According to *the Law of Sino-foreign Equity Joint Venture Enterprise* and its *Implementation Regulation*, joint ventures, after obtaining land use rights, shall pay land use fees per year according to the agreed land use time in contracts. If the land use time for the first calendar year is over half a year, the land use fees should be calculated for half a year. If the land use fee is adjusted within the contract term, it should be paid under the new standard from the year of adjustment. The standard for land use fees are generally fixed by the government of the province, autonomous region or municipal city where the enterprise is located at according to laws and rules and considering actual situations of the place based on elements including the land use purpose, geographic surrounding conditions, expenses for land acquisition, removal and allocation, and the enterprise's request for fundamental facilities, and should be put on records by MOFCOM and the state land administration authorities. The land use fee shall not be changed within the first five years of land use. Later, it may be adjusted according to the change in supply and need and geographic surrounding conditions along with economic development. The interval of adjustment shall be no less than 3 years. If the Chinese party contributes the right to use the land needed by a joint venture as its investment, the evaluated amount shall be the same as the land use fee for same sites. The land use fee, when being the contribution of Chinese party, shall not be adjusted within the contract term. Joint ventures engaged in agriculture and stockbreeding may pay land use fees to local land administration authority calculated as certain percentage of operational incomes under the approval of province, autonomous region or municipal city governments. For developing projects in undeveloped areas, favorable treatment concerning payment of land use fees may be offered under the approval of local governments.

Under *the Law of Sino-foreign Equity Joint Venture Enterprise* and its *Implementation Regulation*, foreign-invested enterprises shall pay land use fees to local land administration authorities when obtaining land use certificates. Foreign-invested enterprises shall also pay land development expenses for use of developed land. Land development expenses are equal to expenses for land acquisition, removal and allocation plus expenses for matching fundamental facility construction. Such expenses may be collected by land developing organizations fully or in yearly installments. Foreign-invested enterprises, if using undeveloped land, may develop land by themselves or entrust relevant Chinese institutions for development. Construction of fundamental facilities shall be uniformly arranged by local governments of county level or above. The standards for collecting land use fees and land development expenses from foreign-invested enterprises shall be in accordance with relevant Chinese stipulations. The land use term shall be the same as the approved operation term of the foreign-invested enterprise.

8.2.4 Term for Land Use Rights

The term for land use right of foreign-invested enterprises shall generally be the same as the enterprise operation term. However, according to Article 12 of *Interim Regulations Concerning Assignment and Transfer of the Right to the Use of the State-owned Land in the Urban Areas* (No.55 Decree), and in implementation from as of the same day, the longest time limits for assignment of land use rights are: 70 years for residence land use, 50 years for industry land use, 50 years for education, science, technology, culture, health and physical training land use, 40 years for commerce, travel and entertainment land use, and 50 years for complex or other land use. Under Article 22 of *Interim Regulations Concerning Assignment and Transfer of the Right to the Use of the State-owned Land in the Urban Areas* (No.55 Decree), the time limit for land use rights obtained through transfer equals to the use term stated in the land use right transfer contract deducted by the time the former land users already used the land.

8.3 Land Risks in Foreign Investment

8.3.1 Legal Risks in Developing Zones' Land Transfer

Since the reform and opening of China, various developing zones have been set up in different places. These developing zones of different forms are always the bridgehead for attracting foreign investment. There are a great variety of developing zones in China. According to the statistics of the State Development and Reform Commission (SDRC), there are total 31 types of developing zones, including economic development zones, industrial parks, logistics parks, college towns, tourism and holiday zones, private economic zones, sample zones for village and town enterprises, economic experimental zones, new cities, processing zones, environment protection industry parks and so forth.[3]

A developing zone is generally managed by one administrative commission, which covers land assignment. During the investment process by foreign investors in developing zones, most of the land use rights are obtained through the assign-

---

[3] The Situation of Clearing up and Straightening Developing Zones on the website of the State Development and Reform Commission (the last visiting in September 2005).

ment by administrative commissions. However, assignment of land by the developing zone administrative commission involves great legal risks.

First, developing zones' status is unstable, especially the illegally set up ones always facing risks of being canceled under tightened national policy. In July 2003, MOLR clear up and straighten various developing zones along with relevant departments of the State Council under *the Notice on Clearing up and Straightening Various Developing Zones for Strengthening of Land Use Administration* by the General Office of the State Council [Guobanfa (2003) No.70]. Up to the end of 2004, 4,813 developing zones of different types have been canceled and the planned area of developing zones has been reduced 24,900 square kilometers, decreasing 70.1% and 64.5% respectively. At the end of 2004, SDRC took over the setting approval work for clearing up and straightening developing zones as suggested by MOLR and approved by the State Council. MOLR and SDRC have publicized lists of 141 approved national level developing zones in three batches.

Secondly, the administrative commission of developing zones is not entitled to assign land according to latest judicatory interpretations. It is clearly stated in Article 2 of *the Supreme People's Court's Interpretation on Law Application Issue Involved in Contract Dispute Cases Concerning State-owned Land Use Right* implemented on 1 August 2005 that the contract for transfer of land use right signed between the administrative commission of developing zones as the assignor and the assignee shall be deemed void. Before the implementation of this *Interpretation,* the contract for transfer of land use right signed between the administrative commission of developing zones as the transferor and the transferee may be deemed as valid if being recognized retroactively by city or county governmental land administration authorities. The *Interpretation* makes different stipulations on recognizance of land use right contracts signed by administrative commissions of developing zones. First, the *Interpretation,* to corporate with the State Council's land market straightening work and further promote the land administration departments' administration of land market, makes it clear that land use right transfer contracts signed between administrative commissions of developing zones as transferors and transferees should be treated as void so as to set up effective norms for future land transfer activities. Secondly, the *Interpretation,* based on the current actual situation in China, adopts certain remedial measures concerning land transfer problems left behind by administrative commissions of developing zones, that is, land transfer contracts signed by administrative commissions may still be deemed as valid if being recognized retroactively by city or county governmental land administration authorities before litigation. Meanwhile, the *Interpretation,* for the prevention of abusing retroactive recognition measures and effectively standardize future land transfer activities, limits the scope of retroactive recognition as those occurred before the implementation of the *Interpretation.* Land use right transfer contracts signed by administrative commissions of developing zones after the enforcement of the Interpretation shall all be treated as void. Reasonable resolution of disputes arising hereof is offered through these lenient and strict stipulations.

> **Zhongshun Land Dispute:** Zhongshun International Hotel Co., Ltd. is a Sino-Hong Kong joint venture. In 2003, Zhongshun signed the land use right assignment contract with the administrative commission of Nanchang Economy and Technology Developing Zone, under which the commission assigned land use right of 66767.7 square meters. Later, Zhongshun paid the land assignment fee and obtained the land use certificate from Nanchang Land Bureau. On 21 July 2005, Nanchang Land Bureau sent the Notice on Taking Back State-owned Land Use Right to Zhongshun, stating that the land use right assignment contract signed between Zhongshun and the administrative commission of Nanchang Economy and Technology Developing Zone is invalid and should be canceled, and requesting Zhongshun handle cancel procedures with the original assignor and write off land use certificate already obtained within 10 days after receiving the notice.

According to the *Interpretation*, the land use right assignment contract signed by Zhongshun and the administrative commission of Nanchang Economy and Technology Developing Zone shall be deemed void. However, land use right assignment contracts signed by administrative commissions of developing zones as assignors and assignees may be deemed valid if being recognized retroactively by city or county governmental land administration authorities before litigation under Article 2 of the Interpretation. There is no conclusion on what behavior constitutes retroactive recognition of transfer contracts. Considering that the company has obtained land use certificate and paid relevant fees while the land use right assignment contract has been performed, especially Nanchang Land and Resources Bureau has issued land use certificate to the company, the land use right assignment contract may be recognized as valid if Nanchang Land and Resources Bureau's issuance of land use certificate is deemed as retroactive recognition of the land use right assignment contract. However, attention should be paid to: first, it is uncertain whether Nanchang Land and Resources Bureau's issuance of land use certificate could be deemed as retroactive recognition of the land use right assignment contract; second, even if Nanchang Land and Resources Bureau's issuance of land use certificate may be deemed as retroactive recognition of the land use right assignment contract, the contract only 'may' be deemed as effective according to law while the court has abundant discretion in final cognizance of the validity of the contract.

Besides the risk due to uncertainty in law, the *Interpretation* actually sanctions great power to local land administration authorities, that is, discretion to decide whether to recognize retroactively. Great power creates big rent-seeking room. When the obtaining of land use right that is essential for the company's existence is fully up to the flexible attitude of land administration authority, the failure of the company is guaranteed.

8.3.2 Legal Risks in Land Requisition

Introduction of Land Requisition System

Land requisition refers to the modification of agriculture land owned by rural collective economic group into construction land owned by the state by way of government requisition. Under *the Law of PRC on Administration of the Urban Real Estate*, the land use right for the collective-owned land within a planned urban district may be assigned with payment only after it is requisitioned in accordance with the law and turned into State-owned land. The land use right of land collectively owned by farmers can not be assigned, transferred or leased for non-agriculture construction. *The Law on Land Contract in Rural Areas* promulgated in August 2002 not only confirms ad announces the protection of farmers' land use right and proceeds rights but also clearly defines farmers' land transfer right. However, the definition of farmers' right of contracting and transferring private land in the *Contracting Law* is limited within the 'agriculture purpose of the land', excluding confirmation and protection of farmers' contacting and operating power when the land is used for non-agricultural purpose. For transfer of part of farmland into non-agricultural construction, the sole method stipulated in *the Law on Administration of the Urban Real Estate* is state monopoly, that is, change of farmland owned by rural collective organizations into state-owned ones through land requisition which is used for industry construction, accomplishing change of land collectively owned system into state owned system.[4] The above legal arrangement decides basic features of China's land requisition system. Once farmland is converted into industry or city land, it is no longer 'civil land' (collectively owned by farmers and contracted and operated by families) but 'state land' instead. This set of land system designed for resolution of occupation of farmland for industry and city construction purpose combines 'land could not be traded and appreciation belongs to the state' (mandatory requisition), 'state industrialization' (extremely low compensation), 'collective ownership by people's community' ('collectivity'

---

[4] Article 44 of the Land Administration Law states that 'For occupation and use of land for construction involving turning agricultural land into land for construction, formalities of examination and approval for turning agricultural land into other uses should be completed'. However, this system has been flexible recently. On 1 October 2005, the Measures on Administration of Transfer of Land Use Rights for Collective Construction of Guangdong Province is to be implemented, under which all the land used for rural collective construction in Guangdong Province may directly enter into the market for trade and share 'same land, same rights and same price' with state owned construction land. This measure is immediately named by experts as the 'directly entrance into market of farmland'. The local rules of Guangdong province allow rural collective construction land in the province to directly enter the market for trade, breaking down the old system of 'farmland could not be legally turned into non agriculture purpose without government requisition' as well as creating a new period with co-existence of land requisition system and farmland's direct entrance of market'. See the Gate Opening for Farmland System', published in Caijing, September 2005.

turns out to be the sole legal representative of farmers) and 'Hong Kong experience' (land batch rent system), forming its own style. This land system with combination has the following features:(a)The decisive factor in supply of land used for agriculture and cities is neither ownership of farmland nor using right of farmland, which means property right of farmland is not legally qualified for land trade or bargaining; (b) The government is responsible for judging the need of land for industry ad cities and decides on the supply of land by administrative authority including planning, approval and land requisition; (c) Power rent instead of right rent for land property rights stimulates farmland turned into land used for agriculture o cities. Above all, the most important issue is that market price factor may be excluded from the allocation of city land resources.[5]

Hidden Legal Risks in Land Requisition for Foreign-Invested Projects

In practice, land used for foreign-invested projects often involves farmland. The problem is solved mainly by way of land requisition. Local governments, for construction of invested projects and realization of cooperation purpose, convert farmland into construction land to be used in foreign-invested projects. It should be noted that land requisition is normally bound with foreign investment. The process is not assignment of land to foreign investors by governments after governments unilaterally accomplish land requisition and convert farmland into industrial use land. The typical operation method is foreign investors pay compensation expenses to governments who accomplish requisitioning and clearing up land (some local governments do not requisition land by themselves but authorize foreign investors to do so) and obtain land for use after accomplishing requisition with governments' cooperation. Due to internal shortcomings of China's land requisition system, disputes always arise from land requisition. Especially if involving local governments' detain of compensation as contribution may most easily intensify conflicts and directly influence proceeding of foreign-invested projects.

> Fujian Automobile Industry Group and Taiwan Yulong Group reached a cooperation agreement in 1995 for establishment of Southeast Automobile City at Qingkou Town, Minhou County, Fuzhou City. The total investment is USD 352,000,000. The planned requisitioned land for the first phase project is 2,400 mu. During July and August 1995, Minhou County and Qingkou Town sent groups of work teams to planned requisition villages, announcing each person whose farmland is requisitioned may get compensation of RMB 10,000 yuan, aged person beyond 50 may get pension of RMB 60 yuan each month and each family may have at least one opportu-

[5] See reports and speeches made by Professor Zhou Qiren at th international seminar on Reform of china's Land Requisition System jointly held by China Economy Research Center of Beijing University and Chinese Law Research Center of Yale University on 27 and 28 February 2004.

nity to work at Southeast Automobile City. About 20,000 local farmers handed over their land for requisition. However, after the project entered into construction period, each farmer only got RMB800 yuan compensation for land requisition. So they felt being cheated and visited relevant organizations in municipal, provincial and central governments. The proceeding of invested project was severely influenced. In March 1997, Fujian People's Congress Meeting was held, during which dozens of farmers at Qingkou Town went to the Congress to reflect problems. However, the governments of Minhou County and Qingkou Town sent policemen to arrest those farmers. Later, the financial department of Minhou County decided to appropriate funds of RMB1,000,000 yuan per year to compensate farmers at Qingkou Town whose land was requisitioned. According to copies of relevant documents of Fuzhou municipal government found by journalists, the land transfer price for this project is RMB33,000 yuan per mu (including compounding taxes and expenses) among which farmers' compensation is RMB10,000 yuan per mu. The governments of Minhou county and Qingkou Town intercepted land compensation fees and use them as investment in Southeast Automobile Town Project.

Typical land requisition disputes arise mainly from the following legal risks which may easily cause discrepancies:

Low Compensation. Social conflict due to low land requisition compensation. According to Article 47 of *the Land Administration Law*, for requisition of land, compensation shall be given in accordance with the original use of the requisitioned land.[6] First, the compensation standard is comparatively low considering

6 Compensation fee for the cultivated land requisitioned include land compensation fee, subsidy for resettlement as well as compensation fee for ground appendixes and young crops. Land compensation fee for the cultivated land requisitioned shall be six to ten times of the average annual output value in the three years prior to requisition. Subsidy for resettlement for the cultivated land requisitioned shall be calculated on the basis of the agricultural population that requires resettlement. The agricultural population that requires resettlement shall be calculated on the basis of the amount of cultivated land requisitioned divided by the average per capita occupancy of cultivated land of the unit requisitioned. The rate of subsidy for resettlement per head of the agricultural population that requires resettlement shall be four to six times of the average annual output value in the three years prior to requisition of the said cultivated land. However, the maximum subsidy for resettlement for cultivated land requisitioned per hectare shall not exceed fifteen times of the average annual output value in the three years prior to the requisition. The rate of land compensation fee and subsidy for resettlement for the requisition of other lands shall be fixed by the provinces, autonomous regions and municipalities directly under the Central Government, taking the rate of land compensation fee and subsidy for resettlement for the requisition of cultivated land as reference. Rate of compen-

the reselling price of governments, which may cause social contradiction easily. Secondly, the so-called 'maintain their original living standards' in the second paragraph of the provision is a vague polity term which actually means that the standard may be higher if requisitioned persons make trouble. Therefore, land requisition dispute is encouraged from the system aspect.

Detain of Land Compensation. Disputes arising out of detainment of land compensation fee by leaders of rural collective economic organizations. Due to the internal system limitation of the management structure of rural collective economic organizations, collectivity may be turned as tools of village leaders for their own benefits. Detainment, embezzlement and personal allotment of land compensation fee by leaders of rural collective economic organizations are common. Compared with leaders' sudden wealth, farmers are quite miserable after requisition. Land still plays role of social guarantee or even survival guarantee in countries. Disputes are almost inevitable if farmers receive no reasonable compensation.

Conversion Without Permission. Conversion of land compensation into contribution by rural collective economic organizations without permission of farmers. In legal sense, land compensation fees belong to rural collective economic organizations under Article 26 of *the Regulations for Implementation of Land Administration Law of PRC*. Therefore, rural collective economic organizations are entitled to contribute land compensation fees for investment. However, foreign-invested projects always face risks inside rural collective economic organizations if accepting land compensation fees as contribution by rural collective economic organizations.

Acceptance for Farmers. Risks in receiving relevant fees by rural collective economic organizations on behalf of farmers. It is stated in Article 26 of *the Regulations for Implementation of Land Administration Law of PRC* that compensation for on-ground appendixes and young crops belong to the owners. The resettlement subsidy for requisition land must be used as special funds for special purpose and cannot be appropriated. People need resettlement shall be resettled by rural collective economic organizations while resettlement subsidies shall be paid to rural

---

sation for ground appendixes and young crops on the requisitioned land shall be fixed by the provinces, autonomous regions and municipalities directly under the Central Government. For requisition of suburban vegetable plots of municipalities, the land use unit should, pursuant to relevant state provisions, pay to the new vegetable plot development and construction fund. Additional subsidy for resettlement may be provided for those peasants who require resettlement and cannot maintain their original living standards on the basis of land compensation fee and subsidy for resettlement the payment of which is effected pursuant to the provisions of the Second Paragraph of this Article subject to the approval of people's governments of the provinces, autonomous regions and municipalities directly under the Central Government. However, the total of land compensation fee and subsidy for resettlement shall not exceed thirty times of the average annual output value in the three years prior to requisition of the land.

collective economic organizations for administration and use. If resettlement is arranged by other organizations, the resettlement subsidies shall be paid to such organizations. If there is no need for consolidated resettlement, the resettlement subsidies shall be provided for resettled persons or be paid as insurance fees for them. However, in practice, these fees are generally paid to rural collective economic organizations at one time for convenience, which brings huge agency risks virtually. Creditors, when failing to receive relevant fees from rural collective economic organizations, are entitled to ask payment from foreign investors. Though foreign investors may request for reimbursement by rural collective economic organizations after making the payment in theory, reimbursement is impractical due to its high cost.

It should be specially noted that most of the above risks are actually not directly related with foreign investors in strict legal sense. For example, liabilities for rural collective economic organizations' detaining compensation fees all rest on the organizations. However, land requisition disputes may just as easily turn into non-rational group event due to non-smooth judicatory remedy channels. Under such situation, subjects whose rights and benefits are infringed may easily criticize foreign investors whose existence leads to change in interest structure in the district. Once land requisition leads to group events, foreign-invested projects would naturally be influenced. At that time, local governments always choose to settle farmers in damage of the interests of foreign investors. So this legal risk in atypical sense should also be perceived.

8.3.3 Legal Risks in Contribution with Collectively Owned Land

Current Chinese laws allow farmland to be converted into construction sites without going through state requisition under the following situation: (a)Land used by farmers for establishment of enterprises, residence, public facilities and commonweal affairs for which collective land ownership remains though farmland is converted into construction sites; (b)For enterprises jointly established by rural collective economic organizations and other organizations or individuals in the form of equity participation with land use right and joint operation, farmland may be converted into non-agriculture construction sites through administrative approval in accordance with land utilization plan; (c)If an enterprise obtains construction sites in legal accordance with overall land use plan and transfers land use right due to bankruptcy, merge and other similar reasons, the transfer may be an exception to the provision that farmers' collective land use right could not be assigned, transferred or leased for non-agriculture construction.

Article 60 of *the Land Administration Law* contains clear stipulation concerning the second situation mentioned above. For the establishment of an enterprise using the land for construction determined by the overall planning for rural(township) land utilization by a rural collective economic organization or joint establishment of an enterprise with other units and individuals in the form of equity participation of land use right and joint operations, an application should be filed at the competent department of land administration of the local people's government at or above the county level with the approval document which shall be subject to the approval of local people's government at or above the county level pursuant to the limits of authority of approval prescribed by the provinces, autonomous regions and municipalities directly under the Central Government; among them, for cases involving occupation and use of agricultural land, formalities of examination and approval shall be completed pursuant to the provisions of Article 44 of this Law. Land for construction for the establishment of enterprises pursuant to the provisions of the preceding paragraph must be strictly controlled. The provinces, autonomous regions and municipalities directly under the Central Government may, in accordance with the different trades and management scale of rural and township enterprises provide respectively for the standards for land use.

The so-called Nanhai Mode appeared in practice is the representation of the above land use way. Since 1992, Nanhai municipal government has made use of the opportunity of large scale factory establishment with local and external capital, allowing collective economic organizations make overall plan of collective land under the precondition of remaining land ownership nature and lease land or factory buildings to enterprises, which breaks the state's monopoly in requisition of farmlands for non agriculture purpose. In 2002, there were altogether 150,000 acres industrially used lands in Nanhai, among which 73,000 acres of land was no longer collectively owned by means of non requisition, accounting for about half of the total. Under the Nanhai mode, farmers enjoy great increase of market value of land through equity participation of land. Nanhai municipal government sums up and pushes forward land system renovation in village level, standardizing land share system as follows: (a)creating a so-called 'three districts' plan and dividing land into a cropland protection district, economic development district and commercial residence according to land functions so as to protect farmland and implement town planning; (b)converting collective properties, land and farmers' land contracting rights into shares, making statutes concerning stock right setting, dividend allocation and stock right management so as to confine village shareholding organizations' operation activities. Meanwhile, Nanhai municipal government announces allocation of land stock rights to be lifelong and inheritable. According to investigation by the research team of the development research center of the State Council, the effect of Nanhai land share system is obvious. First, the threshold for industrialization is lowered through initiation of industrialization with collective land, which may promote the exploration of new industrialization in the Zhu Jiang Delta Area. Second, different from state requisition of land, collective organizations may win land rent value after paying relevant taxes and allocate it to all farmers according to their stock rights. Third, farmers' land contracting rights are turned into permanent rights to collect share dividend, which not only reserves the reasonable core of family contracting system but also extends farmers' land proceeds right into the process of non agriculture conversion of land.

Special attention should be paid to this more and more popular mode in China: (a)Land contributed by rural collective economic organizations as capital contribution or joint operation condition must be within the scope of construction used land determined by the overall blueprint for rural(township) land utilization and could not be determined at discretion of rural collective organizations; (b)Only construction used land within that proposal may be contributed by rural collective organizations as equity participation for joint operation. If impropriation of farming land is involved, rural collective organizations are not entitled to directly change it into construction used land for equity participation or joint operation and shall handle approval procedure according to the land requisition process stipulated in Article 44 of *the Land Administration Law*; (c)Attention should be paid to whether rural collective organizations accomplish internal decision making process before contributing land for equity participation or joint operation. Though there is no provided legal process for internal decision making, regular rural collective organizations normally have documents such as statutes stipulating decision making process concerning important issues. Furthermore, it is stipulated in Article 15 of *the Land Administration law* that for land collectively owned by peasants contracted out for management by units or individuals other than those in the respective collective economic organization, it must have the consent of over two thirds of the members of the peasants' conference or over two thirds of the villagers' representatives and be submitted to the village (township) people's government for approval, which may be taken as reference.

8.3.4 Legal Risks in Land Offered by Local Governments for Free

In practice, some local governments promise to offer land at free of cost to foreign investors in order to attract investment. There are three commonly adopted ways of operation as follows: first, allocation of land to foreign investors for commercial use for free; second, exemption of land transfer fee, transferring land to foreign investors for free; third, promising free use of land by foreign investors in conference minutes or other documents without any legal transfer or assignment proceeding handled.

Local governments' free offers of land to foreign investors lower foreign investors' investment cost, but bring great legal risks to foreign investors at the same time. First, free transfer of land for commercial use conflicts with China's land administration laws in general with few exceptions. It is stipulated in Article 54 of *the Land Administration Law* that use of state-owned land for a construction project should be obtained in the form of payment use such as assignment; however, the following use of land for construction may be obtained in the form of appropriation subject to the approval of the people's government at or above the county level in accordance with law: (a) land use by state organs and land use for military purposes; (b) land use for urban infrastructure and land use for non-profit undertakings; (c) land use for such infrastructure as energy, communications and water conservancy to which the state renders key support; and (d) other land uses prescribed by laws and administrative regulations. China also issued *The Catalog of Allocated Land* for standardization of land allocation. Only construction projects within the scope of the catalog may use allocated land, otherwise breach of law may occur. Once the state tightens its land policy or MOLR investigates, the projects using land in breach of laws would be canceled. Second, *the Land Administration Law* establishes a basic principle of payment use of land. The construction units shall obtain state-owned land through way of payment use such as assignment. Exemption of land assignment fee and free transfer of land to foreign investors also go against *the Land Administration Law*. Third, if a foreign investor appropriates land for free according to negotiation minutes or conference minutes with local governments without any legal transfer or assignment proceeding handled, the investment project may be lacking in stable land basis and legal basis. Under such situation, the stability of land use by foreign investors cannot be ensured. Finally, it needs to be pointed out that the second and third modes lay a dangerous path for foreign investors or foreign-invested enterprises under the interference, control or threat of local governments. Operation place is an essential resource in the sound operation of an enterprise and the land always has enormous value. If the will of the government cannot be realized or enforced in a foreign-invested project, the government may rely on the land to threaten the foreign investor or foreign-invested enterprise to accept its intention. Otherwise, the government may request foreign the foreign investor to pay land transfer fees with magnificent reasons, or take back land appropriated by the foreign-invested project by deeming conference minutes could not form legal basis for the foreign investor's obtain of land use right. Facing risks of paying large amount of transfer fee or losing land, the foreign investor or foreign-invested enterprise must comply with the government's will or sell off the enterprise and withdraw the investment. Therefore, foreign investors should be prudent when accepting local governments' free offer of land. In any case, it is a simple rule that there is no free lunch in the world.

8.3.5 Lack of Judicial Remedy to Land Disputes

Since the land system of China is quite complicated, land disputes may easily occur in foreign investment if no sufficient diligence is paid thereto. However, it is quite a pity that China lacks smooth channels for judicial remedies of land disputes. Many land disputes cannot be accepted by courts and be effectively settled through judicial process, but can only be settled by government mediation.

First, according to Article 16 of *the Land Administration Law*, disputes over land ownership and the right to use shall be resolved by the parties interested through consultation; it shall be handled by the people's government in the event of failure of consultation. Disputes between units shall be handled by people's governments at or above the county level; disputes between individuals and those between an individual and a unit shall be handled by the village-level people's governments or people's governments at or above the county level. The party interested that refuses to obey the decision on the handling by the people's government concerned may, within 30 days starting from the date of receipt of the notice on the decision on handling, file a suit at a people's court. It is generally agreed that the litigation object is the government's handling decision instead of the dispute itself. In another word, the court may only examine whether the government decision is wrong in fact finding or law application instead of the disputed issue itself. Meanwhile, it is stipulated in the article that neither party shall alter the status of land utilization prior to the resolution of the dispute over the land ownership and the right to use. Due to such stipulation, foreign-invested projects may face great legal risks if competitors or other interested parties cause disputes maliciously.

Secondly, land requisition compensation disputes are excluded by courts and can only be settled through government mediation. It is stated in Article 25 of *the Regulations on Implementation of the Land Administration Law of PRC* that disputes on compensation standard shall be mediated by local people's governments at or above the county level and be adjudicated by the people's government approving land requisition if mediation fails. Land requisition compensation and resettlement disputes may not influence enforcement of land requisition plans. The People's Supreme Court of PRC made reply to Zhejiang Higher People's Court's Application for Instructions Concerning the Land Requisition Compensation Allocation Dispute Case of Xu Zhijun and other ten persons v. the Village Commission of the Eighth Village of Longyuan Town, Longquan City with (2002) Min Li Ta Zi No. 4 Notice, clarifying that according to Article 47.2 of *the Land Administration Law of PRC*, Article 25 and 26 of *the Regulations on Implementation of the Land Administration Law of R.R.C.* and relevant judicial interpretation by the Supreme People's Court, compensation for state's requisition of farmers' plowland includes land compensation fee, subsidy for resettlement as well as compensation fee for ground appendixes and young crops. Land compensation fees belong to rural collective economic organizations, could only be used for developing production and arranging employment, and could not be embezzled or misappropriated. Disputes between members of rural collective economic organizations and rural collective economic organizations because of land compensation fees do not belong to civil legal relation between equal subjects and do not fall within the scope of civil litigation accepted by people's courts. Such disputes may not be accepted by people's courts according to law and shall be mediated by relevant administration departments. As to whether people's courts may accept disputes arising out of resettlement subsidies, analysis shall be made according to concrete situations. If resettlement subsidies are paid to, managed and used by rural collective economic organizations which arrange resettlement of persons needing to be resettled, disputes arising thereof do not fall within scope of civil litigation accepted by people's courts and people's courts shall not accept such disputes as civil cases. Disputes arising out of direct payment of resettlement subsidies to persons do not need resettlement arrangement by rural collective economic organizations, rather fall under the category of civil right and obligation disputes between equal subjects and shall be accepted by people's courts as civil cases.

In practice, the most disputed issue is land requisition compensation, but most of land requisition disputes are excluded from channels of judicial remedy. Land ownership disputes are also common in foreign investment, but judicial remedy is still hard to obtain for them. Therefore, once land disputes occur in foreign investment, foreign investors may face collective campaigns of appeal to higher authorities for help with Chinese characteristics or even other ones beyond current system, which may cause problems in social stability and make the disputes complicated. When foreign investors seek government mediation, governments always make consideration from the standpoint of keeping social stability. Thus, foreign investors' interest cannot be effectively protected.

9 Labor Legal Risks of Foreign-Invested Enterprises

Evidences show that conflict between labor and employer-employee with establishing Trade Union as representation has turned to be an unavoidable problem of foreign-invested enterprises.

—— All China Federation of Trade Unions

9.1 Labor Legal Risks Shown in Trade Union Disputes

9.1.1 Widespread Foreign Enterprises' Refusal of Establishing Trade Unions

Walmart has established 37 stores in 18 Chinese cities including Shenzhen, Beijing, Dalian, Kunming, Xiamen and Fuzhou etc, employing approximately 190,000 Chinese. However, these Walmart stores do not have any trade unions established for the reason that Walmart has the tradition of no trade union and the stores in China should not be the exception.[1] All the chain stores of Walmart over the world adopt the same mode, which is, raising production rate, lowering wages and welfare, forbidding trade union and offering goods with lower price than its competitors. Such operation mode has been determined as the special economic term 'walmartization'. America Kodak (Xia'men) Co., Ltd. put forward that establishing trade union organization is the internal agreement of the trade union with no relation with the enterprise. Since Kodak is the brand of the company, no organization could use it without permission and the trade union could not be named as Kodak trade union. The company would not offer facilities to the trade union organization and the trade union could not have its place for work or other activities at the company. The managing personnel of the company could not attend trade union activities. Other enterprises refusing to establish trade unions include Dell, Samsung, McDonald's, KFC and so on. These influential big companies' resistance influences other large-scale foreign enterprises. Even worse, some local governments, to attract more foreign capital, accept foreign enterprises' condition

[1] After my completion of the book, July 29, 2006, Walmart set up the first trade union in Quanzhou city, Fujian province as the result of two years tussling with All China Federation of Trade Unions.

of establishing no Trade Union and include such condition in violation of the Trade Union Law into the investment agreement.

> Trade unions appeared as the opposite of the capital side. For foreign enterprises, it may cost much to establish trade unions. *The Trade Union Law of PRC* stipulates that an enterprise shall bear as much trade union expense as 2% of the total wage. 60% of such expense shall be paid back to the employees as welfare while another 40% shall be submitted to the higher level trade union. This means that the enterprise has to pay the expense at the amount of 2% total wage which cover all employees including foreign ones with high salary in foreign-invested enterprises even if only a small portion of employees attend the trade union. Foreign companies may hesitate about doing so since no one would like to pay for possible enemies.

There were 734,000 non-state-owned enterprises with 24,879,000 trade union members at the end of 2003 but only 13 foreign enterprises have joined federations of trade union. According to a survey in the Pudong New District of Shanghai, there were 10,720 foreign-invested enterprises (including 3,847 offices or agencies) in Shanghai at the end of 2001 with 720,100 employees. However, the constitution of trade union organizations was still lagged far behind. Only 30% of these enterprises had trade unions established and trade union members only accounted 63% of the employees. In practice, some foreign-invested enterprises, especially those invested by large-scale multinationals, refuse to establish trade unions in no regard of Chinese laws.[2]

9.1.2 Risks Increasing in Refusal to Establish Trade Unions

China makes clear legal stipulations about establishing trade unions in foreign-invested organizations. It is stated in *the Regulations for The Implementation of The Law on Sino-foreign Equity Joint Ventures* that 'Staff and workers of a joint venture have the right to set up grass-roots trade unions and carry on trade union activities in accordance with *the Trade Union Law* and the Constitution of the Trade Unions of China'. *The Law on Sino-foreign Cooperative Joint Ventures* stipulates that 'The staff and workers of a Cooperative joint venture shall, in accordance with law, establish their trade union organization to carry out trade union activities and protect their lawful rights and interests'. It is stated in *the Law on Wholly Foreign Owned Enterprises* that 'Workers and staff of enterprises with foreign capital may organize trade unions in accordance with the law, in order to

2 Peng Shulan (2003), The Survey of Trade Union Status in Enterprises with capital from Taiwan, Hongkong or Maicao , Research of Trade Union Theories, Issue 6. In addition, newest statistics shows 39.3 thousands trade unions have been set up by foreign-invested enterprises which just occupy 1/4 of total foreign-invested enterprises.

conduct trade union activities and protect their lawful rights and interests. The enterprises shall provide the necessary conditions for the activities of the trade unions in their respective enterprises'. *The Trade Union Law* states that 'All workers doing physical or mental work in enterprises, public institutions and government organs within Chinese territory who earn their living primarily from wages shall have the right to participate in and form trade union organizations pursuant to the law, regardless of their nationality, race, sex, occupation, religious beliefs or level of education'. It is stipulated in the Constitution of the Trade Unions of China that ' Basic level units in enterprises, public institutions and government organs with over 25 trade union members may establish basic level trade union commissions while those with less than 25 members may choose one organizing member. Organizing members of neighboring or similar units may unite to set up basic level trade union commissions'. *Regulations on Trade unions in Sino-foreign Equity Joint Ventures of Shanghai* and other local regulations even states the basic rights of enterprise trade unions in detail which mainly include the following eight ones: (a) to attend meetings held by the board of directors of the enterprise discussing important issues such as development plans of the enterprise, the production and operation, etc. as observers to reflect the employees' opinions and requests. When the board of directors or the administrative authorities researches and decides such issues as award or punishment of employees, salary mechanism, welfare, labor protection, labor insurance and so on, the trade union representatives are entitled to attend the meeting as observers while the board of directors or the administrative authority shall hear the trade union's opinions and find its cooperation; (b)to represent employees to sign collective employment contract or agreement with the enterprise, guide employees to sign personal contracts with the enterprise, and supervise the execution of the contracts according to law. (c)to supervise the enterprise' execution of the state's rules and regulations on labor insurance, labor protection, protection on women's special interests and so on; (d)to participate in investigation in accidents involving employees' injury of death in work and suggest on the disposal; (e)to supervise the enterprise execution of work time system and vacation system; if the enterprise wants to extend the work time, it shall be agreed by the trade union; (f)to supervise the use of the enterprise welfare funds, urge and assist the enterprise to run well the collective welfare project; (g)the enterprise, when firing or punishing employees, shall consult the trade union in advance; the trade union is entitled to raise objection if it finds such deeds unreasonable and negotiate with the enterprise for settlement; if the negotiation fails, the trade union may support the employees to submit the disputes to the labor dispute arbitration commission for arbitration, and may support the employees to litigate in the people's courts if the employees do not accept the arbitration awards;(h) other rights under laws and regulations.

Since severe problems are exposed in foreign organizations such as foreign-invested enterprises and representative offices, Chinese execution organizations have already started to strengthen the supervision of labor problems, especially taken decisive measures on the issue of establishing trade unions in foreign-invested enterprises. In September 2004, the law execution inspection group of the Standing Committed of the People's Congress carried out the inspection on the execution of the Trade Union Law in 11 provinces. On 25 October 2004, the All-China Federation of Trade Unions made public announcement that a large number of enterprises not establishing trade unions according to Chinese law in long term, including international famous transnational corporations, would be listed in the 'blacklist' of the federation.

On the other side, the international community is bringing pressure to bear on enterprises concerning the trade union issue. On 21 August 2005, the Union Network International (UNI) held meeting at Chicago, U.S.A. to declare war against Walmart, requesting Walmart to negotiate on wages and other issues. UNI represents 900 trade union organization members of over 140 nations all over the world. Mr. Philip Jennings, the Secretary in charge of UNI said that 'trade unions shall adjust them to the globalized world with no boundary of nations'. UNI would associate with trade unions of various nations to organize local Walmart employees, helping them enjoy relevant welfare and preventing the spread of Walmartization in the world.

9.1.3 Reflection of Tense Employer-Employee Relation by Refusal of Establishing Trade Unions

In fact, even without the pressure from the government, labor capital relation has been an obstacle to the development of enterprises in great degree. Since 2003, Chinese labor disputes cases have been increased at the rate of 30-40% per year, which is much higher than the increase of GDP. The internal conflicts of foreign-invested enterprises are more serious than those of enterprises of other types. It is shown in *the Survey Report of Labor Relation in Foreign-invested Enterprises in Guangzhou* made by the special topic investigation group of Guangzhou Municipal Bureau of Justice in 1999 that the labor disputes appeared to be increased year by year in foreign-invested enterprises at Guangzhou. According to the statistics of Guangzhou labor department, there were 180 labor dispute cases involving joint ventures, cooperatives and wholly foreign owned enterprises accepted in 1997, accounting to 21.4% of the total labor dispute cases of Guangzhou. Among the 180 cases, 93.8% ones are raised by laborers. The proportion of labor arbitration cases involving labor disputes in foreign-invested enterprises goes far beyond the proportion of such enterprises' quantities (6.2%) and employees (15%). Concerning the reasons for such disputes, 85 cases involve labor contracts, with much concerned with salaries and social insurance, the proportion are 35% and 12.8% respectively. Furthermore, 55 cases involve cacannies and strikes due to labor disputes, accounting for 36% of the accepted cases. Since more than 60% of the employees of such enterprises are from other places, the employees are of junior level and have less sense of self protection with law. Some conflicts are still not publicized.[3] Labor disputes have turned to be a social problem instead of problem of enterprises. Labor and management relation has great influence on the economic growth, social development and market economy system trend of China. All the evidence show that the labor and management relation contradiction with the establishment of trade unions as representation has been an unavoidable issue for foreign-invested enterprises.

9.2 Overview on Foreign-Invested Enterprise Labor Law Rules

9.2.1 Foreign-Invested Enterprise Labor Legislation

General Provisions

The Labor Law of PRC was promulgated in 1994. *The Trade Union Law of PRC* was promulgated in 1992 and amended in 2001. The National People's Congress and its Standing Committee have not made any specific law for the adjustment of labor relation in foreign-invested enterprises. The above two laws are applicable to foreign-invested enterprises as well. They are the most basic legal provisions for the adjustment of labor relation in foreign-invested enterprises at present.

Labor Law Rules in Foreign-Invested Enterprise Laws

Such rules include the Law on Sino-foreign Equity Joint Ventures issued in 1979, the Law on Sino-foreign Cooperative Joint Ventures issued in 1986, and the Law on Wholly Foreign-owned Enterprises issued in 1988, and their implementation regulations or detailed rules. Before the promulgation of the Labor Law, the adjustment of labor relation in foreign-invested enterprises mainly rely on the above three laws. After the promulgation of the Labor Law, the three laws have not been abandoned. In the sense of the legal effect, the above three laws are basic laws made by the National People's Congress while the Labor Law is only a general law made by the Standing Committee of the National People's Congress. Therefore, if the three laws conflict with the Labor Law, the former shall be applied with priority. However, there is little conflict between them since the Labor Law absorbed certain regulations in the three laws and there is only one principal article concerning the employment in each of the three laws.

---

[3] The Special Topic Investigation Group of Guangzhou Municipal Bureau of Justice (1999), The Survey Report of Labor Relation in Foreign-invested Enterprises in Guangzhou – For Construction of Lawful Employment Environment and Promotion of Steady Social Development, Guangzhou Economic Administration Cadres Institute Magazine, Issue 1.

Labor Administrative Rules and Regulations Applicable to Foreign-Invested Enterprises

Concerning foreign investment, the State Council have altogether made two important labor administrative rules, that is, *the Regulations on Labor Administration for Sino-foreign Cooperative Joint Ventures* promulgated in 1980, *the State Council's Regulations on Encouragement of Foreign Investment* promulgated in 1986. The former is mainly supplementary to provisions in *the Law on Sino-foreign Cooperative Joint Ventures* concerning employment, making general provisions concerning the right and obligation relationship between the labor side and the capital side in Sino-foreign Cooperative joint ventures. The latter mainly purports to encourage foreign investment, stipulating some favorable policies covering employment and other issues. Besides, Chinese labor administrative authorities, foreign economic and trade authorities and other government authorities have made some department regulations. The main regulations applicable to labor issues of foreign-invested enterprises include *the Regulations on Labor Administration of Foreign-invested Enterprises* issued by the former Ministry of Labor (Now the Ministry of Labor and Social Security) and the former Ministry of Foreign Trade and Economic Cooperation in 1994, which contains specific provisions on labor relation and labor administration of various foreign-invested enterprises. Other important regulations include *the Regulations on Administration of Taiwan, Hong Kong and Macao Residence Obtaining Employment in Mainland* issued by the former Ministry of Labor in 1994, *the Regulations on Administration of Foreigners' Obtaining Employment in China* issued by the former Ministry of Labor, the Ministry of Public Security, the Ministry of Foreign Affairs and the former Foreign Trade and Economic Cooperation Ministry in 1996.

9.2.2 Provisions on Labor Contracts of Foreign-Invested Enterprises

According to *the Labor Law* and relevant regulations, foreign-invested enterprises may hire employees by themselves while writing labor contracts shall be executed.

Term of Labor Contracts

Term of labor contracts may be divided into three types, that is, fixed term, non fixed term and term depending on the accomplishment of certain work.

Salary

Foreign-invested Enterprises may decide salary level and bonus allocation way according to their production and operation status and profits level. China adopts the minimum wage guarantee system. Local governmental departments make and announce the local minimum wage level. Salaries paid by foreign-invested enterprises shall be no less than the local minimum wage.

Work Time

Foreign-invested enterprises may adopt the system of standard work hours, complexly calculated work hours or unfixed work hours. Under the system of standard work hours, employees shall work no more than 8 hours per day and no more than 40 hours per week.

Foreign-invested enterprises may extend work hours for production and operation purpose. Under the condition of ensuring employees' health, the extended hours shall be no more than 3 hours per day, 36 hours per month. Foreign-invested enterprises shall pay overtime wage to employees according to the following standards: (a)For overtime work on work days, the overtime wage shall be no less than 150% of the normal wage; (b)For overtime work on rest days without the missed rest made up, the overtime wage shall be no less than 200% of the normal wage; (c)For overtime work in legal holidays, the overtime wage shall be no less than 300% of the normal wage.

Complexly calculated work hour system or unfixed work hour system may be applied to employees of foreign-invested enterprises or other ones to whom the standard work hour could not be applied.

Work Security

Foreign-invested enterprises are obliged to establish work security system, implement work security standards made by the governments, carry out security education of employees, and offer work security condition and labor protection articles.

Cancellation of Labor Contracts

(a) Negotiated Cancellation: foreign-invested enterprises may negotiate with employees to cancel labor contracts by agreement.

(b) Legal Cancellation: there are two kinds of legal cancellation, that is, cancellation with negligence and cancellation without negligence.

Cancellation with negligence: foreign-invested enterprises may cancel labor contracts if any of the following circumstances occur to employees: (1) to be proved to be unqualified for the employment condition during the probationership; (2) to seriously violate enterprises' work discipline or administration system; (3) to severely damage enterprise interests due to serious breach of duty or jobbery; (4) to bear criminal liabilities.

Cancellation without negligence: foreign-invested enterprises may cancel work contracts under following circumstances, but shall notify employees in person 30 days ahead of schedule: (1) if an employee is sick or injured not for work reason and could not be engaged to the former job or other jobs arranged by the enterprise after the expiration of the medical treatment; (2) if an employee is not competent for his work or could not be competent for his work after training or being adjusted to other posts;

(3) if the former work contract could not be performed due to great changes happened to the objective situation under which the contract is executed while the enterprise and the employee could not reach agreement on alteration of the work contract.

(c) Economic layoffs: a foreign-invested enterprise, if facing bankruptcy and having legal reconstruction or facing serious difficulties, may reduce its staff after reporting to the government labor administration department, but shall explain the situation to the trade union or all employees 30 days ahead of schedule.

Compensation

Under any of the following situations, foreign-invested enterprises shall pay labor contract cancellation compensation to employees: (a) If the enterprise bring forward contract cancellation for cancellation through negotiation;(b)cancellation without negligence under legal cancellation circumstances; (c)economic layoffs. The enterprise shall pay the employee compensation equal to one month salary for each year the employee working at the enterprise according to his actual work years. Under certain circumstances, the compensation shall be no more than 12-month salaries. If the employee's monthly average wage is lower than the average level of the enterprise, the enterprise shall pay compensation according to the latter.

Secrecy

Foreign-invested enterprises may agree with employees on issues related to keeping enterprise trade secrets and competition limitation in work contracts.

Collective Contracts and Trade Union

Foreign-invested enterprises may sign collective contracts with employees, stipulating work remuneration, work time, rest and holidays, work security, insurance and welfare, etc. The draft collective contract shall be submitted for discussion and approval by the employee representatives' meeting or by the staff. The collective contract shall be signed between the trade union representing employees and the enterprise. If no trade union is established within the enterprise, the contract shall be signed by representatives recommended by the employees.

Dispute Resolution

If labor disputes occur between a foreign-invested enterprise and its employee, either party may apply to local labor dispute arbitration commission for arbitration. The applicant shall submit written application to the arbitration commission within 60 days after the labor dispute happens. The arbitral award is generally made within 60 days after receiving the application for arbitration. If any party is discontent with the arbitral award, it may litigate in local courts within 15 days after receiving the arbitral award. If one party fails to litigate in courts within the legal period, another party may apply to courts for mandatory enforcement of the arbitral award. Labor arbitration is the precondition of litigation. No party can litigate in courts without going through the labor arbitration procedure.

9.3 Insight into Foreign-Invested Enterprises' Labor Risks

Labor and Management are both contradictory and uniform. No enterprise could escape labor dispute during its production and operation. It is obvious that the normal production and operation of an enterprise may be influenced if it has too many labor dispute cases and many people involved therein. The economic benefit may be damaged and even the loss, production stop and bankruptcy may occur in the enterprise. This is one of the reasons for foreign-invested enterprises' failure in investing in mainland. Many real cases existed showing enterprises' collapse for labor disputes. For example, the book titled *the Research of Cases in Which Taiwan Investors Fail in Mainland* collects 21 cases involving Taiwan investors' failure in investing in mainland, among which 7 cases are because of inappropriate handling of labor capital problems.

9.3.1 Case Analysis of Foreign-Invested Enterprises' Legal Risks

Penalty for Representative Offices' Hiring Employees in China without Permission: An employee complained that the Qingdao Representative Office of a foreign-invested enterprise had not signed labor contract with him nor pay for his social insurance fee during his work in the office from May 1999 to November 2001, and applied for correction of such action. The labor supervision department, after accepting the case, investigated and verified. The department found through investigation that the office is the Qingdao representative organization or the foreign enterprise. It hired 4 unemployed persons in town and 1 migrated worker from 1999 to April 2002 without employment procedures accomplished, labor contracts signed, or social insurance fees paid. According to *the Provisional Regulations on Administration of Foreign Enterprises' Representative Organizations in Qingdao,* 'representative organizations in Qingdao, when hiring Chinese employees within the nation, shall sign employment contracts with the service agencies appointed by the municipal government. The representative organizations in Qingdao shall abide by relevant labor laws, rules and regulations, provide necessary work conditions for Chinese employees, and respect lawful rights of Chinese employees'. In this case, the Qindao

> Representative organization of the foreign enterprise severely breached the above provision and infringed the lawful rights and benefits of the employee. Therefore, the labor supervision department issued *the Labor Guarantee Supervision Correction Order* to the Representative Office, requesting it make correction within specified time and making administrative punishment according to the situation.

Foreign-invested enterprises normally take the form of Sino-foreign Equity Joint Ventures (EJV), Sino-foreign Cooperative/Cooperative Joint Ventures (CJV), Wholly Foreign-owned Enterprises (WFOE), representative offices (RO) or branches of foreign companies (branches). There are different legal provisions for different type foreign-invested enterprises' hiring of employees. Generally speaking, EJV, CJV, WOFE or branches may directly hire employees while the representative offices could not do so. Representative offices shall engage an agent with qualification to sign labor contract as the nominal employer, delegate employees to the representative offices under the name of the offices, and handle all issues concerning employment. Therefore, the representative offices often reserve rights of inspecting and modifying important articles and conditions in labor contracts. The representative offices shall pay for the service of agents while the price is normally fixed by the parties through negotiation. However, such price is mainly up to the remuneration and other welfare the representative offices pay for employees. Foreign companies with no foreign-invested enterprise or representative office in China could no hire employees in China.

For example, *the Regulations on Foreign Enterprises' Hiring of Chinese Employees in Beijing* states that the foreign affair service organizations, after being approved by relevant state departments, may engage in providing Chinese employees to the permanent representative offices of foreign enterprises within the administrative area of the city while no organization or individual could engage in such service without permission (Article 4). If a representative office of foreign enterprise intends to hire Chinese employees, it must entrust the foreign affair service organizations, for example Beijing Foreign Enterprise Service Group Co., Ltd. (FESCO), to handle relevant matters, and could not hire employees by itself or entrust other organizations or individuals to hire Chinese employees (Article 5). Chinese citizens must apply for jobs or be employed by representative organizations of foreign enterprises through foreign affair service organizations, and could not do so by themselves o through other organizations or individuals (Article 6).

9.3.2 Brief of Labor Legal Risks in Foreign-Invested Enterprises

China has published large amount of laws, rules, regulations, regulatory documents and judicial interpretation to regulate the labor employment actions of enterprises. These legal provisions are numerous, complicated and changeful, making foreign investors hard to follow. In addition, many foreign-invested enterprises do not act regularly in labor administration. They are facing plenty of legal risks in labor issues.

Legal Risks for Dismissal of Employees

The reasons for foreign-invested enterprises' dismissal of employees are mainly the employees' violation of internal discipline or incompetence for work, and economic layoffs. According to Article 25 of *the Labor Law of PRC*, if any of the following situations occurs to an employee, the employer may cancel the work contract without economic compensation made: (a) to be proved to be unqualified for the employment condition during the probationership; (2) to seriously violate enterprises' work discipline or administration system; (3) to severely damage enterprise interests due to serious breach of duty or jobbery; (d) to bear criminal liabilities. Under such situation, a foreign-invested enterprise may fire its employee without economic compensation made.

However, in practice, many foreign investors deem that an appropriate 'reason' may be found for dismissal in any way. Such self-confidence originates from the foreign investors' advantageous status against the employees but is sightless and unrealistic because relevant laws, for the protection of the inferior party, set certain conditions for foreign investors' dismissal of employees and aggravate the investors' responsibilities. For example, when the dispute arising out of an employee's discontent with a foreign company's dismissal decision is submitted to arbitration or litigation, the foreign company shall bear the onus probandi to prove that the dismissal decision is based on abundant facts and legal grounds. The foreign company is obliged to submit full and detailed evidence for the facts and laws it relies on for its dismissal decision so as to prove the dismissal reason is 'sufficient'. If such sufficiency could not be fully proved, the dismissal decision may be removed by the arbitration institution or courts. In practice, the losing rate of foreign companies is much higher than that of employees in dismissal disputes.

The judicatory departments generally take two measures against the enterprises' inappropriate dismissal of employees. If the employee prefers to continue work at the enterprise, the enterprise must accept and compensate for his income during the dispute. If the employee does not prefer continuing his work at the enterprise, the enterprise must pay economic compensation under the standard of his monthly average wage. In Guangdong province, the enterprise must pay one month advance notice fee. According to *the Labor Law* and other relevant regulations, if an enterprise dismisses its employee without reason, it shall compensate the employee one month average salary for each work year calculated according to his work time in the enterprise. Therefore, if an enterprise dismisses its employee without sufficient reason, it must pay the compensation. In addition, a foreign-invested enterprise may also fire its employee according to Article 26 and 27 of *the Labor Law,* but shall notify the employee in writing 30 days ahead and pay the compensation, otherwise labor disputes and legal liabilities may be caused.

Resignation Dispute

Resignation dispute refers to the labor dispute arising out of an employee's unilateral cancellation of work contract according to law or directly leaving the enterprise without relevant procedures handled. According to relevant provisions, the employee must follow certain procedures for resignation while the enterprise generally needs to pay no compensation and may request the employee to pay the breach penalty if it is so stipulated in the work contract. The enterprise may even ask for economic compensation if the resignation causes its loss. However, in practice, many foreign-invested enterprises do not act regularly and incur legal disputes.

(a) Set Barriers as Employees' Resignation Approval Wrongfully

At present, many foreign investors and their staff still deem that the resigning employee needs to write resignation application. However, the employee only need to notify the company 30 days ahead of his resignation according to law. There is no other requirement for resignation. The 'apply for approval' stated in the resignation application is only for politeness and has no legal sense. Many foreign companies request that the resigning employees get approval from the companies so as to protect the companies' interests, which infringe the employees' rights. Even if the employee does not hand over his work or has unresolved dispute with the company at resignation, the company could only let him go. If the foreign company deems that its interests are infringed, it may claim its rights through legal approach such as arbitration or litigation, but could not limit the employee's resignation.

(b) Legal Dispute for Refusal to Handle Work Termination Procedure

After the labor relationship is terminated, the employee may request the foreign-invested enterprise to handle work termination procedure. If the enterprise requests the employee pay breach penalty or repay training fees by using the refusal to handle work termination procedure as a measure or a threat in negotiation and such refusal causes the employee unable to find another job, the employee may raise the following requests to the enterprise according to law: first, the enterprise shall handle relevant work termination procedure immediately, including issue of work termination notice, transfer of files and so on; second, the enterprise shall pay the employee salary during the period in which the work termination is delayed and 25% of the salary as compensation calculated according to the employee's former salary standard.

> Mr. Wang is the former financial manager of a joint venture. On 1 January 2000, he signed a two year term work contract with the joint venture. At the end of 2001 when the contract is to be over since the joint venture showed no intent of extending the contract, Mr. Wang transferred his work to Mr. Zhang, an underling financial

> personnel by himself. Upon the second day after the expiration of the contract, Mr. Wang notified the joint venture to handle work termination procedure immediately. The joint venture, after receiving Mr. Wang's notice, refused to handle the work termination procedure for Mr. Wang since he had not submitted any resignation application to the joint venture nor formerly handed over his work. After failed in various negotiations, Mr. Wang submitted the dispute to labor arbitration, requesting the joint venture handle work termination procedure and compensate his losses for the delayed period (3 months) (calculated as the average wage of 12 months before the termination of the contract ×3 months ×125%). The labor arbitration commission, after hearing the case, awarded that Mr. Wang lost the case since he had not handed over the work appropriately and the joint venture may refuse to handle the work termination procedure temporarily for this reason. Mr. Wang was not convinced and litigated in court. The court, after examination, deems that the contract had been terminated since Mr. Wang did not intend to extend the contract at the expiration of the contract and the joint venture should finish the work termination procedure within 7 days after the termination of the contract. The handover of work shall not be relied upon as a defense for the joint venture's refusal of handling the procedure. The joint venture may litigate for it in another case. The court judged that Mr. Wang win the case.[4]

The reason for the employee's winning of the case is mainly that foreign-invested enterprises are obliged to handle work termination procedure within 7 days after the termination or cancellation of work relation under the current Labor Law of China, which is unconditional. It is also stipulated that enterprises shall compensate employees' losses due to delay in handling the procedure. The joint venture lost the case because it falsely regarded handling work termination procedure as its rights and advantages in negotiation. This risk is quite common and should attract attention of foreign investors.

Social Insurance Disputes

In January 1999, China promulgated *the Provisional Regulations on Collection of Social Insurance Fees* which stipulates that foreign-invested enterprises must make insurance registration at local social insurance agencies and pay various social insurance fees for employees according to laws, rules and local government orders while employees also bear certain payment obligations. These insurances all belong to the national mandatory social insurances, including basic employers'

4 From the China Human Resource Legal Website (the last visiting on 23 December 2004).

liabilities, basic medical treatment, unemployment and work-related injuries. Furthermore, foreign-invested enterprises must register at local housing accumulation fund administration organizations to pay housing accumulation fund for employees.

Not long ago, large amount of disputes were caused by foreign-invested enterprises' inactivity in paying social insurance fees. In recent years, such obviously illegal actions of foreign-invested enterprise have been greatly reduced along with the strengthening of supervision and inspection of social insurance. However, legal disputes of this type may still occur due to wrong cognition of details in social insurance. For example, many foreign investors deem that they need not pay social insurance fees for employees since the labor relation is not finally fixed during the probation period, which is not true. During the probation period, the labor relation has been formed though it may be terminated at any time. It is clearly stipulated in law that foreign-invested enterprise shall pay social insurance fees for employees in probation period.

The author summarizes eight common misunderstandings of foreign-invested enterprises over labor laws, which are briefly introduced as follows based on the common dispute features of foreign-invested enterprises:

(a) Wrongfully think that bylaws may bind employees. Effective bylaws must meet three conditions: first, the content of bylaws must be legal; second, the bylaws must be approved by the staff meeting or the staff representative meeting or at least the representatives of employees; third, the bylaws must be publicly announced to employees.

(b) Wrongfully think that enterprises may not be bound if they only sign probation contracts instead of labor contracts during the probation period. Even if a foreign-invested enterprise does not sign labor contract with the employees having labor relation with it, the actual labor relation between them are still protected by law. If the enterprise wants to terminate the actual work relation, it must notify the employee 30 days ahead and compensate him according to law. If only probation contract is signed and the probation period does not exist, the 'probation period' is the labor contract term.

(c) Wrongfully think employee resignation need approval by the enterprise. If an employee resigns, he only needs to notify the foreign-invested enterprise 30days ahead while there is no other condition.

(d) Wrongfully think handling work termination procedure for employees is the enterprises' rights or weights. Foreign-invested enterprises shall handle work termination procedure for employees 7 days after the cancellation or termination of labor relation. If delay in handling the procedure causes employee's losses, the enterprise shall compensate.

(e) Wrongfully think breach penalty may be agreed on by parties. In Shanghai, foreign-invested enterprises could only agree on penalty over breach of labor contract with two kinds of employees, one is the employees hired, trained or offered other special treatment by the enterprise, another is the employees under the obligation of keeping commercial secrets. The enterprises could not agree on breach penalty with other employees. Even if such agreement is reached, it is still invalid.

(f) Misunderstanding leads to expiration of arbitration or litigation period. The system of arbitration before litigation and proposing of arbitration is applied, so labor arbitration is the necessary proposing procedure of litigation, which means that if arbitration period really expires, the enterprise has also lost its right to win the suit even if litigation procedure is initiated.

(g) Wrongfully think foreign-invested enterprise are entitled to adjust posts of wages of employees at any time. The attitudes of the judicature departments are: first, the enterprises' right of self-determination in hiring employees is recognized and protected and the enterprises are allowed to adjust posts and wages of employees according to production and operation needs; second, abuse of such right, such as abusing the right to retaliate, is prevented along with the recognition and protection of the right; third, to prevent such abuse, foreign-invested enterprises shall provide evidence for such adjustment to prove that the adjustment is 'fully reasonable'.

(h) Wrongfully think enterprises may reduce staff when they do not make good profits. Limitations are set in law for foreign-invested enterprises' reduction of staff, including: first, layoffs only apply when the enterprise is close to bankruptcy and in legal reconstruction period or face great difficulties in production and operation and layoffs are really necessary; second, the enterprise shall explain the situation to the trade union or the staff 30 days ahead, hearing the opinions of staff meeting or staff; third, layoffs must be reported to labor administration departments and the departments opinions shall be respected.

9.4 Legal Risks Arising from Controversial China's Draft Labor Contract Law

9.4.1 Highlights of the Draft

The rather large and cheap supply of manpower that is currently available in China plays an important role in the decision making criteria for today's investors. In addition to this, the legal position of local employees is not especially strong and trade unions do not play an active role. To offset the abuses and poor working conditions particularly common to Chinese laborers, as well as to minimize employer-employee disputes, and stabilize the job market, A draft of *The Labor Contract Law* was passed by the State Council in October 2005 and is scheduled for the second reading by the Standing Committee of the National People's Congress. It could become law in the second half of this year. The seven-chapter draft is the country's first law governing the establishment, revision, and termination of labor contracts in PRC. Some of its more significant elements are summarized below.

Non-compete Provisions

There are no non-compete provisions in the existing *Labor Law*, but in practice, non-compete agreements are very common. There is a consensus that it is necessary for the Labor Law to include such stipulation. The current focus of controversy is the amount of compensation the employee shall be entitled to for the non-compete restriction. The Draft reduces the permissible duration for a post-termination non-compete restriction from the current three years to two years. New is that non-competes must have geographical limitations. Most importantly, under the Draft the former employer must pay the equivalent of no less than one hundred percent of the employee's annual salary to make the non-compete restriction enforceable. The Draft is silent on the payment mode. A previous draft fixed the payment at 50% of the employee's salary; it is therefore possible that this requirement will be subject to further discussions. New is a provision on liquidated damages payable by the employee for a breach of the non-compete clause. The Draft limits the damages to three times the amount paid by the employer to enforce the non-compete restriction. It is not clear whether this would be three times the amount already paid by the company at that time, or three annual salaries of the employee.[5]

Shortened Probationary Periods

Currently, probationary periods are limited by the length of the employment contract, not the job function. The draft law dictates that the length of the probationary period must be based upon the type of work conducted by employees. Probationary periods will be: No more than one month for workers in non-technical positions; No more than two months for employees with technical positions; and No more than six months for senior technical professional positions.

Fixed-Term Contracts

Because there is no at-will employment, employees are usually under contract. Currently, employers often use fixed-term employment contracts. Currently, all labor contracts can be terminated, but only in limited circumstances. The current practice is to use short-term contracts: if an employer wishes to let the employee go but has no sufficient termination ground, he could simply let the contract expire, without the need to pay severance. The Draft does not outlaw fixed-term contracts, but it strongly disencourages using them through the following measures: (1) fixed-term contracts cannot be terminated early, except for cause and in the case of mass lay-offs; (2) severance is payable if a fixed-term contract expires and is not renewed.

---

5 Andreas Lauffs (2006), China's Draft Labor Contract Law –Major Changes for Employers on the Horizon, Baker & McKenzie Client Alert, Feb Issue.

Union Consent Required with Mass-Layoffs

The Draft includes revised procedures to reduce headcount. Under current law, mass lay-offs are possible when the employer is on the verge of bankruptcy or where the employer experiences major difficulties in production. Under the draft law, employers are required to negotiate an agreement with the Trade Unions over any mass layoffs, which are defined as the need to lay off more than fifty workers. Failing to do so makes a unilateral lay-off decision voidable. Under the draft law, a "change of objective circumstances" test is required of companies to determine the need for mass lay-offs. This has been interpreted to include relocation of an enterprise, absorption of an enterprise through merger or the transfer of major assets. It would appear that a mere downsizing would not justify mass lay-offs. There is also a new requirement concerning the selection of employees. The company must retain, to the extent possible, employees with longer service years with the company.

Employee Handbooks and Company Rules

Under current rules, employee handbooks, employment manuals, work rules etc. must undergo an ill-defined "democratic procedure" to become enforceable. The Draft requires that company rules must be discussed and approved by the Trade Union or an employee representative body. Rules that are unilaterally issued by the company are void. Especially US-based companies, driven by Sarbanes-Oxley concerns about corporate governance, will need to examine the status of their handbooks and manuals for China.[6]

Role of Trade Unions Strengthened

The Draft confirms an existing requirement that employers notify trade unions prior to terminating a labor contract for any reason, even for cause. The employer must seek and consider the opinion of the Trade Union, and issue a written explanation of its final decision to the Trade Union. Several Shanghai courts have ruled that foreign-invested enterprises that have not established Trade Unions must notify the union at the next higher level; failure to do so would make a unilateral termination voidable. The Draft further strengthens the union's right to engage in collective bargaining and enter into collective contracts. It provides generally that any act taken unilaterally by the company without required union consultation is void, and that the matter shall be handled in accordance with a union proposal instead.

---

6 Id.

Pro-employee Provisions

The Draft includes many provisions that favor employees. Ambiguous labor contract terms should be construed in favor of the employee in the event of a dispute. The Draft also stipulates that if a labor relationship exists without a written labor contract, the term of the contract is deemed to be open-ended rather than fixed. Moreover, the Draft does not provide grandfathering for fixed-term preexisting labor relationships. This may mean that such contracts cannot be terminated other than for cause when the Draft becomes law.

9.4.2 Implications of the Draft

China's top legislature, the Standing Committee of the National People's Congress (NPC), has received more than 190,000 suggestions since it released the draft of the labor contract law to the public on March 21. Among them, the comments from the American Chamber of Commerce in Shanghai (AmCham Shanghai) and the European Chamber are most remarkable, which represent most foreign investors' attitude over the draft. More than 100 Chamber members of the American Chamber of Commerce in Shanghai (AmCham Shanghai) turned out for an expert briefing on China's proposed Labor Contract Law on March 8, 2006. Following extensive consultation with its members, the European Chamber has submitted comments on the draft Labor Contract Law to the Legal Affairs Committee of the National People's Congress. They warn several provisions of the current draft would result in the loss of rights rather than the gaining of rights, as the Draft law intends. The Draft law may also reduce employment opportunities for PRC workers and negatively impact the PRC's competitiveness and appeal as a destination for foreign investment.

The Law, if enacted in the current form, likely will really cause employers, including foreign-invested enterprises, to review and restructure their labor contracts and human resources policies.

In Feb – Mar 2006, Hewitt Associates surveyed 224 companies in China in order to determine how they were preparing for the new law. Among the 224 participants, 79.5% were North American companies, 12.7% were European companies, and the rest were from other geographic regions. The survey report shows that to prepare for compliance with the new regulations, respondents reply as follow table.

Table 9.1. Hewitt Associates Survey Result

Item	**Percent**
Audit or review HR policies	83%
Consult legal counsel for review of implications	79%
Conduct an employment contract audit	76%
Review manpower strategy	56%
Review non-compete agreements	53%

In general, proposed legal challenges arising from the current Draft mainly rest with two aspects, which are respectively the difficulty of intellectual property rights protection by non-compete clause in labor contract and the improvement of cost in hiring and maintenance of suitable employees. More or less, the change of labor legal environment initiated by the pass of the current Draft will augment the extent of which foreign-invested enterprises exposed to legal risks.

In general, proposed legal challenges arising from the current Draft mainly rest with two aspects, which are respectively the difficulty of intellectual property rights protection by non-compete clause in labor contract and the improvement of cost in hiring and maintenance of suitable employees. More or less, the change of labor legal environment initiated by the pass of the current Draft will augment the extent at which foreign-invested enterprises exposed to legal risks.

Part Three:

Legal Risks for Foreign Investment in Specific Industries

10 Modes and Legal Risks of Foreign Investment in Non-governmental Education in China

A non-insider may not be aware of the great difficulties non-governmental education faces in China.

—— By Mr. Ren Jingxi[1]

10.1 Introduction

Since China Social University was established in 1980 in Beijing, Chinese private universities have developed for over twenty years. Non-governmental education, first appearing as the supplement of governmental education in China, has played an active role in vocational training and other non-degree education fields. Owing to insufficient funding in state education and the diversity of educational demands, China's non-governmental schools were set up during the economic system's reform and are progressing with their own characteristics. At present, the main characteristics of non-governmental education in China are diversified, regional, market-oriented and a mix of different models.

Since the 1990's, non-governmental education has developed rapidly under the social background of market-oriented reform in the Chinese economic system. In 2001, there were altogether 61,200 private schools at different levels and in various patterns, holding 11,159,700 students on campus, among which there are 5,362 common middle schools holding 3,059,100 students on campus, 1,085 vocational middle schools holding 470,500 students on campus, 5,122 primary schools holding 2,221,400 students on campus and 48,400 kindergartens with 4,005,200 students on campus.[2] Though non-governmental education has only occupied a small share in the whole Chinese education system, the education resources gathered therefore are quite remarkable now: (a) For the 89 private colleges qualified in issuing diplomas, the total investment shall be RMB 4.5 billion counted in an average investment of RMB 50 million per school. For the 436 experimental schools holding examinations for higher education diplomas, the total investment

[1] Quoted from the Ten Years in the Purgatory of Education written by Mr. Ren Jingxi, the former Chairman of the Board of Directors for the South Ocean Groups.

[2] As reported by the Chinese Education Newspaper on 27 October 2000.

shall be RMB 4.4 billion counted in an average investment of RMB 10 million per school. For the remaining 677 private higher education institutions, the total investment shall be RMB 3.4 billion counted in an average investment of RMB 5 million per school. The afore-mentioned investments amount to RMB 12.3 billion. (b) For the 1,040 private vocational middle schools, the total investment shall be RMB 5.2 billion counted in an average investment of RMB 5 million per school. (c) For the 4,560 common middle schools, the total investment shall be RMB 22.8 billion counted in an average investment of RMB 5 million per school. (d) For the 4,880 private primary schools, the total investment shall be RMB 24.4 billion counted in an average investment of RMB 5 million per school. (e) For the 44,580 private kindergartens, the total investment shall be RMB 22.3 billion counted in an average investment of RMB 5 million per school. From the above, we may conclude that the total value of the fixed assets of schools with non-governmental education investment shall be over RMB 87 billion.[3]

Concerning foreign investment in non-governmental education, there are 59 projects funded by foreign investment in 2004 with an increase of 40.48%. The foreign investment contractual amount is USD 173 million with a decrease of 10.81%. The realized amount is USD 3,841,000 with a decrease of 29.03%. The international cooperation and exchange of education are mainly in the following three patterns: first, projects assisted by international organizations such as the World Bank; second, Sino-foreign cooperation in running schools; third, foreign capital's M&A; among which, the second one has been widely adopted by China in its international educational cooperation and exchange. Statistics show that, at the end of 2003, there were over 800 institutions and projects of Sino-foreign cooperation in operating schools. Currently, the Sino-foreign cooperation projects focus on such specialties as business management and economics while the specialties of engineering and high technology attract little attention, which is caused by concerns over the investment cost. Projects involving specialties of management and economics need less investment cost than those of engineering courses and high technology. China still lacks high quality resources in higher education though it has large amounts of projects of Sino-foreign cooperation in operating schools. Therefore, the relevant authorities such as the Ministry of Education, through a series of reconstruction activities, try to standardize the market and improve the quality of operating schools so that the specialties in urgent need may be introduced into China and the high quality of higher education resource imported into China may be insured. The non-governmental education market in China is developing fast with continuous commercial developmental potential. Foreign private schools and those joint venture capitals investing in the education industry are all eager to share the non-governmental education market in China. Acquiring a Chinese school is regarded as a short cut by them.[4]

---

3 As reported by the Chinese Education Newspaper on 27 October 2000.

4 As from the Ministry of Commerce's website for guidance of investment in China (www.fdi.gov.cn).

The contribution of non-governmental education under the lack of governmental education resource has been widely accepted. Its appearance turns out to be a social reform with great importance at the turn of the century in China. However, the contribution of non-governmental education in the fairness of education has been frequently omitted. Due to some improper propaganda and the high tuition of private schools, private schools were once regarded as schools for nobles. In fact, private schools, in only considering its offering of nearly 10 million education opportunities, has greatly improved the education fairness status in China, which is a typical social progress. As to the exclusion of common families due to high tuition, various reasons exist, including the incomplete market competition. Public schools, after established with governmental investment, may still enjoy benefits such as government subsidies, extra fees for migrants and so on while private schools, under the same treatment as enterprises, can only rely on themselves for fundraising and school running, and shall be responsible for its own profit and loss. Therefore, it is impossible for private schools to charge the same tuition as public schools.

The table below covers colleges and universities of various types approved by the state or provinces, in which the figures in brackets are the approximate numbers of colleges and universities for each type in 2002.

Table 10.1. Colleges and Universities Approved

	Normal Colleges and Universities	Adult Colleges and Universities
Diploma Education (Universities)	**Public (597)**	Public (686)
	Private (8)	
Non-diploma Education	**Public (548)**	
	Private (123)	
Other Colleges	**Private**	
	Public (80)	

(Quoted from the mid-term report on the Research of Private Higher Education in PRC submitted to international finance companies by the Sweden Development Consultation Company)

10.2 Foreign Investment Modes of Non-governmental Education

Non-governmental education investment refers to the investment actions or activities by various investors including individuals and enterprises who allocate part of their resources for the education business in the non-governmental education field in the form of currencies, lands or intelligence etc. The main features of private schools are self-reliance in raising funds, running schools and engaging teachers, and self-responsibility for profit and loss.[5]

The current patterns of non-governmental education investment in China are as follows:

Education Group Franchise

A regular chain has emerged in Chinese non-governmental education, the most outstanding feature of which is direct investment by large-scale education groups for the establishment of schools sharing the same brand and management. The education industry groups with universities as their leading force existing in China include Zhejiang Wanli Education Group, Ningbo Huamao (Education) Group, Kalun Lake Education Group, Wuxi Zhongrui Education Group, Heilongjiang East Asia Education Group, Beijing South Ocean Education Group and so on. Under the service-oriented idea and with the introduction of market mechanisms, these education groups have gradually realized the large scale operation of education.

> From 1994, South Ocean Education Group established 10 South Ocean international schools at Taiyuan, Datong, Luoyang, Chengdu, Qingdao, Kunming, Dalian, Shuyang, Jinan, Lianyungang. South Ocean University, located in China's capital city, Beijing, began in September 2003, with a total investment of RMB1,000,000,000. Occupying an area of 2,000 mu,, it is a Sino-foreign run college and university. The South Ocean Group has over 16,000 students and 2,600 teachers, staff and workers on its campuses. It has an education industry system involving pre-school education, basic education and higher education. An education pattern has been established by the South Ocean Group with its own characteristics, which accords with the non-governmental education tendencies of investment by groups, school-operating in chains, school management by specialties and appropriate industrialization.

College Town Pattern

College towns appeared at various places at the turn of the century, of which Hangzhou Xiasha College Town, Shanghai Songjiang College Town, Capital New Century College Town, Fuzhou College Town, Ningbo College Town, Beijing East College Town, Zhuhai College Town, Shenzhen College Town, etc. have already undergone their programming and startup. For example, East College town has turned to be a college kingdom containing five famous Chinese universities with different running ways.

---

5 Zhang Xuemin (2001), Education Economics, Southwest Normal University Publishing House, p107.

According to the current development trend, the management methods and operating ways of college towns are not the same. Some college towns mainly focus on attracting domestic and foreign universities to be part of them while others combine the independent running of school by the investor and the participation of other universities. Investors' roles in college towns are not clear as well. Some investors act as the managing and financing institution while others have double identities of running the school and investing. The key issue for college towns is obviously not the scale but the operational style and management method.

State-Owned Private Second-Level Colleges

Private second-level colleges held by public universities are emerging in Zhejiang, Jiangsu, Liaoning, Shanghai and other provinces and cities. From the background, we may see that the purpose for setting up second-level colleges is to relieve the pressure brought by enrollment expansion and the lack of education outlays, which is a kind of emergency schedule. However, private second-level college, a new mode, has maintained a strong momentum of development. Private second-level colleges are mainly divided into the following four types: first, solely established by public universities; second, co-established by public universities and enterprises; third, co-established by public universities and foreign educational institutions; fourth, co-established by public universities and domestic private universities. Concerning the above-mentioned four types, debates still exist with regard to the nature of private second-level colleges which have both the characteristics of public universities and running mechanism of private universities. In general, these second-level colleges are within the scope of private higher education since the school running bodies and investors are neither the state nor governments of different levels.

Transformation of Public Universities

State-owned private second-level colleges exist as a subsystem inside public universities. Transformation or restructuring of public universities is a completely new mechanism with a unique mode. For example, Zhejiang Wanli College is an experiment in the transformation of public universities. The predecessor of Zhejiang Wanli College is Zhejiang Normal College of Rural Technology. In 1999, Zhejiang provincial government, as approved by the Ministry of Education, ordered Zhejiang Normal College of Rural Technology to be run by Zhejiang Wanli Education Group. The ownership and the running power of the college are separated while the state-owned nature remains the same. The new investor brought in a market or private mechanism and the system of presidential responsibility under the guidance of the board of directors was adopted. Two years after initiating the transformation, the scale of the college had been enlarged and the level had been enhanced, thus winning it good reputation. With no increases in the input from state finance, the college, through maintaining education with education, created a new way of operating a school.

Shareholding System and Shareholding Cooperative System

Under the shareholding system, investors only invest but do not participate in the management of the school. The increment of capital is realized through stock rights. The company reinvests the funds from investors to establish a school from which the investors may enjoy benefits through their stock rights. Some second level colleges of certain universities are invested by enterprises, companies and governments who do not take part in the management of the colleges but enjoy their stock-rights benefits. A shareholding cooperative system is a form of running a school adopted by some small scale schools at their earlier stage, under which several investors jointly invest in a school and manage it together. These investors are also wage-workers. Acting as both owners and wage-workers, they realize the combination of labor and capital. Such a system is currently the basic pattern of investment in small scale schools.

> Private Hualian University is the first complex shareholding private university in Guangdong Province. It is also the only private university qualified to issue nationally accepted diplomas in China. The education shareholding system adopted by Hualian University, first started as a way of collecting funds under the shareholding system, has grown into a rather perfect education capital organizing system which combines fundraising, transformation of school management mechanism and operation mechanism. In 1993, the plan of setting up Hualian University to put the education shareholding system into practice was framed out. In April 1994, Guangdong Provincial government approved the establishment of Private Hualian University. In the same year, Hualian University obtained the qualification of recruitment as a common university for diploma education. In 1995, the initiators of Hualian University formally proposed to push the education shareholding system. After much discussion and deliberation, the draft of the Articles of Association for the Shareholding System of Private Hualian University came into being, stipulating the property rights, stock structure, operation mechanism, principle of allocating dividends, etc. of Hualian University in details, which is an exploration in standardization. Taking the concrete situation of the university into consideration, they determined the nature of the shareholding system to be a system focusing on the input of knowledge and the stock structure as corporation fund shares (initiators' shares and common shares having 30%, 25% and 45% stock rights respectively). Through this, the value of the initiators' knowledge and intelligence input, the importance of private fundraising, and the features of the private university are confirmed while flexibility is maintained for future share-buying by private funds in addition to strengthening the university's financial ability.

Listed Company Pattern

The pattern of introducing higher education into the capital market adopted by Chinese private universities for indirect financing and making profits through offering abroad has also emerged.

> Chongqing Hailian College and the listed Australian Amnet Company had their public offering successfully in Australia on 28 February 2002. Hailian College has 51% shares of the newly listed company with its assets of college buildings and land evaluated as RMB 340 million. As disclosed by relevant individuals, Hailian College made up its mind for cooperative offering at its establishment in January 2000. Amnet Company was set up in 1994. Its total share capital is RMB 120 million. Its business scope covers information technology and network services. Amnet promised to invest USD 2,100,000 in Hailian for the building of a sports ground and for enlarged enrollment. However, the two parties' cooperation is under the condition that Amnet shall bind Hailian into the listed company. Amnet announced it would spend USD 10 million on acquiring all of Hailian's fixed assets, for which it would offer 45,450,000 shares. Then, Amnet and Hailian would set up a joint venture for the management of Hailian. The president of Hailian College is to be the Chairman of the joint venture. The concrete operation method of Amnet binding Hailian for offering is that Amnet first shrinks its total capital stock of 125 million shares into 31.23 million shares in the proportion of 4:1, then offers 13.5 million shares with the selling price of USD0.2 per share. Those purchasing Amnet's shares shall obtain the stock rights of one share for every two shares with the term of three years at the purchasing price of USD 0.25 per share. Amnet then finally issues 45.45 million shares based on the assets of Hailian so that Chongqing Hailian may be accepted into tbe Australian Federal Exchange. Upon accomplishment, the total capital stock of Amnet will be 90.18 million shares. The fact is that Hailian is listed in a disguised form through acquisition by Amnet. Under such a pattern, Hailian is able to raise funds from abroad while Amnet, without changing its corporation structure, company name, share title, etc., becomes a listed company involving both information technology, website service and education. According to the two parties' plan, Amnet's next step is to issue new shares equal to RMB 20 million in Australia, enlarging stockholders' shares that are equal to RMB 50 million.

Many Chinese private universities are looking towards the capital market for the wider financing channels available through it. Statistics show that Heilongjiang East Asia Group, Xi'an Europe and Asia College, Xi'an Transportation University Siyuan College, Hubei Correspondence University, Hunan Foreign-Related Economy College, etc, have started up their operations for entering into the capital market with different progress levels.

Education Real Estate Pattern

Education Real Estate Pattern refers to the pattern under which a school is built, or jointly operated, by the education institution and investors, with land from the former and funds from the latter parties. After the school is built up, the investors may use a certain proportion of the real estate for business purposes so as to take back their investment.

> Beijing 21st Century Experimental School is a typical work of Xihua Education's, putting the theory of 'education real estate' into practice for its investment in education. It explores and forms a new school running mode in accordance with China's national power and situation, shifting from 'blood input' to 'blood making', which sets a successful example for the reform of non-governmental education. Beijing 21st Century Experimental School is a new-mode-experimental-school for which Beijing Haidian District Education Commission contributed land while Beijing Xihua Enterprise contributed funds. It was approved by the former Beijing Education Bureau in March 1993. The establishment convention was held on 20 May 1993. The foundation for the campus was laid on 8 September 1993. Its first term started on 1 September 1994. The school is located at Enji Village, Haidian District, Beijing with an area of 88,000 square meters and a construction area of 56,000 square meters.

10.3 Summary of Legal System for Non-governmental Education

At the beginning, China's non-governmental education had some spontaneity and evolution. Relevant legislation lagged behind the development of non-governmental education. China's government does not want to copy the model of state education to establish non-governmental education. So it is urgent to establish a relevant legal system to regulate the following aspects: economic nature of non-governmental education, ownership, admittance, rights of school and student, internal management system, evaluation of teaching quality, issuing of diplomas, equality between non-governmental education and public ones, and the management and regulation of transforming schools.

Great achievements have been made in the construction of China's educational legal system in the past 20 years. Starting from *the Ordinance on Academic Degrees of PRC* in 1978, China has altogether made seven education laws including the *Education Law of P.R.C, the Compulsory Education Law of PRC, the Vocational Education Law of PRC, the Teachers Law of PRC, the Higher Education Law of PRC* and *the Law on Promoting Non-governmental education of PRC*. The State Council has promulgated 16 educational administrative rules such as *the Temporary Regulation on Setting Common Colleges and Universities, the Temporary Regulation on Self-study Examination of Higher Education, the Regulation on School Running by Social Force* and so on. The educational administrative departments of the State Council have issued over 200 administrative regulations such as *the Temporary Regulations on School Running through Sino-foreign Cooperation, the Temporary Regulations on Setting Private Colleges and Universities, the Temporary Measure for Implementing Educational Administrative Punishment,* etc., which form the system of educational laws and regulations with *the Education Law* as the core and the specialized laws on education as the backbone. The contents of the system are quite mature while its structure is rather reasonable. At present, standardized legal relations have been set up in each aspect of China's education system. Laws have been made to ensure the strategic status of education which enjoys preferential development, to normalize the administrative conduct of educational administrative departments, to ensure schools' self-determination in operating, and to protect the legitimate rights and benefits of educatees. As to the debated and difficult issues arising out of the reforms on, and development of, education, legal and standard resolutions are being found.

Among them, what most deserves the attention of investors are certain vital laws and regulations with legal force concerning non-governmental education as follows: *the Regulations on School Running by Social Force of PRC* promulgated by the State Council in 1997, *the Law on Promoting Non-governmental education of PRC* promulgated by the National People's Congress in 2002, *the Regulations for Implementation of the Law on Promoting Non-governmental education of PRC* promulgated by the State Council in 2004, and local rules and regulations on non-governmental education issued by provincial, municipal or district People's Congress.

Table 10.2. Changing Non-governmental Education Policy

Name	Time of Issuance	Main Content
Decision on Reform of Education System by the Central Committee of the Communist Party	27 May 1985	Local authorities shall encourage and guide state-owned enterprises, social organizations and individuals in running schools.
		Democratic parties, people's groups, social organizations, retired cadres, intellects, collective economy units and individuals are encouraged to take various forms and methods for voluntary contribution to the development of education in accordance with government documents, guidelines and policies.
Temporary Regulations on School Running by Social Force of the State Education Commission	8 July 1987	Social Force referred to in this Regulation means state-owned enterprises and national organizations qualified as legal persons, democratic parties, people's groups, collective economy organizations, social groups, academic groups and individuals with state approval for running schools.
		School running by social force shall meet the real needs of the local economic construction and social development, hold various types of short-term vocational technology education, post-training, middle school and primary school teachers' training, basic education, social culture and life education, self-study, examination, tutoring schools or classes, and advanced-study courses for continuous education.
		Social force, if holds schools of various levels and types qualified in issuing nationally accepted diplomas, shall abide by the regulations issued by the nation on establishing schools; if holds other schools, including classes or training departments, etc., shall abide by this Regulations.
Key issues of the Ten Year Plan and the Eighty Five Year Project by the State Education Commission	1992	A system where the government plays a principal part in running schools with circles of society playing a supplementary role shall be gradually set up to meet the increasing needs of society. The general idea for such a system is as follows: pre-school education is mainly supported by all circles of society; middle school and primary school education mainly rely on local governments; for vocational technology education and adult education, the backbone schools shall be held by governments while others are held mainly by trades, enterprises, national organizations and other units in cities and with funds raised from different resources in the country under the planning and administration of local governments; higher education is mainly held by the central government and governments of provinces, autonomous regions and municipal cities.

Table 10.2 (continued)

Name	Time of Issuance	Main Content
Program on Reform and Development of China's Education by the Central Committee of the Communist Party and the State Council	Feb 1993	The pattern of governments total responsibility in running schools is to be changed. A system with school running by governments as the principal part and supported by all social circles will be gradually set up. At the current stage, the basic education shall be mainly held by local governments; higher education shall find a new situation of mainly being held by the central, provincial, autonomous region and municipal city governments, while attracting the participation of all social circles. Vocational technology education and adult education shall mainly rely on trades, enterprises, national organizations and the joint efforts of all social circles.
		The policy of encouraging, supporting, guiding and administrating school running by social groups and citizens in accordance with law is being adopted by the nation. China welcomes donations and contributions from compatriots in Hong Kong, Macau and Taiwan, immigrants abroad and friendly foreigners. School running through international cooperation is allowed within the scope of relevant national laws and regulations. An examination and approval process must be undertaken for operating schools of various types qualified to issue nationally accepted diplomas.
Regulations on School Running by Social Force by the State Council	31 July 1997	These Regulations apply to the operating of schools and other educational institutions in society by enterprises, national organizations, social groups and other social organizations and citizens using non-financial education outlays of the state.
		Social force shall focus on establishing educational institutions offering vocational education, adult education, high-level secondary education and pre-school education. The state encourages social force to establish educational institutions offering compulsory education as the supplement of compulsory education by the state. The state strictly restricts social force in establishing higher education institutions.
Project on Reviving Education in the 21st Century by the Ministry of Education	24 Dec 1998	In the following 35 years, a school running system with school running by governments as its principal part, the common participation of all social circles and the joint developments of public schools and private schools, is to be set up.
		Experiments shall be made on the reform of the public school mechanism under the guidance of government educational administrative departments.

Table 10.2 (continued)

Name	Time of Issuance	Main Content
Decision on Deepening Education Reform and Fully Pushing Forward Quality Education by the Central Committee of the Communist Party and the State Council	13 June 1999	We should further unbind our minds and change our ideas to encourage and support social force to run schools in various forms, thus meeting the increasing needs of the people. A structure with school running as the principal part and the joint development of public schools and private schools is to be set up. All forms of school running in accordance with relevant national laws and regulations can be attempted for greater progress in developing non-governmental education. Social force is encouraged to hold senior middle school and high level vocational education in various forms. Private common universities may be established under the approval of the state education administration authorities. Under the precondition of ensuring children and juveniles of the right age enroll in nearby public primary schools and junior high schools, a small number of private primary schools and junior high schools are permitted while the opportunity for choosing schools shall be offered. One school with two mechanisms is forbidden. Infant education relying on residential districts with the combination of public schools and private schools shall be actively developed. Preferential policies such as favorable utilization of land, tax free for compounding fees, etc. shall be made according to the situation of each place to support school running by social force.
Law on Promoting Non-governmental education of PRC	Dec 2002	As the basic law in the field of non-governmental education in China, this law made clear such big issues such as the legal status, school running principal, and management principal of private schools in certain degree, and stipulated private schools' establishment, organization and activities, teachers and educatees, property and finance management, administration and supervision, support and encouragement in details, among which Article 51 stipulates that investors may be reasonably rewarded with the surplus in operating schools.
Regulations on Implementation of the Law on Promoting Non-governmental education of PRC	Feb 2004	The implementation Regulations further make clear certain issues stipulated by the Law on Promoting Non-governmental education.

Resources: Compilation of Laws, Rules and Regulations on Education by the Legal Affairs Office of the Ministry of Education (2004 Edition) and the Development Background of Private Higher Education by Liu Shengji (published on the website of the international relationship research institution of Taiwan Guoli Political University).

10.4 Legal Risks for Foreign Investment in Non-governmental Education in China[6]

10.4.1 Legal Risks Shown by Ren Jingxi's Withdrawal

Mr. Ren Jingxi is the founder of South Ocean Education Group. Shanxi South Ocean International School, invested by Mr. Ren with over RMB 40 million, was formally established on 1 September 1993. Undergoing ten years of difficulties and struggles, South Ocean Education Group was developed into a non-governmental education group involving ten basic education complex schools, each combining primary school, junior middle school and senior middle school with a fifteen-year continuous education program, and two private higher education institutions at the end of 2003. The Group had over 10,000 students enrolled, over 2,000 teachers, a total campus area of 1,800 mu, a construction area of school houses, classrooms and other facilities of 560,000 square meters, account assets of over RMB 0.8 billion, cash of over RMB 80 million, and an evaluation value of over RMB 1.3 billion.

However, Mr. Ren Jingxi unexpectedly withdrew from South Ocean Education Group in its flourishing period. On 25 December 2003, Beijing Mid-Asia Fortune Investment Co., Ltd, invested in South Ocean Group, holding 70% of the shares of the group while Mr. Ren held only 18% of the shares to assist Beijing Mid-Asia Fortune Investment Co., Ltd. in the management during the transition of control rights. On 15 July 2004, Mr. Ren, as decided by the board of directors of South Ocean Education Group, granted his 18% shares of South Ocean to some high level managers of South Ocean, after which Mr. Ren completely withdrew from South Ocean with no stock rights and no further participation in its management.

After his withdrawal, Mr. Ren wrote a recollection article of over 10,000 Chinese characters, titled, "Withdrawn from South Ocean Education Group- I was defeated by the autarchic, monopolized, disgusted and inhumane education",, which is popular online. Mentioning the non-governmental education undertaking of South Ocean Education Group, Mr. Ren stated that "the hardship and difficulties faced with by China's non-governmental education sector may not be understood by outsiders. To summarize my experiences of engaging in non-governmental education for over ten years, I can only describe it as twelve years in purgatory with a tired, bitter and cold heart".

---

6 On the International Seminar of Private Education Facing 21st Century held in the autumn of 1999, Mr. Ma Ruojin, the Chinese representative of IFC affiliated to the World Bank, made a speech, introducing that IFC has offered USD 44 million loans to 11 private education institutions in developing counties while it offers no loan to China, the reason for which is too much limitation. He mentioned four problems of Chinese private education as follows: return of capital stock investment, limitation on investment in compulsory education, public offering of private education enterprises and mortgage of education assets, all seizing the keys of restriction on supply for private education in China.

Mr. Ren's withdrawal from South Ocean Group reflects the potential risk for investment in China's non-governmental education. Chinese non-governmental education investment is like the two sides of a peacock whose beautiful feathers cover the ugly buttock. Various legal risks are just alongside the investment road with the allurement of 30-40% return rate as predicted by James Herkman.

10.4.2 Insight into Legal Risks for Foreign Investment in Non-governmental Education

Unclear Legal Status of Non-governmental Education Institutions

In practice, the registration form of non-governmental education institutions is varied. As shown in the mid-term report of the "Research on Non-governmental Education Market of PRC," submitted by Sweden Development Consultation Company to IFC, among the 59 private universities investigated, 52 universities are registered as private schools, 5 are registered as private shareholding companies and the other 2 operate as private schools but each are mainly or absolutely owned by a public university.

Table 10.3. Legal status of non-governmental education institutions

	Number of Sample Universities	**Illustration**
Registered as private school	52	A legal entity admitted and entitled to execute contracts. Usually registered as private non-profit institution. From 2003, 'investors are allowed to be rewarded from the surpluses.
Private shareholding company	5	Private shareholding profit organization. Dividend distribution allowed. Not tax free.
Secondary college	2	Registered as a private university, but with one public university as the main establisher and investor.
Total	59	

The registration form of private schools, under the existing laws, is special and called 'private non-enterprise legal person'. Under the current legal framework, private schools, under *the Temporary Regulations on Private Non-enterprise Organizations* (No. 251 Decree of the State Council, effective as from 25 October 1998), are registered as 'private non-enterprise organizations' at the Ministry of Civil Affairs. They are non-profit organizations. After being registered according to the Regulations, they may obtain the Certificate for Private Non-enterprise Organization (Legal person), the Certificate for Private Non-enterprise Organization (Partnership) and the Certificate for Private Non-enterprise Organization (Individual) respectively according to their different manner of bearing civil liabilities under law. 'Private non-enterprise organizations are social organizations engaged in non-profit social service that are held by enterprises, national organizations, social groups and other social forces and citizens with non-state assets'. Private Universities are known as 'private' since they are established with non state-owned assets, so they fall into the category of private non-enterprise organizations instead of national organizations. Two matters arise hereof: first, defining all private schools as non-profit organizations and making general stipulations on private schools along with various social service entities are not suitable for standardizing private schools; second, the legal status of private non-enterprise organizations is vague while *the General Rules of Civil Law* of China only stipulates on four kinds of legal persons, that is, enterprise, official organ, institution (Shi Ye Unit) and social group, which means the legal person status of private non-enterprise organizations still needs to be clarified.[7]

Uncertain Property Rights

Property right policy is another important and realistic problem faced by Chinese non-governmental education. The method of treating and dealing with private schools' assets not only influence each private school's life and death, but also directly relates to the healthy development of the non-governmental education investment industry.[8] Property rights are directly related to the rights and benefits of investors for running schools. Unclear property rights are one of the main legal risks for investment in non-governmental education. School property issues are always the focus of non-governmental education legislation.

Private schools are established with the contribution of investors. All assets of a private school shall belong to the investor establishing it and the private property rights of the school ought to be protected. However, *the Law on Promoting Non-governmental Education* only generally stipulates that 'a legal person has the property right' in Article 35, as 'private schools have the legal person property right over the assets invested in by investors, state assets, granted property and operation accumulation'. But this article just clarified the private schools' control rights to the legal person properties, rather than the investors' property rights to

---

7 In the laws and regulations on non-profit entities of many nations and districts, schools and hospitals are generally listed in a separate item due to their specialty in meeting public interests and professional nature. Special legislation is carried out for standardization thereof. For example, the Private School law of Japan and the Private School Law of Taiwan stipulate specifically on school legal persons.

8 Liu Jianwen, the Research on Legal Issues in Higher Education System Reform, Beijing University Publishing House, (2005), p132.

invested private schools. *The Regulations for Implementation of the Law on Promoting Non-governmental Education of PRC* on 5 March 2004 run around this issue, which leaves space for local authorities to make different specific policies and make judgments by themselves during its implementation. The legal risk for investment in non-governmental education is virtually increased.[9]

Article 25 of *the Education Law of PRC* adopted in the third conference of the Eighth People's Congress in March 1995 that "no organization or individual is allowed to hold schools or other education institutions for profit purpose". It is also clearly provided in Article 6 of *the Regulations on School Running by Social Force* in 1997 that social force shall not establish education institutions "for profit purpose(s)". Therefore properties in private schools, held by a party, that are non-profit in nature in accordance with *the Education Law,* shall belong to the State. Such stipulations conflict with the protection of investors' property rights to private schools. The main problem is that the legal system concerning private education does not clearly distinguish the mercantile non-government schools from non-mercantile ones. Furthermore, under *the Law on Promoting Non-governmental Education,* the property right of private schools shall not be distributed, transferred or mortgaged during the existence of the school, the school running profit shall not be used in other investments, and the investors' investment could only be returned at its cost value after the private schools' liquidation. (Also see the analysis in the section of Risks on Investment Withdrawal.) Especially, investors don't have normal residual claims rights similar to that of shareholders to a company, of which the detailed analysis goes as follows.

Risk for Acquiring Investment Return

Uncertainty still exists for acquiring non-governmental education investment returns under the current legal system. Article 51 of *the Law on Promoting Non-governmental Education* on 28 December 2002 gives an answer to the question on non-governmental education investment return. It stipulates that "investors of private schools may acquire reasonable returns from the surplus in running schools after the deduction of school running costs, reserves of development funds and picking up other necessary expenses under relevant regulations by the school. The concrete method of acquiring reasonable returns is to be provided by the State Council". 'Reasonable return' is a way to allow profits from non-governmental education investment, but incurs debates on the definition itself. *The Regulations for Implementation of the Law on Promoting Non-governmental education of PRC* by the State Council on 5 March 2004 provides the way for investors to acquire investment return in Articles 44 to 47. The Regulations abandon the quotation limit on 'reasonable return' and shifts from substantial control to procedural control. First, it requests private schools make public their financial status, stating

9 Chen Guowei (2005), The Private Higher Education Investment Risk and Elusion, Zhongzhou Academy, Issue 4.

'private schools shall do business accounting and make a finance accounting report according to *the Accounting Law of PRC* and under the national uniform accounting system. Second, it sets up a procedure for capital use. The Regulations stipulate that investors requesting for reasonable returns under the Articles of Association of private schools may acquire returns in proportion with the school running surplus at the end of each fiscal year. Yearly net profit with school running costs deducted, assets donated by society or assisted by the nation, reserve for development funds and picking up of other necessary expenses under relevant national provisions shall be accomplished before the acquiring of reasonable return in proportion with the surplus.

Jiang Yanjun points out in his article published on Guangming Daily on 13 November 2003 that the initial issue for non-governmental education investors to acquire reasonable returns is to determine the standard of reasonable returns, before which the school running cost, reserve for development funds and other expenses as provided shall be determined. (a) Determination of School Running Cost. The school running cost of private schools normally consists of four parts, that is, building expenses, staff expenses, market expenses, specialty and brand strategy expense. Building expenses, covering land purchasing expense, capital construction expense, repair and maintenance expense, teaching facilities expense, water and electricity supply expense, is the biggest cost for private schools. (b) Determination of Reserves for Development Fund, Public Welfare Fund and Security Fund against Risks. The purpose of having the reserve for development fund is to ensure the capital reserve for private schools' continual development. It can be used in enlarging the school running scale and increasing capital input for the creation of specialties and brand. (c) Choice of Calculation Base. Generally, there are three options for the calculation base of 'reasonable return': first, the investment amount of investors; second, the school earnings; third, the school running surplus. Mr. Jiang deems the third one most appropriate. (d) Determination of 'Reasonable Return' Rate. There are two views in the theoretical circle. One is to set a rate slightly higher than commercial loan interest rate with the investment amount as calculation base. Another is to set a specific calculation rate after determining the surplus for calculation base. (e) Determination of Payment Term for 'Reasonable Return'. Investors should be allowed to receive investment return distributions at the end of each academic year.

The Law on Promoting Non-governmental Education and the Regulations on Implementation of the Law on Promoting Non-governmental Education failed to stipulate clearly on the way for investors to acquire reasonable return and left the determination of reasonable return still remains unclear. However, Article 49.5 of the Regulations stipulates the approval authority may confiscate the investment return if the investor's return rate in the school running surplus is so high that bad social influence occurs; and criminal liabilities shall be borne according to law if such behavior constitutes crimes. The definition of 'high rate' and the determination of 'bad social influence' remain unknown. The uncertainty in non-governmental education investment return policies and laws along with the liability clause with vague application conditions make an investors' acquiring of investment return an adventure like taking chestnuts out of fire, not even mentioning that private schools are treated as non-profit organizations under Chinese policy and law on education. It is stated in Article 25 of *the Education Law* that 'no organization or individual is allowed to hold schools or other education institutions for profit purpose'. And it is also clearly provided in Article 6 of *the Regulations on School Running by Social Force* in 1997 that social force shall not establish education institutions 'for profit purpose'. Under such a legal environment, the legal risk for acquiring investment return is excessively high.

Risk on Investment Withdrawal

The following actual case could partly reflect the possible risks on investment withdrawal from private schools.

Yucai School at Xinjiang County, Shanxi Province is a private joint shareholding school. It was formally set up under the approval by the former Yuncheng Education Commission in 1999. The school had seven shareholders at that time, and among them Mr. Chen Liying was the president of the school with an investment of RMB 150,000, the other six including Mr. Wang Huaibin, Wang Dengke, contributed RMB 120,000. Later, the cooperation could not continue due to the shareholders' friction. At the beginning of April 2001, Mr. Chen Liying acquired all the shares of the other six shareholders who would withdraw from the school. Due to the tight budget, Mr. Chen Liying contacted with Mr. Zhang Shaobo and Mr. Ning Zhiyi, telling them he had invested RMB 810,000 in the school and would like to transfer RMB 700,000 worth of shares to them, leaving RMB 110,000 worth of shares for himself. Mr. Zhang and Mr. Ning agreed and contributed RMB 700,000. On 29 April 2001, Mr. Chen Liying, Mr. Zhang Shaobo and Mr. Ning Zhiyi formally executed the Stock Transfer Agreement. On 20 May 2001, they submitted the Transformation Report to the Social Force School Running Guidance Team and reported to Xinjiang County Government and Education Bureau on the change of shareholders. It is stated in Article 3 of the Agreement that the registered capital shall be RMB 1,000,000 instead of the real contribution of RMB 810,000. RMB 190,000, the margin between the registered capital and the real contribution shall be registered as free shares under the name of Mr. Chen Liying, which shall only participate in dividend distribution but not be concerned with profit and loss. After the execution of the Agreement, the school immediately issued contribution certificates to the three persons. Then, Mr. Zhang and Mr. Ning started to work at the school. The cooperation lasted till 7 August 2001 when Mr. Chen Liying sent notice and declaration to Mr. Zhang and Mr. Ning, announcing that the Stock Transfer Agreement signed by them was void and Mr. Zhang and Mr. Ning should negotiate with him on withdrawal. He also showed his gratitude to Mr. Zhang and Mr. Ning for their work in the school. Mr. Zhang and Mr. Ning objected to the withdrawal and appealed to the court, requesting for legal confirmation of the effectiveness of the Stock Transfer Agreement and continuous performance of it (not including Article 3). During the hearing, Mr. Chen Liying, the defendant, alleged that the Agreement involved the transfer of school property, which violated prohibitive stipulation on the transfer of school property in Article 36 of *the Regulations on School Running by Social Force* of the State Council, and was therefore void. Mr. Zhang Shaobo and Mr Ning Zhiyi, the plaintiffs deemed that the Agreement only involved transfer of shares among shareholders instead of transfer of school property. Hot debates arose during the hearing of the case. One view is that the Agreement states clearly that the subjects are individuals and the transfer object is shares for individual's investment in school, so the Agreement shall be effective. Another view is that the property invested in school belongs to the school, and any transfer of property invested in the school is a transfer of school property, which violates law and makes the Agreement void.[10]

Withdrawal of investment is the biggest concern of investors. However, under the current legal environment, the withdrawal is not effectively guaranteed. It is stipulated in the Law on Promoting Non-governmental education that private schools have legal entity property rights over the assets invested in by investors. These include state assets, granted property and operation accumulation. During the existence of private schools, all the property shall be legally managed and used by private schools while no organization or individual can infringe it. Such stipulation limits the investors' right to freely transfer invested property. In cooperative school-running, cooperators are not protected by law for transfer or withdrawal if disputes arise among them. If the school transfers shares for fundraising in its enlargement of scale and further development, legal protection is still unavailable. Furthermore, under *the Law on Promoting Non-governmental Education,* the property right of private schools shall not be distributed, transferred or mortgaged during the existence of the school; the school running profit shall not be used in other investment; and the investors' investment can only be returned after bankruptcy or dismissal of private schools, after paying back the tuition fee and incidental expense, salaries of teachers and staff, and other debts, all of which make the asset liquidity and cash changing ability of education investment poor. Once the school running fails, the investors have to bear all the economic loss. Investors shall bear loss caused by devaluation and other elements without enjoying the flow accumulation in school operation.[11]

Policy Risks

The development of non-governmental education is directly influenced by the national education policies. During school running, private schools mainly have contact with education administration authorities and connect with other departments of planning, land, finance, industry and commerce, tax, public health and environment

[10] The Research on Private Education Investment Legal Issues by Fan Wenxia of Shanxi University as her Law Master Degree thesis in 2004.

[11] Wu Daguang (2001), The Analysis of China Private Education Market Characteristics and Policy Trend, China Higher Education, Issue 11.

protection. Therefore, the policies regarding non-governmental education by any one of the administration departments may interfere with the direct benefit of private schools. Obstruction in the development of private schools due to policy change is the so-called 'policy risk'. The school running risk due to policy change faced by private schools may lead to damages to initiators, cooperators, teachers, staff and students in different degrees, turbulence or even closing down of the schools.

Just two cases here could illustrate the policy risks of investment in private education in China: (a) In 2004, the Ministry of Education suddenly cancelled higher education degree examinations of private schools and stopped their enrollment in 2005. The policy adjustment greatly influenced the 436 experimental colleges and universities with higher education degrees. The policy influenced the development of private colleges and universities. A path to success already found by private schools which were experienced therein suddenly disappeared. Waste of human power, financial and material resources occurred. About 300 private universities of the sole school running level were facing their deaths.[12] (b) Since the 1980s, private universities have not been limited except being prohibited to engage in religious activities when setting courses. Under this background, Chinese private universities have set up majors in medicine and other related subjects to solve the lack of doctors and medicines in the rural area. In 2002, the Ministry of Public Health and the Ministry of Education jointly issued a notice forbidding private universities, involved with higher education diplomas and higher education self-study examinations, to recruit students from graduates and past-graduates of senior middle schools and reserving the already-registered students' status till 2005. Such a policy involving the sudden cancellation of a right that was granted since the affected private schools were established is fatal to those with medicine was their only major.

The policy risks for private education mainly involve the following situations. Firstly, a former policy is intentionally violated by private schools due to the relevant authorities negligence in implementation or administration, under which damage may occur when the implementation is strengthened and the violation activity is punished afterwards. Secondly, former local policy made by local government departments or for local industry is not in accordance with national laws and regulations, which must be adjusted after the implementation of *the Administration Permission Law*, and thus resulting in changes to how the school is operated and loss in school running of private schools. Thirdly, no clear stipulation was made before but a new policy is introduced due to the development of a particular situation, which when standardizing school running activities, would surely bring loss. In fact, no matter what happens, the development of private schools would be influenced.[13]

---

[12] Where Is the Way Out for Private Universities after Cancellation of Degree Examination by Hao Guoyin from www.cer.net.

[13] Li Weimin (2005), the Analysis of Policy Risk for Private Universities, the Xi'an Europe and Asia Vocational College Academy, Issue 1.

Investment Proceeds Risk

One of the essential purposes of investors investing in non-governmental education is to obtain proceeds, through which they may gradually take back investment. Investment return in the long term is one of the features of education investment. For example, a private university may not be admitted by the society until it sends out the first graduates. A certain period of time passes before the investment return is realized. Relevant data shows that the cost of training one student is over RMB ten thousand in China, part of which is collected from the student while others are from the state's financial subsidy. Private schools mainly rely on tuition fees due to the lack of state finance allocation or subsidy. Therefore, investment return can not be achieved at the same year of investment.

Tuition fees are the most essential income for private schools. Therefore, different charging methods bring different risk pressures on operating private schools. Currently, the tuition-fee operation method may be briefly divided into the following three patterns: First is the 'education reserve' pattern which was once popular in the Zhujiang River Delta. Students (or their families) are requested to pay a large sum of money (RMB 100,000 – 300,000) at one time. The school promises that students need not pay any other expense at school and the school shall fully repay the 'education reserve' when they leave school. Facts show that such a mechanism has a repayment risk. The school can only continue operating with sufficient students. Second is the collection of tuition fee in each semester, which is mainly adopted by public schools but seldom by private ones. The reason is that such a mechanism heavily relies on the variation of student quantity and is likely to cause short-term financial crisis in the school. Private schools still in their early years of operating are reluctant to take on such risk. However, such a mechanism has its advantage of fully bringing the regulation role of price lever into play for the avoidance of the 'education reserve' repayment pressure and social criticism for collecting a 'sponsoring fee'. It is easier for the families to accept. Through market competition, school earnings may not be lower than the 'education reserve'. The third method combines the 'sponsoring fee for school establishment' and 'tuition fee and incidental expense', and is currently being widely adopted by private schools. Student's families are requested to pay, along with the tuition fee and incidental expense for each semester, the 'sponsoring fee for school establishment of RMB 10,000-60,000 at one time when entering school. This is a compromise between the first two methods. First, it may ease families' payment pressures to a certain degree; second, it helps to enlarge student resources due to its compliance with the commonly-existing consumers' psychology towards paying for nonce; third, the financial status of the school remains stable without repayment pressure; fourth, the real obtained usable capital under such a pattern may exceed the 'education reserve'. Its disadvantage is that families may face higher risks since the 'sponsoring fee' is normally not repayable. If part of the sponsor fee may be returned when a student changes to another school, the pattern combining 'sponsoring fee for school establishment' and 'tuition fee and incidental expense' will be more favorable for families than the 'education reserve', and the market guidance function may be fully exerted.[14]

The economic structure of China makes social economic development out of balance. The current Geordie coefficient of China has reached the pre-warning zone. In recent years, groups of students living in poverty have appeared in both public schools and private schools due to the continuous increases in tuition fees. Little space is left for the rise for tuition fees in private schools. The start-up of scholarships, loan and stipend has basically not solved the tuition fee problem. Private schools even lower their tuition fee due to competition in student resources. Under such conditions, many private schools either seek the 'boundary benefit' with continual expansion of school scale or cut back teaching expense

Table 10.4. Income and Expenses of a Typical Private University with 5,000 students

Income and Expenses	RMB	Percentage in Total Income
Tuition Fee	39,000,000	86%
Accommodation Fee	6,000,000	13%
Other Income	500,000	1%
Total Income	45,500,000	
Expenses		
Teachers' Salaries and Tax Payments	8,190,000	18%
Teaching Materials	1,365,000	3%
Common Expense	1,365,000	3%
House Rental	910,000	2%
Computers, Furniture, etc.	4,095,000	9%
Administrative Staff's Salaries	2,730,000	6%
Accommodation Expenses	2,275,000	5%
Other Expenses	10,920,000	24%
Total Expenses	31,850,000	70%
Operating Profit	13,650,000	30%

(Quoted from the mid-term report of the Research on Non-governmental education Market of PRC submitted by Sweden Development Consultation Company to IFC.)

14 The Summary of Hot Issues and Difficult Problems in Private Education on the website of China Education Newspaper.

inputs at the expense of sacrificing teaching quality, resulting in poor quality, diminished student resources and difficulties in operating the school. Non-governmental education investment risk is further increased.[15]

We may also conclude from the mid-term report of the "Research on Non-governmental education Market of PRC" submitted by Sweden Development Consultation Company to IFC that the return of China's private university investment is still quite low although the profit rate (and cash flow) is much high. A large amount of schools' cash flow (and certain amounts of low cost bank credit) has already been allocated for large scale campus construction. The final result is that only a circle of capital, excluding the even limited investment return for investors. In the finance sense, private schools in China do not fit the norm since they are the most profitable *and* least efficient investments.

[15] Li Weimin (2004), The Research on Private Higher Education Cost, Investment and Tuition Fee, the Private Education Research, Issue 6. Chen Guowei (2005), The Private Higher Education Investment Risk and Elusion, Zhongzhou Academy, Issue 4.

11 Legal Risks for Foreign Investment in China's Water Market

The experience of private investment in infrastructure in China over the past years indicate that risks and pitfalls go together with opportunities.

—— Lu Youjie[1]

11.1 Introduction

11.1.1 Basic Information of Foreign Investment in China's Water Market[2]

During the late 1970s to the early 1980s, the construction capitals of some Chinese waterworks were mainly funded through loans from World Bank, Asia Development Bank and foreign governments. The conditions on such loans were that these waterworks usually had to purchase equipment from appointed foreign water companies or through international bidding, and accept the technical guidance of foreign parties. However, the foreign-invested water business at that time was only at the stage of selling equipment and technologies while the direct introduction of capital did not appear. Until the 1990s, direct investment emerged in the foreign-invested water business along with the policies encouraging foreign investment in China's public utilities construction. The permitted field in water business at this stage was limited to waterworks and sewage treatment factories while the pipeline networks were still untouched. The cooperation mode is mainly Building-Operation-Transfer (hereinafter "BOT") or cooperative companies. Along with the policies pushing forward the opening of the water industry to the outside world, water business giants such as Vivendi, Thames and Suez started

---

1 Lu Youjie is a scholar in Department of Construction Management of Tsinghua University, the sentence quoted from Lu Youjie, Risk Management for Large-scale Infrastructure Projects in China, downloaded from www.building.com.hk/forum/luyoujiepaper.pdf (last visited on Nov. 2005).

2 The data comes from the websites of the Ministy of Commerce, the Investment in China, the Water Information and Asia Development Bank's Final Report on Important Issues and Relevant Suggestions in the Progress of the Water Market in Chinese Cities.

their joint ventures with Chinese waterworks, which formed the second surge in opening the Chinese water industry. Furthermore, Anglian Water Company from Great Britain, Guotai International Group, The China Water Company Limited with Hong Kong as its registration place, Macdonald Water And Environment Company are active in the market as well. There are two methods for foreign water companies' entrance into the Chinese water market. One way is to set up joint ventures to build and operate new waterworks or sewage treatment factories, which has been an essential way of attracting foreign investment. Another is through direct merger and acquisition, under which the foreign company acquires part of the shares of a Chinese waterworks company for reconstruction and operation.

In 2003, there were 25 projects utilizing foreign investment in the water production and supply industry, which was 212.5% higher than the previous year. The contractual foreign investment amount was USD 114.52 million, 0.6% lower than the previous year. The actual utilized foreign capital was USD 121.53 million, 126.06% higher than the previous year. In January to April 2004, there were 7 projects utilizing foreign investment in the water production and supply industry with contractual foreign investment of USD 41.32 million and actual utilized foreign capital of USD 14.11 million. The change in the utilization of foreign capital in the water production and supply industry is indicated in the following chart.

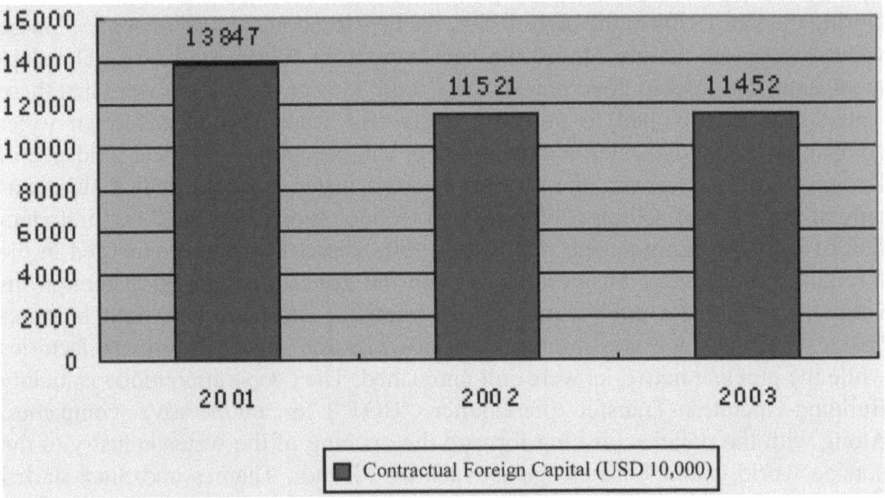

Chart 11.1. The utilization of foreign capital in the water market (Resource: the website of the Ministry of Commerce)

Along with the implementation of *the Measures on Administration of Public Utilities Franchises*, the legal obstacle in foreign capital's way into China's water industry has been removed and the total investment in China's water industry has increased greatly. There were 118 foreign capital utilization projects in 2004, 180.95%

higher than the previous year, with contractual foreign capital of USD 868 million, 435.45% higher than the previous year, and actual utilized foreign capital of USD 187 million, 31% lower than the previous year.

Table 11.1. Water Market Competition Status

	Foreign-Invested Water Company	**Domestic Environment Protection Listed Company**	**District Water Company**
Market Position	Large-Scale Waterworks	Large and Middle Scale Waterworks and Sewage Treatment Factories	Local Water Projects
Market Promotion	Foreign Investment, Government Invitation for Investment	Bidding and Negotiation	Local Resource Advantage
Technology Level	Advanced	Mainstream Technology for General Use	Generic
Management	Advanced	Reducing Employers for Cost Control	Transformation of State-Owned Enterprise
Strategy	Investment in Large-scale Waterworks, Winning with Good Quality, Main Focus on Good Quality Projects	Racing to Control Market, Taking Preferable Projects, Winning with Quantity, The More The Faster The Better	Taking Local Projects, Winning with Resource Advantage
Capital Utilization	Smooth Channel	Investment and Financing	Financing
Brand	Foreign Enterprise Image	Listed Company, High Strength	Local Fame
Comprehensive Strength	Highest	High	Higher

(Resource: Information Website of Water, www.hwcc.com.cn)

The total investment in China's water industry in 2004 was RMB 950 million. Combining the water supply and sewage treatment businesses, a huge market valuing of RMB 10 billion is to be formed in 2010. For the sewage treatment market, all cities must build their own sewage treatment factories in the tenth five-year term under *the Notice on Strengthening City Water Supply, Water Saving and Water Pollution Prevention.* In 2005, the sewage treatment rate shall be over 60% in cities with a population of over 5 million while the rate shall be no less than 70% in municipal cities, provincial capitals, separate planning cities and important scenery-tourism cities. However, according to inspection, grade-three water, which meets the minimum criteria of waterworks, only accounts for 29.5% of water in China's seven water systems while the grade-five water of bad quality accounts for 44%. About half of the Chinese cities suffer from pollution of shallow underground water while about half of the Chinese cities face the problem of severe pollution of underground water. Up to now, 60% of Chinese cities still have no sewage treatment factory. China's sewage-release amount in 2003 was as great as 68 billion tons, which is more than twice that of 1980. At the end of 2003, there were altogether 612 sewage treatment factories in 275 Chinese cities with the treatment capacity of 4,253.6 square meters per day and the treatment rate of 42.38%. About 1/3 of industry waste water and 2/3 of life sewage are directly discharged every year in China. In the 2003 inspection on important sections of the seven major river systems of China, only 38.1% of water was higher than grade-three standard, the standard that is suitable for drinking. About 54% of underground water in plain areas is below the quality standard suitable for life use. Water pollution is severe. China's city sewage treatment rate shall be no less than 60% in 2010, for which 1,000 sewage treatment factories need to be built supplementary to the current 452, with a required total investment of RMB 200-300 billion, excluding the over RMB 10 billion operation expense each year. In 2005, the market value of China's environment protection industry is to be RMB 470 billion,, accounting for 3.7% of the year's GDP, if the market grows at the speed of over 12% on the current base. The capacity of China's water market is amazing.

11.1.2 Big Events in Foreign Investment in the Chinese Water Market

In 1992, French Suez Water Company invested in Tanzhou Water Company at Zhongshan City, Guangdong Province, which was the start of foreign water companies' entry into the Chinese market.

In 1997, Vivendi cooperated with Tianjin authorities to set up the joint venture, Tianjin General Water Company, with 55% of shares held by Vivendi, which was the first time for a franchise to a foreign company operating existed waterworks by Chinese governments.

In 1998, the first waterworks project constructed with foreign investment in China, Shanghai Thames Dachang Water Co., Ltd., successfully accomplished the construction of the first phase water supply of 200 thousands tons and the second phase water supply of 400 thousands tons, supplying water to 1.2 million people in the northern part of Shanghai city. It is famed as an example of Shanghai's successful attraction of foreign capital. In 2000, Thames Water acquired Baowishi Company's 50% share and turned Dachang Project into the first wholly foreign-owned waterworks in China. In April 2004, Thames Water, as the investor of Dachang Waterworks, executed the Stock Transfer contract of Shanghai Thames Dachang Water Co. Ltd. with Shanghai North Water Company, transferring the ownership of Dachang Waterworks to Shanghai North Water Company.

In 1999, Vivendi (French General Water Group) invested a waterworks franchise in Chengdu and another in Tianjin. Chengdu Sixth Waterworks, invested by Vivendi, is the first water supply project adopting BOT mode in China's water field and has been put into use recently.

In 2002, Vivendi acquired 50% of the state-owned shares in Pudong Water Company with RMB 2,000,000,000, triple the asset evaluation price, which is the first large-scale introduction of foreign capita in city water supply network.

On 1 September 2002, Pudong Vivendi Water Co., Ltd. started its operation in Shanghai, which is the first fully joint venture water company in China.

On 7 July 2004, German Berlin Water International Shareholding Co. Ltd, jointly with East China Engineering Technology Shareholding Co. Ltd. of Chemistry Third Institute won the franchise of Wang Xiaozhi Sewage Treatment Factory for 23 years with the highest bid of RMB 480,000,000, defeating other foreign and domestic water companies in the competition.

On 17 March 2004, Hainan Tianya Water (Group) Company and Sino-French Water Investment Co. Ltd. signed the 'Agreement on All Round Cooperation in Operation of City Water Supply'. Each party holds a 50% share in the newly established Sanya Sino-French Water Supply Co. Ltd. Sanya municipal government grants the franchise of water supply to the new company which then monopolizes the water supply business of Sanya City, including construction of waterworks, reconstruction of pipelines, sales of drinking water and so on. The Sino-foreign cooperative enjoys a thirty-year city water supply franchise in Sanyan City. This event marks the first time an entire city's water supply has been under foreign cooperation, in addition to a city's complete openness towards foreign cooperation with regard to an enterprise of such public welfare significance.

11.2 BOT Mode of Foreign Investment in Water Industry

11.2.1 BOT in China

To solve the existing problems in the sewage treatment industry, many Chinese cities have started their market-oriented reform, gradually opening the investment market for sewage and rubbish treatment utility construction. In 2004, the State Planning Commission (Now the National Development and Reform Commission, NDRC), the Ministry of Construction and the State Environmental Protection Administration, under the approval by the State Council, issued *the Opinions Concerning Promoting Industrialization Development of City Sewage and Rubbish Treatment,* encouraging domestic and foreign investment in the construction and operation of city sewage treatment utilities. In recent years, experiments such as BOT, operation-under-trusteeship, combinations of water supply and drainage methods, etc. have been made all over China, among which BOT develops the fastest, emerging as the main mode of foreign investment in China's water market.

Table 11.2. Data of Some Chinese BOT Projects

Project Name	Total Investment (RMB 100,000 yuan)	Treatment Capacity (10,000 tons per day)	Operation Term (years)
Beijing Economy And Technology Development Zone Sewage Treatment Factory	3200	2	20
Waterworks at Suilin County, Heilongjiang Province	USD10,000,000		30
Hubei Wuhan Tangxun Lake Sewage Treatment Factory	19500	5	20
Sewage Treatment Factory in Zibo County, Shandong Province	1860	3	10
Sewage Treatment Factory in Rugao County, Jiangsu Province	3200	2	
Sewage Treatment Factory in Shenyang City, Liaoning Province	3500	3	25
East District Sewage Treatment Factory in Jiangmen City, Guangdong Province	4200	4	20
Xiajia Bay Sewage Treatment Factory in Jingmen City, Hubei Province	11000	10	25
Xinjiang Bazhou Sewage Treatment Project	120000	62	7
Sewage Treatment Factory in Feng County, Jiangsu Province	5700	2-4	25
East District Sewage Treatment Factory in Taicang City, Jiangsu Province	3250	2	
Sewage Treatment Factory in Tongzhou District, Beijing	17000	10	20
Qingshan Lake Sewage Treatment Factory in Nancang City, Jiangxi Province	29000	33	20
Sewage Treatment Factory in Xinle City, Hebei Province	12000	8	
Sewage Treatment Project in Ci County, Handan City, Hebei province	11300		
Jinshan Sewage Treatment Factory in Fuzhou City, Fujian Province	13154.51	5	
Zhuzhuan Well Sewage Treatment Factory in Hefei City, Anhui Province	12023.72	11	
Hanzhong Shimen Waterworks	10000	10-20	20
Qinghuangdao Harbor Zone Sewage Treatment Factory	USD14,000,000	12-38	20

BOT is a new project financing mode appearing in the 1980s. It refers to 'Build-Operate-Transfer' and is also known as 'franchise investment and financing mode' in China, under which a nation or a local government department, through a franchise agreement, authorize the foreign investment enterprise, signatory of the agreement, including Sino-foreign joint ventures and cooperatives, wholly foreign-owned enterprises, to undertake the financing, construction, operation and maintenance of public infrastructure or basic industry projects. Within the term stipulated in the franchise agreement, the project company has ownership of the utilities built with the investment. Such ownership is not in a completed sense. The company may collect appropriate fees from the users of the utilities so as to take back the investment and funds in the project, the operation and maintenance cost and reasonable return. Upon the expiration of the franchise, the project company shall freely transfer the utilities to the government department signing the agreement. BOT projects are the combination of private capital with governments (also called Public Private Partnership, PPP). Its biggest advantage is absorbing large amounts of commercial capital and private funds into the construction of public basic utilities, making up for the shortage of finance funds, mitigating governments' financial burden and debt risk as well as effectively introducing in advanced, technologies and management for enhancing operation management efficiency.

11.2.2 Case Study: Chengdu Sixth Waterworks

Chengdu Sixth Waterworks invested by Vivendi is the first water supply project under BOT mode in China's water industry. The water project at Chengdu has achieved several leading cards. It is the first city water supply project carried out through public bidding within the BOT framework. It is the first formal BOT water supply project in China. It is the first BOT water project for which the contributor and the creditor must bear city planning risk. It is the first project for which the Europe Investment Bank offers credit mechanism for project financing in China. It is also the only project accomplished project financing in China in 1999. With new French technology adopted in the project, the group succeeded in the bid with the lowest water rate. The State Planning Commission took part in the design of the project. This outstanding project has won three world awards including 'best trade', awarded by the International Project Financing Magazine.[3]

Brief Introduction

Chengdu Sixth Waterworks BOT Project is the third experimental BOT projects approved by the State Planning Commission and the first experimental project built under BOT mode in China's city water supply basic utility construction. The

[3] "ADB News from PRCM" from www.adb.org.

project construction scale includes water-taking work of 0.8 million tons per day, water purification work of 0.4 million square meters per day, water transfer pipeline work of 27 km and a franchise period of no more than 18 years, including construction time. The combo of French Water and Japan Marubeni Corporation succeeded in the bid for the project.

Project Contract Structure

During Chengdu Sixth Waterworks BOT project financing process, the project company mainly relies on offering various contracts as the project guarantee. Therefore, the execution of the main contract for the project is of great importance. For the project, the project company has obtained the following contracts:

Franchise Agreement. The project company and Chengdu municipal government signed the Agreement, specifying that the project company shall finance, design and build the project facilities, operate and maintain the waterworks, and stipulate the terms and conditions for transfer of project facilities to Chengdu municipal government or Chengdu Water General Company as designated by Chengdu municipal government.

Water Purchase Agreement. The project company and Chengdu Water General Company designated and authorized by Chengdu municipal government signed the Agreement, stipulating the Water Company's water purchase and payment, under which the project company shall supply 0.4 million square meters pure water per day in accordance with the standard pure water quality stated in the Agreement.

Turnkey Construction Contract. The project company and the general contractor signed this Agreement, stipulating the purchase of equipments, construction of project and so on.

Financing Documents. The project company and each creditor sign an agreement concerning the credit financing part of the project.

Above all, the project and contract structure of Chengdu Sixth Waterworks is much more complicated, which makes risk-sharing arrangement more difficult.

Risk Share Structure

BOT project financing involves accomplishment risk, production risk, market risk, financial risk, political risk, force majeure, etc., which may be divided into two phases according to time sequence, that is, pre-accomplishment period and post-accomplishment period. Chengdu Sixth Waterworks BOT Project risk share consideration mainly focus on original water resource, pure water sale, financial risk, legal risk and force majeure and practical prevention measures have been taken.

11.3 Insight into Legal Risks for Foreign Investment in Chinese Water Market Under BOT Mode

11.3.1 Foreign Water Companies' Failures Under a Flawed BOT Legal Environment

China started research on the application of BOT in the infrastructure industry in 1994 while many foreign investors planned to adopt BOT mode to participate in the economic construction of China. Under such a background, the former Ministry of Foreign Economic and Trade Cooperation issued *the Notice on Relevant Issues Concerning Attraction of Foreign Investment with BOT Mode* in 1995, and the State Planning Commission, Ministry of Electricity (which no longer exists) and Ministry of Transportation jointly issued *the Notice on Relevant Issues Concerning Approval Administration of Foreign Investment Franchise Projects*. The two notices are the main ground for China's guidance of BOT project experimental work. However, the experimental foreign investment franchise project approval procedure under *the Notice on Relevant Issues Concerning Approval Administration of Foreign Investment Franchise Projects* has already been cancelled by the State Council.[4]

Later, relevant authorities issued some administration regulations including: (a) *the Measure for Administration of Project Financing Abroad* issued by the State Planning Commission and the State Administration of Foreign exchange on 16 April 1997; (b) *the Measure for Administration of City Planning Public Utility Franchise Operation* issued by the Ministry of Construction on 1 May 2004; (c) *the Notice on Printing and Distributing Opinions Concerning Promotion of City Sewage and Rubbish Treatment Industrialized Development* jointly issued by the former State Planning Commission, Ministry of Construction and the State Environmental Protection Administration on 10 September 2002; (d) *the Notice on Appropriate Handling of Current Issues Concerning Guarantee of Foreign Investment Project with Fixed Return* issued by the State Council on 10 September 2002, among which the last one has the greatest influence over the legal environment of BOT investment.

Generally speaking, China does not have a complete set of rules and regulations concerning BOT investment mode. First, these rules and regulations rank lower. The main legislatures are the General Office of the State Council or other departments in charge instead of the People's Congress or its Standing Committee. In the sense of legal sources, formal documents issued by the State Council with the same legal effect as administrative regulations and rules and regulations made by the ministries or commissions affiliated to the State Council are of lower legal rank. Second, the contents of these rules and regulations are very simple, leaving

[4] See the Directory of the First Series of Administrative Approval Items to Be Cancelled under the State Council's Decision.

many vacancies in legislation. The legal rules are limited in number and have simple content, not covering many difficult problems existing in BOT project operation. Under such vagueness or vacancy in legal provisions, the executing and judicial authorities have much discretion. Third, some provisions are in contradiction with each other. For example, it is stipulated in Article 3 of *the Notice on Relevant Issues Concerning Attracting Foreign Investment under BOT Mode* that 'governmental authorities normally shall not make guarantee or promise for projects in any form, including foreign exchange guarantee' while it is stated in *the Notice on Relevant Issues Concerning Approval Administration of Experimental Foreign Investment Franchise Projects* that 'the nation ensures exchange and remitting abroad of foreign currencies needed by the project companies for repayment of loan principal, interests and bonus'. Such clear conflict between the two Notices may guide the government nowhere in negotiation of BOT projects. Fourth, the legal provisions contain unclear definitions and lack definiteness. Legal vocabulary should be clear and definite, offering stable expectation to viewers. However, words with unclear meaning such as 'encourage' and 'support' are used in provisions concerning BOT investment mode on many essential issues, making the parties unable to judge the applicability thereof. For example, it is stipulated in Article 3.5 of *the Notice on Carrying out City Rubbish Treatment Charging System for Promoting Rubbish Treatment Industrialization* that 'city governments are *encouraged* to mortgage sewage and rubbish treatment fees for loans for the purpose of raising funds for construction and reform of city sewage pipelines and rubbish collection and transportation facilities'. Literally, it seems to allow parties to mortgage charging rights. However, consideration shall be given here on whether the parties are allowed to mortgage charging rights since the Notice is of lower rank in force and contains no definite affirmation of the legal force of mortgaging charging rights.

China's legal environment for BOT investment mode severely lags behind the practical needs. The flawed legal environment directly increases investment legal risks. The international water giants entering China years ago, such as Thames Water of Great Britain, Suez Ondeo Water from France, Anglian Water from Great Britain and Guotai International from Hong Kong have gradually withdrawn from the Chinese water market. Thames Water sold out its shares in Dacheng Waterworks. Anglian withdrew from Beijing Tenth Waterworks Project. Veolia Water Systems, Ondeo and other foreign companies remaining in the Chinese market have made little investment recently. Japan water companies are facing the same difficult situation. Foreign water companies have borne too many legal risks and failed in too many cases. The widely known case concerning the takeover of Changchun Huijin Sewage Treatment Company is one of the failed cases.[5] All the cases concern three similar stages. In stage one, the local governments 'bravely decided' to sign a franchise operation contract with no risk and high return without consideration of costs and results and without re-

[5] The detailed information of this case included in Chapter 5 of this book.

gard to the State Planning Commission's provision of 'no fixed investment return rate shall be promised for' the purpose of developing water systems and attracting foreign investment.[6] In stage two, the government 'suddenly found' it unfair after the project had been put in use for several years and requested to resign the contract or directly tore the contract just like the Huijin case. In stage three, some local governments, taking *the Notice on Appropriate Handling of Existing Problems in Guarantee of Foreign Investment Fixed Return Projects* (the State Council General Office's No. 43 Decree issued in 2002) as the 'imperial sward', 'settled' the disputes without regard to 'appropriateness'.[7] Above all, simple legal provisions and the inappropriate behavior of local governments and some foreign companies have caused the defeat of foreign companies in their investments in the Chinese water market.

11.3.2 Detailed Analysis on Legal Risks for Foreign Investment in the Chinese Water Market Under BOT Mode

Investment-Proceeds Risk: Is There Always Return for Payment?

Water Price: Key Element for Investment Return

The return for foreign investment in the Chinese water market is dependent on the water price. The water price determination and adjustment method directly influence investment return. Presently, China's water price is still under governmental control.[8] The price is mainly fixed under the government's guidance and with the adoption of a price hearing system. Water supply fees and sewage fees are made in the above way under the principle of recovering costs and gaining tiny profits. The new *Water Law of China* stipulates that the water supply price shall be determined under the principals of recovering costs, reasonable benefits, good quality at a reasonable price and being fairly borne. On 10 September 2002, the Development and Reform Commission, the Ministry of Construction, and the State Environmental Protection Administration jointly issued *the Opinions on Promoting the Development of City Sewage and Rubbish Treatment Industrialization*. Article 3.1 stipulates that local governments or entrusted agencies may, taking the bank long-term loan interest rate standard for the same period as referenced, determine the investment return standard for city sewage and rubbish treatment projects with

6 These contracts with no regard for Chinese parties' interests are usually accompanied by corruption. For example, Chi Ruoyan, the former General Manager of the water supply company involved in the Shenyang Water case, was sentenced for being involved in the 'Mu-Ma Case' (two supreme leaders of Shenyang were arrested), as reported by the 21st century Economy Report on 4 March 2002.

7 From the Economy Reference on 30 June 2004.

8 Li Shilin, The Views on Half Market Orientation, download from the website of Tianze Public Utility Research Center (www.ccppp.org).

social capital investment, and calculate the projects' operation cost, considering the specific conditions to reasonably determine the city sewage and rubbish treatment price, which is to be used as the upper limit for investors' tender base. The best planning and investing and operating enterprise of the projects are to be chosen through bidding. *The Notice on Promotion of Water Price Reform, Enhancing Water Saving and Protecting Water Resources* (the State Council General Office's No.36 Decree issued in 2004) clearly provides the four compositions of water price for the first time, that are, water resource fee, water project water supply price, city water supply price and sewage treatment fee. The variations of water price in different cities are great while the water price in large, middle and small cities are quite different from each other. In 2002, among cities adopting sewage treatment charging systems, Suzhou and Changzhou charged RMB 1.15 per ton, the highest price, while the 14 cities such as Ningbo and Nanchang charged the lowest price of RMB 0.10 per ton, which is insufficient for making up operation costs (about RMB 0.50-0.60 per ton). The principle of recovering costs and gaining tiny profits is still adopted for cities planning sewage projects with foreign investment, under which the internal yield is 8–15%. The internal yield would be stabilized at 8–10% under fiercer competition in a project bidding and tender system. The water price is calculated according to an index concerning investment gross costs, internal yield, local electricity price and residence consumption, confirmed through a price hearing held by the provincial or municipal price administration authorities, and is basically under little influence from the market. Whether waterworks and sewage treatment factories, after entering into the market, can obtain expected profits, will be up to their operation level and cost control level, if under the same charging policy.

Further increases in the water price are the current focus in city water industry administration. China's water price, under governments' control, has been rather low for many years and thus has not reflected the rareness of water. As to water price adjustment, investors are always in a disadvantageous position. Generally speaking, the governments do not promise increases in the water price. Though the market tendency clearly shows the need for price increases, it is still very hard to obtain governmental approval for price adjustments. In other words, governments have absolute control over water price determination and adjustment though governments may usually agree to reimburse investors when water price can not be adjusted due to government interference. Therefore, investors generally regard the obstacle of administrative interference as a no-protection risk. Situations in which governments are incapable of reimbursing water prices, have no intention of reimbursing water prices, or frequently abandon contracts, decreases governments' credit and gives them a bad reputation in the investment circle.[9]

9 The Certain Important Issues and Relevant Suggestions Concerning the Promotion of Market-orientation of China City Water Industry (PPP) (final report) by Asia Development Bank.

Table 11.3. List of Water Price in Major Cities on 1 July 2004

City	Water Price (RMB)	Sewage Treatment Fee (RMB)
Beijing	2.300	0.600
Shanghai	1.030	0.700
Tianjin	2.300	0.600
Chongqing	2.060	0.400
Shijiazhuang	2.000	0.600
Taiyuan	2.200	0.250
Huhehaote	1.500	0.350
Shenyang	1.400	0.200
Dalian	2.300	0.200
Changchun	2.100	0.400
Ha'er'bin	1.800	0.500
Nanjing	0.900	1.000
Hangzhou	1.150	0.600
Ningbo	1.400	0.250
Hefei	0.900	0.540
Fuzhou	1.200	0.450
Xiamen	1.800	0.500
Nanchang	0.880	0.220
Jinan	2.240	0.360
Zhengzhou	1.200	0.600
Wuhan	0.700	0.800
Changsha	1.020	0.400
Guangzhou	0.900	0.700
Shenzhen	2.000	0.500
Nanning	0.840	0.500

Resource: Certain Important Issues and Relevant Suggestions Concerning the Promotion of Market-orientation of China City Water Industry (PPP) (final report) by Asia Development Bank

'Take or Pay' Encounters 'No Fixed Return' Policy

The State Council has ordered the straightening out of fixed return projects three times from 1998 to 2002,[10] forbidding foreign investment projects to adopt a

[10] *The Notice on Strengthening Administration of Foreign Debts in Foreign Currencies and Carrying out Inspection of Foreign Debts In Foreign Currencies* was issued by the State Council in August 1998. *The Notice on Further Strengthening and Improving Administration of Foreign Currency Income and Expenses* was issued by the State Council in April 2001.Local governments took measures to straighten out and put right foreign investment fixed return projects according to the two Notices. *The Notice on Appropriate*

fixed return method, which impacts many BOT projects in city water industry. It is provided in *the Notice on Appropriate Handling of Existing Problems in Guarantee of Foreign Investment Fixed Return Projects* issued by the State Council General Office on 10 September 2002 that the promise of foreign investors' fixed return is not in accordance with the principal of sharing benefits and jointly bearing risks by Chinese and foreign investors and is in violation of relevant laws and regulations on joint ventures and Sino-foreign cooperatives. First, for foreign investment projects with a fixed return, payable with its own proceeds, the Chinese and foreign parties shall modify the contract or agreement through negotiation so as to replace fixed return with a legitimate proceeds allocation method such as 'return of investment' ahead of schedule. Second, for projects at a loss or with insufficient proceeds, in which part or the majority of investment return is paid with capital not related to the project, or under which foreign investors are not paid with the investment return as promised, different measures such as 'transformation', 'acquisition', 'transfer', 'withdrawal' and so on may be adopted according to the project situation. However, there is no clear definition or legal specification of 'fixed return' in current laws and regulations, or governmental documents, which results in obstacles, disputes or confusion in the clearing up of fixed return projects.

There are three investment return models in BOT investment water projects, that is, 'investment return model of assuming sole responsibility for profits and loss', 'investment return with fixed rate model' and 'investment return with flexible rate model'. In the latter two models, the government guarantees the investment return rate. 'The investment return model of assuming sole responsibility for profits and loss' refers to the model under which the project company shall assume responsibilities for profits and losses, and undertake the operation result. In such a model, the government does not guarantee investment return rates while the project company faces the greatest risks as well as the largest possibility for profits. The 'fixed rate model' refers to the model under which the government at the location of the project undertakes investment return payments according to the pre-negotiated return rate without regard to the actual operation status. Beijing Holding, the mainland company listed at Hong Kong, invested RMB 1.5 billion for the acquisition of the first term operation rights of Beijing Water Resource Ninth Waterworks Project. The agreed fixed investment return rate in the contract is 14%. Beijing Water Supply Co. is still in charge of the construction, operation and management of the Waterworks while Beijing Holding takes no responsibility for the operation result. Under this return model, the project company has the minimum risk and profit. Due to comparatively big investment risks in BOT projects, the government guaranteed the investment return rate to be slightly higher than international loan interest rates or daily interest rates on short term private loans for the same period. Under the

---

Handling of Existing Problems in Guarantee of Foreign Investment Fixed Return Projects was further issued by the General Office of the State Council on 10 September 2002, requesting correction of projects with fixed returns in the way of acquisition, transformation, transfer and removal.

'flexible rate mode', the upper and lower limits of the investment return rate is determined. The government shall subsidize the operator when the operation income is lower than the investment return rate, while operation income beyond the return rate shall belong to the government. The project company is entitled to the operation income within the upper and lower limits of the return rate. For the project company, this model has intermediate risks and profit opportunities in comparison with the two other modes and is more reliable.

Payment of fixed returns is the realization of fixed interest rates for commercial loans under the disguise of project financing or share financing. The above-mentioned 'investment return with fixed return mode' is the mode with fixed return However, disputes still exist over whether the 'take or pay' clause contained in BOT water investment agreement falls into 'fixed return'.

In current BOT projects, governments usually promise the lowest water quantity, which is regarded as 'take or pay' or 'either taking or paying' clause in law. Generally, relevant prices are also agreed on in BOT project agreements. Simultaneous guarantees of water quantity and price leads to disputes over whether BOT projects fall within 'fixed return' projects. The Changchun Huijin Sewage Treatment Factory Project Case is the outburst of such conflicts. Chuangchun Municipal Intermediate People's Court deems in the first instance that the project is a fixed return one under disguised form since Changchun Huijin and Changchun Drainage Co. settled on the minimum sewage treatment quantity and price and fixed the exchange rate and price condition in the BOT cooperation contract, which is also the view of Changchun Municipal Government. However, Huijin alleges that the fixed return stipulated in the State Council document mainly refers to the situation under which 'the foreign investors' proceeds are invariable or national interest is sacrificed to promise foreign investors' a minimum income' while the fixed sewage treatment quantity and price are only both parties' cooperation items and have nothing to do with fixed proceeds.

It is stated in the Certain Important Issues and Relevant Suggestions Concerning the Promotion of Market-orientation of China City Water Industry (PPP) (final report) by Asia Development Bank that 'take or pay' and agreement on price are basic features and fundamental guarantees of project financing methods such as BOT. If a government selects BOT as a project financing method, it has to accept the game rules, otherwise it may choose other financing methods. However, the fact is that the government adopts BOT methods but refuses to obey the rules. Especially in the judicial standpoint, the courts tend to deem the 'take or pay' clause to constitute 'fixed return', which leads to higher legal risks for foreign investment return in BOT projects.

Legal Effectiveness of Government Guaranty or Assurance

In current Chinese laws and regulations, the main provisions concerning government guaranty are as follows: first, Article 8 of *the Guaranty Law* stipulates that government agencies shall not be guarantor unless approved by the State Council for reloaning of loans from foreign governments or international economic organizations; second, Article 4 of *the Measures on Administration of Domestic Organizations' External Foreign Exchange Guaranty* issued by China People's Bank in September 1996 stating that no state agency or organization shall make an external guaranty unless approved by the State Council for reloaning of loans from foreign governments or international economic organizations. Except under special situations, governments have no qualification to guarantee against common commercial loans or other debts. It is clear in law that various government guaranty forms such as government finance allover guaranties existing in BOT water projects in practice are void.

Another special government credit form exists along with a government guaranty in BOT water projects, that is, government assurance. Governmental franchise has great importance in BOT legal relationships as the core and basis for the whole BOT operation. Hosting nations greatly influence BOT projects and as such have high political risks. Therefore, foreign investors may not only consider the host state's political environment but also request for certain governmental assurance by the hosting state. Government assurance is different from the guaranty in civil law or guaranty law. It is not a general civil guaranty activity. The two has fundamental distinctions. First, guaranty refers to a person's promise for his own behavior. For example, the obligor promises to supply goods in time and ensure the goods' quality. Second, guarantee refers to a third party's guarantee for parties. For example, the legal system for third party guarantee on obligor's performance of his obligations mainly requests that the third party offers a guaranty for one party's performance in his obligations. However, government assurance means the government makes a promise for its own behavior mainly concerning political risks, breach contract liabilities and so on. Guaranty contracts in civil law are affiliated to the main contracts while the government assurance has no independent guaranty contract. It is directly indicated in the franchise agreement and no relationship between main contracts and affiliated contracts exist here. Government assurance is the hosting state's promise of its own behavior. The purpose is to ensure the smooth process of BOT projects and strengthen foreign investors' feeling of safety and confidence in BOT projects. The core of government assurance is to show foreign investors the hosting state's willingness in bearing obligations under the BOT project franchise agreement. China's government assurance for BOT projects generally covers: first, a promise for favorable taxes or adjustment of product or service prices when changing tax; second, a promise for remittance of foreign currencies;[11] third, non-compete promises; fourth, a promise for a

[11] The hosting state may promise the investors' free remittance of operation proceeds in foreign currencies abroad. Normally there is no foreign currency profit in BOT projects and the currencies collected are normally RMB. If RMB currency can not be exchanged into foreign currencies freely, the foreign currency loan and interests may not be repaid, not mentioning the remittance of profits. It is stated in Article 3 of *the Notice on Relevant Issues Concerning Approval Administration of Experimental Foreign Investment*

certain operation term; fifth, a promise for high quality logistics service; sixth, protection of intellectual property and other secret information. Furthermore, the government may make some additional promises such as granting entry licenses for foreign employees, less limitations on equipment imports, no export limitation on equipments and products, or even national treatment and so on.

It is stated in Article 3 of *the Notice on Relevant Issues Concerning Attracting Foreign Investment under BOT Mode* that 'government agencies generally shall not make guaranties or promises in any form for BOT projects, such as foreign currency assurance or loan guaranty, etc. If a guaranty is in real need for a project, prior approval must be obtained from relevant state authorities'. However, it is provided in *the Notice on Relevant Issues Concerning Approval Administration of Experimental Foreign Investment Franchise Projects* that a project company may be allowed to reasonably raise charging standards or prolong a franchise term if it suffers great economic loss under the influence of China's policy adjustments, and the state ensures exchange and remittance abroad of foreign currencies needed in the repayment of loans, interests or bonuses (Article 3). Such legal conflict results in uncertainty in government assurance. Such a clause may be void without prior approval or relevant state authorities.

Risks in Government's Breach of Faith

BOT is a kind of public private partnership (PPP) in which government credibility is very important. Investors, when investigating a project, pay much attention to government credibility in addition to the project's economic benefits since government credibility determines whether a long-term project operation can be accomplished or whether they can be offered with a reasonable takeover price for a project terminated ahead of time.[12] Considering the district element, investors have more confidence in southeast coastal areas and more developed areas of China where government officers have a better sense of the market and the BOT performance rate is high. The ten top cities elected in the first China Cities with Best Water Investment Potential Competition held by China Water Website in 2004 are Beijing, Shanghai, Shenzhen, Guangzhou, Suzhou, Hangzhou, Tianjin, Xiamen, while Nanjing and Wuhan, and Chongqing and Chengwu shared the same ranking. In less developed districts, government credibility is relatively low. The rate for government breaches of contract under cooperation with private capital is rather high; even personnel changes upon completion of a term may influence the survival of a BOT project. The dire situation in some places can be summarised as, 'opening the door to attract investment but closing the

Franchise Projects that 'the state ensures the exchange and remittance abroad of foreign currencies needed in repayment of loans, interests and bonuses of project companies'.

12 Shen Jiyong, Wang Shouqing and Qiang Maoshan (2005), the Political Risk and Sovereignty Risk in China BOT/PPP Projects: through Case Analysis, the China Commerce: Investment and Financing, Issue 1.

door to terminate it'. Foreign investors may find warning in the following cases involving government breaches against private enterprises: (a) Reconstruction of 107 National Highway in Xianning, Hubei. The private Tan Family Company signed a contract with the transportation bureau under which the company invested RMB 30 million while the bureau took charge of collecting tolls. The bureau failed to pay the company's profit share of RMB 26 million in the four years following 1995. Then, the bureau sold the highway property and relevant rights without notifying the company or paying the company any money. After that, the bureau litigated, requesting the local court to confirm the formerly established relationship between the two parties as a debit and credit as opposed to an investment. The court made such a judgment accordingly. (b) The private Xiamen Rongbin Investment Co. invested in construction of South Xiangjiang Bridge in Changsha. Changsha municipal government first modified the design, leading to an increase of RMB 50 million in project costs, then unilaterally declared as void the former agreement offering land-use right of 2,800 mu. (c) The private Anhui Guozhen Group invested in many projects at Fuyang city. First, the Fulin Road Square Development Project. The company prepaid USD 1.5 million per contract in 1997, but could not obtain the land use certificate. At the beginning of 2000, the government announced it was taking back the land according to law without returning the prepayment made by the company. Second, the Yinglu Advertisement Management Right Project. The company invested RMB 15 million to make Yingzhou Road the Fuyang Image Road and the sample road, but the government cancelled the road naming right stipulated in the contract and ordered the company to remove all the advertisement light boxes. Third, the natural gas utilization project. In 1997, the government publicly announced the designation of the company as the sole tunnel gas operation company in the city. The company made great efforts to list Fuyang in the first group of cities in Anhui Province participating in the national east transfer of west gas project. Afterwards, the government suddenly announced establishment of a state-owned natural gas company to wholly undertake Fuyang city natural gas utilization business.[13] However, the worst case of the government's breach of contract in foreign investment in the Chinese water market is the Changchun Huijin case.

Uncertainty in Legal Effectiveness of Hypothecation of Charging Right

Pledge of charging right is not a guarantee under *the Guaranty Law* in which Article 75 lists pledge rights without containing a charging right. However, it is stipulated in Article 97 of *the Interpretation on Various Issues Concerning Application of the Guaranty Law by the Supreme People's Court of PRC* that the pledge of

[13] Yang Qing (2005), the Research on Various Problems in Applying BOT in China Water Industry, China Market, Issue 1.

proceeds right in real assets such as highway bridges, highway tunnels and highway crossings shall be dealt with according to Article 75.4 of *the Guaranty Law.* Therefore, it may be deemed that highway charging right is clearly included in 'other rights' stipulated in Article 75 of *the Guaranty Law.* Besides, the State Development and Reform Commission and the People's Bank of China approved using the proceeds right in rural electricity network reconstruction projects to pledge for loans. It is also stipulated in *the Opinions on Further Resolving Capital Problem in Construction of University Logistics Service Facilities Including Students' Apartments* issued by the People's Bank of China and the Ministry of Education that students apartment charging rights may be pledged for loans. *The Opinions Concerning Promotion of City Sewage and Rubbish Treatment Industrialized Development* jointly issued by the former State Planning Commission, Ministry of Construction and the State Environmental Protection Administration encourages city governments to pledge sewage and rubbish treatment charging right for loans. It is stated in *the Opinion on Implementing Various Policies and Measures of Developing the West by the State Council* that the loan scope shall be extended for pledges of basic facility project proceeds rights or charging rights, including the use of proceeds rights in the rural electricity network and highways to pledge for loans. Conditions shall be created for gradually expanding the charging pledge loan scope to basic city facility projects including water supply, heat supply, public transportation, telecom and so on, and attempts shall be made for extending loans with project proceeds rights or charging rights pledges for water development projects and city environment protection projects such as city sewage treatment and rubbish treatment with certain repayment abilities. It is obvious that the above-mentioned provisions are only joint administrative regulations not in the level of administrative laws and rules. It may be found in the current laws and national policies that charging rights permitted to be pledged are limited to real asset proceeds. A pledge right is a type of property right. According to the property right legal principle in General Rules of Civil Law, the lawful effect of pledge right shall be in accordance with the clear provision of law. The 'other rights may be pledged under law' stipulated in Article 75.4 of *the Guaranty Law* also embodies such a principle, showing rights to be pledged must be those allowed by law. However, a charging right pledge is not stipulated in *the Guaranty Law.* There is also no clear confirmation in law or rules of other rights for pledges including school charging rights, hospital charging rights, water charging rights, electricity charging rights and so on. Furthermore, some pledges do not have lawful charging rights, which is also one of the legal risks for a charging right pledge. Charging right is a kind of legal right which must be approved or licensed by the administrative authorities. In current charging right pledges, some charging rights have not been approved by administrative authorities or contradict with relevant laws and rules. The pledges do not have legitimate charging rights. For example, the city supporting charging rights and land development charging rights in a city construction project pledge belong to administrative charges, and the fees collected shall be covered by the fiscal budget with two-line administration of income and expenses. Accordingly, pledges on such rights are not protected under law.[14] Furthermore, some pledges do not go through pledge registration, which may cause a charging right pledge to be void. According to existing laws and rules, right pledges, except an exchange, cheque, cashier's cheque, bond, certificate of deposit, storage certificate, bill of lading, and so on, with delivery of right certificate as the effective essential element, generally are under the procedural effective essential element of pledge registration. However, the state has not clearly designated a pledge registration administration authority even up to now, so a charging pledge can not be effectively registered. Furthermore, a project under construction can only obtain a charging license upon its accomplishment, and registration for pledge rights can not be made before obtaining the license. Finally, even if the charging right pledge comes into existence effectively, the realization of it may be difficult when the obligor refuses to perform his obligation, especially in projects with a charging right involving public interest.[15]

Conflict Between Franchise Agreement and Existing Laws and Regulations

The most important document in a BOT project is the franchise agreement. It is stipulated in Article 18.1 of *the Constitution* that 'PRC allows foreign enterprises and other economic organizations of individuals to invest in china under the laws of PRC and cooperate with Chinese enterprises or other economic organizations in various forms', which make clear China's ways of utilizing foreign capital in economic cooperation and specifies Chinese subjects as 'enterprises or other economic organizations' without mentioning the legal status of BOT franchise agreements with a government as one party. The purpose for avoiding a government's direct contract with foreign investors in Chinese law is to prevent the so-called 'national contract' under which the government shall bear national liabilities. Therefore, BOT contracts in China can only be negotiated and executed between a state-owned company with a certain franchise and foreign investors. Such contracts are obviously not franchise agreements. In franchise agreements with no government participation, the parties' request for BOT agreements can not be satisfied. For example, the project tax rate can only be determined by law while no party may offer tax preferences in contracts. It is difficult to get government support and preference with no legal basis, especially for tax, performance guarantee and foreign exchange balance. Even if relevant authorities promise this as an exception, the validity is still uncertain.[16]

---

[14] Heng Huiyong, Hao Cheng (2005), the Risk in Charging Right Pledge and Countermeasure Suggestion, Finance and Economy, Issue 5.

[15] Yang Fan (2003), the Legal Risk in Charging Right Pledge, Henan Finance and Tax Higher College Transactions, Issue 5.

[16] Zhang Xiaoyan, The Conflict between BOT and China's Existing Laws, the People's Court News on 15 December 2004.

Conflict Between Ratio of BOT Project Company's Registered Capital Against Total Investment and Existing Laws and Regulations

Foreign investors have two alternative ways of investing in China's fundamental facility construction under the BOT mode. One is 'sole foreign investment' for a project company. Another is the joint establishment of a project company by the project initiators and investors. In nature, the two are foreign-invested enterprises. Article 3 of *the Provisional Regulations on Ratio of Joint Ventures' Registered Capital and Total Investment* issued by the State Administration of Industry and Commerce in 1987 lists four ratios ranging from 7:10 to 1:3. For project financing, investors mainly rely on loans along with certain investments of self-owned capital in the project company since the project needs a large amount of funds. Generally, project companies' ratio of self-owned capital and long-term debt is between 1:9 and 4:6, much lower than the common share to debt ratio, which contradicts with China's existing laws and rules.

Risks in Bidding

BOT projects in China are carried out through public competitive bidding. Once the project proposal is approved, the bidding process starts. It is provided in Article 3.1 of the *Opinions on Expediting Market Orientation Progress of City Planning Public Utility Industry* issued by the Ministry of Construction on 27 December 2002 that franchise operations shall determine investors and operators through public bidding in a stipulated process. According to *the Bidding Law of PRC*, the content, term, market admittance condition, bidding process and method of the franchise project shall be publicly announced, applications shall be publicly accepted in stipulated time, applicants shall be examined and seriously evaluated for their qualification by experts according to market admittance conditions, and the bidder to be granted with the franchise shall be chosen out of the best. Article 8 of *the Notice on Relevant Issues Concerning Approval Administration of Experimental Foreign Investment Franchise Projects* issued by the Ministry of Construction on 19 March 2004 further specifies the bidding process.[17]

---

[17] The authority shall choose bidders or operators according to the following procedure: first, propose the public utility franchise project and publicly announce bidding conditions after getting approval from the municipality, city or county government, and accept bidding; secondly, recommend qualified bidding candidates through qualification examination and plan pre-examination of franchise bidders according to the bidding conditions; thirdly, organize a bid-evaluation commission to evaluate bids under law, and choose the best franchise grantee after interrogation and public enquiry; fourthly, publicly announce the bidding result with the announcing time of no less than 20 days; fifthly, sign the franchise agreement with bidder if no objection is raised within the public announcing time and after approval by municipality, city or county government.

The Standing Committee of the National People's Congress promulgated the bidding law especially for projects on 30 August 1999. In project procurement, the bidder shall not be responsible for financing. The bidding documents shall specify the concrete technique standard and the bidder shall compete according to the bidding price. Since the law is based on the specialty of project procurement, the bidding law forbids any material alteration to clauses or conditions in the bidding documents. Meanwhile, the law forbids further negotiation in any form after the completion of the bidding evaluation.[18] Once the winning bidder is determined and announced, no further negotiation can be made. However the bidding process of PPP BOT projects is quite different. The bidder needs to prepare plans for project financing, construction, operation and maintenance. In bidding for a BOT water project, bidders' plans need to be evaluated jointly and the final determination of the bidding winner shall be made according to the integrated evaluation. Meanwhile, BOT project participants need to establish a risk share mechanism through a series of contracts. The process is quite complicated. It is hard to ensure all relevant matters be appropriately dealt with in the contract. In the bidding process of a BOT water project, it is impossible to eliminate detailed negotiation after the winning bidder is chosen due to the complexity of project arrangements. The coercive application of *the Bidding Law* in BOT water projects is a 'cutting feet for shoes' style system.

Loan Term Limitation

BOT water projects are generally feature centralized capital, long-term repayment, long-term operation and stable cash flow. The application of long-term debt favors the improvement of financing efficiency, lowering project costs accordingly. In the financing of many international projects, it is common for fundamental facility projects to get 15 to 20 year loans according to the cash flow status in different operation periods. However, long-term financial debt instruments can not find legal support in China. It is stipulated in Article 11 (Loan Term) of *the General Rules for Loans* that 'the loan term shall be determined through negotiation between the debtor and creditor according to the debtor's production operation period, repayment ability and the creditor's capital supplying ability, and be stated in the loan contract. The term for self-support loans shall not exceed 10 years, otherwise the contract shall be submitted to the People's Bank of China for record'. Article 12 (Extension of Loan Term) stipulates that 'the debtor, if unable to repay the loan in time, shall apply to the creditor for extension of loan term before the expiration date. The creditor shall determine whether to extend the loan term.

[18] Article 46 of *the Bidding Law of PRC* states that the bid-inviting party and the winning bidder shall conclude a written contract according to the bid invitation documents and the winning bidder's bid documents within 30 days of the date of issuance of the letter of acceptance. The bid inviting party and the winning bidder may not subsequently conclude other agreements which contravene the substantive terms of the contract.

Extension for short-tem loans shall not be longer than the original loan term, extension for mid-term loans shall not be longer than half of the original loan term, while extension for long-term loans shall not be longer than 3 years, unless the state stipulates otherwise. In another words, the loan term shall be less than 13 years, which obviously falls behind the financing demand in BOT water projects.

Conflict Between Allocated Land and Pledge

BOT water investments mainly adopt the financing method of establishing project companies with share capital investment, combined with project financing, and based on complicated contractual relationships and various guarantee agreements due to the great amount of construction capital needed. A floating mortgage guarantee is usually adopted under loan agreements to permit the debtor to expand the mortgage scope from the total assets of the project company at the execution of contract, to all the assets obtained during the construction and operation of the project including land, buildings, equipments and rights such as creditor's rights, intellectual property rights, mining rights and so on, which is an international practice.[19]

It is stated in Article 3.4 of *the Notice on Carrying out City Rubbish Treatment Charging System for Promoting Rubbish Treatment Industrialization* that 'the land used for construction of newly built city sewage and rubbish treatment facilities may be obtained through administrative allocation. The investing and operating enterprise is entitled to use the allocated land for specified purposes within the contract term'. In China, land for BOT water investment project is generally allocated. The allocated land use right is also a property right, but the core feature of property in civil law, its ability to be tradable, is lost.[20] It is stipulated in Article 44 of *Interim Regulations Concerning Assignment and Transfer of the Right to the Use of the State-owned Land in the Urban Areas* (No.55 Decree) that 'the allocated right to the use of the land may not be transferred, leased, or mortgaged, with the exception of cases as specified in Article 45 of these Regulations'. It is further clarified in Article 8 of the *Measures on Administration of City Real Estate* that real estate for public welfare including education, hospitals and public utilities can not be mortgaged. Article 33 of the *Interim Regulations* states that, 'With the mortgage of the right to the use of the land, the above-ground buildings and other attached objects thereon shall be mortgaged accordingly. With the above-ground buildings and other attached objects, the right to the use of the land within the limits of use of the said buildings and objects shall be mortgaged accordingly'. A floating mortgage in BOT water projects involves real property attached to the land. Land-use right mortgages must be considered in such mortgages.

---

19 Clifford Chance (1996), The Project Financing, translated by Gong Huihong, Huaxia Publishing House, P. 46.

20 Chang Liang, Chen Mei (2005), the Legal Issues Concerning Land in BOT Projects, the Resources and Human Living Environment, Issue 3.

The assigned land-use right and the ownership of the on-land buildings and other attachments may be transferred, rented or mortgaged after the payment of full land-use right assignment amount to the local city or county government, or after the turning-in of proceeds in transfers, rent or mortgage as the land-use right assignment payment. A detailed course of action is stated in Article 45 of *the Measures on Administration of City Real Estate* as follows: in the disposal of real estate mortgage of land-use right obtained through allocation along with buildings attached thereto, the mortgagor can only be repaid preferentially after the amount equal to the amount of land-use right assignment payment is handed over from the proceeds in disposal'. Therefore, legal risks exist for possible confrontations of ineffectiveness or failure in realizing the mortgage in the setting up of a floating mortgage guarantee in a BOT water investment project in China.

Appendix: Laws and Regulations on Foreign Investment in China's Water Market

Issuing Time	Issuing Authority	Title
19 July 1994	Ministry of Construction	Regulations on City Water Supply
16 January 1995	Ministry of Foreign Economic And Trade Cooperation	Notice on Relevant Issues Concerning Attracting Foreign Investment under BOT Mode
21 August 1995	State Planning Commission, Ministry of Electricity, Ministry of Transportation	Notice on Relevant Issues Concerning Approval Administration of Experimental Foreign Investment Franchise Projects
1 January 1997	Ministry of Public Health, Ministry of Construction	Measures on Supervision and Administration of Drinking Water Sanitation
16 April 1997	State Planning Commission, State Administration of Foreign Exchange	Provisional Measures on Project Financing Abroad
4 September 1997	The State Council	Water Industry Policy
23 September 1998	State Planning Commission, Ministry of Construction	Measures on Administration of City Water Supply Price
September 1998	The State Council	Notice on Strengthening Administration of Foreign Exchange and Foreign Debt And Carrying out Inspection on Foreign Exchange and Foreign Debt
1 May 1998	State Planning Commission, Ministry of Construction, State Environmental Protection Administration	Notice on Strengthening Collection of Sewage Treatment Fee, Establishing Good Operation Mechanism of City Sewage Release and Centralized Treatment

27 May 2000	Ministry of Construction	Provisional Regulations on Utilization of Foreign Capital in City Planning Public Utility
April 2001	The State Council	Notice on Further Strengthening and Improving Foreign Exchange Administration
1 April 2002	State Planning Commission, Ministry of Finance, Ministry of Construction, Ministry of Water Facilities, State Environmental Protection Administration	Notice on Further Promoting Reform on City Water Supply Price
29 August 2002	Standing Committee of National People's Congress	Water Law
7 September 2002	State Planning Commission, Ministry of Finance, Ministry of Construction, State Environmental Protection Administration	Notice on Carrying out City Rubbish Treatment Charging System for Promoting Rubbish Treatment Industrialization
10 September 2002	State Planning Commission, Ministry of Construction, State Environmental Protection Administration	Opinions on Promoting the Development of City Sewage and Rubbish Treatment Industrialization
10 September 2002	General Office of The State Council	Notice on Appropriate Handling of Existing Problems in Guarantee of Foreign Investment Fixed Return Projects
11 November 2002	General Office of The State Planning Commission	Notice on Issues Concerning Expediting Prophase Project Work and Active Promotion of city sewage and rubbish treatment industrialization
27 December 2002	Ministry of Construction	Opinions on Expediting Market Orientation Progress of City Planning Public Utility Industry
1 January 2004	National Development and Reform Commission	Measures on Administration of Water Supply Price for Water Projects
19 April 2004	General Office of the State Council	Notice on Promotion of Water Price Reform, Enhancing Water Saving and Protecting Water Resources
1 May 2004	Ministry of Construction	Measures on Administration of City Planning Public Utility Franchise Operation

[Note: The project approval under the Notice on Relevant Issues Concerning Approval Administration of Experimental Foreign Investment Franchise Projects has been called off while the Notice is still in effect.]

12 Legal Risks for Foreign Investment in the Insurance Industry

The best time for foreign life insurance companies' entrance into the Chinese market has passed, but those with nice skills and creative strategies still have a chance here.

—— Bai Defan, Tab Bowers, Rong Juesheng[1]

12.1 Introduction of Foreign Investment in China's Insurance Industry[2]

12.1.1 Brief View on China's Insurance Industry

China's insurance industry achieved the premium of RMB 431.81 billion in 2004, 11.3% higher than the previous year. This included the property insurance premium of RMB 108.99 billion, which was 25.4% higher than the previous year, and the life insurance premium of RMB 322.82 billion, which was 7.2% higher than the previous year. The insurance capital utilization balance at the end of the year was RMB 1,124.98 billion, RMB 287.13 billion yuan more than the beginning of the year. The insurance depth, that is, the proportion of premium in GDP, was 3.4% while the insurance density, that is, the premium per person counted according to permanent population, was RMB 332. At the end of 2004, the gross assets of insurance companies were valued at RMB 1,185.36 billion, RMB 273.07 billion more than in the beginning of the year.

The market structure shows that China's insurance market is still highly monopolized. PICC Property and Casualty Company Limited ("PICC P&C"), China Pacific Insurance (Group) Co., Ltd and Ping An Insurance (Group) Company of China, Ltd. ("Ping An") occupy 95% of China's non-life insurance market. The market share of PICC is 53.34%, 5% lower than 58.09% in 2004. China Pacific Insurance (Group) Co., Ltd listed the second has excellent performance, improving its market share from 12.32% in 2004 to the current 14.50% with an

---

1 Bai Defan, Tab Bowers, Rong Juesheng (2004), The *Selling life insurance to China*, Mckinsey Senior Management Collected Essays, Fourth Issue.

2 Relevant data is from the websites of China Insurance Regulatory Commission and the Ministry of Commerce.

Table 12.1. Property Insurance Premium, Depth, Density and Increase Rate in 2002

Nation/ District	Premium (USD 0.1 million)	Nominal Increase Rate (%)	Actual Increase Rate (%)	Insurance Density (USD/person)	Insurance Depth (%)
U.S.A.	5198.58	12.9	11.1	1799	4.98
Japan	910.28	3.5	1.8	714.7	2.22
Great Britain	770.26	17.3	10.8	1199.7	4.56
Taiwan, China	79.32	8.7	11.4	354.1	2.81
Hong Kong, China	23.42	18.6	22.3	345.2	1.45
Mainland China	118.34	13.8	13.3	9.2	0.96

Resource: Swiss Reinsurance Company, sigma, Eighth Issue in 2003; Data of Mainland China is quoted from the 2003 Year Book of China Insurance.

increase of 2%. It is the sole company enjoying increased market share among the three Chinese insurance giants. 90% of the life insurance market is still monopolized by three Chinese life insurance giants, that is, China Life Insurance Company Limited, Ping An and China Pacific Insurance (Group) Co., Ltd.

The China Insurance Regulatory Commission (CIRC) is the state supervision authority of Chinese insurance industry. It is in charge of the promulgation of relevant regulations on the insurance business. CIRC was established as a ministry level commission under the direct guidance of the State Council in November 1998, replacing the People's Bank of China to administer the insurance market. The duties of CIRC include making insurance policies, implementing laws, punishing persons violating laws and regulations, protecting policy holders' rights and benefits, operating a risk evaluation system, approving the establishment of domestic insurance companies and foreign insurance companies and issuing licenses for operation. According to experience, CIRC has great discretion in issuing new licenses.

Besides, some administration authorities are also responsible for supervising the insurance industry, such as the State Administration of Industry and Commerce (SAIC) and local branches. They are fully responsible for the registration of insurance businesses, protection of fair competition in insurance market and policy holders' rights and benefits. (Note: Functions' overlapping in ensuring fair competition in insurance market and protecting policy holders' rights and benefits exist between the State Administration of Industry and Commerce and CIRC. In most cases, the later plays a more active role.)

12.1.2 Brief View of Foreign Investment in China's Insurance Industry

Since the opening of China's insurance industry, the proportion of foreign insurance companies' premium as a percentage of national premium has increased every year. The premium increased from RMB 1.82 billion in 1999 to RMB 6.73 billion in 2003. The current premium is five times that of five years ago. The total assets of foreign-invested insurance companies in China increased from RMB 4.4 billion in 1999 to RMB 19.78 billion in 2003, 3.2 times the previous one. The market share of foreign insurance companies in Shanghai, Guangzhou and other areas with earlier openness is over 10%.

For the average market share in China, foreign-owned enterprises and joint ventures account for 3%, which means foreign capital has a market share of at least 1.5% if its shareholding proportion is counted as no more than 49%. Furthermore, China Life, PICC and Ping An have all listed abroad while Ping An has been introduced into foreign strategic investors. With simple counting, we may find foreign investors hold 16% of the Chinese insurance market through the three companies and a total market share of 17.5% if one includes the 1.5% market share obtained through joint ventures, which is calculated according to the proportion of ventures listed abroad and the shareholding proportion of strategic investors based on the three companies' Chinese insurance market share of 64% in 2004.

Foreign insurance companies apparently speeded the entering into the Chinese market in 2004. Altogether 40 foreign insurance companies set up 75 agencies, including the ones in preparation in mainland China, up to 8 December 2004, among which are 23 life insurance companies, 14 property insurance companies and 3 re-insurance companies. In the first 10 months of 2004, foreign life insurance companies held 2.4% of the Chinese mainland life insurance market while property insurance companies' market share was 1.1%. Though the market share of foreign life insurance companies is still not a big proportion, the great developmental pace shall not be ignored. The increased rate of premium acquired by foreign insurance companies has been twice or three times that acquired by Chinese insurance companies. Take the first half of 2004 as an example, the premium income of foreign property insurance companies increased 47.1% while that of Chinese property insurance companies only increased 23%; the premium income of foreign life insurance companies increased 51.2% while the Chinese life insurance premium income only increased 6.5%. Obviously, the market share of Chinese companies in the insurance industry is decreasing as the market share of foreign insurance companies are quickly increasing.

Comparing major insurance companies, we may find Generali China Life Insurance Company Limited, a joint-venture between Assicurazioni Generali S.P.A. (Generali) and China National Petroleum Corporation (CNPC), has a premium income only next to China Pacific Insurance (Group) Co., Ltd, who is number one in the Chinese life insurance industry since it succeeded in undertaking RMB 20 billion in group insurance immediately after the lifting of the ban in the first quarter of 2005 that prevented foreign life insurance companies from undertaking group insurance and pension annuity insurance. After the RMB20 billion supplementary pension insurance premium offered to China National Petroleum Corporation, its Chinese shareholder, Generali China Life Insurance Co., Ltd. obtained high premium income of RMB20.153 billion, which is much higher than Ping An Life Insurance Company's premium income of RMB14.9 billion yuan. American International Assurance Company, Limited (AIA), the former number one foreign insurance company also lagged far behind.

Course of Foreign Investment in Chinese Insurance Industry

- ✧ In October 1980, American International Group (AIG) set up its representative office at Shanghai, which marks start of an era for foreign insurance companies' entrance in Chinese insurance market.
- ✧ In September 1992, American International Assurance Company, Limited (AIA) subordinated to AIG was approved to set up a branch at Shanghai, which was the first time a foreign insurance enterprise started business in China since 1949.
- ✧ In July 1994, the Shanghai Branch of the Tokyo Marine and Fire Insurance Company Limited was approved.
- ✧ In 1995, Guangzhou city was approved to be the open city for foreign insurance agencies. In the same year, AIG set up its life insurance and property insurance branch at Guangzhou.
- ✧ In November 1996, Manulife-Sinochem Life Insurance Co., Ltd., the first life insurance joint venture was set up in Shanghai. Later on, Pacific-Antai Life Insurance Company Limited and Allianz Dazhong Life Insurance Company Ltd. were established.
- ✧ In April 1999, CIRC simultaneously approved four foreign insurance companies to enter the Chinese market. American Chubb Group of Insurance Companies set up its branch in China while American John Hancock Tianan Life Insurance Company, British Prudential Corporation PLC. And Canadian Sun Life Assurance Company set up life insurance joint ventures in China.
- ✧ In July 2000, Assicurazioni Generali and ING Insurance International BV obtained their business license in China. In the same year, China Life CMG, CITIC Prudential Life Insurance Company and John Hancock Tianan Life Insurance Company started their formal operations in China.
- ✧ In September 2001, China approved eight foreign insurance companies to carry out or enlarge operation in China. Gerling Group Insurance, Allianz Group Insurance and Swiss Suez Insurance Company were approved for the aim of establishing property insurance companies in China. Commercial Union Assurance Co. PLC, CNP Assurances and General American Life Insurance Company were approved for planning of establishing life insurance joint ventures. Axa-minmetals Assurance Co. Ltd. which has started its operation in

Shanghai and Royal & Sun Alliance Insurance Group PLC were approved to set up one branch respectively in China.

- On 25 October 2001, just before China's entrance into WTO, another eight foreign insurance companies were approved to carry out or enlarge business in China. St. Paul Fire and Marine Insurance Company and American International Association set up representative offices at Beijing and Shanghai respectively.
- In December 2001, Gerling Group Insurance, Allianz Group Insurance and Swiss Suez Insurance Company were approved to plan for the establishment of property insurance company in China. CGNU, CNP and General American Life Insurance Company, New York Life Insurance, Metropolitan Life Insurance Company and Nippon Life Insurance were approved to plan for the establishment of life insurance joint ventures.
- On 7 June 2002, the day of historic importance in China's insurance industry, the first foreign wholly owned insurance company, American International Assurance Beijing Branch was opened in low key.
- In August 2002, Munich Reinsurance Compa, Swiss Reinsurance Company and CIGNA Insurance Company were approved to start business in China.
- On 1 November 2002, Standard Life Assurance Company, Liberty Mutual Insurance Company and Sompo Japan Insurance Inc. were approved to set up agencies in China. AXA-Minmetals Assurance Co., Ltd. and Royal & Sun Alliance Group were approved to set up one branch each. Heng An Life Insurance Company and Standard Life Insurance Company were approved to set up a joint venture which would be the largest life insurance joint venture in China with each party contributing 50%.
- On 20 December 2002, Hai'er New York Life Insurance Company, the joint venture set up by New York Life Insurance, the largest mutual life insurance company in America, and Hai'er group formally entered the Shanghai market. The joint venture has RMB 0.2 billion of registered capital with each party holding 50% of the shares. The preparation period for Hai'er New York Life Insurance is the shortest in all insurance joint ventures, illustrating the efficiency level of both parties. Almost simultaneously, ING Capital Life Insurance Company Limited set up jointly by ING and Beijing Capital Group began selling policies in Dalian.
- In 2003, CIRC, according to China's WTO entrance commitments, permitted foreign property insurance companies to undertake all non-life insurance businesses except legal insurance businesses, and expanded the operation area of foreign insurance companies to 15 cities.
- On 13 February 2004, Mr. Wu Dingfu, the Chairman of CIRC announced at the media meeting held by the State Council Information Office that China would further promote openness in the insurance market, sincerely perform its WTO entrance commitment, and gradually cancel limitation on foreign insurance companies' service objects and operation area.

12.2 Laws and Regulations on Foreign Investment in China's Insurance Industry

Foreign investors mainly take two methods of entering the Chinese insurance market, participation or establishment. The latter includes the establishment of joint ventures, wholly foreign-owned enterprises, branches or representative offices.

12.2.1 Participation in Insurance Companies

Participators in existing Chinese insurance companies must abide by the newly amended the Regulation on Administration of Insurance Companies and the Provisional Regulation on Equity Investment in Insurance Companies.

Participation Subjects and Regulations on Supervision and Administration

According to Article 5 of *the Provisional Regulation on Equity Investment in Insurance Companies* promulgated on 1 April 2000, enterprises registered at the Administrations of Industry and Commerce and qualified as legal persons may invest in insurance companies. Meanwhile, Article 6 of *the Provisional Regulation* stipulates that enterprises abroad or foreign-owned enterprises in China who comply with Article 5 may invest in insurance companies. Therefore, the participation subjects shall be enterprises with legal person qualification, while enterprises without legal person qualification cannot participate therein.

However, it is stipulated in Article 41 of *the Regulation on Administration of Insurance Companies* issued on 16 June 2004 that 'enterprise legal persons or other organizations admitted by law or administrative regulations may invest in and hold shares of insurance companies', which contain 'other organizations admitted by law or administrative regulations'. Article 45 provides that 'financial institutions abroad meeting the requirements under Article 42 of this Regulation may invest in and hold shares of insurance companies under approval of CIRC', which does not make legal person qualification a prerequisite for an overseas financial institution's participation. Under the principal of lex posterior derogat priori, the investor's scope covers other organizations with no legal person qualification at least in the publicized rules. Furthermore, the 'financial institutions abroad' contained in Article 45 seems to differentiate between financial institutions and non-financial institutions, which could not be found in other articles.

Furthermore, special attention should be paid to the different treatment of foreign-invested enterprises in *the Provisional Regulation on Equity Investment in Insurance Companies.* Sino-foreign equity and contractual joint ventures are actually treated as Chinese shareholders while wholly foreign-owned enterprises which also possess Chinese legal person qualification are treated as foreign shareholders in relation to the firm's operational aspects, along with enterprises abroad without regard to their nationality. The proper law standard concerning enterprise nationality which shall be adopted under the General Rules of Civil Law and Civil

Procedure Law is in fact abandoned. The 'capital control theory' is adopted instead. Even a Sino-foreign equity or contractual joint venture holding more than 25% capital share in an insurance company, the insurance company may still not be regarded as foreign-owned companies under *the Regulation on Administration of Foreign-owned Insurance Companies*. However, if an enterprise abroad or a domestic wholly foreign-owned enterprise holds more than 25% capital share in an insurance company, the insurance company shall be deemed a foreign-owned insurance company from the operation and administration aspect and *the Regulation on Administration of Foreign-owned Insurance Companies* shall be applied thereto. In another words, foreign investors' shareholding of less than 25% in a sole Chinese capital insurance company constitutes foreign capital participation while a share holding higher than 25% constitutes a Sino-foreign joint venture. The distinction between foreign capital participation and joint venture lies in the share holding proportion of foreign investors.[3]

However, there are also exceptions to this rule. For example, the foreign capital shareholding proportion of Ping An Insurance Group was 41.3% before its listing, which is high above the stipulated 25% critical point. However, CIRC conceded that Ping An Insurance Group was a Chinese insurance company instead of a foreign-owned one according to the newly amended *Insurance Law* for ensuring the quantity and scale of Chinese capital insurance companies back at the end of 2003. Furthermore, a Chinese capital insurance company with branches at Hong Kong shall not be deemed as having foreign shareholders at its participation in insurance companies. It may not be limited by the above legal proportion and the relevant authorities shall continue to regard the insurance company as being invested by Chinese capital and shareholders. In addition, shareholders abroad, when investing in listed insurance companies, shall not be limited in relation to investment proportions. That is to say, domestic insurance companies listed abroad, even if foreign capital shareholders hold more than 25% of the company's shares, shall still be treated as Chinese capital insurance companies.

Share Proportion

The share proportion for foreign investment in a Chinese insurance company shall be no higher than 10% per shareholder and 25% for all foreign shareholders in the total share capital of the insurance company in accordance with *the Provisional Regulation on Equity Investment in Insurance Companies* promulgated on 1 April 2000. But it is stipulated in Article 43 of *the Regulation on Administration of Insurance Companies* passed on May 13, 2004 that each enterprise legal person or other organization (including its affiliates) investing in an insurance company shall not hold more than 20% of its shares except insurance holding companies or insurance

[3] Qiu Meihui, The China Mainland Insurance Supervision Discretion Influences Market Opening – Further Discussion on Mainland Insurance Opening Policy, download from the website of Taiwan Insurance Industry Development Center (the last visiting on Dec. 12, 2005).

companies approved by CIRC. Article 45 stipulates that financial institutions abroad complying with the requirements of Article 42 may invest in financial companies if approved by CIRC. The total share proportion of all shareholders abroad shall be lower than 25% of the total shares of an insurance company. In another words, each shareholder's share proportion is improved to 20%. Furthermore, after the execution of *the Closer Economic Partnership Arrangement* between Mainland China, Hong Kong & Macao, the upper limit for share holding by each enterprise legal person in Hong Kong or Macao in a sole Chinese capital insurance company increases from the former 20% to 24.9%. There is no investment proportion limitation on shareholders' investment in listed insurance companies.

In fact, foreign shareholders are not forbidden from holding more than 25% share capital in a Chinese insurance company. Any share proportion is permitted if not beyond the China's admittance commitments in WTO regime of insurance industry. However, participation turns into a joint venture if all shareholders abroad hold more than 25% of shares of an insurance company and *the Regulation on Administration of Foreign Insurance Companies* is applicable thereto. In practice, a foreign group holding more than 10% stock of a Chinese insurance company, usually participate in name of various companies under the group so as to elude the provision on the 10% upper limit for sole foreign investor's share in a Chinese insurance company.

Table 12.2. Foreign Equity Investment in Chinese Insurance Companies

Insurance Company	**Foreign Capital Investor**	**Share Proportion**
China Ping An Insurance (Group) Limited	Morgan Stanley Morrisys Investment Co., Limited	6.87%
	Goldman Sachs Group Inc.	6.87%
	HSBC Insurance Holding Co., Ltd.	10.00%
	Subtotal	23.74%
Xin Hua Life Insurance Co., Ltd.	Suez Insurance Company	10.00%
	International Financial Corporation	6.00%
	Meiji Life Insurance Company	4.50%
	Holland Finance Development Company	4.40%
	Subtotal	24.90%
Tai Kang Life Insurance Co., Ltd.	Winterthur Swiss Insurance	10.00%
	Xin Zheng Teda Investment Co., Ltd.	8.33%
	Luxemburg Louy Bank	5.67%
	SoftBank Group	1.00%
	Subtotal	25.00%

Table 12.2 (continued)

Insurance Company	Foreign Capital Investor	Share Proportion
Pacific Life Insurance Co., Ltd.	China Insurance International Holdings Company (Note 1)	50.05%
	Jinbo Investment International Co., Ltd. (Note 2)	12.45%
	Futong International Holdings Company (Note 2)	12.45%
	Subtotal	74.95%
Min Sheng Life Insurance Co., Ltd.	Asia General Singapore	5.00%
Shenming Life Insurance Holding Co., Ltd.	Tokiomarine & Nichido Fire Insurance Co., Ltd and Japan Millea Asia Co., Ltd.	12.45%
	Hong Kong New World Development Co., Ltd.(Zhen Jianyuan)(held by Wanhan Wuxin and Wuhan Yili) (Note 3)	20.00%
	Subtotal	32.45%
Huatai Property Insurance Holding Co., Ltd.	An Da Scale Reinsurance Co., Ltd.	10.00%
	An Da North America Insurance Holding Company	6.13%
	An Da America Holding Company	6.00%
	Subtotal	22.13%
Pacific Insurance (Group) Co., Ltd.	China Insurance International Holdings Company Limited	30.05%
	China Bank of Industry and Commerce (Asia) Co., Ltd.	24.99%
	Subtotal	55.04%

Note: 1. China Insurance International Holdings Company (Hong Kong) is established by China Life Insurance Company in Hong Kong. 2. The two companies are all branches of Futong Group. Futong Group, through its various branches, actually holds 24.9% share of Pacific Life Insurance Co., Ltd. The two companies are only representative of these branches. 3. The two holding companies are domestic companies established by Hong Kong Group. So Pacific Life Insurance Co., Ltd. is still a Chinese capital insurance company. Resource: the China Mainland Insurance Supervision Discretion Influences Market Opening – Further Discussion on Mainland Insurance Opening Policy by Qiu Meihui from the website of Taiwan Insurance Industry Development Center.

12.2.2 New Establishment

Choice of Enterprise Form

Foreign investors have three options for operating insurance businesses in mainland China with the new establishment mode: joint venture, wholly foreign-owned enterprise, or branch.

Joint Venture. An insurance company set up in the form of a joint venture refers to the joint venture with limited liability jointly established by one or more foreign insurance enterprise(s) and Chinese one(s). The foreign insurance company must hold more than 25% of share capital in the joint venture, otherwise participation may occur and the invested enterprise shall be treated as a domestic insurance company by CIRC. The Chinese and foreign investors of the joint venture shall share profits and losses according to their contribution proportion in the paid-up capital of the joint venture. Representatives of the investors form the board of directors in which the number of directors delegated by each party shall be up to their share proportions. The board of director is the highest authority in the joint venture, deciding important issues concerning the joint venture.

Wholly Foreign-Owned Company. A wholly foreign-owned company refers to an insurance company with limited liability whose registered capital is completely owned by one or more foreign insurance companies. Though the operation of foreign-owned companies and branches are all flexible, foreign-owned companies have more advantages than branches. The nature of limited liability ensures foreign insurance companies investing against possible risk for its branches' debts.

Branch. A branch refers to the entity with unlimited liability established by a foreign insurance company in China. The foreign insurance company is the sole investor of the branch and responsible for all the branch's debts. Since a branch is not an independent legal entity, the concept of 'paid-up capital' shall not be applied. The foreign insurance company needs to allocate the minimum operation capital to the branch in the same amount as foreign-invested insurance companies in other forms.

Insurance companies established in the above mentioned three forms are all known as 'foreign-owned insurance companies' and governed by *the Regulation on Administration of Foreign-owned Insurance Companies*. Each form has its advantages and disadvantages. Therefore, the decision on which form is more beneficial is mainly up to the foreign insurance company's operation planning in China.

According to China's WTO entrance commitments, China permits foreign insurance companies to establish foreign-owned non-life insurance companies in the form of wholly foreign-owned enterprises and permits foreign insurance companies to change its branches already established in China into foreign-owned companies under the precondition that the have operated for at least one year since 11 December 2003. The fact is that CIRC had not approved any changing of branches into foreign-owned enterprises until 26 May 2004 when AIU Insurance Company Shenzhen Branch gained approval.

Market Access

Foreign Share Proportion. Since 11 December 2001 when China started its WTO entrance commitments (the WTO commitment day), China has permitted establishment of branches and joint ventures by foreign non-life insurance companies and allowed the foreign share proportion in joint ventures to be 51%. Since 11 December 2003, limitation on foreign capital share proportion has been cancelled. Wholly foreign-owned non-life insurance companies may set up joint ventures. Then, Life insurance companies should have no more than 50% of foreign share capital. Insurance broker companies should also have no more than 50% of foreign share capital. The foreign share capital proportion should be permitted to reach 51% no later than 11 December 2004. Being wholly foreign-owned is to be permitted no later than 11 December 2006.

Table 12.3. Market Access Schedule

Opening Time	Non-life Insurance	Life Insurance	Re-insurance	Broker Company
Upon accession	Foreign non-life insurers will be permitted to establish as a branch or as a joint venture with 51 per cent foreign ownership.	Foreign life insurers will be permitted to hold 50 per cent foreign ownership in a joint venture with the partner of their choice.	Foreign insurers will be permitted to provide reinsurance services for life and non-life insurance as a branch, joint venture, or wholly foreign-owned subsidiary, without geographic or quantitative restrictions on the number of licenses issued.	Joint ventures with foreign equity no more than 50 per cent will be permitted
Within two years after China's accession	Foreign non-life insurers will be permitted to establish as a wholly-owned subsidiary.			
Within Three years after China's accession				Foreign equity share shall be increased to 51 per cent
Within Five years after China's accession				Wholly foreign-owned subsidiary will be permitted

Conditions of Permission

According to China' WTO commitments and the provisions in *the Regulation on Administration of Foreign-owned Insurance Companies,* a foreign insurance company, if intending to engage in the non-life insurance business in China, shall apply to CIRC for establishment of a foreign-owned insurance company.

Subject Qualification. It is stipulated in Article 8 of *the Regulation on Administration of Foreign-owned Insurance Companies,* that the necessary conditions for foreign insurance companies applying to establish foreign-owned insurance companies in China are as follows: (a) have engaged in the insurance business for over 30 years; (b) have established representative offices in China for over 2 years; (c) possess assets at the end of the previous year of application totalling no less than USD5 billion; (d) are being effectively supervised and administered by the local nation or district authorities with a perfect insurance supervision and administration system established there; (e) are complying with repayment ability standard in local state or district; (f) are obtaining an agreement for such application from local state or district authorities; (g) other diligent conditions stipulated by CIRC. The first three conditions seem to be the hardest ones while the others are relatively soft, which in fact leaves the CIRC with the discretion to approve or disapprove the application. Further attention should be paid to subjects when establishing new foreign insurance companies, which are different under participation. Under participation, subjects shall be foreign insurance companies, that is, insurance companies registered out of China territory engaging in the insurance business, as opposed to ordinary financial companies abroad or normal enterprise legal persons or other organizations abroad.

Capital Requirement. The minimum registered capital for setting up joint ventures is the same as that of foreign-owned enterprises, that is, RMB0.2 billion (about USD24.24 million). The minimum registered capital is the paid-up capital. The foreign insurance companies' investment shall be exchangeable foreign currencies. The branch of a foreign insurance company shall have the operation capital of over RMB 0.2 billion (about USD24.24 million). The contribution shall also be in exchangeable foreign currencies. CIRC may increase the minimum registered capital or operation capital amount according to the business scope and operation scale of the foreign insurance company to be established.

12.2.3 Specialties of Capital Contribution

It is stipulated in Article 72 of *the Insurance Law* that 'the minimum amount of registered capital required for the establishment of an insurance company is RMB 0.2 billion. The minimum amount of registered capital for the establishment of an insurance company shall be fully paid-up in monetary form'. It is stated in Article 7 of *the Regulation on Administration of Foreign-owned Insurance Companies* that 'the minimum amount of registered capital required for joint ventures or foreign-owned insurance companies is RMB0.2 billion or exchangeable currencies with equal value. The foreign insurance companies' contribution shall be exchangeable currencies. The branch of a foreign insurance company shall obtain free allocation of operation capital in exchangeable currencies that is no less than RMB0.2 billion from the company. Such provisions are totally different from those in China's foreign investment laws. Further attention should be paid to the minimum amount of registered capital, which needs to be fully paid-up in monetary form. In another words, if the registered capital exceeds RMB0.2 billion, the amount within RMB0.2 billion shall be paid up in one time while the extra amount may be paid gradually.[4]

In addition, there is further stipulation concerning participation in China's insurance companies. It is stipulated in Article 5.4 of *the Provisional Regulation on Equity Investment in Insurance Companies* that the capital invested shall be the self-owned capital of the enterprise with justifiable resources. Furthermore, the contributors of insurance companies shall contribute in currencies while investment in property or invisible assets is forbidden (Article 10). Enterprises or other investors are forbidden to invest in insurance companies with bank loans (Article 11). It is forbidden for participating shareholders and insurance companies to make mutual investment in the form of exchanging stocks (Article 12). In another words, foreign investors shall not only contribute in cash but also contribute in exchangeable currencies.

12.3 Legal Risks for Foreign Investment in China's Insurance Industry

12.3.1 Withdrawal of Foreign Insurance Companies Signals Risks

In the spring of 2002, Lincoln Group left China. In February 2002, America Lincoln Finance Group Re-insurance Company decided to withdraw from China. Mr. Ma Dehao, the chief representative of Lincoln Group at that time, recalling a painful experience, stated four reasons: first, the foreign insurance company was aware that it still took time for the potential consumers in China to realize insurance; second, the limited number of qualified insurance employees restricts the fast development of China's insurance industry; third, foreign companies may restrict the number of foreign employees to cut costs, but it takes a long time to train local employees, especially those with no experience; fourth, the capital market in China is still in its growth stage. Many insurance companies are facing the difficulty of finding appropriate investment forms to match long-term capital with debts, which forces them to

[4] However, the stipulation in Article 5 of *the Detailed Rules on Implementation of the Regulation on Administration of Foreign-owned Insurance Companies* on 'the registered capital or operation capital of foreign-owned insurance companies shall be paid-up currencies' seems to indicate all registered capital shall be paid up in one time.

slow down. The management of joint ventures is carried out according to the majority opinion. Decisions and operations are hard to execute without both parties' consensus. At the end of summer of 2002, Switzerland Life Insurance Company left. From 9 February 2001 to 17 July 2002, 30 representative offices of 22 foreign insurance companies in China withdrew from China.

The withdrawal of foreign insurance companies reflects existing risks in China's insurance industry to a certain degree. In July 2005, the world famous credit evaluation organization-Standard & Poor's issued *the 2005-2006 Report on Prediction of China's Insurance Industry Credit in China.* Stand & Poor's adjusted the life insurance industry risk level from 'excessively high' to 'high'. China's non-life insurance industry risk level is still 'high'. This indicates that China's insurance industry is still in the stage of high risks, including legal risks.[5]

12.3.2 Insight into Legal Risks for Foreign Investment in Insurance Industry

Risks in Managing Joint Ventures[6]

Since Chinese and foreign enterprises are quite different in regards to their capital, management and techniques, disputes may easily arise under cooperation. As such, foreign insurance companies normally do not prefer joint ventures. Basically, foreign property insurance companies all enter China in the form of a wholly-owned subsidiary, which enables them to maintain the most original and basic enterprise cultures and management ideas.[7] However, China requests foreign life insurance companies to enter China in the form of joint ventures. Therefore, a joint venture becomes the sole choice for investment in the life insurance industry. For life insurance companies, the Chinese partners they have found are divided into two types: large scale enterprise groups and insurance companies. The Chinese partners chosen by foreign parties all have three backgrounds: first, political background; second, international background; third, capital background. The Chinese enterprises already cooperated with foreign companies, such as China Minmetals Group, China Chemicals, China Petroleum, CITIC Group, All Bright Group, etc. all have such backgrounds. These Chinese enterprises are managed at the 'vice ministry level' (in political rank) and are ones with certain influence in China's political stage. Foreign companies deem their choice of such Chinese enterprises as possibly helping the joint ventures obtain direct or indirect political

---

5 The Stand & Poor's Warns Risk Expansion in China's Property Insurance Industry and Agrees on Launching out of Insurance Foreign Currencies issued in the Financial and Economic Times on 2 July 2005.

6 Also see the detailed analysis on troubles in managing joint venture in Chapter 6 of the book.

7 Bai Defan, Tab Bowers, Rong Juesheng (2004), The *Selling life insurance to China*, Mckinsey Senior Management Collected Essays, Fourth Issue.

benefits under the special social circumstances of China. However, the combination of strong parties brings about the conflict of no compromise. The foreign party regards itself as experienced in managing insurance enterprises perfectly since it comes from a mature market while the Chinese party thinks it is more familiar with the particularities of China and understands better the pulse of the Chinese market due to its local advantages. The two parties diverge on issues including operation ideology, market operation, products, and even power allocation. For example, most joint ventures have each party holding 50% of shares. Since the foreign party is experienced in the industry and has advanced technology, the general manager is usually delegated by the foreign party. To balance, the Chinese party may delegate the Chairman of board of directors. According to international practice, the general manager controls the actual operation power. However, due to different enterprise cultures, the Chinese party deems the Chairman as the legal representative and only the legal representative has the decision power in controlling the enterprise, which leads to the embarrassing situation of each party having its own power center.[8]

Company management is the essential factor in the development of insurance companies and the insurance industry. If the management structure of an insurance company is not sound, the risks may accumulate gradually and burst out upon reaching a certain degree of accumulation. The core of company management is the internal distribution of rights and obligations, the balance of power, and risk control. Sound company management structure actually forms an internal correction mechanism for the company. Any divergence in the coordination of the relationship among owners, operators, consumers and relevant parties may be found immediately and adjusted accordingly. If the company management structure is not sound, certain resources or power in the company may be controlled and taken advantage of by some persons or groups. The company finance system may be full of errors and the finance report of the company may contain disclosure of false information. When the internal correction mechanism is destroyed, the mistakes will accumulate day by day and an outburst will inevitably eventuate after reaching a certain degree of accumulation. The exposure of the most astonishing risks is related to the long period of risk accumulation while the accumulation of such nature is due to the concealment and complexity of risks. The inborn nature of the insurance industry is such that risks are concealed and complex, and have the possibility of accumulating over a long time period. Therefore, the risk in an unsound and imperfect insurance company management structure should not be overlooked in this sense.[9]

---

8 Lin Hua (2002), The Inside Investigation of Foreign Insurance Companies' Withdrawal, Foreign Investment in China, Issue 12.

9 The China Insurance Industry: Contradictory, Challenge and Countermeasure, the important research subject report of Beijing University, by Sun Qixiang, etc.

Legal Risks Coming from Insurance Market

Policy Risk in Premium Rates Control. In August 2000, CIRC issued *the Provisional Measures on Administration of Property Insurance Premium Rates,* stipulating all insurance companies in the territory of China shall adopt the terms and premium rates stipulated by CIRC and could not alter the basic terms and premium rates for major insurance varieties, emphasizing the strict unification of premium rates. Article 107 of *the Insurance Law* stipulates that the basic insurance clauses and premium rates for types of insurance concerning public interests, compulsory under law, or newly developed life insurance shall be approved by CIRC, which means the insurance companies may make their own insurance clauses and premium rates under the precondition of approval by CIRC.[10] Article 8 of *the Measures on Administration of Property Insurance Companies' Insurance Clauses and Premium Rates* adopted by CIRC on 3 November 2005 limits the scope of property insurance clauses and premium rates approval scope as: first, compulsory insurance types under law; second, other types of insurance deemed to be related to public interests by CIRC. CIRC determines the scope of insurance types for approval and may adjust according to the real situation. Property insurance companies, when fixing insurance clauses and premium rates of other types of insurance beyond Article 8 of the *Measures*, shall submit them to CIRC or its delegated companies for record within 10 days after operational use thereof. Generally, China's premium rates are still highly controlled by the government and far from being market-orientated.

Under market orientation of premium rates, insurance companies have the freedom for determining the rates and may fix the premium rate for each item on its own according to the supply and demand situation of the market, the operation and management strategy, the business risk level, the target profit and other factors. If so, the insurance companies' premium rate risks are mainly market risks and operation risks. However, under the control of insurance premium rates, the insurance companies' premium rate risks are mainly policy risks, under which the insurance companies have to obey the unified insurance clauses and premium rates set by the supervision authorities. If the premium rates are adjusted higher, the insurance companies may easily profit while lower rates may cause loss. The insurance companies can only passively accept the premium rates and cannot freely adjust the rates according to the operation status and risk situation of the insurance

---

10 Now, China is pushing forward the market orientation process of premium rates. Since 1 January 2003, CIRC have made public announcements concerning its reply to various insurance companies regarding the adjustment of vehicle insurance premium rates, implementing open policy in vehicle insurance premium rates. A thirty-percent-floating scope is allowed for premium rates. Each insurance company may decide the price for its own major types of insurance under the approval of CIRC. Operation risk control is also strengthened. Later, CIRC issued the Measures on Administration of Personal Insurance Product Approval and Record in April 2004, opening premium rates for other types of insurance and realizing the all-round openness of premium rates for vehicle insurance.

objects. They may only take disguised measures such as large amounts of return, high commission charges, increases in value-added of the insurance policy such as promising extra services besides compensation obligation under the policy, etc. to compete in the market.

Unfair Competition. Unfair competition in China's insurance market is very serious, mainly illustrated through the irrational price competition between insurance companies. For example, a surge of unfair competition appeared in the vehicle insurance market after the vehicle insurance reform. The tendency of vehicle insurance premium rates to be determined via market forces is good and may improve the management level, is advantageous for the consumers' interest and stimulates demand. However, in the implementation process, some insurance companies compete with each other to lower the vehicle insurance price, occupying the market with discounts and higher commission fees, which results in the whole-industry price war. Low premium rates, high returns, large guarantee scopes, insurance through negotiation and other manners violating laws and regulations are unstoppable, increases the operation risk of insurance companies, and thus finally damaging the whole benefit of having an insurance industry and the legitimate rights and benefits of insured parties.

Risk in Partners' Insufficient Ability of Insurance Indemnity

It is pointed out in a research report by China International Finance Company that insufficient 'Ability of Insurance Indemnity' is the main problem in China's insurance industry. Taking PICC as an example, it disclosed the information when listing in Hong Kong at the beginning of November 2003 that the minimum legal ability of insurance indemnity shall be RMB 594.3 million until 31 December 2002 under CIRC's stipulation on supervision and administration of ability of insurance indemnity; however, the actual ability of insurance indemnity on that day was only RMB 280.2 million, still lacking RMB 314.1 million yuan. The reasons for low repayment ability include: first, lack of capital; second, narrow investment channels; third, bad debts left behind by the blind investment in the economy's over-heating period; fourth, inherited loss in interest spread.[11] Though

[11] The pre-set interest rate of China's life insurance products always takes the bank interest rate as the main reference. Since China's reform and opening, the bank interest rate has always been high, which is influenced by the pre-set interest rate of life insurance products being commonly high with the peak reaching 8.8% yearly compound interest. Along with the lowering of bank deposit interest rates seven times, the yearly interest for fixed term deposits goes down from 10.98% to 2.25%. A high interest rate is promised for insurance products being sold while the capital utilization is mainly in the way of bank deposits. Insurance companies suffer great loss for the pre-set high interest rate products due to the lowering of interest rate. It is estimated that the highest pre-set interest rate for domestic life insurance policies is 9%, the lowest is 4.5%, and the weighted average is 7.8%. The yearly proceeds rate in insurance companies' capital utilization is

the listing of PICC, China Life Insurance and Ping An may make up for the lack of capital in a certain degree and the insurance capital investment channels are expanding, the current repayment ability risks for China's domestic insurance companies still exist. According to Standard & Poor's evaluation at the end of 2003, RMB 15-20 billion (USD1.8-2.4 billion) was needed as capital for the domestic life insurance industry to achieve the sufficient capital level amount while RMB 7-10 billion (USD 0.8-1.2 billion) was needed as capital for the domestic non-life insurance industry.[12]

Comparing *the Circular of CIRC Soliciting Comments on Amendment Standard for the Minimum Ability to Indemnity of Insurance Companies' Property Insurance and Short Term Life Insurance* on 22 August 2005 with Article 4 of the *Regulations on Administration of Insurance Companies' Ability to Indemnity and Supervision Guideline* (2003 No.1 Decree), we may find an amazing increase in the requested insurance companies' minimum ability of insurance indemnity from '18% of the part below RMB 100 million in the company's self-remaining premium deducted by sales tax in the recent fiscal year, and 16% of the part above RMB 100 million; 26% of the part below RMB 700 billion in the company's average complex indemnity amount of the latest three years and 23% of the part above RMB 700 billion' to '9% of the part below RMB 5 billion in the company's self-remaining premium deducted by sales tax and value added and 8% of the part above RMB 5 billion; 22.5% of the part below RMB 2.5 billion in the average complex indemnity amount of the latest three years and 12.5% of the part above RMB 2.5 billion'. In the former provision, an insurance company with an operating time of less than three consecutive fiscal years shall directly adopt the standard of the latest fiscal year which is adjusted to double the latest fiscal year's standard in the Circular.[13]

If foreign investors invest in China's insurance industry through new establishment, the problem of insufficient ability of insurance indemnity may be slid over. However, for investment by participation in existing domestic insurance companies, attention should be paid to the participating object's ability of insurance indemnity situation, otherwise the investor may be easily trapped in the 'ability of insurance indemnity' hook.

Shortage of Experienced Talents

Currently, competition in the insurance market is growing more fierce. There are over 20 life insurance companies in Beijing. In cities such as QingDao and NanJing where the insurance market was late to start, there are almost 10 life insurance companies competing with each other. However, opportunities still exist to

lower than 3%. The total interest rate loss difference for China's insurance industry may reach RMB50 billion. Resource: the Insurance Website.

12 See 'how huge is China Insurance Industry's Risk', China Securities Paper on 3 December 2003.

13 From the website of China Insurance Regulatory Commission www.circ.gov.cn.

enter the insurance industry at a low cost.[14] Along with the further opening of China's insurance market, more and more foreign investors will surely enter the insurance market. In some open cities such as Beijing, Shanghai and Guangzhou, the later an investor enters the market, the higher is the cost and the more difficulties there are to face. Such costs and difficulties are mainly relate to selecting and employing people with experience in the insurance industry. Due to the specialties of China's insurance market, foreign insurance companies greatly rely on local employees for their fast development. Foreign investors normally have confidence in investing in the insurance industry, but worry about suitable local talent for their branches in different places. Now, the competition for talented persons are being carried out among foreign insurance companies, newly established Chinese insurance companies and old Chinese insurance companies. Foreign insurance companies are hiring people from PICC and China Life on a large scale. According to a survey, group job-hopping of high-level management staff have occurred several times in PICC at Jiangxi, Jiangsu and other provinces. It is even circulated in the insurance industry that PICC has been the training base for foreign insurance companies.[15] It is known that the management level at Hezong Life Insurance and the general manager of its branches are all from insurance companies in the same industry.[16] Hiring talent from companies in the same industry is not only expensive but also brings about labor disputes. Due to the limited number of people with suitable qualifications, late entrance in the market not only means a doubled 'transfer fee' but also enhances the possibility of labor disputes. During the early stage, insurance companies with an old brand face less pressure concerning the flow of trained personnel, and therefore usually neglect labor administration. Under the current situation, these insurance companies are improving labor administration and further forbidding resigned employees entrance into the same industry in competition. Foreign insurance companies are facing higher labor law risks in attracting talents. Once management personnel occupying key posts cannot carry working due to legal disputes, the business operation and other work would be severely influenced.

Sales persons may also incur labor law risks. Competition for market share in China's coastal cities is getting fierce. It may take a long time to re-establish sales agent groups. Just like finding an attractive Chinese cooperative, it is not easy for foreign investors to find high quality sales agents. Unless newcomers have excellent

[14] In European and American developed nations, the number of insurance companies is over 1,000 per nation. Even in Hong Kong district, the number of insurance companies of different types is about 200. As a comparison, there are less than 100 insurance companies in China now. Obviously, there is still space for more.

[15] See the Survey Analysis Report through Questionnaire of Special Topics on Salary System and Human Resources Construction by the Jiangsu Changzhou Branch of PICC.

[16] Wan Yun (2005), The Disclosure of Hidden Shareholders Sharing Insurance Market and Long Run Industry Capitals Rushing to Grabbing from Each Other, China Operation Newspaper on 8 October.

skills in hiring and training, are capable of rapidly establishing agent groups, can enhance sale production rates, and can retain sales personnel better than their competitors, thus making up for the disadvantage of entering the market late, then it may not be appropriate for the newcomer to enter the Chinese market in the form of a joint venture. Participation is a shortcut to achieving whole-nation network coverage. Achieving the transfer of over 100,000 sales persons is no less difficult than self-establishing sales channels in each city.[17]

Agent Risk

The good and bad are intermingled in China's insurance sales groups. Most insurance salesmen lack specialty knowledge and some flow quickly without regard to long-term planning, considering short term benefits only. Their service and quality level are not satisfactory. The Second Civil Tribunal of the People's High Court of Jiangsu Province issued *the Survey Report of Hearing on Insurance Dispute Cases in The Province in 2004,* indicating that manipulation is the main reason of insurance legal disputes. It is common for insurance agents to fill in the insurance policies or even sign the policies for the policy holders. Once the insurance company refuses payment of compensation for such reasons as pre-insurance diseases, policy holders and insurants often argue against the insurance company on the ground that the insurance agent has not performed his duty of illustrating the insurance clauses. Other disputes may arise out of insurance agents' embezzlement of premiums, taking discount shopping coupons as payment for premiums, making out an invoice ahead of payment, or even making false policies.

Insurance Legal Disputes Harassment

According to the survey, the biggest problem in China's insurance industry from the consumers' view is contractual disputes, as opposed to difficulties in being insured or the lack of insurance companies. Recently, insurance legal disputes have been the focus of complaints and have become the biggest problem in China's insurance industry.[18] It was shown in *the Circular of Letter Visits Complaint Situation of National Insurance Supervision and Administration System* in the first half of 2005 by CIRC that the total number of letters and visits handled by the national insurance supervision and administration system was 4,484 in which 2,741 were complaints against insurance companies including 1,273 against property insurance companies and 1,468 against life insurance companies. Among the complaints, the letter and visit items were 2,898, among which 1,435 were about contractual disputes, accounting for 49.5%, and an increase of 3.7% from last year. The 22 life insurance companies under complaint included 8 Chinese and 14

---

[17] Bai Defan, Tab Bowers, Rong Juesheng (2004), Selling life insurance to China, Mckinsey Senior Management Collected Essays, Fourth Issue.

[18] From Xin Hua Net (last visit on 5 October 2005).

foreign companies, and joint ventures where there were 112 disputes involved. The increase in complaints is due to the great increase in the number of insurance legal litigation cases.

However, in the handling of insurance cases in the current judicial practice, courts obviously have the judicial tendency of one-sided emphasis on 'protection of vulnerable groups'. Many judicial personnel are bias towards insurants and policy-holders since judicial personnel deem insurance companies to be the dominant group with much money, while the insurants and policy holders are deemed as vulnerable groups that the courts should protect.[19] The unfavorable treatment of insurance companies include: (a) improper request for evidence. The improper evidence-request for insurance companies generally exists in case hearing; (b) abuse of 'doubtful point benefit' interpretation principle. Article 31 of *the Insurance Law* stipulates that the courts or arbitration institutions shall make interpretation favorable to insurants and beneficiaries when insurance companies have disputes with insurants, policy holders or beneficiaries over clauses of insurance contracts. However, the clause is severely misused in judicial practice, especially at the basic level, which results in insurance companies losing cases at an abnormally high rate.[20]

Special attention should be paid to circumstances involving life or property insurance cases where death occurs since the court may improperly adjudicate insurance companies to undertake compensation liabilities due to the consideration of factors beyond law for the purpose of avoiding victims' troubles or maintaining social liabilities.

Tax Change Risk

Before the 1983 tax reform, the insurance industry was once regarded as a special industry by the nation with an enterprise income tax rate of 55%, half of which went to central finance while the other half went to local finance. In addition, a 15% fixed-asset investment orientation adjustment tax and 5% sales tax were

---

19 See the Survey Report on Hearing Situation of Insurance Dispute Case in The Province by the Second Civil Court of Jiangsu Province Higher Court.

20 A typical example is set in *the Survey Report on Hearing Situation of Insurance Dispute Case in The Province by the Second Civil Tribunal of Jiangsu Province High Court in 2004.* A person purchasing life insurance for serious illness in China Life Insurance Company was in hospital for acute peritonitis. He applied for compensation from the insurance company. The insurance company, through examination, deemed that the scope of serious illness was made clear in the insurance clauses which did not include the insurant's disease, so the company refused payment. The first trial court decided in the first instance that the insurance company compensate RMB 100,000 since interpretation favorable to the insurant shall be made when the insurance company had disputes with the insurant on whether the insurant's disease was serious illness, that is, the insurant thought acute peritonitis as serious illness while the insurance company did not agree. After the insurance company appealed, the second instance court changed the original sentence.

collected. After the tax reform, a 55% enterprise income tax rate was applied to China People's Insurance Company, a 33% enterprise income tax rate was applied to Pacific Insurance Company, and a 15% enterprise income tax rate was applied to Ping An Insurance Company. At the beginning of 1997, the income tax rate for Chinese insurance companies was consolidated to 33%, but the sales tax rate was adjusted from 5% to 8%. From 2001, the sales tax rate decreased by 1% each year, hence the tax rate was lowered from 8% to 5% in three years. By 1 January 2003, the tax rate had reached 5%. However, insurance companies are charged a 1-2% insurance regulatory expense by CIRC. For foreign insurance companies, if the foreign investors' investing capital or the branch's operation capital from the head office exceeds USD 10 million and the operation term is over 10 years, the income tax rate for the company's sales income shall be 15%. Through application approved by tax authorities, the company may be exempted from enterprise income tax in the first year after making a profit and exempted from half of it in the second and third years. Even after the five year exemption term, the income tax rate is 15%. However, the current consolidated income rate for Chinese insurance companies is 33%. Furthermore, if a foreign insurance company re-invested the company's operation profits in the company to increase the registered capital or to use the profits as capital for establishing other foreign investment enterprises, 40% of income tax already paid for the investment part may be returned if the operation term is longer than 5 years. The tax for city maintenance and construction is only applied to Chinese insurance companies instead of foreign ones.

To carry out the national treatment principle, China intends to cancel preferential tax for foreign insurance companies and combine them into the tax collection scope of Chinese insurance companies. Meanwhile, different sales tax rates may be adopted for different insurance products. Such enormous tax policy changes are a legal risk that foreign investors have to consider before investing in China's insurance industry.

Appendix: List of Chinese Insurance Laws and Regulations

- Opinions on Reform and Development of Insurance Industry [Guo Fa (2006) No. 23]
- Notice on Strengthening Construction of Honest System and Enhancing Service Quality of Vehicle Assurance Settlement [Bao Jian Fa (2005) No. 24]
- Notice on Relevant Issues in Insurance Institution investors' Stock Investment Trade
- Guidance on Trusteeship of Investment Companies' Share Assets (On Trial)
- Provisional Measures on Administration of Utilizing of Insurance Foreign Exchange Abroad [Insurance Supervision Commission Decree (2004) No.9]

- ✧ Notice on Several Issues Concerning the Measures on Administration of Personal Insurance Product Approval and Record [Bao Jian Fa (2004) No.76]
- ✧ Measures on Administration of Personal Insurance Product Approval and Record [Insurance Supervision Commission Decree (2004) No.6]
- ✧ Notice on Adjusting Proportion of Insurance Company's Investment in Secondary Bank Bond, Secondary Bank Term Debts and Enterprise Bond [Bao Jian Fa (2004) No. 77]
- ✧ Regulation on Administration of Insurance Companies [(2004) No.3] by CIRC
- ✧ Detailed Rules on Implementation of the Regulation on Administration of Foreign Insurance Policies of PRC [(2004) No.4]
- ✧ Notice on Relevant Issues Concerning Adjustment of Life Annuity [Bao Jian Fa (2004) Mo. 31]
- ✧ Notice on Relevant Issues Concerning Forbidden Assisting Insurance Companies Abroad in Selling Insurance Policies Secretly [Bao Jian Fa (2004) No.29]
- ✧ Notice on Relevant Issues Concerning Compulsive Vehicle Insurance Against Third Party Responsibilities [Bao Jian Fa (2004) No.39]
- ✧ Notice on Relevant Issues Concerning Implementation of Property Insurance Company's Terms and Rates Post Record System [Bao Jian Fa (2004) No.34]
- ✧ Guidance Opinions on Promoting Popularization of Personal Insurance Terms [Bao Jian Fa (2004) No.33]
- ✧ Establishment of Departments and Divisions in CIRC's Agencies and The Main Responsibilities [Bao Jian Fa (2004) No.25]
- ✧ Notice on Printing and Distributing the Guidance Opinions on Strengthening Insurance Industry Association by CIRC
- ✧ Emergent Notice on Strengthening Supervision of Aviation Insurance Market
- ✧ Notice on Administration of Insurance Guarantee Fund [CIRC Decree (2004) No.16]
- ✧ Regulation on Administration of Insurance Companies [CIRC Decree (2004) No.15]
- ✧ Measures on Administration of Insurance Companies' Reserve for Non-life Insurance Business [CIRC Decree (2004) No.13]
- ✧ Regulation on Administration of Insurance Companies (2004) [CIRC Decree (2004) No.14]
- ✧ Regulation on Penalty for Violation of Finance Law [State Council Decree (2004) No.427]

- ✧ Emergent Notice on Relevant Issues Concerning Adjustment of Terms and Rates for Vehicle Insurance Against Third Party Liabilities and the Insurance Against Additional Risks [Bao Jian Fa (2004) No.44]
- ✧ Notice on Printing and Distributing the Guidance for Risk Control of Utilizing Insurance Capital (On Trial) [Bao Jian Fa (2004) No.43]
- ✧ Provisional Regulation on Administration of Insurance Assets Management Companies [CIRC Decree (2004) No.2]
- ✧ Measures on Administration of Representative Offices of Foreign Insurance Companies in China [CIRC Decree (2004) No.1]

13 An Insight into Foreign Investment Dispute Resolution in China

Currently, there are lots of problems, as well as the efficiency and function of judicial work obstructed, but also the effectiveness is greatly affected.

— Xiao Yang[1]

13.1 Insight into Commercial Dispute Resolution in China

13.1.1 Introduction

As China's social and economic circumstances become increasingly complex, it is increasingly important to improve its commercial dispute resolution system. There is an urgent need for a practical and efficient mechanism that protects both the parties to a dispute and the public. In order to provide an accessible and effective system, China's civil justice system must embrace the basic principles of an effective commercial dispute settlement mechanism: (a) Specialised – judges or arbitrators should have sufficient commercial knowledge; (b) Proportionate – procedures and costs should be proportionate to the nature of the issues involved; (c) Efficient – cases should be dealt with efficiently; (d) Just – the end result and the procedure should be just; and (e) Effective – the mechanism should be adequately resourced and organised so as to give effect to the foregoing principles.

13.1.2 Assessment of China's Civil Justice System

Bearing the above standards in mind, we can assess China's civil justice system as a means of resolving commercial disputes.

---

1 Mr. Xiaoyang is the President of Supreme People's Court of China. Xiao Yang (2005), Adherence to the Administration by law, Improvement of the Quality of Government, Qiu Shi (one of most important official magazines), Issue 1.

Non-specialisation

A commercial dispute settlement mechanism can only be effective if it includes a group of judges with sufficient commercial knowledge and who consider issues in a manner widely accepted by the business community. However, the Chinese courts, including the People's Supreme Court, are lacking in such specialists.

The present situation is a consequence of longstanding ties between the military and China's ruling regime, as retired soldiers have long been the main pool from which judges are drawn. At the same time, qualified law school students do not become judges because the salary is too low. Given these conditions, the business community may well find that very few judges or their assistants are familiar with commercial practices in China. Furthermore, judges especially those in the lower level courts are still unaccustomed to or incapable of analysing issues from the viewpoint of businesspeople – an extremely important skill for resolving commercial matters.

Cost Analysis

Commercial dispute litigation costs can be split into monetary and non-monetary costs. The monetary cost, including legal fees and court costs, is often insignificant when compared to the non-monetary costs such as negative publicity and damage done to commercial relationships and connections. However, it is impossible to make an accurate calculation of such non-monetary costs. An analysis of the monetary cost follows below.

Court fees and charges. On the whole, commercial litigation court fees and charges are unremarkable, and the courts' operating costs are paid mainly with public funds. When submitting a complaint, the plaintiff must pay a filing fee to the court, the amount of which is determined in accordance with the value ascribed to the complaint:

Table 13.1. Court fees and charges

Value of the complaint	**Filing fee**
RMB 1 –RMB 1,000	*RMB 50*
RMB 1,000.01 – RMB 50,000	4%
RMB 50,000.01 – RMB 100,000	3%
RMB 100,000.01 – RMB 200,000	2%
RMB 200,000.0 – RMB 500,000	1.5%
RMB 500,000.01 – RMB 1,000,000	1%
Above RMB 1,000,000	0.5%

Attorney's fees. Articles 6 and 7 of the 'Provisional Administrative Method on Attorney's Fees' provide that counsel's fees should be calculated in proportion to the amount in dispute and may vary according to the difficulty and complexity of the case, the potential risks involved and the time and manpower required. China Attorney's fees are relatively low.

Long Duration and Delay

Despite the authorities taking measures to combat the problem of excessive delay, protracted commercial cases are still a serious problem in China. Inefficiency, lax attitude and the poor structure of the courts are often blamed and the reasons can be categorised as follows: (a) Inadequate structure, unqualified judges and poor organisation; (b) Complex and rigid procedures; (c) Difficulty allocating resources; and (d) Delay in delivering reserved judgements.

The following data give some insight into the operation of China's civil justice system:

Table 13.2. Economic Contract Cases from 1998 to 2000

Year	Accepted	Concluded	Mediated	Conciliated	Ignored	Withdrawn	Others
2000	1,184,613	1,203,410	416,039	484,959	15,518	248,859	38,035
1999	1,410,107	1,417,074	585,394	502,495	11,843	273,295	44,047
1998	1,329,020	1,332,932	575,391	460,925	8,439	250,860	37,317

Data from the Legal Yearbook of the PRC (2001)

Litigation proceedings are taking longer and longer, mainly due to the increasing number of cases and the limited capacity of the courts. Such delays result in high legal costs and the distraction of the parties from their main business.

Fairness, Justice and Neutrality

Given the role of the civil justice system in dispute resolution, the main concern of the business community (and especially foreign participants) is the fairness, justice and neutrality of the system as opposed to its speed, cost and application of domestic laws or precedents.

The Supreme People's Court (as well as lower courts) is somewhat similar in nature to an administrative governmental department in that it has certain connections with political and governmental organisations on behalf of which it is responsible for undertaking certain duties. This means that in reality, the Court carries out its duties together with its judicial functions like a bureaucratic administrative agency charged with law enforcement and dispute resolution.

Despite the Chinese judicial system undergoing a decade of modernisation, Chinese courts have yet to prove themselves as independent and powerful bodies. Local courts rely on the financial support of local governments and local authorities nominate judges. The result is that courts have no choice but to serve as guardians of regional interests. Therefore, it is difficult for courts to pass fair verdicts in cases involving regional interests.

Access to Justice

Naturally, the deficiencies in China's judicial system disturb those interested in access to justice. Although people may choose not to subject commercial disputes to litigation, this does not mean they are not interested in access to justice. If legal rights are unenforceable, they are meaningless. In China, access to the just resolution of commercial disputes has been hindered by: (a) Non-specialisation of the judiciary; (b) Problems in litigation procedures; (c) High cost of legal services; (d) Delays in proceedings; and (e) Systematic unfairness of the judicial system.

13.1.3 Current Reform and Further Proposals

Enhancing Specialisation

Uniform judicial test for selecting judges. The 'Provisional Implementing Measures for the National Judicial Test' adopted in 2001, requires all judicial candidates to have a bachelor's degree. The requirement is much higher than the old standard for judicial nomination and will help to create a team of learned judges.

Introduction of expert lists. The introduction of expert lists will ensure appropriate management of cases both in interlocutory stages and at trial. Expert judges, that is, judges with certain knowledge and experience, should be responsible for the trial and management of cases. A record of judges nominated for expert lists should be kept so that they may be allocated according to their special capabilities. Further training should be offered to the expert judges through co-operation with the legal profession and law schools.

Case Management

Case management refers to the practices and procedures which ensure maximum efficiency with the minimum time and energy. Such procedures include the keeping of management records, convening court-supervised conferences, limiting discovery and asking parties to consider early settlement.

The introduction of case management in China's civil judicial system is the focal point of my recommendations for improving the system. Under the current system, the procedures applied to all cases are the same, regardless of differences in monetary sums, complexity or importance. I recommend that cases be accepted and handled by appropriate judges under the case management system to facilitate and encourages prompt settlement through strict scheduling of procedures and the immediate identification and determination of the issues involved. Effective case management is more likely to provide just treatment of litigants, prompt and economical case settlement, improved commercial litigation processes and increased public confidence in the courts.

Case management measures have been in place for two years and many courts, including lower level courts, have successfully established a case registration court to allocate cases and supervise the court's operation by electronic means.

Fair Adjudication

The fairness and impartiality of judges is essential in the reform of China's civil justice system. In 1999 the Supreme People's Court put forward the 'Five Year Court Reform Compendium' to mark the beginning of this profoundly meaningful process accompanying market economy reform.

It is difficult for Chinese judges to earn respect because they play what is essentially an administrative role. The situation could be improved by expanding the juridical role and powers.

The greatest challenge for judicial reform is keeping courts independent from the governmental authorities whose financial support and power of appointment have a significant influence. Only after this problem is resolved will courts be able to handle commercial disputes impartially. However, at present, any move in this direction is likely to stir up trouble as judicial reform is tightly bound up with the evolution of China's political regime.

13.1.4 Alternative Dispute Resolution (ADR)

Litigation, the traditional manner of dispute settlement, may not be the first choice in resolving contemporary commercial disputes in China. Alternative methods both within and outside the judicial system may be more timely, cost-effective and satisfactory. Experimentation with innovative dispute resolution methods has been the main theme of the modern business community. In reality, under the influence of traditional Chinese culture, so-called ADR dominates China's dispute resolution system.

Mediation

Mediation is the cornerstone of the Chinese dispute resolution system. It has played a prominent role throughout history as well as in recent times. Generally, the business community prefers to submit disputes to mediation, which may be adopted separately or in combination with litigation or arbitration proceedings.

Ad hoc mediation. Under the laws and regulations of the PRC, the parties can settle their commercial dispute through ad hoc mediation before submitting it to arbitration or litigation. If the mediation is successful, the settlement agreement is deemed to constitute a private contract.

Institutional mediation. The Beijing Conciliation Centre (BCC), established in 1987, and the provincial conciliation centres, in recent years, developed institutional mediation to deal specifically with commercial disputes. The BCC provides institutional conciliation services pursuant to the 'Conciliation Rules of the Beijing Conciliation Centre'.

Mediation in arbitration processes. The China International Economic and Trade Arbitration Centre (CIETAC) has a long established tradition of mediation during arbitration, which encourages the parties to conciliate throughout the process.

Mediation in civil procedures. Under the Civil Procedure Law of the PRC, courts must attempt mediation during proceedings, and may request the assistance of relevant parties or individuals. A mediated settlement has the same binding force as a court decision.

Arbitration

Arbitration is an important method of dispute resolution in China – especially when commercial disputes are involved. China only allows for institutional arbitration when ad hoc arbitration is unacceptable under the Arbitration Law of the PRC. The main Chinese arbitration institutions accepting commercial cases are CIETAC and the China Maritime Arbitration Commission (CMAC), both of which are independent branches of the Council for the Promotion of International Trade (CCPIT), which acts as the Chinese Chamber of International Commerce. Both institutions have their own arbitrator lists and arbitral rules, and possess the special characteristic of combining arbitration with conciliation to absorb the advantages of both. Arbitral tribunals may conciliate cases before or after commencing arbitration proceedings if the parties so desire. Arbitrators may act as conciliators in the same proceedings.

The fees and charges of Chinese arbitration institutions are quite low compared to those of other major international commercial arbitration institutions. In addition, the awards of all commercial arbitral institutions are final, which means that courts cannot accept appeals concerning such awards. More importantly, arbitrators are less influenced by governments than are judges and so, on the whole, are more fair and impartial.

13.1.5 China's Perspective on Commercial Dispute Resolution

Litigation has certain advantages such as well-established systems, a uniform set of rules and sophisticated laws to produce predictable and enforceable results.

Also, parties do not need to pay court costs such as judicial expenses and courtroom rentals. However, litigation can be a long and complex process with formal and technical delays. Commercial litigation in China tends to be costly, time-consuming, cumbersome and inefficient. It seems that in the end litigation may actually obstruct rather than facilitate the resolution of commercial disputes. Business relationships and confidential information may be exposed during the adversarial process. This increasingly adversarial nature of China's judicial system means that simply being involved in a dispute may adversely impact unrelated transactions.

Non-binding mediation by a neutral third party may be more appropriate than litigation. Mediation proceedings are informal, quick and inexpensive and parties tend to feel that their concerns are being heard and fairly considered. One advantage is that mediation is applicable to almost all kinds of conflicts originating from one party's perception of another's failure to perform duties or meet responsibilities, and such perceptions may be dispelled by the participation of a neutral third party for a quick resolution of the dispute. Another advantage is that the parties may achieve a more creative outcome. In addition, parties can enjoy complete control over the mediation process and prevent confidential matters from being disclosed. This form of dispute resolutions relies more on the parties' voluntarily performing the obligations declared by the mediator as part of the "solution", which facilitates the enforcement of the decision made by the mediator. Thus, mediation creates a 'win-win' atmosphere, generates creative solutions and facilitates their enforcement.

The focus of arbitration is the resolution of underlying problems as opposed to the defeat of one's opponents. This focus is supported by arbitrators chosen for their expertise in the specific subject matter of a dispute. As a result, the business community has long recognised that arbitration, through which disputes are settled in a private business-like manner, is generally preferred in China.

However, the advantages of arbitration may be overstated. For example, arbitration may be costly since the parties must pay arbitration fees, rental costs of the hearing room, travel costs, translation fees and other administrative expenses. Procedural delays are also prevalent as the absence of a clear set of rules gives the parties more room to manoeuvre and may result in more procedural disagreement than in litigation. Another downside of arbitration is that arbitrators in China do not have authority to grant injunctions or interim relief, even in regard to the preservation of property and evidence. Even strong proponents of commercial arbitration complain that it can be distressingly slow and extremely expensive. Parties to commercial disputes who choose arbitration are usually motivated by considerations other than those of time and money such as neutrality, informality, flexibility, confidentiality, the ability to choose the arbitrators or a desire to promote a conciliatory atmosphere conducive to future business relations.

The following chart illustrates some of the strengths and weaknesses of litigation, mediation and arbitration as a means of commercial dispute resolution.

Table 13.3. Effectiveness Comparison

Item	Litigation	Mediation	Arbitration
Flexibility	C	A	B
Cost	B	A	C
Duration	C	A	B
Confidentially	C	B	A
Enforceability	A	C	B

A=Good, B=Average, C=Bad

13.1.6 Conclusion: How to Choose an Ideal Commercial Dispute Settlement Mechanism in China

Four factors should be considered:

- the specialised nature of the commercial dispute;
- the need for relationship maintenance;
- the effectiveness of the civil justice system; and
- the available ADR.

China's civil justice system will remain ineffective for resolving commercial disputes until the following shortcomings are overcome:

- an unspecialised judiciary;
- excessive procedural delays; and
- the miscarriage of justice.

Reform measures such as judicial tests and improved case management will eventually lead to a modernised commercial dispute resolution system. But in the short term, China's civil justice system will remain time-consuming, cumbersome and inefficient, and the adversarial atmosphere will severely harm relationships.

In contrast, mediation and arbitration provide effective alternative structures within which the particularities of commercial disputes may be sufficiently considered. ADR also accords more closely with China's deep-seated societal and philosophical preference for solutions agreed in a harmonious manner that tend to preserve, rather than damage, the relationship of the parties involved.

In a nutshell, mediation or arbitration is superior to civil litigation in resolving commercial disputes in China.

13.2 Characters of a Chinese-Style Judicial Decision-Making Process

In theory, a judge should make judicial decisions based on his or her own judgement on the issues in dispute in accordance with the principle of independence which is a fundamental keystone to any modern judicial system. The independence suggests that judges remain impartial to form legal ascertainment without any outside interferences. The decision-making process of the judge should not be interfered by other political institutions, social groups and persons. Organization of the tribunal and how arguments concerning a dispute progress in court both fall into the judge's discretion. The resulting judgement developed by the judge should be solely influenced by the law and particular facts of the case. Furthermore, the judge should not be influenced by any illegal intervention into the system as a result of any unofficial activities. Ultimately, the judge should be fully responsible for the final ruling upon a case.[2]

In contrast to this ideal model, judicial decision-making in China is a very complex process in which many kinds of characters play different roles. Almost all judicial decisions, some minor cases excluded, are not made by judges who have independent control of the cases upon which they preside. In most cases, there are many participants other than judges who take part in the process some of which are more powerful players than the judges themselves. A case involving a foreign investment dispute usually includes the chief judge of a tribunal, the president or vice president of a peoples' court, the adjudication meeting of that court, the branch Committee of CPC in that court, the local Committee of Political and Legislative Affairs of CPC in the jurisdiction, the higher-level court, people's congress at the same and higher level, local government, local Committee of CPC, experts outside the court, lawyers, the press, the public and so forth. In this sense, judges of the trial panel are only nominal decision-makers on the front stage. Behind this game, there is a myriad of different powers balancing one another to attain the final result.

13.2.1 The Government-like Judicial System and Judicial Decision-Making

Strictly speaking, each court is independent from each other court, which means no court has the power to govern another. A court can guide its direct subordinate courts concerning legal matters in accordance with the *Law of People's Court Organization of PRC*. But in present practice, China's judicial system is government-like which means that the constitution and operation of the judicial system are alike to that of a governmental system. It includes the following four aspects:

---

[2] Gao Hongbing (2000), Exploration of Independent Judge's Decision, Politics and Law, Issue 1.

government-like courts and judges, interrelationship among the courts, internal operation of courts and internal personnel administration system.[3]

The feature of the government-like courts and judges manifests in that the courts and judges at every legal have homogenous official ranks like governments and cadres. The Chinese culture is orientated upon a feudal structure where Chinese people are accustomed to mechanically apply official ranks to classify almost everything. Such a tradition is also popular within the judicial system, even if this concept conflicts with the *Law of People's Court Organization of PRC*. The courts, from the lowest level courts to the People's Supreme Court, have all been formatted according to the political ranking system. The rank of the People's Supreme Court is higher than a Ministry who is positioned in the middle of the hierarchy. And the official rank of the chief judge of the People's Supreme Court is higher in the middle of the hierarchy is higher than a minister. The rule is similarly applicable to provincial courts, intermediate courts, and grass root courts.

The characteristic of a government-like interrelationship among the courts means that an inferior court will treat a higher court as its governor rather than a body that merely provides guidance, which is akin to the bureaucracy present in governmental organs. Especially in complicated and intricate cases, inferior courts may ask for instructions and opinions of its higher court. The reason for this is mainly because judges of inferior courts are punished for their so-called "mistakes" as a consequence to a decision being rectified in a higher court. In theory, every judge should rule upon cases independently without being punished for reaching decisions that are ascertained independently. But to prevent judicial corruption, the People's Supreme Court issue a rule named *Penalty of Mistakes in Cases* which take the ratio of the cases rectified by higher courts as the criterion to assess the level of corruption amongst inferior judges. Such rules entitle superior courts and judges power to govern over its inferior courts and judges. Consequently, a lower level court will treat its higher level court as a governor.[4] Superior courts are generally content to enjoy such power. Sometimes, the superior court may unilaterally give its opinions concerning particular cases to its inferior courts as orders.

The government-like operation of the courts means that a court will be divided into certain tribunals, such as the civil tribunal, criminal tribunal and administrative tribunal. The presiding judge of these tribunals have the power to govern the trial panel and approve controversial cases. The civil tribunal will be further divided into the first, second, third and fourth tribunal. Cases that involve so-called foreign elements are handled by the fourth civil tribunal. If the trial panel find it hard to make a decision over a legal issue or grant judgment, the case file may be submitted to the presiding judge of the tribunal to settle the

---

3 He Weifang (1997), Two Problems in Judicial Administration of China, China Social Science, 6:117-130.

4 He Weifang (1998), the Interrelationship between Superior and Inferior Courts in Judicial Reform, Jurisprudence, Issue 8.

matter. Then under superior direction, the judge may make the final judgment and report back to the tribunal panel. In the same means, a presiding judge may solicit directions or orders from the vice president or president of the court in some extremely intricate cases.

The government-like personnel administration system implies that the president, vice president, presiding judges of a court have exclusive authority to inferior judges of the court in areas such as promotion, award and punishment etc. A judge will usually choose whether to go to trial according to the will of the president, vice president, presiding judges in order to get a promotion, award or avoid being punished. In this case, the judge does not have any substantial independence in making decisions. Usually, the intention of the president or vice president of the court or presiding judges of tribunals can manipulate the direction of a lawsuit.

The four features of the government-like judicial system in China result in the trial panel not being able to independently make judicial decisions. In practice, judges of a case's trial panel seem to control the adjudication process, but the president or vice president of the court or presiding judges of tribunals, and the higher court and its president or vice president or presiding judges, all can officially meddle in the adjudication of a case. Judges with higher rank outside the trial panel always have a fateful influence upon a case where the direct consequence is that judges lose their independence. With the many manipulations occurring under the table, the uncertainty and complexity of the final result are drastically increasing. In this sense, an unjust and unfair result seems to be unavoidable.

13.2.2 Decision-Making by the Judicial Committee

According to explicit provisions of the *Law of People's Court Organization of PRC*, there are three types of judicial organizations in the court: sole tribunal, collegial bench and judicial committee. The judicial committee is responsible for the review of some complicated and significant cases and judicial experiences and instruction on relevant judicial work. Its establishment and function is one feature of the group decision-making system. For a long time, the committee takes on an extremely important role in Chinese judicial work. Generally, it is comprised of a president and vice-presidents of the court, some major presiding judges of tribunals and experienced judges. The committee takes on substantial judicial responsibilities, even if it does not *per se* appear on the bench. In addition, the collegial bench must follow any complicated and major decisions it makes.[5]

---

[5] He Waifang, Reviews to Judicial Committee, Peking University Law Review, Vol. 1 Issue 2, pp 365-374.

13.2.3 Local Governments and the Peoples' Congress' Influence on Decision-Making of Localized Courts

The fact that the court has been localized is evidence through its finance being reliant upon the support of the fiscal revenue of local governments. In addition, the Local people's congress is responsible for the appointment of judges. In this vein, the court has no choice but to be subject to the rein of local interests as dictated by local governments and people's congresses. Particularly in some major and significant cases, the court and judges are willing to accept the letters of opinion from certain local officials. What is more, they freely like to report cases to superior officials for the sake of building up so-called "social influences". The judicial committee thus becomes a convenient and invisible conduit for the communication between them. The opinions of superior officials – outer authority – shall be one hundred percent followed down to the end. This also implies that the plaintiff often loses its lawsuit handled by local courts when local governments or officials are charged at that case. Similarly, the local congress may make use of its supervisory power on specific cases currently established to formally intervene in the trial of cases. In recent years, the congress is willing to give instructions and opinions without any enquiry from the courts.

13.2.4 CPC's Committees or Committees of Political and Legislative Affairs' Influence on Judicial Decision-Making

In 1949, all laws and legal traditions of the old Chinese government were abolished without any exception in accordance with the "*Common Guidelines*". In addition to the Financial and Economic Committee and Cultural and Educational Committee, the State Council of Administration set up the Committee of Political and Legislative Affairs to replace unborn judicial organs. In 1954, the systematical judicial institution was established in the *Constitution* of the year under the principle "to independently make judgment; only comply with the law". However, on December 24 1957, in *the Report of Regarding Judicial Work Symposium and the Anti-Rightist Struggle in the Supreme People's Court* checked by the Central Committee of CPC to the CPC Committee of the Supreme Court and Ministry of Justice, the policies changed – "All judicial activities must firmly obey by the superintendence and leadership of CPC Committees at every levels; CPC Committees have authority to look over all cases". The opinions were entirely disloyal to the principle of judicial independence set in the *Constitution.* From then on, the CPC Committees started to overstep into judicial work until 1979. the two *Constitutions* of 1975 and 1978 both abandoned the policy "to independently make judgment; only comply with the law". Until 1979, the specification in *the Instruction of the Central Committee of the Communist Party of China to Implement Criminal Law and Criminal Procedural Law* abrogated the censorship by the CPC Committee. Instead, the Committee of Political and Legislative Affairs of the CPC Committees at different levels took on the authorities of leadership, superintendence and personnel over judicial work. The changed system lasts till today.[6] In addition, even the CPC Committee of a court generally does not participate in discussions concerning specific cases because of the existence of the Judicial Committee inside the court, but its great influence cannot be overseen for its discretion to exclusively decide on major affairs and personnel appointments.

13.2.5 Lobbying and Judicial Decision-Making

There is no so-called "Friends of the Court" (*Amicus Curiae*) institution in China. However, more and more persons with specialties have stepped onto this stage. The fact that there are more and more letters of expert opinions demonstrates that the concept of outside counsel is increasingly becoming accepted. Export opinions have had significant influence upon greatly debated cases.

Furthermore, public opinion is allowed to be involved in the judicial decision-making process under some conditions. Commonly, local governments and courts may be subdued to public opinions in cases involving employment and social stability. And with the voice of asking for judicial openness, the press may act as the forth power in decision-making.[7]

In the case of Liu Yong, the final result was completely formed by a group decision process including outside experts, the press and public opinions. In the initial trial, he was sentenced to death penalty with a reprieve; however, when the news was released, he did not escape from the death penalty at last under public pressures.[8] In addition, the same stories happened in the case of Sun Zhigang's death and BMW collide with persons.

Multiple participants in the judicial decision-making process signify the fact that the judicial systems are localized and government-like. It is one of the social and political characteristics in a country undergoing transition. It is undoubtedly marked the sign of "Made in China". As addressed in the article on the Periodical named Finding Facts (*Qiu Shi*): *Adherence to the Administration by law, Improvement of the Quality of Government* written by Xiao Yang, the president of the Supreme Court of China, there are many challenges, difficulties and problems facing with Chinese judicial system. These mainly include:

- arrangement of the judicial system is not scientifically reasonable;
- It cannot be at present unbound from a variety of outside influences and local interests;

---

6 Wang Yi, Questions for Committee of Political and Legislative Affairs of CPC, Economics Club Website.

7 He Waifang (1998), Three Issues in the Relationship between the Court and the Media, Jurisprudence Research, Issue 6; He Waifang (1998), Oppositions to the Live Broadcast of Trial, China Lawyers, Issue 9.

8 Refer to related reports about Liu Yong case.

- It may take some time to redistribute judicial resources to reach the goal of establishing a system of "checks and balances" among the courts;
- Substantial independence and fairness in judicial work seems not to be achieved in a short time, where there is a shortage of institutional and procedural judicial safeguards in the courts, particularly in the courts at the root level;
- The quality of the whole judicial profession is not high as expected;
- The cases involving personal relations, bribery scandals or authoritative intervention emerge unceasingly, some of which even related to commitment of the crime;
- The monitory system needs to be fortified including interior supervisory systems and exterior systems;
- The difficulties in the execution of effective judgments are not overcome;
- The problems above mentioned not only grossly affect the results of judicial work, but also the achievements of "administration by law and judicial work for the best of the people" being realized.[9]

Appendix: A Typical Chinese Judicial Process[10]

Hubei Zhongsheng Pharmacy Ltd. (thereafter, the "Zhongsheng Pharmacy") is an enterprise of pharmacy products in Qianjiang, Hubei province. Wuhan Qirui Technological Development Ltd. (thereafter, the "Qirui Ltd") is a company that has diversified businesses in the chemicals, consultation and services. In Oct. 1998, both reached a contract to set up a joint venture, named Ruikang. The joint venture opened in July, 1999, and achieved the total output value of 71.88 millions RMB, the sale of over 32 millions RMB and the payable tax of nearly 7 millions RMB in the year of 2000. However, the distrust and suspiciousness began pervading. Due to the disorder in the operation, they broke the chain of the production and sale to separately run them. On June 30, 2001, the joint venture was actually under sole operation of Zhongsheng. They both proposed each of their claims to the Party Committee (Hubei Province) and provincial government by the media or in writing directly. The atmosphere of the time was on edge. In Jun. 6, 2001, Zhongsheng filed the lawsuits in court, and Qirui Ltd. also counterclaimed during the litigation.

---

[9] Xiao Yang (2005), Adherence to the Administration by law, Improvement of the Quality of the Government, Qiu Shi, Issue 1.

[10] I make the bolds, and the italics are my editorials for the case.

Eight attempts to mediation failed in the end [the mediation is largely promoted in China's judicial practice]. For the continuity of this profitable joint venture being halted due to the lawsuit, the collegial panel made its preliminary ruling opinion that the company did not terminate its businesses and would call the liquidation by a temporarily fixed date. In the address made by Yu, Zhengsheng, the Secretary of Provincial Committee of CPC, addressed his opinions on the report of the provincial court: "I agreed on opinions of the provincial court. To uphold the principle of judicial work by law, and consider the social effects as well, it is necessary for our government to go to help the court in the case ... [*in Yu's assenting view, we can see the actual intervention to judicial system from local superior officials, and the influences of so-called "social effects". The usage of "help" implies that the participation in the trial process of the local government is encouraged in judcial work.]*

Later, Wu Jiayou, the president of the People's High Court of Hubei Province, chaired a consulting meeting including officials of the Supervisory Office of Provincial Committee of CPC, Committee of Political and Legislative Affairs of Provincial Committee of CPC, Economic and Trade Committee of Hubei Province and the CPC Committee and Municipal Government of Qianjiang City. In the session, they formulated an opinion as the foremost option that Qirui was advised to quit the joint venture and offered its shares for sale. Furthermore, since one reason for causing their dispute was the attitude of the local regulatory department of medicine that handled the outsourcing of medicines related to the joint venture, the Supervisory Office of Provincial Committee of CPC particularly held another consulting meeting where officials in charge of the provincial regulatory department of medicine and thc Office of Legal Affairs of provincial government attended [*the decisions formed in the consulting meeting have consequently concluded the opinions from each departments of the local CPC Committee and local government. By this, the active participation of the CPC Committee into decision-making or ruling is obviously seen*].

After several attempts of failed mediation, officials of the Supervisory Office and the CPC Committee of Qianjiang City and judges of the People's High Court of Hubei Province met together to have a face-to-face talk on Nov. 22, 2002.

Afterwards, officials of the Supervisory Office and judges of the People's High Court of Hubei Province went especially to the Intermediate Court of Hanjiang City to call legal representative of the disputed parties to attend mediation for the second time. In negotiations, they concentrated on the disposals of outsourced medicines and the proprietorship of some related equipment. In the Memorandum of Mediation, every attending leader signed their names. Finally, after mediation lasting, from the morning to 3 o'clock in the afternoon, both parties signed the agreement of mediation.

On Nov. 28, with fulfillment of the last obligation in the agreement of mediation by Zhongsheng to deliver the highly-efficient liquid phase chromatograph to Qirui, the dispute was resolved in a peaceful manner. During the litigation that lasted over one year, the leaders of Hubei Provincial CPC Committee, Provincial Government and the People's High Court expressed their opinions and instructions several times, even taking part in mediation in person *[this demonstrates again the complexity of a diversified decision-making process]*. A great amount of legal and administrative resources were consumed, but the consequence of a large number of lay-offs, bankruptcies and loss of market share was avoided. Thus the desired social effects was eventually achieved. *[The final judgment's social effects have been a particular concern for a long time in judicial work. The influences of political factors such as local interests, employments and social stability are particularly paid attention to in the adjudication.]*

It was reported that Zhongsheng had engaged in the privatization of the previous joint venture without any halt in the operation. The new enterprise had run its usual course. Qirui completely walked away from the dispute and started a new medicine program. The program was estimated to be prosperous. *[The last paragraph of the report tells us that the judicial work of the People's High Court of Hubei Province was highly prized. It suggests that in the media the judicial work of court is appraised by the standards including the factor of social effect. The general values of procedural justice and statutory fairness are hereby ignored. Worse than all, it will be underrated where the court makes judgment simply according to the facts and laws, resulting in ill social effects. They may be regarded as being shortsighted, too simple, lack of political awareness and alike.]*

13.3 Insight into Chinese-Style Arbitration

Commercial arbitration, as an alternative dispute resolution ("ADR") mechanism, has the features of privacy, autonomy, flexibility and efficiency. Now it plays more and more of a significant role in the modern commercial society featuring elements of high market-orientation and internationalization. China's arbitration system is composed of China International Economic Trade Arbitration Commission ("CIETAC") and China Maritime Arbitration Commission ("CMAC") as two leading sheep, and local arbitration commission as the main body hereof. During the developing years, the CIETAC achieved a good reputation in the international business circle. However, it encountered an unparalleled crisis since the finding of corruption involving its main leaders shocked us in early 2006. Some black holes behind China's arbitrations were accordingly disclosed.

13.3.1 A Crisis in China's Arbitration History

As the eldest child of China's arbitration, the corruption in 2006 was the largest disaster for the CIETAC since it was established. Wang Shengchang, the former director of Legal Department and the Secretary-General of CIETAC, was prosecuted for the charges of committing the crime of "private misappropriation and bribery". As a well-trained young arbitration expert, Mr. Wang participated in hundreds of cases involving international commercial arbitration. He was credited as a new star in the Chinese arbitration profession. In the well publicized Case of

"Pepsi arbitration", Wang was designated by Pepsi as the arbitrator and made a notorious role of it. His impartiality in that case was therefore seriously doubted.[11]

However, Wang's arrest was just the preview of a quake in the entire staff of CIETAC. Afterwards, the Council for the Promotion of International Trade (CCPIT), as the superior organ of CIETAC, made a large cross-sectional reorganization, or declared a reshuffle of the arbitration commission. In the rearrangement, it put CIETAC back into the administration system of China's public institutions, which indicates the drastic decline of salaries and termination of bonuses and subsidies. As a result, it caused a large amount of brain drain and emotional sabotage among its remaining employees in the CIETAC. The CIETAC encountered a halt after the striking corruption crisis.

Similarly, a 25-second video was played on a website on Jan. 17, 2006 that exposed a scene where Qi Tianchang, the arbitrator of the Arbitration Commission of Tian Jin, illegally had dinner with the representative attorney (Zhang Decai, Attorney of Being Zhonglun Jintong Law Firm) and legal counsel of Fuji Xerox involved in an ongoing case. On Feb. 2, Mr. Qi was laid off and never re-enrolled. Mr. Zhang was subsequently punished later. It is learned that Qi was the first previous arbitrator who was banned from re-entering for life. In the case "Tianjin Guangyi Real Estate v. Fuji Xerox", Qi, designated by Fuji Xerox as the arbitrator, with chief arbitrator appointed by the director of Tianjin Arbitration Commission and the arbitrator designated by the opponent jointly comprised the arbitration tribunal. In the evening of Jul.6, 2005, Qi privately met with Chen Zhenwei and Zhang decai, the representatives of Fuji Xerox (counterclaimant in the case), and accepted their invitation for dinner.

These two events ruined China's established reputation in international business arbitration at one point in time. China arbitration came across its worst point.

13.3.2 Chinese Characters of Arbitration

From 20 Feb. to 24 Feb., 2006, the National Arbitration Symposium was held in Beijing. Because the Office of Legislative Affairs of the State Council is the highest supervisory organ to China's arbitration commissions at every level, the address by Lu Yunhua, a leader of the Office of Legislative Affairs of the State Council, undoubtedly drew much attention at this time. In his address, he came up with the goal of a second phase of growth for the arbitration industry. Also, some innovative measures were underlined such as the practice of open arbitration carried on in Guangzhou and Qingdao Arbitration commissions, pre-trial notice taken by Deyang Arbitration commission and the inspection taken throughout northwestern areas.

The privacy of arbitration is considered an advantage when compared with litigation. However, in Guangzhou and Qingdao arbitration commissions, they broke

[11] "Wang Shengchang was arrested for the bribery charge in Pepsi Arbitration dispute" , 2006, Apr.24, www.people.com.cn.

the "closed-door" principle by having open arbitration. The measures were positively affirmed by the superior authority for its innovativeness. Moreover, as done by Deyang Arbitration Commission, the pre-trial notice is an absurd creation but exalted for the same reason. The core of this practice is that arbitrators shall disclose the final result before the official written award of arbitration is released. Even the parties can claim for the result and make adjustments by negotiation (or do not adjust), then the arbitrators publicly release their written opinions after absorbing the parties' reply. This measure not only lacks in legal basis, but also substantially opens the door to the corruption in arbitration. As for the administrative inspection, it provides official access for outside authorities to overtly intervene the arbitration.

This is China's real situation in relation to commercial arbitration. Their measures are seriously aberrant from basic principles of arbitration. Current practice is ruining its foundation. Besides the ignorance of some professionals, the whole profession is actually pushed into the corner under the pressure incurred by the corruption case. A poem (cited as follows) written by an anonymous person in CIETAC expresses somewhat concerns about so-called Chinese features in the arbitration.

What Can We Do

What can we do
When somebody says
Arbitration shall open its door
Everyone can attend oral hearings
Though
Arbitration has its feature of
Confidentiality

What can we do
When somebody says
Arbitration shall disclose its result
Before awarding
Parties may supervise and negotiate better
Though
Arbitrational tribunal has its authority
Making award independently

What can we do
When we find
Once familiar arbitration
Has a totally new face
Though
China arbitration is rushing into
Golden Age of its own characteristics

WHAT CAN WE DO???

13.3.3 The Root of Risk in Chinese Arbitration

The root of risk in Chinese arbitration, if any, exists in two fields, one is the appointment of the chief arbitrator; another is the lack of a monitory system on the overstepping authority of the Secretary in the arbitral tribunal.

The sound operation of the arbitral system is not only dependent on a set of good rules, but also on the goodness of professionals whose quality has decisive effects on the result of arbitration. According to present rules, the arbitrator for a case is selected by the party at point. The party is usually inclined to select the arbitrator he knows well. Thus, in most of cases, the arbitrator elected in this way may tend to make the decision in favor of its selector, instead of on the basis of its expertise, no matter what the rule of independence require. In this sense, both parties select the arbitrators who are separately favorable to them. The point of balance is centered on the attitude of the chief arbitrator. Similarly, appointment of the chief arbitrator is a tug-of-war. According to the arbitral rules of CIETAC and other local arbitration commissions, chief arbitrator shall commonly be initially selected by both parties; otherwise, it shall be appointed by the arbitration commission if they cannot reach the consensus. In practice, both parties are often opposite on who is the chief arbitrator. Therefore, the Commission has a final decision for its appointment. In this vein, the director or other chief officials of the commission are exposed to sticking in the mud. It is known that Wang in the corruption mentioned above did hold the appointment of chief arbitrator with another official. Foreign investors are advised to pay one hundred percent attention to this issue.

Furthermore, the Secretary of the arbitral tribunal played a crucial role in the arbitration process. In terms of arbitral rules, theoretically, the secretary is only responsible for some of procedural issues. The main part of arbitration is taken on by the arbitrators. However, participation in an arbitration case is just their part-time job, most of whom are experts or successful men in different areas. They would rather take more time focusing on their major businesses than the arbitration with grants lower pay. Hereby, the secretary practically becomes an essential part in the arbitration. Particularly, in some cases, they are even responsible for drafting the arbitral awards. The arbitrators just finish their share of responsibilities: to attend the hearing and make opinions on the decision. The secretary substantially becomes solo arbitrator controlling over some of the cases. Besides, there is no strict institution regarding the supervision on the secretary, particularly in the case where it has taken on the arbitrator's responsibilities. For this, the secretary may be immune from any charge of its role in the arbitration. The secretary and its influences have come to light and become the eye of the typhoon day by day, which deserves much attention of foreign investors involved in arbitration in China.

13.4 Mediation in China

All kinds of voluntary resolutions to a dispute are encouraged by the American Arbitration Association (AAA). In addition to arbitration, AAA acted as a forerunner in promoting alternative resolutions such as mediation, conciliation and other closed-door methods. Since it was established in 1926, the approach of mediation, has been an effective alternative. And the "*Rules of Business Mediation*" issued by AAA applies very often.[12] In fact, the mediation is a primary dispute resolution in China, in accordance with the theory of "*peace is the best*" in traditional culture and thought of as a "Harmonized Society" exalted by China's highest authority.[13] Chinese mediation includes mediation in court and mediation outside court in litigation, arbitration or mediation center.

13.4.1 Mediation in the Litigation Process

Judicial mediation is the resolution that certain people's courts organize mediation in which both parties negotiate with each other and reconcile peacefully to reach the agreement of settlement. Because mediation can preclude the possibility of judges being charged for making so-called "errors" in adjudication and their decision being overruled in the appellant court, almost all courts have been motivated to promote arbitration.[14]

The mediation includes either amicable settlement outside court and in court. Outside court mediation is where both parties negotiate their disputes and reconcile peacefully to finally reach the agreement of settlement. Afterwards, the plaintiff may withdraw its filing in terms of the agreement. The court also encourages parties to do so by merely charging half of the filing fees in this case. The only pitfall in outside court mediation is that the agreement of settlement cannot be used as the basis for forcible execution but a form of contract. As for any dispute in the fulfillment of a said agreement, the party has to file the lawsuit again via litigation procedures. On the contrary, the in-court mediation is chaired by judges of the trial panel, as an intermediary, in the attempt to reach an agreement. And the agreement in court can be relied on to be the basis for final ruling. The court proffered official affirmation for possible forceful execution.

---

[12] Robert Kerson (2000), Mediation in Business Disputes, translated by Huang Yanming, Southern Economy, Issue 2.

[13] Justice Robert F. Utter, Tribute: Dispute Resolution in China, 62 Wash. L. Rev. 383.

[14] Weng Xiaobin (2000), The Reforms on Judicial Mediation Institution, Modern Law, Issue 5.

13.4.2 Mediation in the Arbitration Process

The combination of mediation with arbitration is an outstanding character in China's arbitration. It means: In the arbitration, the autonomy of parties at dispute is fully respected. The arbitral tribunal may organize the mediation on the basis of clear facts.

The combination of two resolutions has its specific advantages as follows, whether it is in practice or in theory. Firstly, it helps parties save time. The tribunal may make the final arbitration result based on the agreement if the mediation succeeds. If not, the ongoing arbitration may well resume in ordinary procedures. Secondly, the agreement reached in the tribunal is included into the written arbitration result that can be referred to as proof for judicial execution. Furthermore, this peaceful way may provide a possibility for parties to continue their commercial cooperation.

The Arbitration Law of PRC neither requires compulsory mediation, nor provides its specific principles and procedures. Thus, it runs totally on a voluntary basis at the discretion of the parties concerned. The role of arbitrators also converts from an adjudicator to an intermediary in the settlement. In practice, mediation in the arbitration generally includes three methods: negotiation presided by the arbitral tribunal where both parties concerned jointly participate; the arbitral tribunal separately negotiates with each party for the settlement; the arbitral tribunal just provides its plan of settlement for the parties' reconciliation.

13.4.3 Mediation in the Mediation Center

Case Study. A arbitral dispute concerning a Sino-foreign equity joint venture: Jiangsu Jierui Plastic Tubes and Pipes Ltd.

> On Oct. 27, 1997, China Huaiyin Transportation Investment General Company (thereafter, "Huaiyin Transportation") and China the First Auto (Huaiyin) Special-purpose Vehicle Factory (thereafter, "First Auto Huaiyin") signed an agreement of joint venture with Liu Zeshan, the legal representative of New Zealand UNILAND Ltd. (thereafter, "UNILAND"). According to the agreement, they all agreed to invest in setting up a joint venture – Jiangsu Jierui Plastic Tubes and Pipes Ltd. (thereafter, the "Joint Venture"), carrying its primary business in production, sale and consumer service of pipes and tubes for tap water. The total registered capital is 1,400,000 US dollars. The ratio of contribution is: 45% for Huaiyin Transportation, in the sum of 450,000 US dollars; 30% for First Auto Huaiyin, in the sum of 300,000 US dollars, 25% for UNLAND, in the sum of 250,000 US dollars. The difference between the registered capital and total contribution shall be paid by the mortgaged loan under the

name of Joint Venture. In the Joint Venture, UNLAND is supposed to provide the technology of PE water pipes and tubes from New Zealand. Later, the equities of two Chinese shareholders were transferred to Huaiyin Transportation Holding Ltd. Because the unsettled disputes regarding the fulfillment of technological development and design, capital shares, management became more serious, Huaiyin Transportation Holding Ltd. filed the suit to the Huaian Office of Mediation Center of Jiangsu under the Council for the Promotion of International Trade (CCPIT). According to relevant provisions of "CIETAC/Chinese Chamber of International Commerce Mediation Rules (2000)", the office accepted the case and then appointed arbitrators. After contact with the foreign investor, Liu Zeshan agreed to participate in the mediation under the Office separately on Jul. 29, Aug. 6 and Oct. 8, 2004. By the negotiation of several rounds, both parties were involved in deep discussions and finally reached the agreement on the basis of reciprocal reconciliation and compromise at most. By the check of mediators, every article of the agreement is confirmed in accordance with provisions of laws and regulations. Thus, the dispute that had lasted for years was finally settled by mediation.

At present, the specific institutions relating to commercial mediation involving foreign factors is the mediation centre located in different provinces and cities, among them, Beijing Mediation Centre under the leadership of CCPIT / Chinese Chamber of International Commerce as an example. In practice, the mediation is initiated. In the centre, they generally function to promote reconciliation between parties based on their applications in accordance with related laws and international commercial practices. The final agreement is built on the basis of reciprocal compromise and voluntary consent. In addition, the facts including responsibilities stipulated in related contracts will be ascertained and fully respected. The basis of acceptance for the mediation application is the agreement to file for mediation that both parties reach in advance. There is no restriction on the nationality, geography or classification in its jurisdiction. It usually accepted filings concerning international trade and economic transaction, finance, investment, technology licensing, construction contracting, transportation, insurance and commercial and maritime disputes.

14 Managing the Future – The Strategy for Foreign Investment Under Power-Oriented Economy

An in-depth understanding of China's current overall economic, social and legal environment is essential for foreign investors to make wise judgments of their legal risks in China.

The whole purpose of China's economic reform is to transform the so-called planned economy to a market economy, which is the typical statement by the Chinese government and is also bureaucratic propaganda. However, the division of a planned economy and a market economy covers the actual side of China's economic environment. Chinese economy, in its nature, is a power-oriented economy. Both the planned economy and the market economy are only disguises to cover the power-oriented economy.

During the negotiation for China's entry to the WTO, China's market economy status became one of the hottest issues although the final resolution reached through compromise will artificially delay the acceptance of China's market economy status for 15 years. The Chinese government has always insisted on China's compliance with the market economy standard and it has continuously requested that other nations admit China's market economy status based on the government's assertion that over 97% of China's product price has been fully free, and that input, output and sales processes of vast majority of Chinese enterprises are no longer under state control. However, such a statement only encompasses part of the reality inasmuch as the price and control of resources are intentionally omitted. In fact, the extent of price control over resources as production input is the criterion for judging whether the economy is free of state interference and operates independently. Viewing the reality of the situation, the pricing and circulation of various resources, including land, oil, coal, electrical power, labor, currency, market access, etc., are all under strict governmental control. Under such circumstances, China lacks assurance in declaring itself as a market economy nation.

Therefore, should China be regarded as a planned economy since its resources are under strict plan control? Actually, this question itself is confined between dividing the market economy and planned economy. Behind the division of resources under the plan, the true disposition is allocation according to political power. A market participant, whether a state-owned enterprise, a private enterprise, a foreign enterprise or individual, fully depends on its relationship with political authority for the quality and quantity of economic resources it is able to obtain. Power-oriented, diversity-orderly structure is formed in China's economic resource allocation process. Just as asserted by Guy de Jonquieres, a columnist of the *Financial Times*, the China economy may realize its openness, when the central plan system has been gradually abandoned, the competition mechanism has been set up and state-owned shares have been sold out; however, the vital control right is still in the hands of the State. If one sought to obtain a bank loan, foreign currency, new factory land or scarce raw material, that individual must have friends in the 'correct' position.[1] Such conclusion is illustrated by many examples, while the obtaining of land may be the best case in point. Furthermore, China Mobile and China Unicom's competition in pursuing information industry resources is more typical illustration of allocation according to power.

In this sense and only in this sense, we may conclude bravely that a true planned economy has never existed in China. Rather at all times, the power-oriented economy has always been the economic operation mechanism playing the actual role in China.

In fact, power-oriented economy may be regarded as the destiny of Chinese economy in the sociology sense. The origin for this destiny lies in the lack of political power balance mechanism which may be the constitution to a certain degree instead of the political power oriented culture lasting for thousands of years in China's feudalistic society. Unrestricted power must extend into economic, social and cultural fields besides the fight in the political stage. Tracing back to thousands of years ago and viewing current situation, the standard pattern of power in various fields have not changed much. Chinese economy, in its nature, is neither market economy nor planned economy, but a power-oriented one.

Political power is the dominant focus of China's economic, social and legal environment. The nature of Chinese economy is a power-oriented economy and the nature of Chinese society is a government official standard society while the nature of Chinese legal system is rule by law under the authority. Up to now, China's process of law modernization is still under the level of 'law instrumentalism'. In China, the political power instead of law enjoys the highest authority while the law is only the tool and servant of power. Law fails to tame power. On the contrary, under the control of power, law leaves way for abuse of power and provides a legitimate cover for the authority's control of Chinese economy and society.

The origin for most legal risks described in each and every chapters of this book is closely related to power. For example, ambiguities in legal rules will incur risks as the statement in Chapter 1. In an international conference held by OECD, many foreign investors could not understand why Chinese government insists on keeping *the Guidance Catalog of Foreign Investment Industries* with no clear boundary. In fact, the vagueness of rules just intends to meet the very need of authorities. On one hand, the existence of legal rules satisfies people's appeal for

---

1 Richard McGregor, Business and politics converge in China, Financial Times, July 31, 2006.

legal modernization and the WTO's request for transparency. Meanwhile, vagueness of legal rules leaves enough space for power's manipulation of whole economy and society. Under such situation, foreign investors have to seek answers from relevant authorities and officials during their investment process, which not only creates opportunities for power to seek rent but also opens door for power's control of investment projects. In the Carley Case mentioned in Chapter 2, we may find Article 7 of *Several Administration Regulations on the Capital Contribution by the Parties to Sino-foreign Equity Joint Enterprises* directly empower the 'power' (Beijing Municipal Bureau of Commerce) to deprive foreign investors' qualification as shareholders. In the merge and acquisition issues involved in Chapter 3, political power turns out as the legal risks maker. The author has handled two cases in Qing Hai Province in which the local government sent a work team to administratively take over a normally operating enterprises established through merge and acquisition, locked down the gates and refused the entry of managers delegated by the acquiring party based on the reason that the acquiring party failed to settle all the employees and employees' quarrels which may influence social stability. China Water Company Limited (Hui Jin) case mentioned in this book is another typical example. In foreign-funded merge and acquisition, even if foreign investors offered sufficient capital for employee settlement, the concerned governments would still easily manipulate changes to drive away foreign investors on the occasion that employees made difficulties to impair public interests. The so-called employees' making problems or causing damages of public interests are sometimes even intentionally caused. Chapter 5 focuses on the most typical approach by political power's interference of economy, that is, economic policy. In the event that an economic policy is adjusted, foreign invested projects with marvelous prospect may be terminated easily. The failures of Carlyle's acquisition of shares in Xu Gong and Huang Qiao Case are both results of the state policy changes. Besides, land use right, labor, tax and other issues discussed in other chapters all contain possibilities of legal risks caused by the political power abuse. Therefore, we can conclude that, in current situation, the biggest risk for foreign investment in China does not lie in law itself but in 'power'.

And then, who is the owner of power? The answer is Communist party of China (CPC), the sole governing party in China, who is the monopoly of political powers. Current China is a state with the tri-unity of political party, government and religion. The Communist Party of China not only controls government, but also has power similar to that of western religion through the sole legitimate ideology—Marxism, which may be even more powerful than general political power. China's private enterprises are familiar with game rules of Chinese society through their growth in social cracks. Since the Central Committee of Communist party of China allowed privately-owned companies with three CPC member employees to establish party branches since 2002, more than 85% of them currently have branches of the Communist Party of China, which underline the growing convergence of interests between China's private sector and its communist rulers. At present, there seems to be no tendency of allowing foreigners to be CPC party members. However, the practice of privately owned enterprises becoming 'intimate' with power may be learned by foreign investors to certain extend. To entry or keep legs in Chinese markets, it is important to please authorities who may not only bring non-substitutable resources for enterprise developments but also for the 'protection umbrella' of enterprises so as to avoid triggering many legal risks. However, foreign investors should also learn from the tragic results of too close combination of Chinese privately-owned enterprises with political power. Though China is a sole party nation, the political power structure is still easily changeable. Therefore, too close combination with political power will naturally lead to negative effects and even legal troubles to the enterprise development by the changeable political power structure.[2]

To conclude, it is quite a pity to say that even legal risk management measures are helpful to the preventing of legal risks faced with foreign investment in China, but the better way is 'to keep right relation with right persons at right time', which is essential strategy for foreign investment under the power-oriented economy of China.

[2] In June 2006, stepping down of Mr. Liu Zhihua, the vice mayor of Beijing, led to collapse of large amount of real estate development enterprises in Beijing.

References

1. Andreas Lauffs (2006) China's Draft Labor Contract Law –Major Changes for Employers on the Horizon. Baker & McKenzie Client Alert, February Issue
2. Bai Defan, Tab Bowers, Rong Juesheng (2004) The Selling life insurance to China. Mckinsey Senior Management Collected Essays, Issue 4
3. Basel II: International Convergence of Capital Measurement and Capital Standards: a Revised Framework.
4. Chen An (1998) Discussion on Limitation, Integration and independence of the Subject of International Economic Law. In: Series of International Economic Law. China Law Press, Vol.1
5. Clifford Chance (1996) The Project Financing. translated by Gong Huihong. Huaxia Publishing House, pp. 46
6. Chen Guowei (2005) The Private Higher Education Investment Risk and Elusion. Zhongzhou Academy, Issue 4
7. Chang Liang, Chen Mei (2005) The Legal Issues Concerning Land in BOT Projects. the Resources and Human Living Environment, Issue 3
8. Chen Zhiwu (2002) Who obstructs our business? New Fortune, December Issue
9. Ewald, F. (1991) Insurance and risk, In: Burchell, G. Gordon, C. and Miller, P. (eds) The Foucault Effect: Studies in Govermentality. Chicago University Press
10. Gao Hongbing (2000) Exploration of Independent Judge's Decision. Politics and Law, Issue 1
11. Gao Zhanyun, Zhu Yaning (2003) Origins and Regulations of Disqualified or Deceased China's Investors in Sino-foreign Equity and Cooperative Joint Ventures. China Business Management Study, Issue 10
12. Geringer, J.M. and L. Herbert (1991) Measuring Performance of International Joint Venture. Journal of International Business studies, 19:365-388
13. Geringer, Kogut, Killing. Geringer, J. M. & C. A. Frayne (1990) Human resource management and international joint venture control: A parent company perspective. Management International Review, 30:103–120
14. Heng Huiyong, Hao Cheng (2005) The Risk in Charging Right Pledge and Countermeasure Suggestion. Finance and Economy, Issue 5

15. He Weifang (1997) Two Problems in Judicial Administration of China. China Social Science, 6:117-130
16. He Waifang (1998) Three Issues in the Relationship between the Court and the Media. Jurisprudence Research, Issue 6
17. He Weifang (1998) The Interrelationship between Superior and Inferior Courts in Judicial Reform. Jurisprudence, Issue 8
18. He Waifang (1998) Oppositions to the Live Broadcast of Trial. China Lawyers, Issue 9
19. Hu Xiangting (2004) Traps in Local Favorable Polices for Inviting Investment, the Essay of China's Economics Annual Meeting
20. John P. Karalis (1992) International Joint Ventures: A Practical Guide. St. Paul,Minn, West Publishing Co., pp.138
21. Killing, P. (1988) Understanding alliances: The role of task and organizational complexity. In: Cooperative Strategies in International Business. F. Contractor & P. Lorange (eds) Lexington: Lexington Books
22. Kogut, B. (1989) Why joint ventures die so quickly? Chief Executive, May/June issue: 70–73
23. Li Wei'an and Wu Xianming (2002) The Analysis of Sino-foreign Joint Venture Parent Company Guiding Type Company Management Mode. World Economy and Politics, Issue 5
24. Li Weimin (2004) The Research on Private Higher Education Cost, Investment and Tuition Fee. Private Education Research, Issue 6
25. Li Weimin (2005) The Analysis of Policy Risk for Private Universities. the Xi'an Europe and Asia Vocational College Academy, Issue 1
26. Lin Hua (2002) The Inside Investigation of Foreign Insurance Companies' Withdrawal. Foreign Investment in China, Issue 12
27. Liu Jianwen, (2005) The Research on Legal Issues in Higher Education System Reform. Beijing University Publishing House, pp.132
28. Lu Changcong, Zhen Wenquan, Li Zhongguang (2004) The Property Right Variation and Proceeds Dispute in Sino-foreign Joint Ventures. China Industry Economy, Issue 11
29. Lu Feng, Feng Kaidong (2004) the Foundation for Failure in Automobile Industry. the Internal Reference of Reform, Issue 13
30. Luan Jianqi (2003) Discussion on Problems in Transfer of Trademark Rights in Foreign-invested Enterprises. Contemporary Law, Issue 3
31. Masahiko Aoki and Qian Yingyi (1996) View the Corporate Governance in Transition Economy. China Economy Publishing House, pp213
32. Michael Pennington (2000), M&A in China - Where, how and which onion not to buy! Lehman Brown, Shanghai, Issue 5

33. Mure Dickie(2006) Chenming scraps deal with foreign equity fund. Financial Times, July 31
34. Ping Xinqiao (2003) Motive and Effect of Governmental Umbrella – Positivism Analysis. China Center for Economic Research (CCER) at Peking University Discussion Paper (No. C200332)
35. Richard A·Posner (2003) Anti-Trust Law. translated by Sun Hongning. China University of Political Science and Law Press, pp.138
36. Justice Robert F. Utter, Tribute: Dispute Resolution in China, 62 Wash. L. Rev. 383
37. Robert Kerson (2000) Mediation in Business Disputes. translated by Huang Yanming, Southern Economy, Issue 2
38. Shen Jiyong, Wang Shouqing and Qiang Maoshan (2005) the Political Risk and Sovereignty Risk in China BOT/PPP Projects: through Case Analysis. the China Commerce: Investment and Financing, Issue 1
39. Tang Shume (2003) Research on Capital Structure of Foreign-invested Limited Liability Company. Tianjin Social Science, Issue 5
40. Wang Xiaoling (2004) The Carrying on Joint Venture by Chinese Automobile Companies to the End? Commerce Weekly, Issue 2-3
41. Wang Xiaoling (2004) Re-thinking of FDI Strategy. Commerce Weekly, Issue 3
42. Weng Xiaobin (2000) The Reforms on Judicial Mediation Institution. Modern Law, Issue 5
43. Wu Daguang (2001) The Analysis of China Private Education Market Characteristics and Policy Trend. China Higher Education, Issue 11
44. Wu, Zhipan (2003) Legal Issues in Foreign-funded Purchase of State Shares. CASS Journal of Law, 6:83
45. Xiao Yang (2005) Adherence to the Administration by law, Improvement of the Quality of the Government. Qiu Shi, Issue 1
46. Xie Wangyuan et al. (2005) How to Judge the Case of Foreign Company Using the Loan to Make Contributions and Withdrawing them. People's Prosecution, Issue 1
47. Yang Fan (2003) The Legal Risk in Charging Right Pledge. Henan Finance and Tax Higher College Transactions, Issue 5
48. Yang Peng (2002) A Official's Experience – The State of Industrial Policy in China. Strategy and Management, Second Issue: pp. 54
49. Yang Qing (2005) The Research on Various Problems in Applying BOT in China Water Industry. China Market, Issue 1
50. Yang Yunlong and Fu Qiang (2005) From Joint Venture to Harmony. the Science and Technology Brainpower, Issue 8

51. Yao Meizhen (1993) Comparative Foreign Investment Law. Wuhan University Press
52. Zhang Shiwei, Li Shoushuang (2004) The Offshore Company Law. China Law Press.
53. Zhang Weiying (1995) The Entrepreneurs in Enterprises-Contract Theories. Shanghai Sanlian Bookstore and Shanghai People's Publishing House
54. Zhang Weiying (1999) The Enterprise Theories and Reform on Chinese Enterprises. Beijing University Press, pp. 122
55. Zhang Weiying (2005) The Property Rights, Incentives and Company Management. the Economy and Science Publishing House, pp. 2-3
56. Zhang Xiaoyan (2004) The Conflict between BOT and China's Existing Laws. the People's Court News on 15 December 2004
57. Zhang Xuemin (2001) Education Economics. Southwest Normal University Publishing House, pp.107
58. Zhang Ya (2005) The Legal Dilemma of Property Right Transaction. The Report of State-owned Enterprises Reforms Vol. 2.
59. Zhao Daibo, Deng Juan (2002), Traps in Investment. Shangjie, October Issue.
60. Zhao Jingxia (1995) The Micro Comparison of Investment Laws for Chinese and Foreign Capital and Revelation. International Economic Cooperation, Issue 4
61. Zhao Yumin, Wang Baojun (2002) Views to Management of Contributions in Foreign-invested Joint Ventures. Study on China Administration for Industry & Commerce, Issue 2

MIX
Papier aus verantwortungsvollen Quellen
Paper from responsible sources
FSC® C105338

If you have any concerns about our products,
you can contact us on
ProductSafety@springernature.com

In case Publisher is established outside the EU,
the EU authorized representative is:
Springer Nature Customer Service Center GmbH
Europaplatz 3, 69115 Heidelberg, Germany

Printed by Libri Plureos GmbH
in Hamburg, Germany